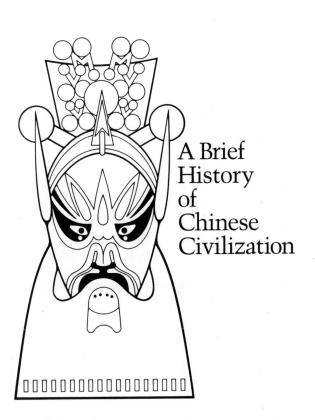

A Brief
History
of
Chinese
Civilization

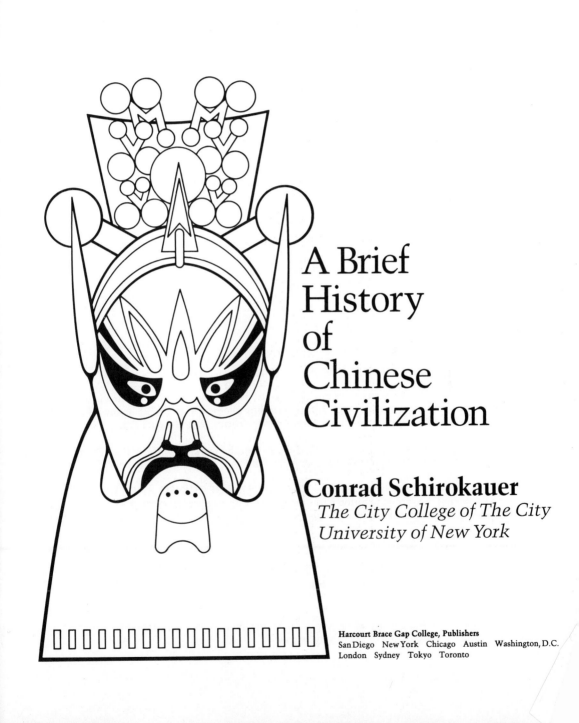

A Brief
History
of
Chinese
Civilization

Conrad Schirokauer
*The City College of The City
University of New York*

Harcourt Brace Gap College, Publishers
San Diego   New York   Chicago   Austin   Washington, D.C.
London   Sydney   Tokyo   Toronto

Calligraphy by Dr. Leon L. Y. Chang
Maps by J. P. Tremblay

Some material previously published: A BRIEF HISTORY OF CHINESE AND JAPANESE CIVILIZATIONS, Second Edition by Conrad Schirokauer, copyright © 1989, 1978 by Harcourt Brace Jovanovich, Inc.

ISBN: 0-15-505568-2

Library of Congress Catalog Card Number: 90-81893

Printed in the United States of America

 6 7 8 9 016 10 9 8 7 6

Preface

The reasons for studying China can be subsumed under three broad headings: the richness of its long historical record, which forms such an important part of the total history of the human race and illuminates the nature of the human condition; the enduring value of Chinese cultural achievements; and the contemporary importance of the world's most populated land. Setting aside China's contemporary importance, surely some acquaintance with its civilization is required of one who would be an educated person, for to be educated means to be able to see beyond the narrow geographic, temporal, and cultural bounds of one's immediate neighborhood. Indeed, to be educated entails the ability to see oneself in a broader perspective, including the perspective of history. And in this day and age, that means not only the history of one's own tribe or state or even civilization but ideally of all human history — for it is all our history.

That history is woven of many strands, and so we have economic and political history, the study of social structure, of thought, and of art. This text is based on the belief that an introduction to the history of a civilization requires consideration of all these facets of human activity, a general mapping out of the terrain so that the beginner may find his or her bearings and learn enough to consider in which direction to explore further, with some idea of the rewards to be gained for the effort. An introduction then is certainly not a catalog (although it should contain basic data) or a personal synthesis or summation, nor is it the proper vehicle for extending the expanding frontiers of present knowledge. Instead, it should, among other things, introduce the reader to the conventions of a field of study and attempt to convey the state of our present understanding. The basic aim of this text then is to serve as a work of orientation. Thus, for example, where applicable, the standard dynastic framework has been used to provide the basic historical chronology.

History is the study of change and continuity, and both elements are always present, for no generation starts off with a blank slate, nor can even the most fervid traditionalist block changes wrought by the passage of time. In looking at a given segment of history, the scholar does not confront a choice between change and continuity but faces the more difficult task of weighing the change in the continuity, the continuity in the change. Such a determination requires, in the final analysis, as much art as science, and no assessment is ever final. This is so not only because of the continual discovery of new evidence (the dramatic finds of recent Chinese archaeology are a good example) or of new techniques (for example, in the dating of materials) but also because scholars' intellectual frameworks and analytic concepts change, and they learn to ask new questions. Even if that were not the case, history would still have to be rewritten at intervals, inasmuch as the ultimate significance of any individual historical episode depends in the final analysis on the whole story: as long as history itself is unfinished, so is its writing.

If this is true of all history, it seems especially the case with the history of China, about which we know a great deal more now than we did just a generation ago, but the areas of our ignorance continue to be enormous. Etienne Balazs (1905–63) once compared students of China to Lilliputians clambering over the Gulliver that is Chinese history, and his words are still apt. Indeed, one of the continuing attractions of the field is that it offers great opportunities to the intellectually adventurous and hardy to work on major problems. Our hope is that the very inadequacies of a text such as this will spur some readers on to these endeavors. Thus for this text to succeed, it must fail: readers must come away hungry, their appetites whetted but not satiated.

Fortunately, the past decade has been an especially lively one for the study of Chinese civilization. Indeed, scholarship has been so productive, as well as specialized, that it is extraordinarily difficult to keep up with all that is going on. Perhaps that is itself a sign that the field has come of age, but the effort to maintain a broad view is as rewarding as it is necessary. It is hoped that students will benefit from a book that speaks with a single voice and perhaps even from the temerity of a single author who tries to do it all!

A broad survey such as this is by necessity based on the studies of many scholars (indeed the author's pleasure in wide reading is matched only by his fear of inadvertent plagiarism). No attempt has been made to list all the works consulted. The suggested readings in the appendix have been drawn up in the hope of meeting some of the readers' needs, not of acknowledging the author's indebtedness, although there is considerable overlap. It is also impossible here to list all the individuals who have contributed to this textbook by offering suggestions, criticism, and encouragement, or who helped by suggesting references, supplying a date or a translation for a term, and so forth, or to acknowledge individually the teachers, students, and colleagues who have influenced my thoughts about the broader problems of history and China and the teaching of these subjects. I do, however, want to single out for special mention Professor Arthur F. Wright (1913–76), scholar and humanist, whom I had the privilege of knowing as both teacher and friend.

For their outstanding contributions to the first edition and their continued influence in the second, I am indebted to William A. Pullin, without whose gentle persuasion this book would never have been written, Kwang-Ching Liu, William F. Morton, Robert M. Somers, H. Paul Varley, Gary Ledyard, Henry Sirotin, Avery M. Colt, Marion Corkett, Patricia Smythe, Carla Hirst Wiltenburg, and Jean Paul Tremblay. In addition, Maurice Meisner and Lee Sands made suggestions that were first incorporated into *Modern China and Japan: A Brief History* (1980).

It is a great sadness that William A. Pullin and Robert M. Somers, who contributed so much to the first edition of *A Brief History of Chinese and Japanese Civilizations*, did not live to see the second edition or the present volume. I miss them both and hope they would have been pleased.

The high cultures of China are profoundly visual, and the highest art is calligraphy. It therefore gives me particular pleasure to thank Dr. Léon Long Yien Chang (Chang Lung-yen) for gracing this book with the art of his brush.

Special thanks for helping make this textbook possible go to Drake Bush, acquisitions editor; Robert Watrous, manuscript editor; Cheryl Solheid, designer; Lynne Bush, production manager; Avery Hallowell, art editor; and Leslie Leland, production editor.

My greatest debt is to those who have lived with this book for so long, my forbearing family, for the project ate badly into the time available for me as son, father, and husband. My son Oliver helped in reading final proof of the first edition — his sharp eyes spotted errors that had eluded everyone else. My wife, Lore, as always, not only helped in innumerable direct and indirect ways but also contributed greatly to the art work, which includes a number of her own photographs.

CONRAD SCHIROKAUER

Note on Names and Romanization

In Chinese, surnames precede given names, and that has been the order followed in this book, except for modern Chinese scholars who, writing for a Western audience, have adopted the Western name sequence.

The transcription of Chinese terms is a troublesome matter, because there are two systems in wide use: Hanyu Pinyin, the system adopted by the People's Republic of China, is generally employed by newspapers and magazines as well as in many scholarly books, especially those on modern and contemporary China. However, since the older Wade-Giles system remains in use among scholars and on Taiwan and is, futhermore, employed in the vast majority of English-language publications prior to 1979, it is indispensable for the serious student.

The practice in this text is to use the Pinyin transcription with the Wade-Giles version supplied in parentheses on the first occurrence in each chapter except in those cases where the two versions are identical or where the only difference between them is the presence of a hyphen or umlaut. However, geographical names are given in Pinyin only, and we have used names such as "Canton," "Tibet," "Confucius," and others that have clearly entered the English language. There are also a few Southern names (Sun Yat-sen, Chiang Kai-shek) that conform to neither Wade-Giles nor Pinyin. Common usage has been followed in transcribing names used on Taiwan.

With the exception of Chang 'an (modern Xian), the modern geographical names have been used throughout. This has been done for easy identification even though it results in some anachronisms.

Note on Calligraphy on the Chapter Title Pages

In drawing the titles, Dr. Léon L. Y. Chang selected calligraphic forms appropriate for the contents of each chapter. Thus Chapters 1 and 2 are written in the Da Juan (great seal) form used during the Shang and Zhou. The title for Chapter 3 is in the Xiao Juan (small seal) form, which was promulgated as standard by the first emperor of the Qin. The title for Chapter 4 is written in two styles: the characters in the single column at the right are in the Li (clerical or official) form, which dates from the third century B.C. and was used until the middle of the third century A.D.; the characters at the left are in the Zheng (standard) form, which began during the Three Kingdoms period. Thus the first of these characters designates Wei, one of the Three Kingdoms. The next is Jin, which briefly reunified China. This style of calligraphy was called Jinli during the Tang and is now commonly called Kaishu. The titles of all subsequent chapters are written in the Zheng, Xing, or Cao forms (standard, longhand, or cursive), which are illustrated in Figure 4-3.

Hanyu Pinyin to Wade-Giles Conversion Table

Pinyin	Wade-Giles	Pinyin	Wade-Giles	Pinyin	Wade-Giles	Pinyin	Wade-Giles
a	a	chuai	ch'uai	feng	feng	ji	chi
ai	ai	chuan	ch'uan	fo	fo	jia	chia
an	an	chuang	ch'uang	fou	fou	jian	chien
ang	ang	chui	ch'ui	fu	fu	jiang	chiang
ao	ao	chun	ch'un			jiao	chiao
		chuo	ch'o			jie	chieh
ba	pa	ci	tz'u	ga	ka	jin	chin
bai	pai	cong	ts'ung	gai	kai	jing	ching
ban	pan	cou	ts'ou	gan	kan	jiong	chiung
bang	pang	cu	ts'u	gang	kang	jiu	chiu
bao	pao	cuan	ts'uan	gao	kao	ju	chü
bei	pei	cui	ts'ui	ge	ko	juan	chüan
ben	pen	cun	ts'un	gei	kei	jue	chüeh
beng	peng	cuo	ts'o	gen	ken	jun	chün
bi	pi			geng	keng		
bian	pien	da	ta	gong	kung	ka	k'a
biao	piao	dai	tai	gou	kou	kai	k'ai
bie	pieh	dan	tan	gu	ku	kan	k'an
bin	pin	dang	tang	gua	kua	kang	k'ang
bing	ping	dao	tao	guai	kuai	kao	k'ao
bo	po	de	te	guan	kuan	ke	k'o
bou	pou	deng	teng	guang	kuang	kei	k'ei
bu	pu	di	ti	gui	kuei	ken	k'en
		dian	tien	gun	kun	keng	k'eng
ca	ts'a	diao	tiao	guo	kuo	kong	k'ung
cai	ts'ai	die	tieh			kou	k'ou
can	ts'an	ding	ting	ha	ha	ku	k'u
cang	ts'ang	diu	tiu	hai	hai	kua	k'ua
cao	ts'ao	dong	tung	han	han	kuai	k'uai
ce	ts'e	dou	tou	hang	hang	kuan	k'uan
cen	ts'en	du	tu	hao	hao	kuang	k'uang
ceng	ts'eng	duan	tuan	he	ho	kui	k'uei
cha	ch'a	dui	tui	hei	hei	kun	k'un
chai	ch'ai	dun	tun	hen	hen	kuo	k'uo
chan	ch'an	duo	to	heng	heng		
chang	ch'ang			hong	hung	la	la
chao	ch'ao	e	o	hou	hou	lai	lai
che	ch'e	en	en	hu	hu	lan	lan
chen	ch'en	er	erh	hua	hua	lang	lang
cheng	ch'eng			huai	huai	lao	lao
chi	ch'ih	fa	fa	huan	huan	le	le
chong	ch'ung	fan	fan	huang	huang	lei	lei
chou	ch'ou	fang	fang	hui	hui	leng	leng
chu	ch'u	fei	fei	hun	hun	li	li
chua	ch'ua	fen	fen	huo	huo	lia	lia

Pinyin	Wade-Giles	Pinyin	Wade-Giles	Pinyin	Wade-Giles	Pinyin	Wade-Giles
lian	lien	nian	nien	qu	ch'ü	shuo	shuo
liang	liang	niang	niang	quan	ch'üan	si	ssu
liao	liao	niao	niao	que	ch'üeh	song	sung
lie	lieh	nie	nieh	qun	ch'ün	sou	sou
lin	lin	nin	nin			su	su
ling	ling	ning	ning	ran	jan	suan	suan
liu	liu	niu	niu	rang	jang	sui	sui
long	lung	nong	nung	rao	jao	sun	sun
lou	lou	nou	nou	re	je	suo	so
lu	lu	nu	nu	ren	jen		
lü	lü	nü	nü	reng	jeng	ta	t'a
luan	luan	nuan	nuan	ri	jih	tai	t'ai
lüan	lüan	nüe	nüeh	rong	jung	tan	t'an
lüe	lüeh	nuo	no	rou	jou	tang	t'ang
lun	lun			ru	ju	tao	t'ao
luo	lo	ou	ou	ruan	juan	te	t'e
				rui	jui	teng	t'eng
ma	ma	pa	p'a	run	jun	ti	t'i
mai	mai	pai	p'ai	ruo	jo	tian	t'ien
man	man	pan	p'an			tiao	t'iao
mang	mang	pang	p'ang	sa	sa	tie	t'ieh
mao	mao	pao	p'ao	sai	sai	ting	t'ing
mei	mei	pei	p'ei	san	san	tong	t'ung
men	men	pen	p'en	sang	sang	tou	t'ou
meng	meng	peng	p'eng	sao	sao	tu	t'u
mi	mi	pi	p'i	se	se	tuan	t'uan
mian	mien	pian	p'ien	sen	sen	tui	t'ui
miao	miao	piao	p'iao	seng	seng	tun	t'un
mie	mieh	pie	p'ieh	sha	sha	tuo	t'o
min	min	pin	p'in	shai	shai		
ming	ming	ping	p'ing	shan	shan	wa	wa
miu	miu	po	p'o	shang	shang	wai	wai
mo	mo	pou	p'ou	shao	shao	wan	wan
mou	mou	pu	p'u	she	she	wang	wang
mu	mu			shen	shen	wei	wei
		qi	ch'i	sheng	sheng	wen	wen
na	na	qia	ch'ia	shi	shih	weng	weng
nai	nai	qian	ch'ien	shou	shou	wo	wo
nan	nan	qiang	ch'iang	shu	shu	wu	wu
nang	nang	qiao	ch'iao	shua	shua		
nao	nao	qie	ch'ieh	shuai	shuai	xi	hsi
nei	nei	qin	ch'in	shuan	shuan	xia	hsia
nen	nen	qing	ch'ing	shuang	shuang	xian	hsien
neng	neng	qiong	ch'iung	shui	shui	xiang	hsiang
ni	ni	qiu	ch'iu	shun	shun	xiao	hsiao

Pinyin	Wade-Giles	Pinyin	Wade-Giles	Pinyin	Wade-Giles	Pinyin	Wade-Giles
xie	hsieh	yi	i	zei	tsei	zhua	chua
xin	hsin	yin	yin	zen	tsen	zhuai	chuai
xing	hsing	ying	ying	zeng	tseng	zhuan	chuan
xiong	hsiung	yong	yung	zha	cha	zhuang	chuang
xiu	hsiu	you	yu	zhai	chai	zhui	chui
xu	hsü	yu	yü	zhan	chan	zhun	chun
xuan	hsüan	yuan	yüan	zhang	chang	zhuo	cho
xue	hsüeh	yue	yüeh	zhao	chao	zi	tzu
xun	hsün	yun	yün	zhe	che	zong	tsung
				zhen	chen	zou	tsou
ya	ya	za	tsa	zheng	cheng	zu	tsu
yai	yai	zai	tsai	zhi	chih	zuan	tsuan
yan	yen	zan	tsan	zhong	chung	zui	tsui
yang	yang	zang	tsang	zhou	chou	zun	tsun
yao	yao	zao	tsao	zhu	chu	zuo	tso
ye	yeh	ze	tse				

Source: *People's Republic of China: Administrative Atlas* (Washington, D.C.: Central Intelligence Agency, 1975), 46–47.

Wade-Giles /Pinyin Table

Each entry in the Wade-Giles column represents the initial letter or letter pair of a syllable or word. Unless otherwise indicated, conversion is accomplished simply by changing that initial letter. Where other changes are necessary or the conversion is irregular, the entire word or syllable is listed.

Wade-Giles	Pinyin	Wade-Giles	Pinyin	Wade-Giles	Pinyin	Wade-Giles	Pinyin
a	a	ch'en	chen	i	yi	p'ien	pian
		ch'eng	cheng				
cha	zha	ch'i	qi	j	r	s	s
chai	zhai	ch'ia	qia	jih	ri	shih	shi
chan	zhan	ch'iang	qiang	jo	ruo	so	suo
chang	zhang	ch'iao	qiao	jung	rong	sung	song
chao	zhao	ch'ieh	qie			ssu, szu	si
che	zhe	ch'ien	qian	k	g		
chen	zhen	ch'i	chi	ko	ge	t	d
cheng	zheng	ch'in	qin	kuei	gui	tieh	dieh
chi	ji	ch'ing	qing	kung	gong	tien	dian
chia	jia	ch'iu	qiu			to	duo
chiao	jiao	ch'iung	qiong	k'	k	tung	dong
chieh	jie	ch'o	chuo	k'o	ke		
chien	jian	ch'ou	chou	k'ung	kong	t'	t
chih	zhi	ch'u	chu			t'ieh	tie
chin	jin	ch'ü	qu	l	l	t'ien	tian
ching	jing	ch'uai	chuai	lieh	lie	t'o	tuo
chiu	jiu	ch'uan	chuan	lien	lian	t'ung	tong
chiung	jiong	ch'üan	quan	lo	luo		
cho	zhuo	ch'uang	chuang	lüeh	lüe	ts, tz	z
chou	zhou	ch'üeh	que	lung	long	tso	zuo
chu	zhu	ch'ui	chui			tsung	zong
chü	ju	ch'un	chun	m	m	tzu	zi
chua	zhua	ch'ün	qun	mieh	mie		
chuai	zhuai	ch'ung	chong	mien	mian	ts', tz'	c
chuan	zhuan					ts'o	cuo
chüan	juan	f	f	n	n	ts'ung	cong
chuang	zhuang			nieh	nie	tz'u	ci
chüeh	jue	h	h	nien	nian		
chui	zhui	ho	he	no	nuo	w	w
chun	zhun	hung	hong	nüeh	ne		
chün	jun					y	y
chung	zhong	hs	x	o	o	yeh	ye
		hsieh	xie			yen	yan
ch'a	cha	hsien	xian	p	b	yu	you
ch'ai	chai	hsiung	xiong	pieh	bie	yü	yu
ch'an	chan	hsü	xu	pien	bian	yüan	yuan
ch'ang	chang	hsüan	xuan			yüeh	yue
ch'ao	chao	hsüeh	xue	p'	p	yün	yun
ch'e	che	hsün	xun	p'ieh	pie	yung	yong

Contents

PART TWO
CHINA IN A BUDDHIST AGE

PART THREE
LATE IMPERIAL CHINA

PART FIVE

POST-IMPERIAL CHINA

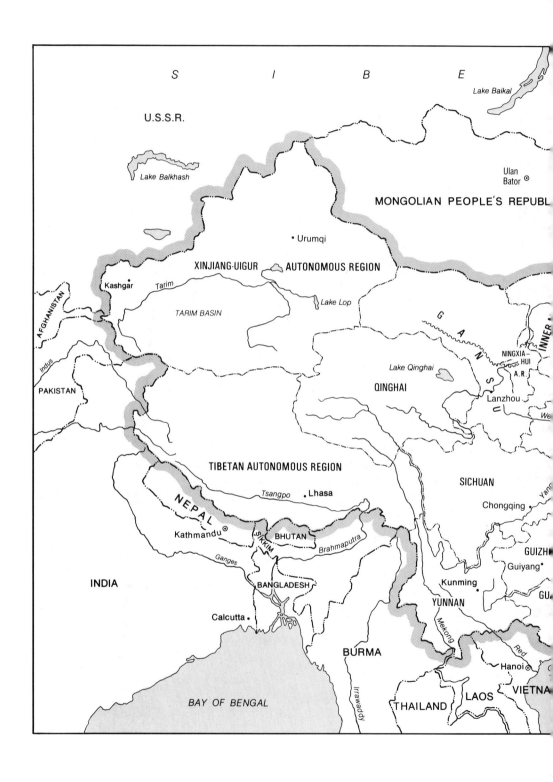

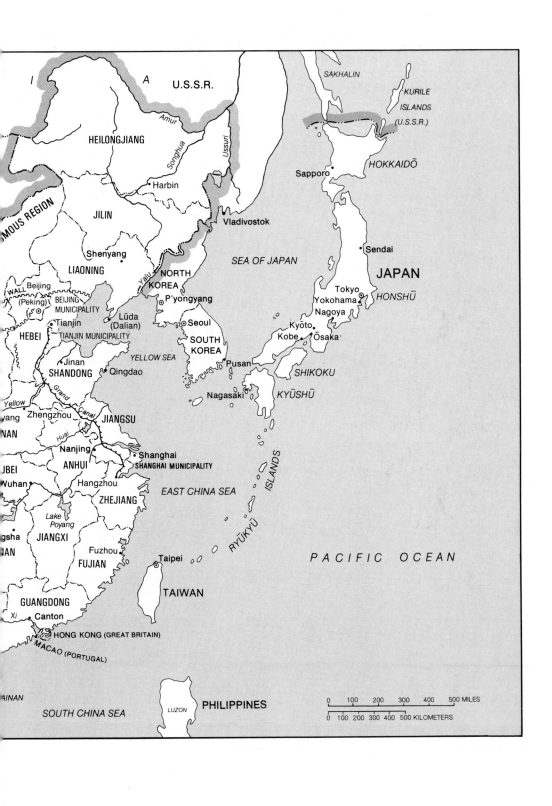

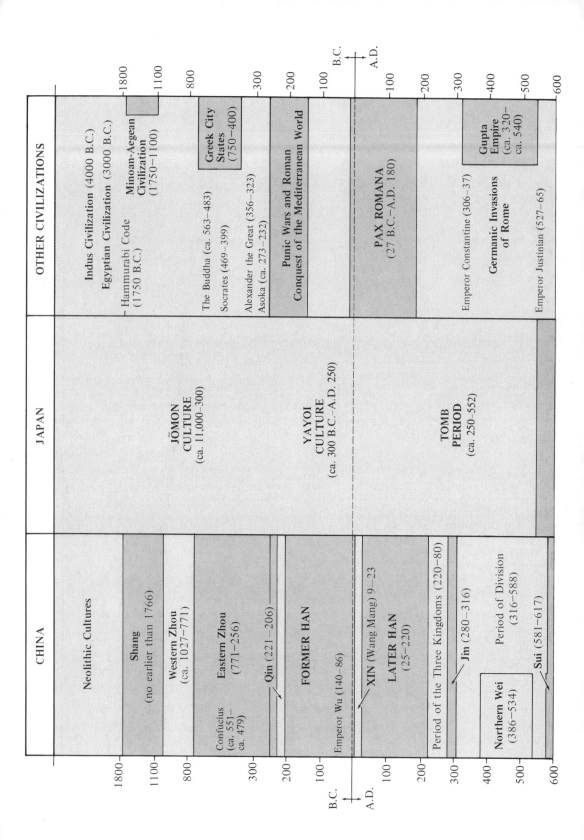

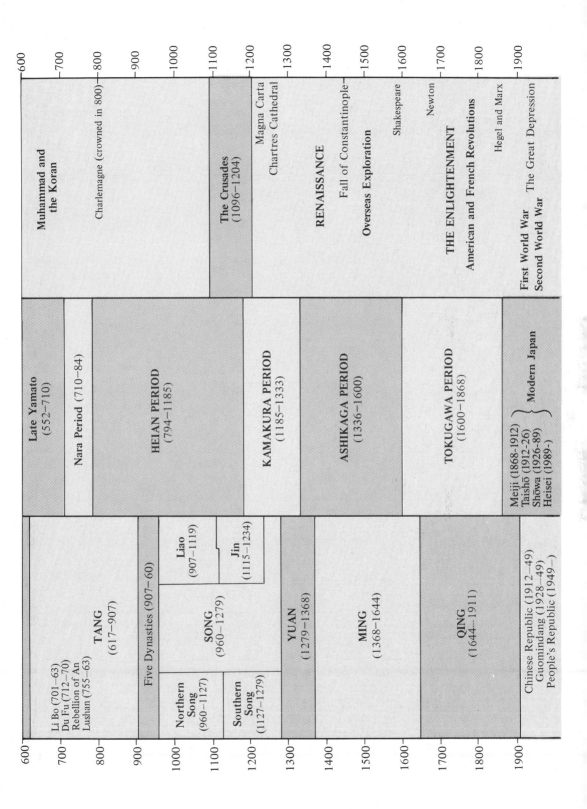

PART ONE

The Classical Civilization of China

Flying Horse. Bronze, Wu wei, Gansu, second century A.D., 34.5 cm × 45 cm.

1
Chinese Antiquity

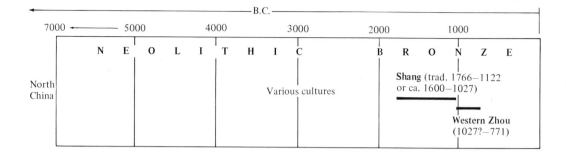

	B.C.						
7000	5000	4000	3000	2000	1000		

N E O L I T H I C   B R O N Z E

North China   Various cultures

Shang (trad. 1766–1122 or ca. 1600–1027)

Western Zhou (1027?–771)

*T*he earliest civilization in East Asia originated in China. Although in many ways uniquely Chinese, it established the foundations for the culture that later spread its influence throughout the rest of East Asia and in this respect provides a starting point for the study of the history of the entire region.

Geographic Parameters

In China, as elsewhere, the physical environment provided the opportunities and challenges out of which civilization was wrought, and civilization, in turn, over many centuries shaped and altered the environment. Geography not only provided the setting for history but itself became part of history as new lands were opened to agriculture, marshes were drained, canals were built, mountains were terraced, dikes were constructed to contain rivers, and a complex ecosystem evolved. In this sense, Chinese history consists of the interaction of man and nature, each leaving a deep imprint on the other. Yet the basic configurations of the land remained the same.

Because Chinese civilization was based on intensive farming, it spread, over the centuries, into areas suitable for agriculture but did not take hold in regions too dry for farming. It seems that a culture creates its own frontiers. We must, therefore, distinguish between the homeland of Chinese civilization — the agricultural regions that comprise China proper — and the vast areas of Inner Asia and other lands beyond the Great Wall that are part of China today but were traditionally inhabited by non-Chinese, generally nomadic, peoples.

Within China proper, the basic geographical division between North and South gave rise to different agricultural traditions as far back as the fifth millennium B.C. The outstanding geographical feature of the North is the Yellow River, which flows from the highlands of the west, through the alluvial lowlands of the Great Plain, to empty into the sea near the Shandong Penin-

4

sula. It is a region of temperate climate, cold winters and warm summers, but rainfall is scarce. This is particularly true in the arid west, but in the moister areas as well the annual rainfall is extremely variable. Although the area is subject to drought, the soil is fertile. It is a region suitable for growing millet, kaoliang (a kind of sorghum), and, in the moister parts, wheat and beans.

Very different conditions prevail south of a line which runs roughly along the 33rd parallel, following the Qinling Mountains and the Huai River. Here rain is abundant, the climate is subtropical, and the soils are leached. The dominant river is the Yangzi, which is about 3,200 miles long, roughly 500 miles longer than the Yellow River. Once the necessary technology was developed and the land laboriously drained, a process that took many centuries, this region proved ideal for intensive rice culture. This grain, destined to become the favorite staple throughout East Asia, was already important in the Neolithic cultures of South China.

North and South the agricultural regions were bordered by areas unsuitable for agriculture; and not until the establishment of the People's Republic in 1949 was there a concerted attempt to integrate the steppelands of Manchuria and Mongolia, the arid regions of far western Xinjiang, or the Tibetan highlands into China proper. These regions, like the jungles and mountains of Guizhou and Yunnan in the southwest and the world's largest ocean on the east, formed formidable barriers to communication with other Asian civilizations. This was particularly the case during the formative period of Chinese civilization prior to the domestication of the camel (first mentioned in Chinese texts in the late fourth century B.C.).

Neolithic Cultures

Reports concerning a few fossil teeth discovered in Yunnan Province in 1965 indicate that a humanoid may have lived in southwestern China around a million years ago and had the use of fire. More ample archaeological data exist for the humanoid known as Peking man (Homo erectus pekinensis) whose remains, found not far from modern Beijing (Peking), indicate that he may have lived half a million years ago between two periods of glaciation. Although in terms of cranial capacity and other physiological criteria Peking man was only a protohuman, he used fire and worked with flaked and pebble stone tools. However, any connection between this precursor of Homo sapiens and the historical Chinese people is purely speculative. The origins of China's civilization are best looked for in its Neolithic cultures.

A stream of archeological discoveries continues to change our picture of the Neolithic in China. Whereas once one culture, the Yangshao, was considered nuclear, now it seems clear that a number of cultures, each with its own phases, contributed to the formation of Chinese civilization (see Figure 1-1). Most extensive in the North was the Yangshao culture, with sites found on terraces on river banks where over the centuries wind had deposited fine-grain

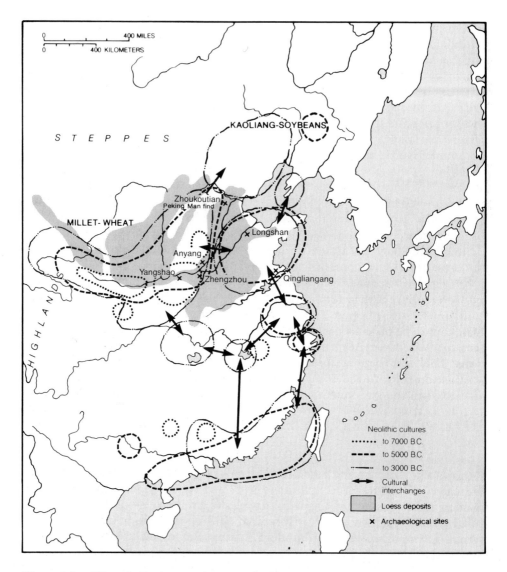

Figure 1-1   Climatic Regions and Areas of Earliest Settlement

sand to form loess. In the highlands of Shanxi, Shaanxi, and Gansu, the layers of loess reach a thickness of 350 feet. Because loess is fertile, retains moisture, and is easy to work, it favored the development of agriculture and encouraged settlement.

Other Neolithic settlements also are usually located on high ground near a stream, close enough to use the water but safe from flooding. This problem was particularly acute in the lower reaches of the Yellow River, which received its name from the heavy load of loess carried in its sluggish waters. Down to the seventh century B.C., people's response to this dangerous river was to evade flooding by moving their settlements upland and to propitiate the river spirits by sacrifice.

Sites such as Banpo (Pan-p'o) near present Xian in Shaanxi Province reveal that the Yangshao people lived in small villages, practiced agriculture, raised pigs, made painted pottery, and buried their dead in a special burial ground. They, and their contemporaries to the east, hunted and fished, but their main sustenance came from growing millet, the grain which remained the foundation of the diet of the ordinary person in North China. Another element of continuity is the Chinese emphasis on raising grain crops together with small animals like the pig (and later the chicken) to supplement the diet. This was the basis of the agricultural technology that, refined over the centuries, provided the economic foundations for Chinese civilization.

Southern and Northern cultures shared in a general Neolithic technology but were distinguished by distinctive artifacts, ornaments, burial practices, and most visibly by styles of pottery varying in shape, color, and decoration. Some were painted, some not. Some were cord marked, others embellished with comb impressions or stamped designs. Pottery with cord marking was apparently once common throughout East Asia — remains have been found on Taiwan and in Japan where the earliest have been dated back to 10,000 B.C. In shape, however, and in appearance, the Chinese and Japanese cord-marked pottery are very far apart. Similarly, Yangshao painted pottery has not been linked to any produced outside of China. This ware was usually decorated with symmetrical abstract designs, although fish and human faces also appear. Figure 1-2 exemplifies the decorative process of abstraction and also serves as a reminder that fish was an important supplementary source of food throughout East Asia.

Interchange among the various cultures accelerated after around 4000 B.C. forming what Kwangchih Chang has termed an "inter-action" sphere[1] even as the various cultures were becoming increasingly complex (see Figure 1-1). The Longshan (Lung-shan) cultures of North China shared such technological developments as building walls of stamped earth, and they used the potter's wheel and improved high temperature kilns in which to produce predominantly undecorated grey ware. That they also shared in a common fund of beliefs is indicated by their practice of scapulimancy, divination by applying heat to animal bones (oracle bones) and interpreting the resulting cracks.

There is evidence of the beginning of metallurgy in Longshan cultures, but nothing on the scale of the discoveries at Erlitou, in central Henan, which includes remains of a bronze foundry as well as the foundations of two very large houses. It is clear that this Erlitou culture developed out of Longshan, but its relationship to what came after remains subject to dispute. Some scholars say that Erlitou belongs to early Shang, but others identify it with the Xia (Hsia) "dynasty" traditionally thought to have preceded the Shang. They point out that its sites coincide with those traditionally given as the capitals of the Xia and that prior to archaeological discoveries made in the 1920s many

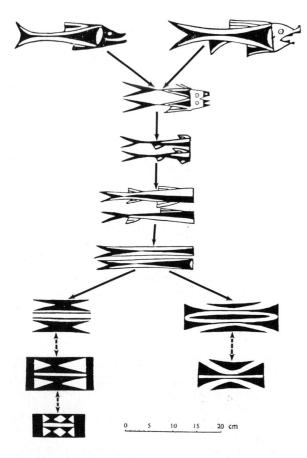

Figure 1-2   Evolution of Yangshao fish designs (from site at Banpo).

modern scholars had also dismissed the Shang as a later fabrication. However, whereas everyone now accepts the historicity of the Shang (but not its idealized image) the Xia issue remains unresolved.

Civilization: The Shang

With the Shang, China entered a significant new phase of development, for there now appeared all the characteristics usually associated with the emergence of civilization: the formation of cities, the use of writing, an increase in occupational specialization, and a more complex organization of society. China entered this stage late compared to the ancient civilizations of the Middle East, but indications are that the process occurred without significant external influence.

Although the Shang became the predominant power in North China, other peoples and cultures remained in control of pockets of varying size (see Figure 1-3). The core of the Shang state was northern Henan, where two sites have

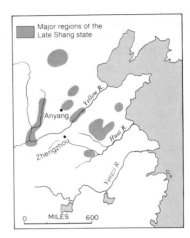

Figure 1-3   The Shang State

yielded particularly valuable information. The earliest of these, Zhengzhou, contains Longshan remains beneath those of the Shang, providing evidence of the continuity between the two cultures. The later site at Anyang is rich in archaeological materials including oracle bones used for scapulimancy (see Figure 1-4). These, along with tortoise shells used for the same purpose, bear a

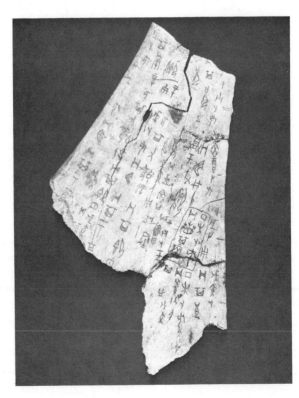

Figure 1-4
Inscribed oracle bone.

fully developed language. The exact dates of Shang civilization and of the Shang state remain to be determined. Although 1766 B.C.–1122 B.C. are the dates traditionally accepted, there are good arguments in support of the view that the Shang began around 1600 B.C. and came to an end in 1027 B.C.

In addition to the presence of writing and bronze, archaeology reveals other major differences between the Shang and its Neolithic predecessors. One of these is the horse-drawn chariot; another is the size and scale of the Shang's capital cities. The walls surrounding Zhengzhou are estimated as 2,385 feet long, 60 feet wide, and 30 feet high. It might have taken 10,000 laborers working 330 days a year no less than 18 years to complete such a wall given the technology of the time. Obviously, this was a society that was capable of mobilizing considerable human resources over a long period.

Written Language

The language that appears on the Shang oracle bones and tortoise shells already included almost all of the grammatical principles of later classical Chinese. The function of words in a sentence is determined basically by placement; for example, the subject precedes the verb, the possessive comes before the possessed, and so forth. This is a positional grammar not unlike modern English as contrasted with such highly inflected languages as Greek, Latin, or Russian. The Shang further possessed a developed script, which was later stylized and greatly expanded but which nonetheless formed the starting point for writing throughout East Asia.

In its origin and fundamental orientation, this script was strongly visual (see Figure 1-5; Figure 4-4), and writing became the most highly prized of the visual arts, as well as being a means of communication. From early pictograms (stylized pictorial representations of things) and from ideograms (visual representations of a thing or concept through association), the student can learn much about early Chinese culture. The pictogram for "book," for example, suggests that the first books were made of slips of wood or bamboo held together by a thong. The symbol also suggests that the written language, originally developed for communication with the gods in the form of burnt offerings, was now used for human communication as well.

The interpretation of pictograms and ideograms, particularly those for abstract terms like "good" (woman and child), is fascinating but fraught with danger, for many etymologies accepted for centuries have conclusively been shown to be false. Furthermore, many symbols or characters are neither pictograms nor ideograms, but phonograms. The simplest of these are phonetic loans, symbols borrowed for their sound rather than for their meaning. An imaginary English counterpart might be the use of a symbol representing a bee to write the verb "to be," and we could go on and combine "bee" and "leaf" to write "belief," but it would hardly do to conclude from this that people in England conceived of "being" in terms of insect and vegetable life.

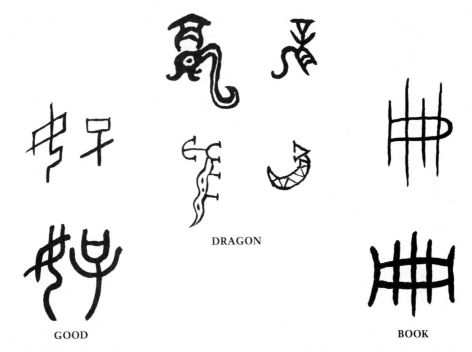

DRAGON

GOOD   BOOK

Figure 1-5   Early Chinese writing: inscriptions on bronze (heavy ink) and bone (lighter ink). Drawn by Dr. Léon L. Y. Chang.

Most phonograms are more complex, and the majority of Chinese characters are composed of a combination of pictogramic and phonetic elements, although this was not yet true in the Shang. The development of such compound characters was no doubt a response to the proliferation of phonetic loans, which must have caused great confusion in a language that has an unusually large number of homonyms. In the compound characters, one element (the phonetic) indicates the pronunciation of the word and another (the radical or signific) designates the general category to which the word refers. This principle is illustrated by the word for "black horse." The radical, "horse," is on the left; the phonetic, "li," on the right: together they inform the reader that the "li" under discussion has something to do with horses. The presupposition is, of course, that the reader already knows that there is a word in the language with this sound and meaning. Over the course of time the significs were standardized and their number reduced, finally resulting in the 214 that still provide the basic organization for most Chinese dictionaries. However, the language has undergone numerous phonetic changes over time, with the result that in modern times the phonetic element is no longer a sure guide to pronunciation.

BLACK
HORSE

The inventor of the character used to represent "black horse" had a wide range of emblematic symbols for this very common sound from which to choose. Naturally a symbol with appropriate overtones — in this case "elegant and beautiful" — was selected. In this way, at least at the beginning, the phonetic element was not a completely neutral indicator of sound like the letters of an alphabet or the syllabaries developed much later in Korea and Japan.

The failure of the Chinese to develop a wholly phonetic script shows that the existing system, complex as it is, was adequate to their purposes. The consequences for Chinese thought of this written language are important. The average literate Chinese in later times were no more conscious of the etymology of the words they wrote than are modern English speakers writing about Oxford (where oxen ford the river). Yet the Chinese symbols, unlike their alphabetic counterparts, tended to acquire an identity and life of their own and to function as potent emblems. An example is the rule, effective down to the twentieth century, prohibiting the use of a character that appeared in the name of a ruling emperor or any of his dynastic predecessors. Thus, again in imaginary contemporary terms, Oxford would have to change its name and such words as "afford" would be banned, at least in the United States, because a Gerald Ford had been president.

Like later classical Chinese, the language on the oracle bones is very compact. Because it contains a large number of homophones, classical Chinese is aurally incomprehensible without a visual reference. The spoken language uses many more compounds. Thus the compactness of oracle bone inscriptions suggests that, even at the beginning, there was a gap between the spoken and written languages, a distinction that the visual orientation of the latter helped to perpetuate.

The spoken and the written languages continually influenced each other, but until the twentieth century they remained distinct, and literacy was the highly prized monopoly of a restricted cultural elite who prided themselves on working not with their hands but with their brains. On the other hand, the written language was a unifying element geographically. There was one system of writing (with some local variations prior to 221 B.C.) even though people spoke mutually unintelligible languages. Thus, in modern times, a speaker of Cantonese could not converse with a Mandarin speaker from Beijing (Peking), but they could communicate in writing and read the same newspapers. And beyond China, scholars in Vietnam, Korea, and Japan were able to participate in Chinese literary culture although they usually did not learn to speak Chinese.

About 100,000 Shang oracle bones have come to light, and some 50,000 inscriptions from these bones have been published. Of the roughly 5,000 characters used in the inscriptions, approximately 1,500 have been deciphered. The bones were used to address questions to the spirits, usually on behalf of the ruler, and the nature of these questions provides important insights into Shang religion and the activities of the ruler. They ask about the proper timing of military expeditions, hunts, and journeys; inquire about ceremonials and omens; and ask about the weather, the course of an illness, or the sex of an unborn child. The oracle bone inscriptions have also been used to confirm the Shang genealogy contained in the *Records of the Grand Historian* by the great Han historian Sima Qian (Ssu-ma Ch'ien) (see Chapter 3).

Students of the Shang continue to work on the oracle bones, and new discoveries continue to be made. Of equal or even greater importance, however, are the Shang dynasty bronzes, which furnish dramatic proof of technological advances and provide further information concerning other aspects of Shang civilization.

The Bronzes

Bronze was worked in foundries outside the cities, and the artisans who cast it also had their quarters beyond the city walls. Their houses, provided with floors of stamped earth, testify to a way of life superior to that of the common people who lived in semi-subterranean dwellings.

The peasantry apparently continued to use stone tools, and there was little change in agricultural methods from the Neolithic. At least this seems to be the case, for very few bronze tools have been discovered, and the metal was apparently used mostly for weapons, chariot fittings, and above all for ritual vessels. These were constructed of pieces cast separately in clay models and then joined together. The Shang bronzesmiths are noted for the clarity of detail and perfection of their craftsmanship.

The bronze vessels were cast in many forms (see Figure 1-6), some derived from old pottery traditions, others going back to containers made of more perishable materials such as wood, and still others apparently new with the Shang. They were receptacles for storing or serving various solids and liquids

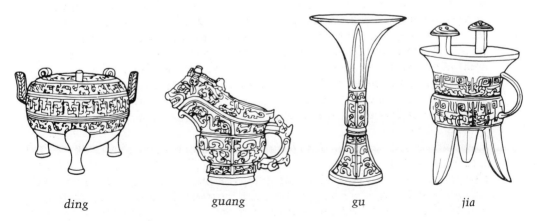

| *ding* | *guang* | *gu* | *jia* |

Figure 1-6   Four types of Shang bronze vessels. The *ding (ting)* is a cooking vessel; the *guang (kuang)*, a wine container; the *gu (ku)* and *jia (chia)*, drinking vessels.

used in the performance of sacred ceremonies. Many of them probably belonged to altar sets such as the one illustrated in Figure 1-7. The pieces in this set date from the late Shang or early Zhou (Chou), and the set includes vessels in various styles, probably accumulated over a period of time by the family that built the tomb from which it was excavated. One type of vessel represented is the tripod, a shape that goes back to the Neolithic and is particularly ingenious in its hollow-leg variety, which is a most effective way of heating liquids rapidly with minimum heat loss. The tripod also appears under a pot with a perforated base to form a steamer.

It is typical of the developed Shang style that all available space is decorated, with the forms of real and imaginary animals figuring prominently. Most clearly visible in the illustration of the altar set are the heads (perhaps of rams) on the handles of the two ritual vessels at the top and the single-legged dragon-like creature that decorates the altar itself. Some of the abstract forms also derive from animals. For example, in the *gu (ku)* (the vessel directly in front of the altar at the very center), the vertical decoration, somewhat like the petal of a flower, is a stylized cicada. Since the life cycle of this insect includes a long period of dormancy in the ground, it forms an appropriate symbol for the rebirth of an ancestor in the spirit world, and it was not uncommon, among the wealthy, for a corpse to be buried with a jade cicada in its mouth. The significance of other forms is more difficult to fathom, and this is true of the most common motif of them all, the *taotie (t'ao-t'ieh)* (see Figure 1-8). This mytho-

Figure 1-7   Bronze altar set. (Altar table, 19.7 cm × 89.9 cm × 46.4 cm.) Metropolitan Museum of Art, New York.

Crest   C-horn   Tail   Quill

Lower jaw   Forehead   Fang   Snout   Upper jaw or trunk   Beak or fang   Eye   Leg

Figure 1-8   *Taotie (t'ao-t'ieh)* design.

logical being is always presented frontally as though squashed onto a horizontal plane to form a symmetrical design. In the modern language the term *taotie* signifies glutton, and in the late Zhou dynasty it was considered a covetous man banished by the Shang to guard a corner of heaven against evil monsters or, more fancifully, as a monster equipped with only a head who tries to devour men but hurts only itself. The trouble with these explanations is that it was only much later (during the Song [Sung] dynasty: 960–1279) that the form appearing on the bronzes was identified as a *taotie* at all.

It was also during the Song dynasty that Shang bronzes first became objects of study by the student of antiquity and of pride for the collector of art and artifacts. They have ever since been appreciated as works of art, prized not only for their shape and design but also for the various green, blue green, and even reddish patinas created by chemical action as they lay buried in the ground. Unfortunately, the forging of bronzes also has an old history, and a patina is no guarantee of old age; at least one family made forgery a hereditary occupation, burying bronzes in the ground to be disinterred two generations later.

The detailed study of the changing types and styles of bronzes from early Shang through late Zhou and into the Han is a fascinating but specialized field of art history. The main stylistic development during the Shang was away from rather controlled decoration kept within the bounds of the vessel toward the more bristling and protruding forms and flanges found in the Late Shang. Some of the Shang forms such as the *gu* are very graceful, but the most powerful pieces have about them an air of ferocious majesty. It is an art that is not easily accessible but that can be most rewarding:

> Our first reaction to the art of the ritual bronze may well be that we are coming into contact with something thoroughly unfamiliar, not to say hostile. The shape of the vessels, and the strangely potent beings they advertise, convey the impression of a spirit that is almost barbaric, and we perhaps have to remind ourselves that they are, after all, highly civilized works of art. But the more prolonged our examination of structure and content, the less acute does this feeling of strangeness and hostility become. We find that we are acquiring a new and first-rate aesthetic experience.[2]

The beauty of these objects lives on even though the religion they served has died.

Shang Religion

Some of the Shang bronzes are decorated with representations of the animals sacrificed in religious ceremonials, and this may also be the significance of a human head that appears on the decoration of a recently excavated vessel as well as of a number of bronze axes found in various tombs. More direct evidence of human immolation is provided by the contents of royal tombs. Some of these are immense. They contain the remains not only of animals but also of people buried alive. In one tomb there are the remains of a chariot complete with horse and driver; in others whole entourages accompany the ruler in death. Human victims were also sacrificed below the foundations of buildings. The people marked out for such grisly deaths were non-Shang "barbarians" captured in war and reduced to slavery. Presumably they were believed to accompany the dead on a journey to the afterworld.

It is not known what kind of sacrifices the ruler made to his ancestors, but it is certain that such sacrifices were an important part of his life. Actually, the names by which the Shang kings are known represent the days assigned for sacrifice to their spirits. Not only was the good will of the ancestral spirits essential for the well-being of the living, the performance of these solemn rituals was also a source of legitimacy for the ruler and helped to sanctify the living hierarchy as an extension of the dead. And just as a ruler presided over mundane society, there was a principal deity, the supreme god or god-on-high, *Shangdi (Shang-ti),* whose powers far exceeded those of the ordinary spirits. *Shangdi* controlled the basic forces of nature and human destiny and was so elevated that earthly rulers approached him through the intermediation of their ancestral spirits.

Many other deities were worshipped by the king and his people. Jade disks representing a circular heaven have been preserved from the Shang dynasty, as have small square jade pillars that represent the earth. Indeed, jade, respected for its strength and clarity, had its own mystique and was considered to possess protective powers.

To the people of the Shang, the world seemed populated not merely by humans, but also by ghosts, spirits, and mythical monsters. It is probable that various animal gods served as tribal totems. The legend that the progenitor of the Shang was a black bird is very likely of Shang date even though not written down until later. Another later source tells of a god who may be identical with the deity who dispatched the black bird and whose wives gave birth to ten suns and twelve moons. Fortunately, a great archer saved humanity from the overwhelming heat and light by shooting down the excess celestial spheres. Such legends, however garbled in the retelling, are the remnants of what must have been a rich mythology.

Furthermore, there is no reason to suppose that folk religion during the Shang was any less rich in gods of the house and hearth, of the field and well, of mountains and rivers than was the case later on. Unfortunately, there is no access to this material now, and students of folk religion, unlike archaeologists, have no carbon 14 tests for dating the antiquity of their materials.

The elements of Shang religion known to have survived into later times include reverence for ancestors and a concept of the ruler as having important religious functions, expressed in the centrality of his sacred places (already oriented north-south, east-west in the Shang) and in ceremonials that, although in adumbrated form, Chinese rulers continued to perform for three millennia after the end of the Shang.

Government and Society

In the Shang as in other ancient cultures there was no distinction between the sacred and the secular, and David Keightly has suggested that we think of the Shang as a "political-religious force field"[3] varying in intensity over time which may or may not have had a single capital throughout the period. At the center of this force-field was the king. Kingship was hereditary, but intragenerational succession from older to younger brother was as frequent as intergenerational inheritance, usually from uncle to nephew. Aside from his religious duties, the king was the leader in time of war. In time of peace, he spent much of his time in hunting. Major hunts might go on for months and provided good preparation for warfare, as well as provisions for the table and the altar.

The Shang may well have originated as an alliance, and loyalty was to the king rather than an abstract "state." There was not at this early date a distinction between the king as a private and a public person; the government can best be thought of as modeled on a patriarchal family in which the king as father had undisputed authority; the running of the state was not considered essentially different from operating a household. Beyond the central area, however, his authority was in frequent need of reassertion, for he spent much of his time in travel to reinforce the kin and religious ties with local leaders. The capital then may have been "a base of operations, a cult center, a necropolis, an industrial and artisan center, rather than a fixed administrative and redistributive center."[4]

To assist the king there were officials who served in various capacities as needed. They acted as generals in war, served on royal missions, supervised building projects, managed the royal stables and palace, directed the artisans, and took charge of outlying territories assigned to them. The highest officials were no doubt drawn from the nobility that lived in the capital. In war the nobles fought from chariots, using bows and arrows and spears. The less fortunate served as foot soldiers.

Other officials were specialists in divination who may also have been responsible for setting the calendar, a vital function in agrarian society since the correct timing of sowing and reaping and other farm tasks is a matter of life or death. The Shang used a system of counting days in repeating cycles of sixty, which much later, in the second century B.C., was also adopted for keeping track of years.

Less privileged than the nobility but better off than the majority of peasants were the artisans who worked in jade, bronze, bone, and leather; wove hemp and silk; made pottery; built chariots; and otherwise fashioned a material culture richer and more sophisticated than that of previous eras. Most people, however, lived in villages, tilled the land, and lived in houses that were only partly above the ground. Their lives probably did not differ much from those of their descendants in the Western Zhou period.

The Western Zhou (1027? – 771 B.C.)

The Zhou was based to the west of the Shang and seems to have shared in the developed culture of the time even before it conquered the Shang. Consequently there was no sharp break in technological or cultural continuity. Its capital cities, like those of the Shang, were surrounded by stamped-earth walls made of layers of compressed earth hammered down by the workmen. The cities were oriented according to the points of the compass. Important buildings were built on stamped-earth foundations and faced south. During its period of vigor, the court shifted the capital six times, but until the eighth century it remained in the area just west of modern Xian. After the dynasty was forced, in its decline in 771 B.C., to flee from barbarian attack and shifted the capital east, near present Luoyang, it officially continued but without real power.

During the early Western Zhou, bronze was used for the same purposes as under the Shang, and even in style it is difficult to distinguish Late Shang from Early Zhou pieces (see Figure 1-7). But change soon set in. Even early Zhou bronzes sometimes carry lengthy inscriptions in contrast to the simple indications of ownership that appear on some of the Shang vessels. Certain Shang shapes, the elegant *gu* for instance, disappear as do some Shang motifs including the *taotie* and the cicada, which are gone by the tenth century. Among animals introduced by the Zhou, birds figure prominently. One indication of change is a greater coarseness, a loss of sharpness in detail.

In the late Western Zhou (often called Middle Zhou by art historians), animal forms tend to dissolve into purely decorative patterns and ribbons. The stripes on the tiger shown in Figure 1-9, however, are not purely decorative since they suggest the skin of the animal and help to create a sense of movement. Such free standing figures first appeared in the Shang and became quite popular during the Zhou. The opening on top suggests that such tigers may have been used as structural supports, and this is born out by their sturdiness. Seen from the front, however, the lowered head and bared fangs reveal that this art had not yet lost its bite.

The vessel shown in Figure 1-10, which dates from the middle of the ninth century B.C., clearly illustrates how animal forms were transformed into purely ornamental, repetitive patterns that, like the Yangshao designs derived from fish, retain only hints of their origin. The effect is decorative rather than awe inspiring, and the inscription on this vessel states that it was commissioned as a bridal gift to a firstborn child. It ends with the words, "may sons and grandsons forever treasure and use it." [5] From their origin as sacred vessels used in solemn (and bloody) religious rites, the vessels have been transformed into treasured family heirlooms. Such changes in the appearance and function of the bronzes are evidence of a slow and gradual process of secularization in the upper reaches of society, a process which was to accelerate in the centuries immediately following the move to the east. It does not imply a weakening of religion but does suggest an expansion of the secular realm and a more worldly attitude toward life.

Recognition of this trend must not obscure the general continuity of religious belief from Shang to Zhou. On the one hand, in the late Shang there was already a decline in the frequency of divination and in the range of questions asked. On the other, *Shangdi* continued to be venerated, although he was

Figure 1-9 Tiger. Zhou dynasty, ninth century B.C., 25.2 cm × 75.2 cm. Freer Gallery of Art, Washington, D.C.

Figure 1-10 *Hu*, ceremonial
wine vessel. Mid-ninth
century B.C., 60.6 cm high.
Asian Art Museum of San Francisco,
Avery Brundage Collection.

increasingly referred to as *"Tian"* (*"T'ien"*), or *"Heaven,"* which gradually
replaced the older term. Burial practices also changed. The number of humans
and animals buried alive in tombs decreased; greater stress was placed on the
observance of proper rites and ritual in dealing with both gods and men. The
ruler, styled "Son of Heaven" (a term later applied to emperors), still derived
ultimate authority from the divine. One of the key concepts of Chinese political theory, the idea that the sovereign ruled by virtue of a Mandate from
Heaven, very likely originated from a Zhou justification for their overthrow
of the Shang. Furthermore, political relationships were more extensive and
complex than those of the Shang and required solemn sacrifices to ancestors
for the necessary sanctification.

The Zhou Political System

After its victory over the Shang, the Zhou never attempted to rule the conquered areas directly. Instead, it invested members of the royal family,

favored adherents, and allies with the authority to rule over more than 100 separate territories, which these men were free to administer without interference from the Zhou king. These subordinate rulers were given ranks later systematized into a hierarchic order, and they were placed under an obligation to render military service and tribute. Among those granted territory in this manner were the descendants of the Shang royal house, who were thus enabled to continue the performance of their ancestral rites (perhaps relieving the Zhou from the threat of supernatural reprisal). In practice these positions were hereditary under a system of primogeniture, but the investiture had to be renewed each generation to legitimize the inheritance, and this was done with solemn rites addressed to ancestors accepted as common to both king and local lord.

The relationship between the Zhou kings and the subordinate territorial authorities resembles, to a certain extent, that between lords and vassals in medieval Europe. As a result the Zhou political system has often been identified as feudal. Nevertheless, there are major differences, such as the absence in China of subinfeudation (vassals having their own vassals) and the Chinese appeal to bonds of kinship rather than to contractual agreements. Furthermore, the contrasts between the history of postfeudal Europe and post-Zhou China make it very difficult to apply to both the term "feudalism" in the sense of a stage of development in a universal historical process. Awareness of the differences between them further serves to restrain the temptation to overinterpret the Zhou evidence, which is much more meager than that available for the student of Europe almost 2,000 years later. The difficulties are further compounded by disagreements over the definition of "feudalism" itself. This is not the place for a study of comparative feudalism, but, in any case, post-Heian Japan presents a much richer and more fruitful field for such a study than does China's Western Zhou because the parallels between Japan and Europe are far more numerous. Nevertheless, the Western Zhou will continue to figure in comparative analyses because this was the period when the Chinese political system most resembled the Western feudal order.

About the structure of local village life during the Western Zhou and the routine activities of the common people, we are not well informed. This was not the kind of information those who were literate considered important to preserve in writing, and as a result our knowledge of ordinary life in China before relatively recent times remains strictly limited. However, we can learn something from the folk poetry included in one of China's oldest and most revered classics, *The Book of Songs*, containing poems composed between 1000 and 600 B.C.

The Book of Songs

Folk songs are only one part of the poetry in *The Book of Songs*. There are also religious hymns and stately songs to accompany royal festive and ceremonial occasions. There are prayers evoking Lord Millet, reputed ancestor of the

Zhou, and songs of courtship and love, ceremonial greeting and warfare, feasting and lamentation. Originally these were sung, but by the Han dynasty the music, unfortunately, had already been lost. Tradition held that Confucius as editor determined the selection of poems for inclusion in this book that became part of the classic canon of Confucianism,* a text to be memorized by anyone aspiring to be considered educated. Even before China had an official orthodoxy, failure to recognize an allusion to a poem in this anthology marked out a man as a hopeless boor and ignoramus. For the modern student of Chinese civilization, these poems provide both valuable information and aesthetic pleasure.

Some songs show ordinary people at work: the men clearing weeds from the fields, plowing and planting, and harvesting; the girls and women gathering mulberry leaves for the silkworms, making thread, carrying food hampers out to the fields for their men to have lunch. There is much about millet — both the eating variety and that used for brewing wine for use in rites. We hear about wheat and barley and rice. There are joyful references to granaries full of grain, and to the men gathering thatch for their roofs in off-season. Mention is made of lords' fields and private fields and a bailiff is referred to, but the details of the system are not provided. There are also poems of complaint against the government. One compares tax collectors to big rats. Another tells of the hardships of military service, men constantly on the march, living in the wilds like rhinoceroses and tigers, day and night without rest. Sometimes a soldier survives the hardships and dangers of war and returns home only to find that his wife has given him up for dead and remarried.

The love poems are among the most appealing in the freshness and innocence of their language and in their frankness, for this was a time when girls were not yet restricted by etiquette from expressing the wish to be married or their longing for a sweetheart:

> That the mere glimpse of a plain cap
> Could harry me with such longing,
> Cause me pain so dire![6]

Some poems tell of the anguish of the lovelorn or protest against neglect. The following tells of seduction:

> In the wilds there is a dead doe;
> In white rushes it is wrapped.
> There was a girl longing for spring
> A fine gentleman seduced her.
>
> In the woods there are tree stumps;
> In the wilds lies a dead deer,
> Wrapped and bound with white rushes.
> There was a girl fair as jade.

* *The Book of Songs* is one of the *Five Classics*. The others are *The Classic of Change (Yi Jing)*, *The Classic of History*, *The Spring and Autumn Annals*, and the *Ritual* (a set of texts including the *Records of Rites*). Sometimes a now lost classic of *Music* is added to form the *Six Classics*.

"Ah, not so hasty, not so rough!
Do not move my girdle-kerchief;
Do not make the dog bark." [7]

As always, much depends on the vision of the translator. For Liu Wu-chi, whose translation appears above, the poem tells of "the tragedy of love." In the mind of another contemporary scholar, Wai-lim Yip, it is an "animated pastiche of a lovely rural seducement song":

In the wilds, a dead doe.
White reeds to wrap it.
A girl, spring-touched:
A fine man to seduce her.
In the woods, bushes.
In the wilds, a dead deer.
White reeds in bundles.
A girl like jade.
Slowly. Take it easy.
Don't feel my sash!
Don't make the dog bark! [8]

It is a truism that to translate is to interpret, and much is inevitably lost in the process. But to read is also to interpret, and in reading these poems, later literary and scholarly Chinese "translated" them to conform to their own ideas of what a classic should be, namely a repository of lessons in social and political morality. And commentators worked hard to show how this should be done. For example, the song of longing for the plain-capped youth quoted above was transformed into a lament for the decline in mourning rites, an indication of the decay of filial piety, for white is the color of mourning in China. Thus, in a nineteenth-century English translation following Chinese commentators the poem begins:

If I could but see the white cap,
And the earnest mourner worn to leaness!
My toiled heart is torn with grief! [9]

No matter which translation of the poem about the dead doe we select, it is not the traditional interpretation: *The Book of Songs* we read today is not the same as that read by traditional Chinese scholars, for *all* modern readers bring a different vision to the text. But the study of Chinese civilization cannot even begin without an attempt to understand traditional views and images. This is true of all periods, but it is especially pertinent to a consideration of Chinese antiquity; for the gap between the classical understanding of the poems and the modern is not any wider than that between the account of China's beginnings presented in this chapter and the traditional view once held by educated persons in China and East Asia, people whose own understanding of themselves was intimately linked to their view of history.

The Traditional Chinese View of Antiquity

Virtually all known cultures develop creation myths at an early stage in their growth: myths to explain the origins of the earth and of their peoples. One looks in vain for such myths in the earliest Chinese texts, however, for in the beginning the classical Chinese view was more concerned with great semidivine culture heroes than with a theory of beginnings. Pangu (P'an-ku), a creator figure, does not appear in literature until quite late, and then he appears in the South rather than the North China Plain. He is first mentioned in a text of the third century A.D., and his story is elaborated still later. Born of a cosmic egg, he continually grew for 18,000 years and separated heaven and earth (he is often shown wielding an axe). When he died, his eyes became the sun and moon; his blood, the rivers and oceans; his hair, the grasses and trees. Humans and animals derived from his body lice.

As exemplified by Pangu, it seems, generally, that the earlier a figure is placed in mythological time, the more godlike its attributes; it also seems that the earliest legendary figures were the most recent creations. The result is an inverse ratio between ascribed and actual age: the older, the younger. Thus, the next group of semidivine beings who are placed in the third millennium B.C. were all current during the Han, and perhaps earlier, but do not appear in China's earliest historical record, *The Classic of History*, also known as *The Book of Documents*. To them is attributed the creation of the basic elements of civilization that we now view as the products of a long historical evolution. Fu Xi (Fu Hsi) was believed to have been the founder of animal husbandry, marriage, the calendar, and musical instruments. The construction of the eight trigrams of *The Classic of Change (Yi Jing, I Ching)*, an ancient divination text (see Chapter 2), is also ascribed to him. Fu Xi and his sister, or wife, Nügua (Nü-kua, also Nüwa) are depicted in the Han with serpent bodies and human heads. Shennong (Shen-nung), whose name literally means "divine farmer," taught men agriculture and also set up markets and began commerce. Huang Di (Huang Ti, the Yellow Emperor) defeated the "barbarians" in North China. He invented government institutions and was credited with a long list of inventions. His wife taught silk culture and domestic work, and his minister invented the first written signs.

Huang Di was the first of five emperors, the last two of whom, Yao and Shun, appear in *The Classic of History*, a collection of documents purportedly compiled by Confucius. Such a collection did exist at the time of Confucius and his disciples, but more material was added later. The pre-Zhou materials in this book cannot be used as historical sources, but the information it contains about the early Zhou is more usable. However, the historicity of Yao and Shun remained unquestioned until modern times. They were accepted as paragons of imperial virtue, as sage-emperors, perfectly just and wise. It was a mark of Yao's impartiality that he passed the throne on not to his son but to Shun, a poor man. Shun was selected because he remained an obedient son even though his wicked stepmother and blind father treated him miserably and even tried several times to kill him. As a final test, Yao married his two daughters to Shun, and when the latter demonstrated his ability to live in harmony with them, Yao was confirmed in the wisdom of his choice. Shun, in turn, passed the throne on to the worthiest official under his reign, Yu, who worked single-heartedly for thirteen years fighting the Great Flood that had long threatened and devastated the land. To channel the waters, he dug great drainage canals.

When Yu died, the people did not accept his designated successor but turned to Yu's son, thereby beginning the practice of hereditary succession and creating the first dynasty, the Xia (Hsia). When after many accomplishments the Xia line produced the brutal and wicked Emperor Jie (Chieh), the dynasty was finished, and a new man of virtue appeared to found the Shang. Again, after a long time, the Shang deteriorated and produced Zhou Xin (Chou Hsin) who killed people in abandon, ripped up pregnant women, and otherwise behaved atrociously. The portrait of the wicked last ruler of the Shang is probably a Zhou attempt to justify their destruction of the previous dynasty, and very likely, the story of the Xia decline was also manufactured by the Zhou to give their story greater weight. The virtuous founder and the bad last ruler remained stereotypes of Chinese historiography.

Yao, Shun, and Yu may be late reflections of early gods or heroes, but with the Duke of Zhou we encounter a genuine historical personage. To him, as a devoted regent for a child emperor, was assigned the credit for fashioning the institutions of the Zhou, the last of the Three Dynasties (Xia, Shang, and Zhou), which were considered *the* age of greatness and perfection. Although the Duke of Zhou did contribute much to the establishment of the dynasty, his reputation was greatly embellished in later times until he became a figure larger than life. He was turned into a model statesman and philosopher, the hero of Confucius, who was disturbed when the Duke of Zhou failed, for an extended period of time, to appear in his dreams. Among the works later attributed to him was *The Rites of Zhou*, which presented a schematic and ideal picture of Zhou government, a source of inspiration for reformers throughout the history of imperial China. Herrlee G. Creel has well summed up the traditional image of the duke: "Ruler, statesman, cultural innovator, scholar, philosopher: for thousands of years, the Duke of Zhou has been regarded as one who succeeded in realizing not one but all the highest Chinese ambitions." [10] In the Confucian view, he was the last of the sages to be emulated by later men, the last man fully to put his lofty ideals into operation.

Decline of the Zhou

Traditional Chinese scholars attributed the decline of the Zhou to human foibles, but modern historians are more apt to point to institutional trends such as the loosening of the bonds that tied the territorial lords to the king at the center. In any case, by the ninth century, Zhou rulers could not prevent fighting among their territories and were even more troubled by the incursions of non-Chinese peoples. To evade the latter, the decision was made to move the capital to the east away from the line of outside attack.

After this move the Zhou continued to reign nominally for another 500 years even though the court no longer had real military, political, or economic power. That it survived so long was partly because no state appeared that was capable of completely supplanting it and founding a new dynasty. But its survival also testifies to a moral authority that faded only slowly over the centuries.

NOTES

1. Kang-chih Chang, *The Archeology of Ancient China*, Fourth Edition (New Haven: Yale Univ. Press, 1986), Chapter 5. Chang acknowledges Joseph R. Caldwell as the originator of the concept and term "interaction sphere."

2. William Willetts, *Foundations of Chinese Art: From Neolithic Pottery to Modern Architecture* (New York: McGraw-Hill, 1965), p. 95.

3. David N. Keightley, *The Origins of Chinese Civilization* (Berkeley: Univ. of California Press, 1983), p. 529.

4. *Ibid*, p. 552.

5. Michael Sullivan, *The Arts of China* (Berkeley: Univ. of California Press, 1973), p. 47.

6. Arthur Waley, *The Book of Songs* (New York: Grove Press, 1960), p. 10.

7. Liu Wu-chi, *An Introduction to Chinese Literature* (Bloomington: Indiana Univ. Press, 1966), p. 20.

8. Wai-lim Yip, *Chinese Poetry* (Berkeley: Univ. of California Press, 1976), p. 53.

9. James Legge, *The Chinese Classics, IV: The She King* (Reprinted Hong Kong: Hong Kong Univ. Press, 1960), p. 216.

10. Herrlee G. Creel, *The Origins of Statecraft in China*, Vol. 1, *The Western Chou Empire* (Chicago: Univ. of Chicago Press, 1970), p. 72.

2
The Age of Philosophers

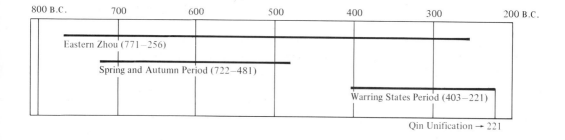

800 B.C.	700	600	500	400	300	200 B.C.

Eastern Zhou (771—256)

Spring and Autumn Period (722—481)

Warring States Period (403—221)

Qin Unification → 221

*T*he 550 years from 771 to 221 B.C. were a time of social change and
political turbulence, during which no one state was able to dominate
China. Not only later scholars, but the philosophers of these times, who
believed in a harmonious, noncompetitive world order with a single rather
than multiple sources of authority, considered this period an age of decline
from the heights of the early Zhou (Chou). The great majority of articulate
people who lived through these turbulent centuries did not consider themselves fortunate to have been born into an age when great changes were underway, changes that were to lead to a stronger, more extensive, and more prosperous civilization. They could not know what the future would bring.
For them, it was a bewildering and disturbing time. Old beliefs and assumptions were challenged, prompting questions never before raised and stimulating intellectual exploration in many directions. Some of these new concepts
were later abandoned; others became the guidelines for Chinese thought
for centuries.

The period from 771 to 256 B.C. is known as the Eastern Zhou. Historians
also divide the period into the Spring and Autumn Era (722–481 B.C.) and the
period of the Warring States (403–221 B.C.). The latter term well describes the
history of those years. The former is derived from the *Spring and Autumn
Annals*, a chronicle of the years indicated. The *Annals* are alleged to have been
edited by Confucius, who is believed to have died in 479 B.C., not long after the
Annals end. Commentaries were later written to elucidate and give meaning
to this dry text. The most interesting of these because of the richness of its
historical narrative as well as the nobility of its literary style is the *Zuo Zhuan
(Tso Chuan, Zuo Commentary)*, which carries Zhou history down to 468 B.C.

The Early Eastern Zhou (Spring and Autumn Period)

The early Eastern Zhou, a time of cultural advance and political trouble,
introduced several important changes to Chinese life. Soybean cultivation,
which had originated northeast of China proper in Manchuria, home of a
non-Chinese tribal people, spread to China proper in the second half of the

28

seventh century B.C. A rich source of protein and an important addition to the Chinese diet, this new crop plant also contains nitrogen-fixing bacteria that helped augment the fertility of the soil in which it was grown. During the sixth century B.C., individual states began experimenting with new techniques of governing. The small state of Lu, the home of Confucius, enacted an agricultural reform in 594 B.C. that required peasants to pay land rents directly to the government rather than to their lords. This amounted to an early system of direct taxation. Written law codes date to the second half of the sixth century B.C. and the first textual evidence for iron is in the *Zuo Zhuan*'s statement that in 513 a state inscribed its laws on an iron tripod. (Bronze, however, continued to prevail since iron, cast not forged, was soft.)

Notwithstanding these advances, political relations of the time were troubled. It was a visible sign of the feebleness of the Zhou court after its move east that the territorial lords no longer bothered to journey to the court for the ceremony of investiture, and that the king could do nothing about it. China was now divided into a number of independent states that negotiated their differences when they could and fought each other when diplomacy failed. Among the most important states of the seventh century B.C. were Qi (Ch'i) in Shandong and Jin (Chin) in Shanxi, as well as the semi-Chinese state of Chu (Ch'u), which was centered on the Yangzi River and tried unsuccessfully to dominate the North. In the northwest, in Shaanxi, Qin (Ch'in) was beginning its process of growth and development (see Figure 2-1).

For a time in the seventh century, the inherent instability of a multistate system was remedied by the formation of a league headed by a strongman (*ba, pa*) and sanctioned by the Zhou court, but unlike the Japanese shogunate of much later times, this arrangement never developed into an institutionalized system. The failure of multistate alliances led to an increase in international tensions among the Chinese states of the time and created a general aura of suspicion and betrayal in the sixth century. Although treaties were supposedly sanctified by being inscribed on bronze vessels, they were broken at will.

There was as little political stability within states as between states. Here, too, solemn promises and even family connections were not allowed to interfere with political ambition. The old sanctions no longer worked. The secularization already reflected in the late Western Zhou bronzes had progressed to skepticism. The old gods were dead; the world in crisis. It was under these conditions that Chinese philosophy developed — conditions very different from those which were stimulating Greeks at about the same time to speculate on the nature of the world.

Confucius

Confucius (ca. 551–ca. 479 B.C.) was apparently of aristocratic lineage and received a traditional education in learning, deportment, and music that

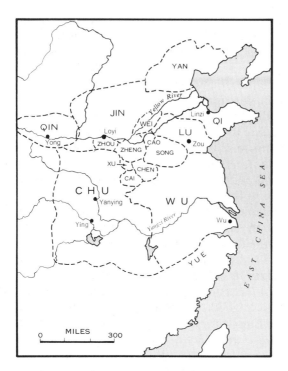

Figure 2-1   China in the Spring and Autumn Era

would not have been accessible to commoners. His ambition was to play an important role in public affairs, to become a trusted adviser to a ruler, but he never became more than a minor officeholder. In his middle years he traveled, unsuccessfully, from court to court in search of a ruler who would follow his guidance. In place of a political career he turned to teaching. He was not a wealthy man and supported himself from his pupils' tuition fees. In accepting students he did not consider class distinctions. But he did insist on students making a serious effort: he would not teach those not eager for learning, those not striving for understanding. "If I hold up one corner of a square and a man cannot come back to me with the other three, I won't bother to go over the point again."[1] Not only instruction but much of Chinese literature and art has operated on this principle, conveying a message by suggestion, relying on readers or viewers to work out the full implications by their own efforts.

No known writings of Confucius have been discovered. To study his teachings we must turn to the *Analects (Lun Yu),* a collection of his words as passed on by his disciples and assembled after his death. The *Analects* do not consist of systematic philosophical treatises or even students' lecture notes. They are an unorganized collection of statements and conversations, open to varying interpretation. In their totality, however, they give a surprisingly full picture of the man and his ideas.

Confucius believed that his teachings merely transmitted the traditional wisdom and values of Chinese culture, but he was a creative transmitter, a man who understood the old traditions in terms suitable for his own age and thereby revitalized and transformed old values. A good example is his redefinition of nobility as something acquired through virtue and wisdom, not through birth. Confucius' ideal man or true gentleman (*junzi, chün-tzu*) is humane, wise, and brave. He is devoted to virtue in contrast to the petty man out for gain. His standard is righteousness. The ultimate virtue is *ren (jen)*, which, like most of the central terms of Chinese philosophy, defies translation. It is the ground for all the other virtues, the condition of being fully human in dealing with others — the Chinese character for *ren* consists of "man" and "two."

For Confucius the interaction between men is governed by *li*, a term which encompasses the meaning of sacred ritual, ceremonial, propriety, and good manners. The *li* (like all Chinese words it can be read either as a singular or as a plural) are traditional and, because of their religious associations, had been sanctified and imbued with a quality of magic that they retained even after literal belief in the old religious ideas faded away. For Confucius the *li* themselves, when performed with true sincerity, are what make the individual human. Sacrifices should be performed as though the spirits were present. On the spirits themselves Confucius was noncommittal.

All dealings between people should accord with *li* performed in perfect good faith. Then everyone would perform his role with genuine understanding and devotion. Harmony would result, and there would be no need for physical sanctions, no necessity for laws and punishments. Of crucial importance was the initiative of the ruler, who by following the advice of true gentlemen could initiate benevolent government and win over the people. The people's confidence was essential to the state, more important than arms or even food.

Among the virtues and *li* most important for Confucius were those connected with the family, and he placed special emphasis on filiality, the wholehearted obedience child owes to parent. For Confucius obligations toward a father have priority over those to the state: a son should not turn his father in for stealing a sheep. The relationship between father and son formed one of the classic Five Relationships of Confucianism. The other four were between ruler and minister, husband and wife, elder brother and younger brother, and between friend and friend. They emphasize the importance of reciprocal obligations between people of superior and inferior status and illustrate the existence of these values at the family level, at the community level (friendship), and in state relationships (ruler and minister). The Confucian view of society was essentially hierarchical; while Confucians felt that the values expressed in the Five Relationships applied to all, that did not mean they favored an egalitarian polity. Quite the contrary. Similarly, the Way (*Dao, Tao*) to perfection was open to all, but only the morally and intellectually cultivated could understand it. The common people could only be made to follow.

For Confucius and his disciples there was only one, valid and true, eternal and universal Way. The idea that there might be a number of legitimate ways was foreign to people who had no contact with any highly developed, literate civilization radically different from their own. There was one civilized way and that was the Way of antiquity, of the sages, of the Duke of Zhou.

Confucius idealized the Duke of Zhou and in turn became a model for his own followers. It remained characteristic of Chinese culture that model emulation played a very large part in education and in the search for self-improvement. Confucius himself appears in the *Analects* as a man of moderation: gentle but firm, dignified but not harsh, respectful but at ease. He displays a nice sense of balance, as when he warns both against learning without thinking and against thinking without learning. In one place Confucius gives an account of his own intellectual and spiritual progression, culminating when he reached 70 and was able to follow his heart's desires without transgressing against morality. Like the master of ceremonial who has internalized every movement or the great musician who has become one with his instrument, the Confucian sage perfects his own moral wisdom until he reaches a point at which he no longer needs to worry about a wrong gesture, a missed note, an improper act. In all three cases the efficacy of the performance depends on the authenticity of the state of mind of the performer.

As in the case of all seminal thinkers, there was much Confucius did not say, questions he did not raise, issues he left open; and his language permitted various interpretations. Thus ample opportunity was provided for future elaboration and for disagreements among Confucians. Confucius was only the beginning of Confucianism. His followers honored him but developed his teachings in ways he could not have foreseen. There were also those who disagreed with Confucius. In the light of later history, it is important to realize that, during the entire period under discussion here, his teachings never won official acceptance in any state. They remained a minority view. One vigorous challenge to Confucianism originated with a man thought to have been born at the end of the decade in which Confucius died. That man was Mo Zi (Mo Tzu).

Mo Zi

Mo Zi (ca. 470–ca. 391 B.C.), like Confucius, apparently traveled from court to court to find a patron for his teachings, but little else is known about his life. His ideas are contained in the *Mo Zi*, a work which also includes writings by later members of his school.

Like Confucius, Mo Zi emphasized ethics, but the content of his ethics differed radically from those of his predecessor. In place of the Confucian emphasis on filiality and loving one's family first, Mo Zi advocated universal love. People should love each other impartially regardless of kinship bonds. He argued that the absence of such love accounted for the evils of the age, emphasized that such love is practical, and maintained that it is in accordance with the will of Heaven. For Mo Zi, Heaven was an intervening deity that punishes the wicked and rewards the good. In Mo Zi's view all people should pattern themselves on their superiors in a hierarchy leading up to the ruler, who himself should obey Heaven. Universal love did not, for Mo Zi, mean the abandonment of hierarchy or obedience. Like Confucius, he argued that government posts should go to the capable not to the wellborn. He also resembled Confucius in appealing to the authority of antiquity, although he placed his ideal further back in time, in the era of the mythical Xia (Hsia).

Mo Zi's criteria for judging the validity of a concept or practice were whether it had been employed in antiquity, the evidence of the senses, and its utility. If universal love were not useful, Mo Zi said, he himself would reject it. On these grounds he passionately denounced offensive warfare. He also bitterly condemned elaborate funerals and rites as wasteful, and attacked the Confucians of his day for waxing fat on the profits they made from managing extravagant funerals. On similar grounds he dismissed music; in his narrow utilitarianism there was no appreciation for the aesthetic side of life. Among the ideas and policies that satisfied his criteria were the use of rewards and punishments and the belief in the retributive power of ghosts and spirits, both helpful in inducing the people to be good. Mo Zi favored frugality and measures, such as early marriages, that would increase the wealth and population of the state.

Mo Zi's rejection of aesthetic considerations is evident in his prose style, which lacks variety and adornment but hammers away at his point repetitiously with a kind of relentless logic. Some of his later followers made important contributions to the art of logic, but none took the further step of distinguishing between logic (the principles of reasoning) and rhetoric (the techniques of persuasion). For centuries after the master's death, Mohism lived on as a tightly knit, organized order that provided support for those of its members who attained office and sought to advance the founder's teachings. Some Mohists became experts in defensive warfare ready to come to the assistance of any state threatened by attack. More united than the followers of any other thinker, the Mohists formed a quasi-religious and quasi-military order during the period of the Warring States.

The Warring States: Growth and Conflict

During the Warring States period (403–221 B.C.) and the 78 years that intervened between it and the Spring and Autumn era, the trends already visible earlier accelerated. Competition among the states became ever more intense, more bloody and ruthless. The number of states declined, but those that survived grew bigger until at the end of the period there was only one great state: the Qin.

War chariots, which stuck in mud and were clumsy in hilly terrain, were replaced by cavalry, and the invention of the crossbow (easy to use but difficult to produce) further made warfare more lethal than ever. Accompanying the chariot into oblivion were the vestiges of a gentlemanly code of fighting that, in an earlier day, had reportedly reduced the brutality of warfare. Now infantry did most of the fighting: peasant conscripts commanded by professional officers. States fielded giant armies, some said to have numbered a million men, although that may have been hyperbole. Given the proliferation of armed struggle, it is hardly surprising that one of the world's military classics, *The Art of War* (the *Sun Zi, Sun Tzu* or *Bingfa, Ping-fa*), should date from the fourth century. It is noteworthy that *The Art of War* stresses the psychology of battle as much as it does the importance of terrain and technical matters. Thus, it stresses the need for a general to know his enemy and to rely for victory more on cunning than on brute force. The true art of winning consists in inducing the enemy to destroy himself.

It was a period for professionals in other fields also. It took a skillful diplomat to maneuver a state through the treacherous waters of international relations and an eloquent voice to win a debate. Rhetorical exercises of this sort are preserved in the *Intrigues of the Warring States (Zhanguoce, Chan-kuo ts'e)*. Other men developed expertise in agriculture, various fields of science, and in statecraft. Operating in a hazardous international environment and faced with internal threats as well, the rulers of states tended to be interested more in the competence than in the pedigree of those whom they employed.

Society was in flux as aristocratic families fell into decline. Some officials, warriors, and landowners died in war or were replaced when their state was conquered by another. Other aristocrats were unable to compete successfully in a world where the old rules no longer prevailed, and men of humble origins could rise provided they were blessed with ability and luck. Both aristocrats in decline and commoners on the way up became *shi (shih)*. This term, originally used for the lower aristocracy of fighting men in the Western Zhou, was then expanded to include not only warriors but also men outside the high aristocracy who were conversant with traditional learning and participated in traditional rituals. Some were small landowners; others served noble patrons in various capacities or assumed minor government posts. During the Warring States period the term became further demilitarized. Among the *shi* were various unattached experts, politicians, and thinkers whose disputations brought about a quickening of intellectual life.

Military and social changes were inseparably linked to economic changes, the one reinforcing the other. Economic growth was essential to produce the surplus needed to maintain large armies, and to provide opportunities for men of initiative; conversely, economic growth was itself stimulated by demands for more production to serve new needs. As always, agriculture was the basic enterprise. Reclamation projects opened new lands. Although there are references to irrigation in the seventh century B.C., it did not become important until the Warring States period, and truly ambitious plans had to wait until the third century B.C. A beginning was made in applying iron to agricultural use, for example, to make the cutting edges of spades. Systems of taxation and labor-service were widely adopted and refined as states became increasingly proficient at marshaling the economic resources of the areas under their control. Land became a commodity to be bought and sold.

Among those who did the buying were men who made their fortunes in commerce, for, with the increase in the size of states, merchants could travel freely over wider areas than previously. Roads built for military purposes could also be used for trade. The most notorious merchant of the period was Lü Buwei (Lü Pu-wei, d. 235 B.C.), who for many years was the chief counselor of Qin and was even rumored to have been the real father of the ruler who united all of China in 221 B.C. Increased trade spurred the development of metallic currencies, which replaced the cowrie shells used earlier. Figure 2-2 shows an assortment of early Chinese coins: spade money, knife money, and round coins with a hole in the center so that they could be strung together. Strings of cash, usually with a thousand coins to a string, later became standard. As a result of the increase in trade, cities, growing in commercial importance, expanded physically by constructing new outer walls to accommodate more people. As for the items exchanged in trade, they included various kinds of textiles, a wide range of metals, special timbers, bamboo, jade, and other regional specialties, such as seafood and pearls from the southeast and even wild animals (bears, foxes, and so forth) from the Sichuan region. Additional evidence of the richness of the material culture of the period comes from the arts.

Figure 2-2   Ancient Chinese coins.

The Arts

In the visual arts the fashion was for the exquisite, the refined, and the expensive. In this last stage of their lengthy development, bronze vessels became objects of aesthetic enjoyment and, most likely, also of ostentation and display. Some were decorated with scenes of the hunt or war; others, more numerous, displayed abstract patterns inlaid with gold, silver, or precious and semiprecious stones to add to their sheen and sparkle. Beautifully made bronze belt hooks, inlaid with silver and gold, and fine ivory carvings confirm the era's sophistication of taste, craftsmanship, and design. Figures were often gilded. The little tapir (Figure 2-3), his body covered with intricate designs, exemplifies this stage of artistic development. He is a delightful ornament or toy, but it is difficult to recognize him as a descendant of the majestic and fierce Shang figures that were his progenitors.

The Warring States bronzes and those of the Shang belong to different worlds. Although humans were as brutal to each other as ever, at least the spirits had somewhat relented. Now the noble dead accepted stylized sculptured figures representing humans — images made of clay (in the north) or wood (in the south) — as substitutes for the actual people found in earlier tombs. Tombs, however, continued to hold large quantities of fine objects. This remained the tradition, at least for imperial burials, to the end of the last

Figure 2-3
Tapir. Late Spring and Autumn
or Early Warring States period, 10.2 cm
×17.8 cm. Asian Art Museum of
San Francisco, The Avery Brundage
Collection.

dynasty. By that time, however, lesser folk were content to burn paper money and objects for the departed.

Music was also an important art. Here, too, there was a change between the Spring and Autumn era and the Warring States period, with string and reed instruments becoming more prominent and percussion instruments less so. Mo Zi was virtually alone in his rejection of music. A number of writers on music made good use of the fact that the character used to write the word for music *(yue, yüeh)* was the same as that for joy *(le, lo)*. For Confucians the importance of music ranked with that of the *li*, for it had the power to transform people. It could make them harmonious, well balanced, well behaved, good subjects or, conversely, cause them to be abandoned, quarrelsome, and depraved. Thus according to Xun Zi (Hsün Tzu, whose philosophy is discussed later in this chapter) music is as important as the rites. Another writer, the tough-minded Legalist Han Fei Zi (Han Fei Tzu), paints a vivid picture of what happened when an unworthy duke insisted that a great music master play a piece created by the Yellow Emperor and meant only for the ears of sages:

> As he played the first section of the music, black clouds began to rise from the northwest. With the second section, a fierce wind came forth, followed by violent rain, that tore the curtains and hangings on the terrace, overturned the cups and bowls, and shook down the tiles from the gallery roof. Those who had been sitting in the company fled in all directions, while the duke, overcome with terror, cowered in a corner of the gallery. The state of Jin was visited by a great drought that seared the land for three years, and sores broke out all over Duke Ping's body.[2]

Our understanding of Zhou music has been advanced by the excavation of great bronze bells. Chinese bells were sounded by being struck, not from the inside as are Western bells, but from the outside with a piece of wood. Sets of bells, numbering as many as thirteen, were suspended in wooden racks. Inside the bells there are grooves and marks of scraping and scratching made as the bells were tuned to the right pitch. The bell reproduced in Figure 2-4 has an ornamental dragon handle; the bosses, important for the quality of tone, are in the form of coiled snakes; and at the bottom the *Taotie* reappears treated in a playful, ornamental manner. After this age, it disappears entirely.

The division of China into numerous different states encouraged the development of regional cultures and the introduction of foreign elements, such as the animal styles of the steppes. The richest regional culture, however, developed not along China's northern and western frontiers, but in the southern state of Chu.

Chu and the Culture of the South

The origins of the state of Chu are obscure, but already by the eighth century it boasted a ruler who called himself a king. During the Eastern Zhou, Chu

Figure 2-4   Bronze bell.
Warring States period, 66.4 cm
high. Freer Gallery of Art,
Washington, D.C.

became a major factor in Chinese politics until it was finally destroyed by Qin in 223 B.C.

It is not surprising that a major power should develop in the lush region south of the Huai and around the Yangzi River, where warm weather and ample water from rainfall, rivers, and lakes provide ideal conditions for rice cultivation. Rice and fish were staples in the diet of the people of Chu. Their technological level was on a par with that of the North: they had iron as well as bronze, made fine ceramics, and employed bronze coins.

Archaeological excavations, especially those from Changsha in Hunan province, reveal a highly sophisticated culture. Chu tombs were surrounded by a layer of charcoal and a thicker layer of white clay. Although they became waterlogged, their contents are remarkably well preserved. The finds include not only a large number of stylized, painted wooden figures of human beings but also jade disks, glass beads, pieces of linen and silk, bows, bamboo mats, slips of bamboo written on with a brush, shields of lacquered leather, musical instruments, and an assortment of lacquerware: bowls, dishes, low tables, and toilet boxes which when opened reveal a set of combs, whisks, hairpins, hair-puffs, and even hairpieces. Many of the lacquer objects are finely painted, red on black or black on red. Changsha is also the site of the oldest painting on silk discovered to date, although that may, of course, be an accident of archaeology. It shows a woman accompanied by a phoenix and a dragon. The dragon became one of the most prominent mythological animals throughout East Asia. Another dragon, called by Max Loehr "partly organism, partly ornament,"[3] appears on the walls and on the lid of the lacquer box known as the Laughing Dragon Box (Figure 2-5). Since the dragon is a majestic and rather awesome animal, however, laughing dragons are exceedingly rare. In East Asia

Figure 2-5
Cover, Laughing Dragon
Box. Wood and cloth cov-
ered with painted lacquer,
diam. 26.5 cm, height of
box, 10 cm. Museum of
Fine Arts, Boston.

the dragon is always associated with water, not with fire as in the West. It does not belch flames, but is the lord of lakes, rivers, and oceans. It is therefore particularly at home in the watery region of Chu.

Other tantalizing glimpses into the world of the supernatural are afforded by drum or gong stands consisting of two birds, standing back to back, either on tigers or on serpents (perhaps the ancestors of dragons), and these may provide a mythological and artistic link with the early culture of North Vietnam. Even more striking are monster heads with antlers, bulging eyes, and long tongues, eating a snake (see Figure 2-6). Like the so-called *taotie* monster of the Shang, these mythological beings offer just a hint about a world of beliefs and observances later disowned and discarded.

Something more about that world can be learned from an anthology of Chu poetry translated by David Hawkes as *Chu Ci (Ch'u Tz'u): The Songs of the South.* Included in this collection are nine shamanistic songs. Shamanism, widely practiced in Central, North, and Northeast Asia, is based on the belief that a priest, or shaman, when in an inspired trance can summon spirits to appear or, conversely, can release his soul to go on a spiritual journey to the land of the gods. Shamans may be of either sex: in Korea and Japan they were women. The songs in the anthology employ erotic imagery, inviting the spirits as to a rendezvous, but neither the sex nor the number of people calling on the gods is known. Shamanism was later derided, but the songs were preserved because they appealed to antiquarian interests and because they could be reinterpreted as the pleas of a loyal minister to his ruler rather than those of a priest to a god.

Figure 2-6
Mythical creature. Excavated in Xinyang District, Henan, Late Warring States period, 195 cm high.

The *Chu Ci* contains China's first nature poetry and was a prime source for the fantastic landscapes beloved by the Han rhapsodists (see Chapter 3). One poem is dedicated to the orange, a reminder of the South's contribution to the diet of China, and to judge by such words as "tangerine" and "mandarin" to the western diet as well. The anthology also contains the longest poem in pre-Han China, the 374-line "Li Sao," or "Encountering Sorrow." A powerful but difficult poem, it is strong in rhythm and in flights of magic and fantasy. This poem, reputed to have been written by Qhu Yuan, a rejected minister, is interpreted as a political allegory, consistent with the story of his life.

Qhu Yuan (Ch'u Yüan), who served his ruler faithfully and wisely but fell victim to slander, personifies the tragedy of the loyal but rejected minister. Banished from court and powerless to change a muddled world, he chose death as the means to preserve his purity and to serve as a model for worthy men. Clasping a large stone, he jumped into the Milo River and thus became China's noblest suicide. In time, his story fused with the stories of others who had drowned, and it is remembered in the Dragon Boat Festival, a festival held on the Double Fifth, the fifth day of the fifth month of the lunar calendar. As part of the festival, celebrated from at least the Han dynasty on into the twentieth century, rice cakes were thrown into the water as offerings to Qhu Yuan's spirit.

Neither the achievements of the South nor its contributions to Chinese culture should be underestimated, but events in the third century B.C. were to demonstrate that power belonged to the North. It was also in the North that intellectual life was at its liveliest.

Mencius and the Development of Confucianism

Like Confucius, Mencius (371 – 289 B.C.?) traveled in vain from court to court, trying to find a ruler to implement his program, and then turned to teaching as another way to propagate his ideas. He was a great admirer of Confucius and, living at a time of lively debate, was spurred to refine and develop the master's teachings. He shares with Confucius the distinction of being known in the West by the Latinized version of his name, a reflection of the status accorded him by Song and post-Song Chinese Confucian scholars. His teachings are contained in the book that bears his name, the *Mencius.*

Mencius contributed importantly to the theory of human nature, a subject of perennial concern to Chinese philosophers. He starts with the position that people are basically good, as shown, for example, by the instantaneous, uncalculated compassion we feel when we see a child about to fall into a well. We are naturally endowed with a sense (or heart) of compassion that is the beginning, the germ, from which grows our benevolence or humanity *(ren)*. Similarly our sense of shame is the germ for dutifulness; our sense of courtesy, for modesty; our sense of right and wrong, for wisdom. These four senses are as much a part of the person as are his four limbs. Challenged with the proposition that human nature is neutral and can, like water, be channeled in any direction, Mencius retorted that the goodness of human nature was like the tendency of water to flow downward.

This view of human nature opened the way for a deepening of the philosophy of individual self-perfection, since "all things are already complete in oneself." [4] Everyone can become a sage by recovering his original nature or finding his lost mind, and thereby know Heaven itself. Mencius thus provided a source of inspiration for the development of Confucian theories of self-cultivation that stimulated later theorists, particularly those of the post-Buddhist age. Additional psychological and metaphysical depth was provided by the "Doctrine of the Mean," a chapter of the *Records of Rites (Li Ji, Li Chi),* compiled around 100 B.C. from earlier materials. Still another chapter of the same work, "The Great Learning," stressed the link between self-cultivation and government, viewing the perfection of the individual as the prerequisite for the perfection of society:

> when the personal life is cultivated, the family will be regulated; when the family is regulated, the state will be in order; and when the state is in order, there will be peace throughout the world. From the Son of Heaven down to the common people, all must regard cultivation of the personal life as the root or foundation.[5]

For Confucians of all persuasions, sagehood was by definition expressed in society.

Mencius looked for a perfectly humane prince who would, by his acts and example, transform all with his benevolence. Such a prince was needed, according to Mencius, to bring out and nourish human goodness. Given his belief in human nature, Mencius needed to explain the all too obvious failure of individuals to be good in actual life. His solution was typically Confucian in its insistence that the germs of goodness must be cultivated if they are to grow and flourish. In an eloquent passage he compared the human heart to Ox Mountain. Once, in accordance with its original nature, Ox Mountain was green and covered with vegetation, but it became bald because of the abuse inflicted by man and beast, until anyone looking at it would conclude that its intrinsic nature was to be barren.

To Mencius, it was the function of government to provide the environment for the nurture of human goodness. He vigorously defended familial virtues against Mohist attack and, like Confucius, thought in terms of a political and social hierarchy based on virtue and ability. He made it explicit that those who work with their brains are to be supported by those who work with their hands. But he insisted that the government was responsible for the well-being of all its subjects, that it provide for their material as well as spiritual needs. As the ideal form of land distribution, Mencius advocated the well-field system, thought to have been practiced in antiquity. Under this system, eight families each farmed an outside field and joined together to cultivate the inside field for their lord. The system took its name from the Chinese character for "well," 井 which resembles the arrangement of the nine fields. Once the people's material wants were satisfied, schools should be established to educate them.

Drawing on such sources as *The Classic of History* and *The Book of Songs*, Mencius refined the concept that government is based on divine and moral sanctions by insisting that a dynasty rules by virtue of a Mandate of Heaven, which can be revoked if the ruler does not conduct himself as a ruler should. In one place, Mencius suggests that such a ruler is not a ruler at all, an argument consistent with the principle of the "rectification of names," contained in the *Analects*, which holds that the world could be set in order if only actualities conformed to names, for example, if princes were really princes. In any event, Heaven in making its judgment follows the voice of the people. Mencius quotes a now lost portion of *The Classic of History*: "Heaven sees with the eyes of its people. Heaven hears with the ears of its people."[6] This right of rebellion became a permanent part of Chinese political thought, used by reformers to frighten recalcitrant rulers as well as by those who took up arms against the government. "Removing the mandate" (*geming* or *ke-ming* in Chinese; *kakumei* in Japanese) became the modern word for revolution.

Daoism

Although Daoism, especially in its first formulation, has a political dimension, its primary emphasis has been on natural harmony more than on the social harmony of the Confucians. For a Daoist, social harmony follows from a return of man to harmony with nature and its underlying reality, the *Dao*, eternal, self-activating, omnipresent, the only and the ultimate reality. The first great Daoist classic, the *Daodejing (Tao Te Ching)*, or *Lao Zi (Lao Tzu)*, dated from the third century although Daoist tradition attributes it to an older contemporary of Confucius called Lao Zi, or Old Master. There is no reason to doubt the antiquity of its ideas, but a true Daoist philosopher would dismiss such matters as precise dating as inconsequential.

The *Daodejing*, much of which is in verse, is cryptic, paradoxical, highly suggestive, and has been the subject of more Chinese commentaries than any other single text. It is also the most frequently translated Chinese book, for its language invites a multitude of interpretations, notwithstanding that, or perhaps because, one of its messages is the inadequacy of language. The *Dao* cannot be named or defined, for to do so is to make distinctions and thereby miss the totality which is the *Dao*.

Among its themes and images there is a preference for the negative over the positive, nothing over something, the weak over the strong, the soft over the hard, the yielding over the assertive. Non-being is of a higher order of reality than being. Water triumphs by yielding, as does the feminine. Non-action accomplishes more than action. It is the empty center that gives value to the wheel, the pot, the house. Silence is more meaningful than words, ignorance superior to knowledge. The sages admired by Confucians really did society a disservice by introducing moral distinctions, family relationships, learning. Apprehension of the *Dao* is through an incommunicable intuitive identification: "those who know do not speak; those who speak do not know."

The *Lao Zi* had as its political ideal a return to primal simplicity, when people were content, ignorant, and lived in tune with nature. To attain this ideal, the ruler must conduct his government with great delicacy and restraint, like a cook boiling a small fish. He must not interfere with the *Dao* and, by taking no action of his own, must allow everything to happen.

The other great Daoist text, the *Zhuang Zi (Chuang Tzu)*, turns its back on politics. The wise man knows that it is better to sit fishing on the banks of a remote mountain stream than to be emperor of the whole world. Zhuang Zi (ca. 369–286 B.C.), the reputed author of the book, had a keen sense of paradox, as when he argued the usefulness of the useless. For him, too, language and debate are not the source of truth. If two men disagree, who is to decide which one is right? The *Dao* is everywhere and in everything, not excluding piss and dung. To understand is to be like Cook Ding, so familiar with every turn and twist in the anatomy of an ox that, over 19 years, he cut up thousands of oxen without ever having to sharpen his knife. He simply slid his knife through the spaces between the joints.

One of Zhuang Zi's favorite themes is the relativity of ordinary distinctions. He tells a story of waking up from a nap and being unable to tell whether he was Zhuang Zi dreaming he was a butterfly or a butterfly dreaming he was Zhuang Zi. Which is dream and which is "real"? For him, true comprehension leads to ecstatic acceptance of whatever life may bring. Consider Master Yu, who fell ill and became all crooked and contorted, "My back sticks up like a hunchback and my vital organs are on top of me. My chin is hidden in my naval, my shoulders are up above my head and my pigtail points at the sky."[7] True sage, he accepts it all with joy and speculates on what may happen next.

Perhaps his left arm will turn into a rooster. If so, he will herald the dawn. Or his right arm may become a crossbow pellet. Then, he will shoot himself a bird. Or his buttocks will turn into cartwheels, "then, with my spirit for a horse, I'll climb up and go for a ride." [8]

There is in Zhuang Zi an ecstatic acceptance of the *Dao* and a celebration of spiritual freedom that expresses itself in soaring flights of imagination. He transcends even the distinction between life and death, and sees both as parts of a single process to be welcomed equally. Only the foolish mourn.

The Daoist sympathy for nature and the natural remained a source of inspiration for Chinese poets and free spirits and provided refreshment for men wearied by the routines of official life. It contributed greatly to the strain in Chinese culture that produced great nature poetry and fine landscape painting.

Apart from the philosophical Daoism of the *Daodejing* and *Zhuang Zi*, there later developed various forms of religious Daoism that built on the lore of the Daoist sages able to ride the winds and live forever. In the Han and after, the search for longevity contributed to the development of Chinese science, and Daoist religious bodies provided havens for displaced peasants. Had Zhuang Zi foreseen the future, he would have indulged in full his fondness for paradox.

In his book, Zhuang Zi's wit and wisdom are often displayed to best advantage against the foil of a logician called Hui Shi (Hui Shih, 380 – 305 B.C.?) who inevitably gets the worst of the argument. Hui Shi was one of a number of men who pursued the study of logic as far as it was ever to go in traditional China.

The Logicians

Among those interested in logic were the later members of the Mohist school. Their acuity is revealed in their critique of Zhuang Zi's treatment of all statements as mistaken. This, they point out, is itself a statement. Therefore, if Zhuang Zi's statement is true, it is false; if false, it is true.

Hui Shi delighted in paradoxes, some not unlike those of the Greeks, but the most discussed logical conundrum was the statement by Gongsun Long (Kung-sun Lung, b. 380 B.C.?) that a white horse is not a horse. The seeming paradox can be explained in terms of the differences between categories of shape (horse) and color (white) or as arising out of a confusion between discussing a term and using it (the term *white horse* is not a horse), but it is perhaps best understood in modern terms as originating out of confusing class membership and identity. A white horse is a member of the class of horses, but this does not imply that it shares all attributes with all members of that class.

During the Warring States period, professional dialecticians won patronage through the brilliance of their debating tactics and their dazzling mental gymnastics, but it was widely felt that their displays had little bearing on practical issues. Since, for other reasons, Mohism also did not survive as a living school after 221 B.C., the logicians had little permanent influence on Chinese thought.

Theories of the Natural Order

In their scientific and philosophic speculations about the world, the Chinese thought of nature in dynamic rather than static terms and considered man a part of the natural process. Animating this process were *yin* and *yang*, paired, complementary opposites whose interaction keeps the world going. *Yin* is associated with the feminine, the passive, the negative, the weak; *yang*, with the opposite qualities and forces: the masculine, the active, the positive, the strong. Perhaps reflecting the rhythm of agricultural life, *yin* is cold and winter, *yang* hot and summer. *Yin* is response; *yang* is stimulus. The two terms range widely in application from the popular to the technical, from the concrete to the abstract, and if phenomena are conceived in terms of polarities, the list can go on endlessly.

Similar in some ways to the concept of interaction between *yin* and *yang* is the Chinese conception of the Five Agents, or Five Phases: wood, fire, earth, metal, and water. Since the components of this concept recall the four elements of Greek philosophy, for a long time the Chinese term was translated as the "Five Elements." This translation is misleading, for it implies inertia and passivity rather than the dynamism and self-movement inherent in the Chinese conception. Furthermore, the translation "Five Agents, or Five Phases" more accurately reflects the Chinese view that the processes of nature occur in regular sequence.

Yin and *yang* and the Five Agents, or Phases, have a long history in Chinese thought. Early speculation concerning them is traditionally attributed to Zou Yan (Tsou Yen), who supposedly lived in the fourth century B.C. Unfortunately the earliest information concerning him comes from the *Records of the Grand Historian* by Sima Qian (Ssu-ma Ch'ien, ca. 145 – ca. 90 B.C.). According to Sima Qian, Zou Yan held that ever since heaven and earth separated, time has been dominated by each of the Five Phases in turn. A cyclical view of time and history is consistent with the practice of counting time in cycles, confirming the experience of an agricultural people patterning their lives on the annual cycle of seasonal change.

The idea of change is important in Chinese thought. The ancient divination text that was incorporated into the Confucian canon and became the textual reference for much of later metaphysical speculation is called *The Classic of Change (Yi Jing, I Ching)*. Sixty-four hexagrams and the commentaries on them form the heart of the book. Each hexagram was created by combining two trigrams, each of which consists of three lines, either broken or unbroken.

Since each trigram has three lines of only two kinds, that is, broken or unbroken, only eight combinations are possible:

Combining the eight trigrams into hexagrams in turn yields 64 unique figures. A common method of divination was to select the appropriate hexagram by counting the stalks of the milfoil. The very concept of divination is based on the conviction that nature and man are interrelated.

By identifying the *yin* with the broken line and the *yang* with the unbroken, the *Yi Jing* illustrates the way this pair of concepts applies to everything. For example, the first hexagram represents heaven, all *yang*, the second hexagram represents earth, all *yin*. The rest consist of combinations of the two. In addition to the hexagrams and their explanations, *The Classic of Change* includes influential appendixes that traditionally were ascribed to Confucius. Although this attribution is no longer accepted today, it helped to assure the status of the *Yi Jing* as a Confucian classic long treasured by those interested in speculations concerning the workings of nature. There were, of course, also Chinese philosophers not given to such speculation. One of the foremost of these was Xun Zi (Hsün Tzu).

Xun Zi

Xun Zi (fl. 298–238 B.C.), along with Confucius and Mencius, counts as one of the three classical Confucian thinkers. If Mencius developed the "tender-hearted" aspects of Confucianism, Xun Zi is his "tough-minded" counterpart. Of a critical, analytical turn of mind, he depicts an impersonal world that proceeds according to its own ways oblivious of humankind. It will rain or not rain regardless of people's prayers. The heavenly bodies rotate the same way whether a sage or a villain is on the throne. In a departure from previous Confucian tradition, Xun Zi rejects the intrinsic validity of names. He regards the meaning of terms as a matter of conventions instituted by kings. He is also modern in his attitude toward the *li*, which for him provide a necessary and proper outlet for emotions such as joy, grief, reverence, and respect.

Xun Zi's emphasis on the psychological aspect of *li*, and of music, is in accord with his theory of human nature. Unlike Mencius, he sees human nature as fundamentally antisocial. But it can be trained. The individual has the potential of consciousness, and Xun Zi, like Socrates, assumes that once a person recognizes what is good he will follow it. Moreover, it is precisely because people are bad that they want to become good, just as the ugly yearn for beauty or the poor for wealth. Like his predecessors, he feels that society must be rehabilitated from the top down and emphasizes the importance of rites, music, and education. His ideas were particularly influential during the Han dynasty, although later he was overshadowed by Mencius.

Consistent with his views on human nature, Xun Zi accepted the need for coercion and, unlike Confucius or Mencius, counseled that strict laws and punishments be established. Here there is an element of congruity with the last group of thinkers to be discussed in this chapter, the Legalists. It is perhaps not entirely accidental that both the greatest Legalist theorist, Han Fei Zi, and the greatest practitioner, Li Si (Li Ssu), began as students of Xun Zi, although he had no more control over his students than do most teachers.

Han Fei Zi and Legalism

Han Fei Zi (d. 233 B.C.) agreed with his teacher that human beings are inherently selfish and antisocial. Even in the family, the parents rejoice when a boy is born, since he will be a support in their old age; but a girl baby may even be put to death since she is a liability. Thus, if calculations of self-interest enter even into the attitudes of parents toward children, how much more is this the case for relationships not bound by ties of natural affection. Unlike the Confucians, Han Fei Zi did not believe that the solution to governance lay in a return to an idealized past. He held that conditions had radically changed and that new problems demanded new solutions. He tells of a farmer who while working in the fields one day observed a rabbit dash itself unconscious against a tree stump. That evening the farmer and his family had a feast. The next day and every day thereafter the farmer waited by the stump for the next rabbit. To Han Fei Zi this farmer was no more foolish than the Confucians waiting for the next sage-ruler. He agreed that benevolent government had worked in antiquity when men were few and their desires did not clash; but, he taught, this was no longer possible in the competitive, struggling world of his time.

Han Fei Zi was particularly attracted to the concept of practical statecraft that originated in the fourth century B.C., which stressed rationalization of administration, managerial techniques, and the strict enforcement of severe punitive laws. Although Han Fei Zi referred to the techniques of personnel management associated with such thinkers as the statesman Shen Buhai (Shen Pu-hai, d. 337 B.C.), he drew more heavily on the doctrines which stressed law, hence the designation "legalist." He emphasized that people should be controlled by the two handles of punishments and rewards. Given the proper legal system, the ruler will not have to do anything and yet will be all powerful. In his advice to the ruler as well as in his general principles, there was an amorality that Confucians always found extremely shocking.

In later times Legalism continued to be associated with institutional innovation but especially with harsh punishments. Its reputation became inseparably identified with that of the regime which implemented a Legalist program. For it was the only doctrine of the Warring States period actually to be put into operation.

The Qin: Legalism Applied

The state of Qin was located in the west of North China, with its heartland in the Wei River Valley in modern Shaanxi. This is the same region from which the Zhou had conquered North China, and it was to serve as a power base again in the future. The area provided a suitable economic base on which to build a strong political and military apparatus. It was also strategically advantageous, since it was protected from attack by mountains whose passes were easy to defend and yet provided avenues for offensives to the east. In 316 B.C. Qin increased its resources without adding to its vulnerability when it expanded into Sichuan, a fertile area well protected by mountains.

When in the eighth century B.C. the Zhou retreated to the east, the northwest became a buffer area between the civilization of China and various warlike tribal peoples. The Qin made the best of this situation, toughening its armies by fighting the tribesmen at the same time drawing on the techniques and expertise developed in the centrally located states. Never invaded itself, it welcomed men from war-torn states. Among them were its most famous and most innovative statesmen.

The transformation of Qin into a Legalist state is traced back to such a foreigner, a man commonly known as Lord Shang (d. 338 B.C.). Following the example of the most advanced states to the east, he introduced a direct tax on the peasantry, devised a centralized bureaucracy, and divided the state into administrative districts (xian, hsien). The hereditary nobility was suppressed, and noble ranks were conferred on those who excelled militarily. Everything was geared to make the state rich and strong.

Lord Shang was also known for the harshness of the legal system he instituted in Qin and for establishing a system of mutual responsibility. According to the Han *Records of the Grand Historian*, anyone who failed to report the perpetrator of a crime would be cut in two at the waist, but an informer would receive a reward equal to that given for decapitating an enemy soldier. Lord Shang, like the later Legalists, insisted that the laws apply equally to all regardless of status and followed this dictum when he punished the crown prince for an infraction of the law and had the prince's teacher branded. Later when the prince became king of Qin, he had his revenge: Lord Shang reportedly suffered dismemberment, his body torn apart by chariots pulling in opposite directions. By that time, however, he had laid the foundations for Qin strength, and perhaps also for the *Book of Lord Shang*. This Legalist text was probably composed not long after Lord Shang's death; quite likely it is based on his words and ideas.

The Warring States period was a ruthless time, and Qin was not alone in using bribery and treachery in international relations or in building up a great military machine at home. According to the *Book of Lord Shang*, the people should be made to welcome war. This can best be achieved by making their peacetime lives so harsh that war will seem to them a release. As it was, the Qin succeeded not only in mobilizing people for war but also in organizing them in great numbers for projects such as the construction of irrigation networks in the Wei River Valley (Shaanxi) and the Red Basin (Sichuan), projects which gave the state added economic muscle.

During the third century B.C., Qin military might and economic strength were translated into territorial expansion at the expense of rival states. The conquest of China was accelerated and completed under the direction of the man who had become king of Qin in 247 B.C. and later became the first emperor of a new China. After 237 B.C., he was assisted by the Legalist minister Li Si (d. 208 B.C.), who had once studied under Xun Zi but whose policies were more consistent with those of Han Fei Zi who himself traveled to Qin where he died in prison. There is no clear evidence to substantiate the tradition that this was Li Si's doing.

In 221 B.C. the conquest was completed, and with its completion ended China's longest experiment with a multistate system. The existence of a number of states made for intellectual and artistic diversity and encouraged economic and political experimentation. It enabled a "hundred schools" to flourish. But it was also a period of instability and warfare, sadly lacking in the harmony that all the Chinese philosophers prized.

NOTES

1. Wm. Theodore de Bary, Wing-tsit Chan, and Burton Watson, comps., *Sources of Chinese Tradition* (New York: Columbia Univ. Press, 1960), p. 26.

2. Burton Watson, trans., *Han Fei Tzu—Basic Writings* (New York: Columbia Univ. Press, 1964), pp. 55–56.

3. Quoted in Jan Fontein and Tung Wu, *Unearthing China's Past* (Boston: Museum of Fine Arts, 1973), p. 76.

4. Wing-tsit Chan, *A Source Book in Chinese Philosophy* (Princeton: Princeton Univ. Press, 1963), p. 79.

5. *Ibid.*, pp. 86–87.

6. *Mencius*, V, pt. A, chap. 5, translated by D. C. Lau, *Mencius* (Baltimore: Penguin Books, 1970), p. 144.

7. Burton Watson, trans., *Chuang Tzu—Basic Writings* (New York: Columbia Univ. Press, 1964), p. 80.

8. *Ibid.*, p. 81.

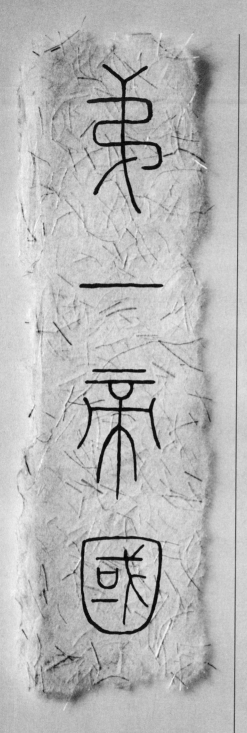

3

The First Empire: 221 B.C. – A.D. 220

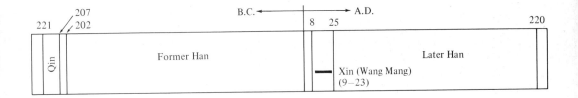

The Qin (Ch'in) unification of China in 221 B.C. was the beginning of some 400 years of imperial rule, even though the Qin itself barely survived the death of its first emperor. Building on Qin foundations, although overtly rejecting many of that regime's policies, the Han erected a more lasting political structure. Under the Han, Chinese civilization was reshaped, and China became a great imperial power comparable in achievements and historical significance to the Roman Empire (see Figure 3-1). Considering the importance of the period, it is perhaps not inappropriate that our English word "China" is ultimately derived from the name of this dynasty. On the other hand, the Chinese refer to themselves ethnically as the Han people.

The Qin Integration

After defeating its rivals and completing its conquests, the Qin applied to all its territories the principles first implemented in its own state. Under the direction of the First Emperor and his advisor Li Si (Li Ssu), China was divided into 36 commanderies (jun, chün), which were in turn subdivided into counties (xian, hsien). Administration was entrusted to officials whose assignments, promotions, and demotions depended on their performances. To guard against a revival of feudalism and prevent a resurgence of local opposition, many old and prominent families were forcibly moved to the Qin capital where the government could keep a close watch on them.

The physical integration of the realm was fostered by a program of road building. The roads were used by the army but also helped to strengthen economic ties between different regions by encouraging trade. To facilitate travel on the dirt roads, axle lengths were standardized so that the ruts formed by cart wheels in the soft soils of North China would be uniform. The Qin further unified its territories by standardizing weights and measures and by issuing a single official coinage to supplant the many different moneys then in circulation. Written communication was facilitated by Li Si's standardization of Chinese characters.

The government did not stop at standardization of the script but also sought to control what was written and read. Its opposition to those, who like the Confucians, "used the past to criticize the present," led to the suppression of

51

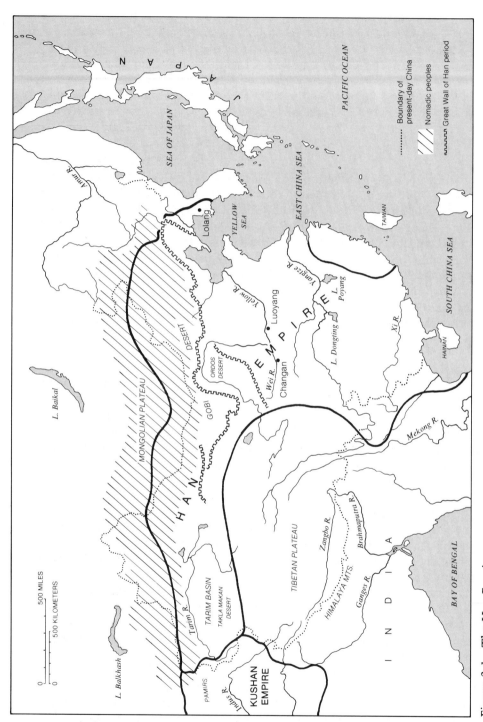

Figure 3-1   The Han Empire

scholars and the banning and burning of books deemed not to be useful. On the other hand, academicians were not confined to a narrow orthodoxy, and the state associated itself with old familistic values as when it made unfiliality a crime. Qin hostility to Confucianism was reciprocated by Confucian hatred of the dynasty. As a result the historical accounts have a strong anti-Qin bias and must be used with great care. We cannot really know, for example, whether 460 scholars actually were buried alive by the Qin, but this became part of the historical record accepted by Chinese scholars for over two millennia, consistent with the ruthless iconoclasm attributed to the Qin.

The founders of the unified empire were highly conscious of their break with the past and set out to establish a regime they hoped would last "ten thousand generations." Since the old title of "king" (wang) had lost much of its luster through overuse by the rulers of even small principalities during the long period of Zhou breakdown, it seemed hardly adequate for the head of a vast empire who claimed sovereignty over all peoples. Therefore, a new designation was adopted, combining two characters previously used for culture heroes and deities, to convey the full majesty of the ruler. Usually translated "emperor" (huangdi, huang-ti), the title remained in use until 1912.

In theory the emperor's sovereignty had no geographical limit, and he sent military expeditions to establish a Qin presence on the coast of South China and in Vietnam, as well as into Inner Mongolia to fight against the Xiongnu tribes. Rather than expansion, however, the Qin emphasized consolidation of its rule over China, and it tacitly recognized the limits of its powers when it built the Great Wall as the demarcation between China and "barbarism." The wall was constructed partly by linking segments that had previously been erected by individual states for defensive purposes. Although the present wall dates from the fifteenth century, the Qin wall is its ancestor, making the dynasty responsible at least in part for China's most spectacular structure.

The Great Wall was only one of a number of large public works projects undertaken by the Qin. In addition to the network of roads already mentioned, the dynasty was active in the construction of canals for transportation and for irrigation. All these projects demanded the services of conscript laborers, as did the building of the imperial palace and of a great, lavish tomb for the First Emperor. Excavation of the central tomb has not yet begun, but a subterranian army of life-sized pottery soldiers, guarding access to the main tomb, has been uncovered. The men are astonishing in the individualism of their facial features, and the horses too are magnificent (see Figure 3-2).

The emperor, known as "First Emperor of the Qin" is depicted in the admittedly hostile historical records as a fierce, suspicious and superstitious man who became increasingly obsessed with the search for an elixir of everlasting life, although that did not diminish his concern for the completion of his tomb. He also reportedly sent a mission of young men and women out to sea in search of the mythical islands of immortality. To assert his sovereignty, symbolically as well as physically, he toured the empire a number of times. On his first eastern tour in 220 B.C., he visited China's most sacred mountain, Mt. Tai

Figure 3-2   Terra-cotta warriors and horses guard the tomb of the First Emperor.

in Shandong, where he performed sacrifices to Heaven. Several other journeys took him to various parts of the empire, and on his fifth tour, he became ill and died. Li Si and a eunuch named Zhao Gao (Chao Kao), however, contrived to keep his death secret until they could return to the capital, forge an order for the heir apparent to commit suicide, and place on the throne the emperor's malleable second son. The alliance between Li Si and Zhao Gao was short-lived, however, ending in the former's death after imprisonment and torture.

The few remaining years of the dynasty were disruptive. Traditional accounts give a picture of murder and intrigue at court and depict an empire torn by rebellion as people sought to escape heavy taxes and demands for labor-service or were driven to arms by fear of execution for minor lapses. However, much of this may be Han propaganda, and it may suffice to note the enormity of the task the Qin set itself. Such a massive unification and restructuring was bound to evoke bitter hostility. In any case, the disintegration of the empire was rapid. The third of the line no longer dared to call himself "emperor," and this "king of Qin" surrendered to rebels in 206 B.C.

The Founding of the Han

As the number of rebellions against the Qin increased and coalesced, the contest for supremacy among the rebel forces gradually narrowed to two groups: one led by Xiang Yu (Hsiang Yü, 233–202 B.C.), a southern aristocrat of great courage and charisma; the other under Liu Bang (Liu Pang, 247–195 B.C.), who had a village background and was a shrewd judge of men. The contrasting personalities and backgrounds of the two main protagonists lends color to the drama of their struggles. In the end, Liu Bang's skill in handling men proved more significant than Xiang Yu's military abilities, and in 202 B.C. Liu Bang emerged victorious, one of only two commoners in all of Chinese history to succeed in founding a major dynasty. The dynasty was the Han, and Liu Bang as emperor is usually referred to by his posthumous imperial title, Han Gaozu (Kao-tsu).

Xiang Yu had shown signs of wishing to restore the old feudal order. During the struggle Liu Bang also found it expedient to reward his generals and allies generously by granting them vassal states, and he also established "kingdoms" in eastern China for members of his own family. However, once he was in power, he took care to forestall any ambitions his former generals and allies might have entertained. Under one pretext or another, he regained control over the lands assigned to them. These lands were then incorporated into the empire. This left the territories assigned to members of the imperial family. Although these "kingdoms" were managed by court-appointed officials, Gaozu's successors kept a close watch on them and followed a policy of reducing and eliminating them when possible. The showdown came in 154 B.C. when seven of these states, goaded into revolt, were crushed by the dynasty with unexpected ease.

The Pattern of Former Han History

The fact that it took so long for the Han emperors to eliminate the kingdoms is an indication that the new rulers were only gradually able to consolidate their power, and that the Han system was not created all at once at the beginning of the dynasty. Nor was all change in a single direction. Indeed, for a time, the fate of the imperial Liu family was in doubt; for after the death of Gaozi, his strong-willed widow, Empress Lü, took control of the throne and promoted the careers of members of her own family. The Lü family did not, however, gain the throne, and after the empress died in 180 B.C., her clan was massacred. The ambitions and political manipulations of empresses on behalf of their families reemerged during the first century B.C. as a source of dynastic weakness, but under Emperor Wen (180–157 B.C.) the dynasty gained in stability. Then, in Emperor Wu (140–86 B.C.) the Han found its most vigorous ruler, who initiated important changes in domestic and foreign policies. Much of the official symbolism and ritual of his reign indicates that he saw himself as making a new beginning. There was also a notable flowering of culture during this period.

Emperor Wu's reign of over half a century was the longest of the dynasty, more than twice that of Emperor Xuan (Hsüan, 75–48 B.C.), who was noted, among other things, for the favors he showed Confucian scholars. These later years of the Former Han were marked by the rise and fall of a number of families with palace connections, and it was a member of such a family, the controversial minister and usurper Wang Mang, who brought the Former Han to an end when he assumed the throne and established the short-lived Xin (Hsin) Dynasty (A.D. 9–23). This was followed by a period of confusion and rebellion, and ultimately establishment of the Later Han. This reemergence of the Han dynasty is a testament to the prestige of the Han and its aura of legitimacy.

Government and Society

In the Han political system ultimate authority was vested in the emperor, although when minor or weak emperors occupied the throne their power might be exercised by empresses or regents. As under the Qin, actual administration was entrusted to a bureaucracy. Officials were graded by rank and salary and were controlled from the capital, which under the Former Han was located in Changan (modern Xian). At the head of officialdom was the Chancellor, who presided over court conferences attended by other high officials. Such officials, and especially the Chancellors, enjoyed considerable authority, although they had no recourse against a despot such as Emperor Wu, who had five of his last seven Chancellors put to death. Another powerful official was the Director of the Secretariat, who until 68 B.C. was able to determine which documents received the emperor's personal attention. The third great official was the Great Commandant, who was in charge of the military although no strict division was made at this time between the military and civil service. Under these three highest officials were nine ministers, who supervised the business of government and also were charged with palace administration and the conduct of ritual observances.

In theory the formal government of emperor and bureaucracy concerned itself with all aspects of the lives of the people, who, for their part, owed their taxes and labor-services directly to the state. In practice, however, the state usually confined itself to matters vitally affecting the welfare and security of the empire or jeopardizing the dynasty. Local matters were mostly handled by the families of notables, who dominated the local power structure. Some of these owed their eminence to old family lands and connections in a given area; others were founded by wealthy merchants who invested in land; still others acquired their base through holding of high office. In addition to the support of their kin, such families enjoyed the backing of a circle of clients bound by favors and protection rendered over the years, and also maintained permanent "house guests" whose services were particularly useful during the frequent vendettas.

Only exceptional, "harsh" officials tried to combat or ignore this local power structure. Cooperation between officials of the central government and those members of the powerful families who held lower posts in the local administration was the more usual pattern, and local matters were largely left in the hands of the local elite in return for their support. In this way, the central government and the local power holders both supported and restricted each other.

Crucial to the functioning of government was the background of its officials, for government service during the Han was a career largely limited to families of means. Not all such families sought to place members in government, but it was primarily they who could afford the investment in books and instruction required to prepare their sons for a government career. Although the top officials could have one or more sons accepted into the service automatically through "hereditary privilege," most recruiting was done through a system of recommendation by central or, more generally, by high local officials. Initially, calls for capable men went out from the capital sporadically, but under Emperor Wu local authorities were asked every year to send up the names of "filial and honest" men. Already in 165 B.C. Emperor Wen (r. 180–157 B.C.) had personally given written examinations to the men recommended to the government, and such testing later became the rule. Also designed to help prepare men for government service was the imperial university, which was established by Emperor Wu with a student body of 50. By 8 B.C. it had 3,000 students and is said to have reached 30,000 under the Later Han. Here too entry was by recommendation.

Emperor Wu's establishment of the university was one aspect of his patronage of Confucianism. Prior to this, Confucians had already been active in government. Actually the dynastic founder, Gaozu, had little patience with pompous and pretentious scholars and once expressed his disdain for the breed by urinating into a pedant's hat. But after he became emperor, Gaozu found a need for precedents to guide him and for ceremonies to create a proper air of majesty and decorum at court — and Confucian scholars were experts par excellence in these matters of ritual. More than that, Confucianism offered to the Han emperors a body of classical learning and theory that could legitimize their dynasty and prompt ministers to faithful service. Their patronage of Confucianism did not by any means prevent Emperor Wu or other Han emperors from employing ideas derived from other traditions, and, as we shall see, Confucianism itself was transformed during this period, amalgamated with various cosmologies in theory and combined with Legalist measures in practice.

The dynasty's institutional and ideological policies contributed to the formation of a bureaucracy staffed by men who shared not only a generally similar family background but also an education grounded in classical learning, a common set of historical references, and a fund of basic ideas and widely held values. They were not faceless functionaries simply carrying out directives from above, but men with their own family interests, and heirs to a tradition that, however adulterated, did not teach unthinking compliance to the whims or policies of the ruler. The government's dependence on such officials, armed as they were with economic and moral power, restricted the power of the central government and tended to soften the impact of absolutism, even though it did not save the lives of Emperor Wu's Chancellors. On the other hand, the cohesiveness of officialdom should not be exaggerated. The diversity of geographic and family ties among the officials encouraged the formation of factional political groupings, and the intellectual heritage left ample room for disagreements, including serious policy differences.

A major area of controversy concerned government financial and economic policies. There was general agreement that the prosperity of government and society was based on agriculture, and from the beginnings of the dynasty a land tax and a head tax were the main sources of government revenue. Adult males were also obliged to render a month's labor-service and to serve in the army. Under Emperor Wu the government expanded its economic role and its income. In an attempt to stabilize prices, the government set up a system of official warehouses for the storage of commodities. It is not clear whether grain was included, but it definitely was in the Ever-Normal Granaries established in 51 B.C. By purchasing grain when it was plentiful and prices were low and selling it in times of scarcity, the government would prevent prices from soaring out of sight. This plan, designed to make a profit for the government, also helped to secure the agrarian tax base by enabling small cultivators to remain solvent. It also served to curb the great merchants whose wealth contrasted with their theoretically low social status. A more direct means of channeling into government coffers some of the wealth gathered by the merchants was the establishment of government monopolies, especially of salt and iron. These affected everyone, for salt was a dietary necessity for peasants living on a largely vegetarian diet and iron, too, was vital since it was needed for tools.

These measures aroused considerable controversy and in 81 B.C., not long after Emperor Wu's death, gave rise to a famous debate at court. The government's economic policies were defended as fiscally sound and necessary by practical-minded men whose realistic arguments had Legalist overtones. Their opponents, suspicious of government interference, warned against official greed and argued for the primacy of moral values. These policies underwent various changes after that, but the tendency during the later years of the Former Han was to abandon the measures. They were later briefly revived, in modified form, by Wang Mang and continued to appear, in one form or another, in subsequent regimes. All the major dynasties enacted official monopolies.

An important aspect of the debate on the government's economic and fiscal policies concerned the dynasty's foreign policy, since it was Emperor Wu's military spending that created the need to increase government income.

Relations with Foreign Peoples

From early times the Chinese traded, negotiated, and fought with neighboring peoples. During the Warring States period such contacts became quite extensive, including relations with tribal confederations in Manchuria and Korea in the northeast, with the inhabitants of the steppes to the northwest, and with the peoples of the south. Prior to the reign of Emperor Wu, Han foreign policy was generally conciliatory, but that emperor adopted expansionist policies and by force of arms asserted Chinese control over the southeast, including

Northern Vietnam, and established Chinese colonies in Korea where they greatly accelerated the diffusion of Chinese culture into that peninsula and beyond to Japan. Emperor Wu's main efforts, however, were reserved for the most troublesome and challenging area of foreign relations, the northern and northwestern frontiers. This was the home of the Xiongnu (Hsiung-nu) tribes, who had caused trouble to Chinese frontier states as early as the fourth century B.C. and had more recently been the object of a military expedition sent out by the First Emperor of the Qin.

Nomad peoples like the Xiongnu were often formidable opponents because of their skill in warfare. For them war represented merely a special application of the skills of horsemanship and archery that they practiced every day in guiding and defending their flocks. In contrast, military service for a Chinese peasant required that he interrupt the normal pattern of his life, leave his work, and undergo special training. The mobility of the nomads was an asset not only in attack but also in defense for, traveling lightly with their flocks and tents, they could elude Chinese military expeditions and avoid complete destruction or permanent control, even when the Chinese were able to mobilize their superior resources in manpower and wealth. The interaction between the Chinese and the nomadic peoples they considered barbarian thus became one of the major themes of Chinese history.

One Chinese policy alternative was to apply military force as the Qin did, but Gaozu, the founder of the Han, decided on a more prudent, conciliatory course. He and his immediate successors wooed the Xiongnu leaders through generous gifts, took care to address them as equals, and cemented friendly relations by sending them imperial princesses as brides. Emperor Wu reversed this policy and sent large armies into the Ordos Region, Inner Mongolia, Gansu, and Chinese Turkestan. To maintain surveillance over these areas, he established military colonies in strategic places and pressured local rulers and chiefs to enter into tributary relations with the Han. In addition to accepting Chinese suzerainty, they were required to send princes to the capital, ostensibly to receive a Chinese education, but actually to serve as hostages. There were also exchanges of gifts, in which practice the Chinese emperor more than matched the generosity of the "barbarian" tributaries.

The Xiongnu were slow to accede to tributary status but did so in 53 B.C., during the reign of Emperor Xuan. By that time the tribes had split into northern and southern federations, and it was the latter which gave its allegiance to the Han. The leaders of the steppe had always found it difficult to achieve and maintain political coherence among independent-minded tribesmen thinly spread over vast areas. The Chinese also did what they could to foster division among their neighbors, "using barbarians to control barbarians." Chinese brides continued to figure in the diplomacy of the Han. The most famous was Wang Zhaojun (Chao-chün) who was married to a Xiongnu chief in 33 B.C. and became a much beloved tragic heroine, the central figure in *Autumn in the Palace of Han*, a drama written well over a thousand years later.

More important, at least economically, than the bestowal of brides on "barbarians" were the opportunities for trade that accompanied the tributory system. Much of this trade was conducted in border markets, and Chinese exports included lacquerware, ironware, bronze mirrors, and silk, some of which was woven for the export trade in two imperial workshops in the capital. It was during the Han that Chinese silk first reached Europe over the famous Silk Road; there it became a major luxury article in imperial Rome. The silk was carried to Rome by various middlemen; neither Chinese merchants nor diplomats traveled that far west.

Chinese envoys did cross the Pamirs, however, in search of allies against the Xiongnu. Again it was Emperor Wu who took the initiative, sending missions to the Chinese Far West and even a military expedition across the Pamirs to obtain the famous western "blood sweating" horses. (The origin of the term is uncertain.) From even further afield came such exotic luxury items as glass and amber as well as foreign jugglers and slaves. Closer to home, tributory states aided the diplomatic and military expeditions by supplying their needs and also contributed to the upkeep of Chinese garrisons.

Flourishing and Decline

Emperor Wu's vigorous expansionist policy extended Chinese influence further than ever before, but it was an expensive policy that led to tax increases and controversial new fiscal measures. After Emperor Wu's death, taxes were lightened and the new measures modified and softened. This took place under the direction of He Guang (Ho Kuang), who began his career under Emperor Wu, controlled the government as regent for Emperor Zhao (Chao, 86–74 B.C.), engineered the dethronement of that emperor's heir-apparent after a reign of only 27 days, and replaced him with Emperor Xuan. He Guang remained in control of the government until his death in 68 B.C. Among the treasures lavished on him in death was a jade suit of the kind shown in Figure

Figure 3-3   Jade burial suit of the Princess Dou Wan, wife of Liu Sheng (d. 113 B.C.). Man-cheng, Hebei, 172 cm long.

3-3, but his family soon got into political trouble and did not survive him for long. The dynasty continued to enjoy foreign triumphs, including the submission of the Xiongnu, and remained culturally productive, but below the surface there were signs that all was not well.

In the traditional Chinese view of the historical process, the end of a dynasty is foreshadowed by a decline in the quality of the rulers, who are depicted as either weak or tyrannical. In the case of the Former Han, the last emperor was a child, not a monster. Other signs of decline included intrigues at court and factionalism in officialdom, a general increase in maladministration, and the spread of corruption. A particularly dangerous development was the narrowing of the dynasty's tax base. Although some statesmen saw the growth of large estates as providing greater opportunities for taxation, powerful and well-connected local notables largely managed to avoid taxation while the tax burden on the free peasantry increased to the point where many lacked the resources to cope with poor harvests or unusual family expenses. Frequently an unpaid mortgage resulted in the loss of their land to the large tax-evading proprietors. When this happened the burden on the remaining peasants increased still further. Peasants and government were caught in an accelerating and vicious cycle. When the number of landless peasants exceeded the number of opportunities available for farming as tenants or hired laborers, the unfortunate had to survive as best they could, perhaps selling wives and children into slavery — although slaves did not constitute more than 1 percent of the Han population. When all else failed, they took to the hills, living as bandits or rebels while the government floundered.

The Han peace helped to increase agricultural productivity. So did technical improvements such as plows that, according to Fransesca Bray, had by Han times reached, "a perfection and sophistication that had been achieved nowhere else in the world."[1] Han plows were notable for their variety and for such advanced features as adjustable struts allowing control of the depth of furrows, improved iron plowshares, and curved metal mould-boards, which reduced friction so that two animals (and later one) could draw a plough whereas in pre-eighteenth century Europe it took from four to eight animals to form a plough team. This and other innovations improved productivity but benefitted those who could afford the necessary draught animals and could diversify their crops rather than the poor peasant struggling to feed his family and pay the tax collector. Complaints about the hardships borne by the peasantry were voiced as early as the late second century B.C. The eminent Confucian theorist Dong Zhongshu (Tung Chung-shu) contrasted the wealth of the rich and the lot of the poor "left without enough land to stick an awl into," burdened by both rents and government exactions, reduced to "eating the food of dogs and swine." He told Emperor Wu:

> Ownership of the land should be limited so that those who do not have enough may be relieved and the road to unlimited encroachment blocked. The rights to salt and iron should revert to the people. Slavery and the right to execute servants

on one's own authority should be abolished. Poll taxes and other levies should be reduced and labor services lightened so that the people will be less pressed. Only then can they be well-governed.[2]

Dong Zhongshu's proposal to limit the size of land holdings was turned down. Even a vigorous emperor might hesitate before attacking the economic base of those who staffed his government. It was not until 7 B.C. that an edict was issued limiting the size of estates to around 500 acres, and even then no attempt was made to enforce this measure. The reigning emperor himself exceeded this quota in the amount of land he bestowed on his favorite catamite.

Deterioration in the quality and effectiveness of government, together with an accompanying pattern of agrarian decline, is a recurrent feature of Chinese history. It fits in well with the traditional Chinese concept of dynastic cycles, although the traditional Chinese scholar placed his emphasis more on the moral factors. Since it fosters the notion that history is merely the repetition of things that happened before, the cyclical view of history distracts attention from straight-line change and can even lead to the conclusion that nothing really new ever happened in Chinese history. It is the modern historian's task to remain sensitive both to recurrent patterns of change and to the movement of history in new directions.

Wang Mang and the Xin Dynasty (A.D. 9 – 23)

The Wang family first rose to prominence through the influence of the consort of Emperor Yuan (48 – 33 B.C.), suffered an eclipse under Emperor Ai (7 – 1 B.C.), and came into its own under Emperor Ping (1 B.C. – A.D. 6), for whom Wang Mang served as regent. He retained this position for another three years until, with a proper show of reluctance, he consented to follow the advice of ministers and the omens of Heaven and mount the throne himself, establishing the Xin dynasty. Although "xin" is usually translated "new," renewal rather than innovation was the hallmark of his reign. Wang Mang tried as far as possible to reinstitute the Zhou order as represented in idealized form in *The Rites of Zhou*. Not only did he change the official nomenclature, reintroducing archaic titles for officials and ancient place names, but he cited ancient precedents in reaffirming imperial ownership of the land and in setting limits to the amount that could be held by any one family, the excess to be assigned to those with inadequate holdings. In this way he tried to prepare the way for a return to the "well-field" system mentioned previously. He also attempted to abolish slavery, initiated an expanded monopoly system, reintroduced price stabilizing storehouses, changed the coinage, and modified the salary system of officials, whose pay was to vary from year to year according to the harvest. It was a complex set of measures, not all pulling in the same direction, and, under the circumstances, hardly enforceable. The land measure, for instance, was revoked after only two years.

Instead of renewing and strengthening the state, Wang Mang's policies disrupted the social and political order, and his policies also disturbed the Xiongnu and other non-Chinese peoples whose titular status was now lowered. The dynasty's greatest problems were caused by nature, however. A great crisis was created when the Yellow River spread destruction during one of its periodic shifts in course. Soon Shandong and then the entire Central Plain were in turmoil. Among the most prominent group of displaced peasants pushed into rebellion were the Red Eyebrows, first organized by "Mother Lü." Their choice of red, the color of the Han, reflected their hopes for a restoration of the old dynasty, but they did not have the field to themselves. Other restorationist insurrections arose, often supported by the power and resources of local notables. During the fighting, Wang Mang was killed in the capital. Troops cut his body to pieces and then ate it; his head was placed on display in the marketplace. Civil warfare continued until victory went to a leader belonging to a branch of the imperial Liu family that had settled in Henan.

The Later Han (25 – 220)

The Later Han is also called the Eastern Han because it moved the capital from Changan east to Luoyang. This choice of capital suggests the influence of the Henan notables who backed the new government in its formative stage and implies a less vigorous policy toward the non-Chinese peoples to the West. Notables and "barbarians" eventually helped to destroy the dynasty, but during its first three reigns, that is up to the year 88, the new Han enjoyed political stability, a cultural flourishing stimulated by the patronage of education and Confucianism, and all the benefits of economic recovery after the terrible years during which natural disasters and warfare had substantially reduced the population of North China. During the first century A.D., China also reasserted its suzerainty over the Southeast and over Northern Vietnam and reestablished its supremacy over Central Asia, a project facilitated by the split of the Xiongnu into a northern and a southern confederation. Ban Chao (Pan Ch'ao, 31-102), brother of the famous historian Ban Gu (Pan Ku), led a Han force over the Pamirs and marched all the way to the Caspian Sea. Since the Later Han took a lenient attitude toward merchants, trade flourished as never before. The international caravan trade continued long after the dynasty ceased to exist.

Despite the initial brilliance of the Later Han, it soon became apparent that the dynasty had no lasting solution for the weaknesses that had undermined its predecessor. The fourth emperor came to the throne as a child, and the first of a succession of consort families monopolized high offices in the capital. In the provinces the estates and clientele of great landed families grew at the expense of the small peasants and the state treasury, occasional warnings by some Confucian officials notwithstanding.

A new element in the complicated politics of the period was the growth of eunuch power. Palace eunuchs, like consorts, enjoyed easy access to the emperor, but, unlike consorts, they did not belong to powerful families well connected in officialdom. Eunuchs were deliberately chosen from insignificant, often aboriginal families to ensure that they would have no outside loyalties but would be solely dependent on imperial favor. This dependency commended them to strong-willed rulers like the founder of the Later Han; his weaker successors, however, sometimes became the instruments rather than the masters of the eunuchs. Earlier, in the Qin and during the last half century of the Former Han, individual eunuchs had become powerful, but never before had eunuchs as a group attained the prominence they achieved in the second century. They were even granted the right to perpetuate their power by adopting "sons" to create ersatz families.

Confucian scholars and officials despised eunuchs as less than complete men and strongly disapproved of their access to power through palace politics rather than normal official channels. Since the scholars wrote the histories, the depiction of the eunuch is a stereotype: a man who overcompensates for his physical impotence by giving full vent to his lust for wealth and power. Nevertheless, there are occasional indications that at least some eunuchs, during the Han and later, enjoyed considerable respect and prestige, and some can be credited with genuine accomplishments.

Much of the history of the second century is filled with the ups and downs of the fortunes of consort families, eunuchs, and scholars playing a deadly political game for the highest stakes, a game that, in the end, they all lost. No single consort family managed to establish itself let alone avoid a bloodbath. When scholars denounced eunuchs, the literati suffered persecution, first in 166, again and with more vigor in 169 and after. Punishments ranged from house arrest to death, and among those arrested in 172 were more than a thousand students at the state university. In 189 it was the eunuchs' turn to suffer and die. More than 2,000 were killed, including some beardless but otherwise virile men who were mistaken for eunuchs. Five years earlier, in 184, the Yellow Turban Rebellion had demonstrated that dynastic disintegration was well advanced, and the following decades showed that the process could not be reversed simply by slaughtering eunuchs. What was coming to an end was more than a political dynasty — an entire epoch of Chinese civilization was drawing to a close. The end of the Han was one of the great watersheds in the history of Chinese civilization. Much survived, but only in changed form. Before we examine the dynasty's closing years, it is time to explore the texture of that civilization and consider some of its salient features, both those which survived and those which perished. Among the great works that survived to inspire and delight future generations of readers throughout East Asia, none has been more admired than Sima Qian's great history.

Han Historiography: Sima Qian and Ban Gu

Sima Qian (Ssu-ma Ch'ien, ca. 145 – ca. 90 B.C.) devoted his life to the completion of a work begun by his father, a history of his world from the legendary

Yellow Emperor to his own day. Even after suffering castration, the price he paid for defending an unsuccessful general against the views of the court and in conflict with Emperor Wu's own opinion, Sima Qian continued with his great undertaking. Through his writing he sought to fulfill his obligation to his father and to bequeath to posterity a literary and moral legacy of permanent value.

His efforts resulted in the *Shiji (Shih Chi, Records of the Grand Historian)* consisting of five sections: Basic Annals, Chronological Tables, Treatises, Hereditary Houses, and Memoirs. The treatises include essays on rites, music, pitch pipes, the calendar, astronomy, the solemn *feng* and *shan* sacrifices performed at Mt. Tai, the Yellow River and canals, and economics. The memoirs contain accounts of the lives of famous men, important political and military leaders, philosophers, and such groups as imperial favorites, merchants, and so forth. They also include accounts of non-Chinese people. Sima Qian's work became the pattern for later histories. Its form, somewhat modified, was followed by later historians including Ban Gu (d. 92), author of *The History of the Former Han.* This history, which is a record of the preceding dynasty written during and sanctioned by the succeeding dynasty, was the first in a series of such dynastic histories. Although the works of Sima Qian and his successors emphasized political history and subjects of concern to officials, in scope they compare favorably with the works of the historians of classical Western antiquity.

Like all good historians Sima Qian and Ban Gu strove for objectivity. One device employed by all Chinese historians was copious quotation from original documents. Another was a careful separation between the narrative text and their own editorial comments. However, historians in China could no more transcend their times and origins than could their counterparts elsewhere. The very process of selection reveals their own values and ideals. Sima Qian freely expressed his enthusiasm for political valor and virtue, his delight in clever stratagems, his fascination with character and personality. His deep feelings give life to his prose. A fine stylist and gifted raconteur, he did not hesitate to invent dialogues or turn to poetry to convey the full force of a historical personage's feelings or personality. His flair for the dramatic is exemplified by the following account of a battle:

Tian Dan then rounded up a thousand or more oxen from within the city and had them fitted with coverings of red silk on which dragon shapes had been painted in five colors. He had knives tied to their horns and bundles of grease-soaked reeds to their tails, and then, setting fire to their tails, had them driven out into the night through some twenty or thirty openings which had been tunneled in the city wall. Five thousand of the best soldiers poured out after them. The oxen, maddened by the fires that burned their tails, rushed into the Yan encampment which, it being night, was filled with terror. The oxtail torches burned with a dazzling glare, and wherever the Yan soldiers looked, they saw nothing but dragon shapes. All who stood within the path of the oxen were wounded or killed. The five thousand soldiers, gags in their mouths so they would make no noise, moved forward to attack, while from within the city came an accompaniment of drumming and clamor, the old men and boys all beating on bronze vessels to make a noise until the sound of it shook heaven and earth. The Yan army, taken completely by surprise, fell back in defeat, and the men of Qi were able to capture and put to death its commander, Qi Jie.[3]

Ban Gu's style is more sober and restrained, in keeping with his more austere Confucianism.

There is a great deal we would dearly like to know, which the Han historians do not tell. Moreover, portions of their texts, especially some of the annals, are at times dry and dull. Nevertheless, they convey an impressive amount of information and, at their best, they remind us that the study of human beings is what history is all about. For the modern reader it is perhaps especially salutary to read of people who rejected the general pattern of their times, for example, of Yang Wangshu, a wealthy student of Daoism who, in an age when the highest elite went to their graves dressed in jade, dismayed his family and shocked the world by insisting that he was to be buried naked. Ban Gu reports that he had his way.

The two histories are read for their literary as well as historical qualities. The elegant simplicity of their prose is more in tune with modern tastes than is the elaborateness cultivated in much other Han writing. In their histories Sima Qian and Ban Gu also helped to preserve many poems that otherwise would have been lost.

Han Poetry

Among the poetic remains of the Han are the verses collected by the Music Bureau established by Emperor Wu. These include hymns and songs for ceremonial occasions and also a group of fresh and simple folk songs. Originally they were sung to the accompaniment of such instruments as the flute, a bamboo mouth organ known as the *sheng*, the drum, the lute, and/or a stringed instrument that was the ancestor of the Japanese koto. The music has been lost, and the words alone remain. The dynasty also produced good and important poems in a form limiting lines to five words each. The most characteristic and popular form, however, was the rhapsody, a uniquely Chinese genre.

The rhapsodies *(fu)* often ran to great lengths and combined poetry with prose. There were prose introductions and conclusions, and there might be prose interludes between the streams of verse. They were frequently in the form of a poetic debate and drew on both the rhetorical tradition of the Warring States period and on the rich metaphors and fantastic allegories of the Chu tradition. Exotic terminology, verse catalogs, and ornamental embellishments enriched the verse, but in the hands of less than a master, the form was apt to degenerate into mere ostentation and artificiality. Its thematic repertoire included royal hunts and ceremonies, landscapes, the capital, fauna and flora, female beauty, and musical instruments.

The most highly regarded Han rhapsodist was Sima Xiangru (Ssu-ma Hsiang-ju, 179–117 B.C.), a colorful man who as a young and poor scholar eloped with the widowed daughter of a wealthy merchant. Eventually his poetic gifts were recognized by Emperor Wu, and the poet received a post at court. One of his greatest *fu* describes the imperial park. It is too long to quote in full, but the following segment, in Burton Watson's translation, is sufficiently substantial to suggest the scope and flavor of this style of verse.

> Within the park spring the Ba and Chan rivers,
> And through it flow the Jing and Wei,
> The Feng, the Hao, the Lao, and the Jue,
> Twisting and turning their way
> Through the reaches of the park;
> Eight rivers, coursing onward,
> Spreading in different directions, each with its own form.
> North, south, east, and west
> They race and tumble,
> Pouring through the chasms of Pepper Hill,
> Skirting the banks of the river islets,
> Winding through the cinnamon forests
> And across the broad meadows.
> In wild confusion they swirl
> Along the bases of the tall hills
> And through the mouths of the narrow gorges;
> Dashed upon boulders, maddened by winding escarpments,
> They writhe in anger,
> Leaping and curling upward,
> Jostling and eddying in great swells
> That surge and batter against each other;
> Darting and twisting,
> Foaming and tossing,
> In a thundering chaos;
> Arching into hills, billowing like clouds,
> They dash to left and right,
> Plunging and breaking in waves
> That chatter over the shallows;
> Crashing against the cliffs, pounding the embankments.
> The waters pile up and reel back again,
> Skipping across the rises, swooping into the hollows,
> Rumbling and murmuring onward;
> Deep and powerful,
> Fierce and clamorous,
> They froth and churn
> Like the boiling waters of a caldron,
> Casting spray from their crests, until,
> After their wild race through the gorges,
> Their distant journey from afar,
> They subside into silence,
> Rolling on in peace to their long destination,

> Boundless and without end,
> Gliding in soundless and solemn procession,
> Shimmering and shining in the sun,
> To flow through the giant lakes of the east,
> Or spill into the ponds along their banks.[4]

The poet has turned the park into the cosmos fulfilling the intent of the landscape architect who designed it. The poem ends with the emperor virtuously giving up his luxuries in order to benefit the people. The *fu* often concluded with a moral message, although only in the case of really serious Confucian poets does that become the main focus. Conversely, one of the most gifted but also most earnestly Confucian of the rhapsodists, Yang Xiong (Yang Hsiung, 53 B.C. – A.D. 18), eventually gave up the form because he felt it was not really suitable for moralizing.

The flair for ornamentation, the cosmological outlook, and the dramatic rendering of movement so striking in Sima Xiangru's rhapsody are also prominent in the visual arts.

The Visual Arts

Like the imperial park, Han palaces were intended to mirror the universe. Heirs to an ancient tradition of celestial symbolism, the Han built their palaces on a north – south axis (for the emperor always faces south) and recreated on a small scale the symmetry of the cosmos. Especially significant was the Ming Tang (Ming T'ang, Sacred Hall) where many important ceremonies were performed. Its round roof representing heaven was set on a square structure representing the shape of the earth. Some accounts of the building are replete with numerological symbolism: 8 windows for the 8 winds, and 4 openings for the seasons; 9 apartments for the divisions of the world; 12 halls and 36 doors representing the number of months and of ten-day periods in a year; 72 windows, one for each five-day period. The aesthetic result was an architecture of formal symmetry and geometric balance.

But it was not a severe architecture. As in classical Greece, the buildings were decorated in rich colors. Red lacquered wooden supports sustained roofs of sparkling glaze, or sometimes of bronze tiles, contrasting with walls of shining white. Sculpture everywhere contributed to the flamboyance. Columns were carved with human and animal forms, and paintings decorated the interiors. In architecture, as in poetry, people enjoyed intricate patterns, colors galore, and lush variety.

Unfortunately, Han buildings no longer exist, but clay models, preserved in tombs, confirm the impressions created by literary descriptions. Among the most interesting are the models of watchtowers (see Figure 3-4), frequently still showing some paint, roofed in tile, and testifying not only to the style of the period but also to the need for security. Other models show such utilitarian buildings as granaries and store-houses and even a combination privy-pigsty (see Figure 3-5), an example of the Chinese genius for recycling.

Among the favorite subjects of the Han painter was the human figure, especially por-traits of exemplars of virtue and other famous men. Most of this art has been lost, but enough remains to document the artists' skill in draw-ing and placing figures so as to create a sense of interaction even in the absence of a landscape or architectural setting. Examples appear on tiles and also on a famous lacquer basket found in Lelang, the Han colony that Emperor Wu established in Korea (see Figure 3-6). Histori-cal and semihistorical scenes are depicted in low relief in Han tombs, giving further indica-tions of formal painting styles. These low re-liefs reveal the use of a convention which translates depth into height so that the upper figures are to read as being located behind rather than above the lower. A more naturalis-tic perspective is found in some tiles discov-ered in Sichuan. One depicts in detail the pro-cess of recovering salt from wells, a process still in use today. The tile shown in Figure 3-7 presents a harvest and threshing scene in the bottom panel, a hunting scene at the top. Ex-cept for the oversized fish, the figures are in scale. They move in real space, and the sense of space receding into the distance is remarkable for such an early work. The striking rhapsodies of Sima Xiangru, the technique revealed in the tile paintings, and the fineness of its lacquer-ware, all testify to the advanced state of the culture of Sichuan.

Figure 3-4   Model of a watch tower. Pottery covered with a green iridescent glaze, second century A.D., 88 cm high. Nelson Gallery — Atkins Museum, Kansas City, Missouri.

Tomb tiles and figures provide much infor-mation on Han music, pastimes, and the lives of ordinary people. There are models of wells and stoves, people playing board games, scholars receiving instruction seated on the floor, as is still the custom in Japan. There are models of carts and dogs and tiles depicting everyday activities such as a woman cooking fish.

There are also horses, for in art as in life, horses were cherished. One painter won renown for painting an ideal horse, combining the best features of actual horses owned by several different families, that is, the mouth of one horse, the

Figure 3-5   Model of a privy-pigsty. Clay, Han Dynasty.

nostrils of another, and so on. The flying horse shown on page 1 is in bronze. Balanced on a swallow, it gallops through the air. At the opposite pole of Han sculpture are monumental figures: grand, dignified lions, other animals, and mythical beasts.

In the Han, as earlier, the fantastic and mythical were never far from human consciousness, and the dragon (see Figure 3-8) remained a favorite motif throughout Chinese history, giving full play to the artist's talents and imagination. Dragons appear also on the backs of Han mirrors where they represent the east, balancing the tiger on the west. A popular form of mirror design is the "TLV" type, so called because shapes similar to these letters are repeated in the design (see Figure 3-9). The square earth *(yin)* at the center is surrounded by circular heaven *(yang)*, while the central axis of the world is represented by the mirror's raised boss. The central square also contains the twelve symbols used for computing the lunar calendar, and in the space between heaven and earth move the directional animals and various spirits. The T, L, and V shapes have been variously interpreted as representing the four corners of the world, the seasons, and points of the compass — or alternatively, the mountains and gates of the universe. Similarly the pattern ringing heaven may represent

Figure 3-6   Exemplars of filial piety. Lacquer painting on basketwork box, Luolang, Korea, Later Han dynasty, approx. 5 cm high.

Figure 3-7   Rubbing from a pottery tile. Guanghan, Sichuan, Han dynasty, 42 cm high.

mountains or waves. Such mirrors were valued by the living and (it was believed) by the dead alike, for they were thought always to tell the truth. No demon, no matter what form he assumed, could escape detection by the mirror.

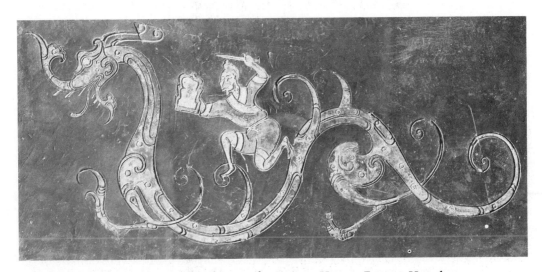

Figure 3-8   Impressed and painted gray tile. Jincun, Henan, Former Han dynasty. Wadsworth Atheneum, Hartford, Connecticut.

Figure 3-9   Mirror back.
Bronze, Later Han dynasty,
diam. 17.2 cm. Metropolitan
Museum of Art, New York.

The Intellectual Order

The establishment of empire resulted in the channeling of intellectual as well as political life. Some varieties of thought, that of the Mohists and the dialecticians for instance, disappeared. On the whole, it was not a time for radical new departures but a period of working out the implications of older ideas and of blending them in new ways. As previously indicated, Confucianism won official endorsement under Emperor Wu, but this did not inhibit the government then or later from employing Legalist policies, including the promulgation of an extensive law code. Confucian ideas shared the political realm with concepts derived from Legalism; similarly, Confucianism shared the intellectual world and interacted with Daoism and various cosmological theories. As a result of its political and intellectual position, Han Confucianism developed in ways that would have startled, perhaps dismayed, its founder.

One corollary to imperial patronage was imperial interference, as when in 51 B.C. scholars were summoned to court to assist the emperor in establishing the "correct" texts of five classics. Textual studies remained a major scholarly preoccupation, generating a dispute between Modern Text scholars, who accepted texts that, early in the dynasty, had been written down in modern characters, and the advocates of Ancient texts, composed in archaic script, that had been "discovered" during the first century B.C. Philosophical and political issues complicated the debate. Of the two groups, the scholars of the Modern Text school were more deeply identified with Han cosmological speculation and the dynasty's claims to cosmic sanctions. Post-Han scholars, however, turned to the more sober antiquarianism of the Ancient Text school. Among the lasting contributions of Han scholarship were China's first real dictionary and the commentaries on the classics, among which those by Zheng Xuan (Cheng Hsüan, 127 – 200) were particularly valuable.

From the beginning, moral teachings have been at the core of Confucianism, and this remained the case during the Han. Of works in this genre, few have been more influential than *The Classic of Filial Piety*, generally thought to be of Han date. Its exemplars of filial piety (see Figure 3-6) have been held up as models for two millennia. Similar in its stress on obedience and selfless service was the *Lessons for Women* by Ban Zhao (Pan Chao, 45 – 114?), the sister of Ban Chao, who won fame in Central Asia, and of the historian Ban Gu. After the latter's death, Ban Zhao completed his history. Her own book emphasizes a woman's obligations to her husband and parents-in-law, and projects an ideal of wifely devotion that extends beyond the grave. In her condemnation of widow remarriage, Ban Zhao went beyond the ideas and practices of the time, for such marriages were both frequent and entirely respectable during the Han.

A major Han intellectual enterprise was the construction of a philosophical order to account for all reality, just as Sima Qian included all of history in his work, and the emperor ruled for all mankind. In their quest for an all-encompassing explanation of the political and moral as well as natural order of things, the Han thinkers were necessarily eclectic, joining Confucian moral and political values to cosmological explanations derived from other schools. Basic to their effort was the conviction that the world was an organic whole passing through time in identifiable phases. All phenomena, no matter how diverse, which shared any particular temporal phase were held to be interrelated in a set of extensive correspondences.

There were various versions of such correspondences, employing *yin-yang* theory, Five Agents concepts, the diagrams of *The Classic of Change*, and similar systems. Table 3-1 is based on the order by which the Five Agents were thought to produce each other. Another Han arrangement was fire-water-earth-wood-metal, the sequence in which the Agents overcome each other. Although not included in the table, this technique could also be used to explain history, past and present. To signify a new beginning, Emperor Wu adopted earth and the corresponding color, yellow, for the dynasty. Another theory, developed near the end of the Former Han, held that the dynasty corresponded to fire and red. This was used by Wang Mang to justify his regime and continued to be accepted even though Wang Mang was discredited.

The acceptance of the idea that all phenomena are interrelated in a set of correspondences gave great satisfaction. Not only did it explain everything, it enabled men to feel at home in the world, part of a temporal as well as spatial continuum. It provided both an impetus to the development of science and the basis for a sophisticated theoretical framework for explaining the world. Since it made Chinese investigators sensitive to phenomena that interact without

Table 3-1   Correspondences for the Five-Agents System

THE FIVE AGENTS

Correspondence	Wood	Fire	Earth	Metal	Water
Seasons	Spring	Summer		Autumn	Winter
Divine Rulers	Tai Hao	Yan Di	Yellow Emperor	Shao Hao	Zhuan Xu
Attendant spirits	Gou Mang	Zhu Yong	Hou Tu	Ru Shou	Xuan Ming
Sacrifices	inner door	hearth	inner court	outer court	well
Animals	sheep	fowl	ox	dog	pig
Grains	wheat	beans	panicled millet	hemp	millet
Organs	spleen	lungs	heart	liver	kidneys
Numbers	eight	seven	five	nine	six
Stems	jia/yi	bing/ding	mou/ji	geng/xin	ren/guei
Colors	green	red	yellow	white	black
Notes	jue	zhi	gong	shang	you
Tastes	sour	bitter	sweet	acrid	salty
Smells	goatish	burning	fragrant	rank	rotten
Directions	East	South	center	West	North
Creatures	scaly	feathered	naked	hairy	shell-covered
Beasts of the directions	Green Dragon	Scarlet Bird	Yellow Dragon	White Tiger	Black Tortoise
Virtues	benevolence	wisdom	faith	righteousness	decorum
Planets	Jupiter	Mars	Saturn	Venus	Mercury
Officers	Minister of Agriculture	Minister of War	Minister of Works	Minister of Interior	Minister of Justice

From Wm. Theodore de Bary, Wing-tsit Chan, and Burton Watson, *Sources of Chinese Tradition.* vol. I (New York: Columbia Univ. Press, 1960), p. 199.

apparent physical contact, it enabled them to discover and explain such phenomena as the sympathetic vibration of musical instruments and the workings of magnetism, phenomena most perplexing within the context of the Aristotelian physics that Galileo was the first to challenge in the West. Among the most noted scientists was Zhang Heng (Chang Heng, 78 – 139): mathematician (he calculated the value of pi), practical and theoretical astronomer, cartographer (inventor of the grid system for map making), and inventor of a seismograph that registered the direction of earthquakes far from the capital.

The most influential philosopher of the period was Dong Zhongshu, a Modern Text scholar who helped persuade Emperor Wu to sponsor Confucianism. He shared the Han conviction that the architecture of the human body, like that of the Ming Tang, was the universe in microcosm. Man's head corresponds to heaven, similarly round in shape; his eyes and ears resemble the sun and moon; his body has four limbs, five internal organs, twelve major joints, 366 small joints, corresponding to the four seasons, the Five Agents, the months and days in a year. Man also functions like the universe: his breathing, the opening and closing of his eyes, his mental and emotional processes all have their cosmic counterparts.

This is explained in Dong's book on the *Spring and Autumn Annals*, the scriptural point of reference for his moral and metaphysical ideas. In his view there was correspondence not only between the individual and the universe but between society and nature. This was, of course, an old idea, and it was current in the Han prior to Dong Zhongshu. According to one famous anecdote, one spring a high minister under Emperor Wen passed a group of brawlers who had killed or wounded one another but took no notice of them whatever. Yet when he later saw a man leading an ox panting in the heat, he made it a point to question the man closely. Later he explained that there were lower officials to deal with brawlers, but an unseasonable heat wave causing an ox to pant, that was a matter for the highest officials charged with harmonizing the *yin* and *yang*. Dong emphasized the crucial role of the emperor in educating people who without such guidance could not realize the potential goodness that was in their nature. He also elaborated the doctrine that Heavenly omens such as unseasonable weather, eclipses, earthquakes, and the like were warnings to a ruler. During the later part of the Former Han dynasty and throughout the Later Han, the theory of portents, auspicious as well as ominous, stimulated the development of a whole literature incorporating many folk beliefs, numerological theories, and abstruse teachings.

On the other hand, the more sober tradition associated with Xun Zi's scepticism did not die out. On the contrary, in Wang Chong (Wang Ch'ung, 17 – 100) it found a great exponent. Wang asserted that Heaven could not possibly be concerned with a creature as insignificant as man, a mere flea or louse in the fold of a garment, a cricket or an ant in a crack. In Wang's writings, Dong's optimism gave way to a fatalistic pessimism. In this he was perhaps ahead of his time, for a century later there was every reason to be pessimistic.

The Fall of the Han

The beginning of the end came for the Han when thousands of desperate people, driven by poverty and plagued by natural calamities, joined a messianic antidynastic movement dedicated to the "Way of Great Peace" *(Taipingdao, T'ai-p'ing tao)*. This movement offered a potent mixture of folk beliefs and religious Daoism (one of its sacred texts was the *Daodejing*), together with organization and leadership. Located in Shandong, Henan, and six other provinces, the members of this sect were called "Yellow Turbans" after the color of their kerchiefs. The color, in turn, was of religious and political significance. Unlike the similarly Daoist "Five Bushels" sect that flourished in Sichuan, the Yellow Turbans tried to overthrow the dynasty by force, launching their rebellion in 184, the first year of a new sexagenarian cycle.

The dynasty managed to survive this challenge — but only barely, for power now shifted to military leaders supported by the great families who had carved out for themselves solid bases in the provinces. It was a military leader who was responsible for the slaughter of the eunuchs in 189. The official demise of the dynasty was postponed until 220 by the rise of another military strongman, Cao Cao (Ts'ao Ts'ao), famous for his brilliance, ruthlessness, and poetry, but his authority was limited to the North. The diplomatic and military maneuvers between Cao Cao and his two rivals in the South and Southwest were embellished by storytellers over the centuries and inspired the much beloved *Romance of the Three Kingdoms*, compiled in its definitive form in the fourteenth century. Among its most famous personalities, in addition to Cao Cao, were two men who served the rival state established in Sichuan: Zhuge Liang (Chu-ko Liang), one of the most brilliant strategists of all time, prototype of the wise, clever, and loyal minister and also admired as a writer, and Guan Yu (Kuan Yü) so renowned for his strength and valor that he eventually became the god of war in Chinese popular religion.

When Cao Cao died so did the fiction of Han rule. His son deposed the last Han emperor and proclaimed himself founder of a new dynasty, the Wei, but was unable to reunify the country, now divided into three kingdoms.

This time, in contrast to the demise of the Former Han, it was impossible to revive the dynasty. The deterioration of the old order revealed its weaknesses — intellectual as well as political. During the second century there were thinkers who hoped through Confucian and/or Legalist reform to reinvigorate the dynasty, but the end of the Han turned men's minds to more private quests for truth and fulfillment. Han Confucianism had become so strongly identified with the dynasty that it could not long survive without it, and theories that had satisfied intelligent and sensitive men living in an orderly, stable period were perceived as inadequate by those who lived through the turbulent and bloody confusion of the last years of the dynasty and suffered from a sense of civilization in crisis.

NOTES

1. Joseph Needham, *Science and Civilization in China*, vol. 6: *Biology and Biological Technology*, Part II: *Agriculture* by Fransesca Bray (Cambridge: Cambridge Univ. Press, 1984), p. 169.

2. Wm. Theodore de Bary, Wing-tsit Chan, and Burton Watson, comps., *Sources of Chinese Tradition* (New York: Columbia Univ. Press, 1960), pp. 233–34.

3. Burton Watson, trans., *Records of the Historian: Chapters from the Shih-chi of Ssu-ma Ch'ien* (New York: Columbia Univ. Press, 1969), pp. 32–33.

4. Burton Watson, *Chinese Rhyme-Prose* (New York: Columbia Univ. Press, 1971), pp. 38–39.

PART TWO

China in a Buddhist Age

Monk. Stone, Northern Qi,
167.6 cm high. University
Museum, Philadelphia

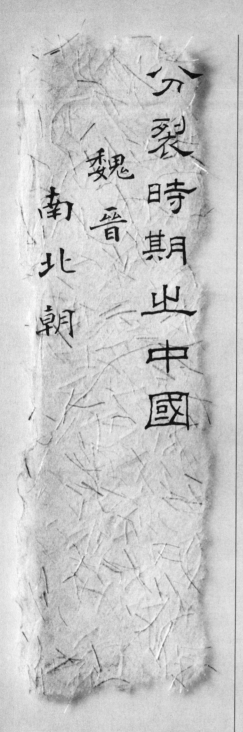

分裂時期中國

魏晉

南北朝

4
China During the Period of Disunity

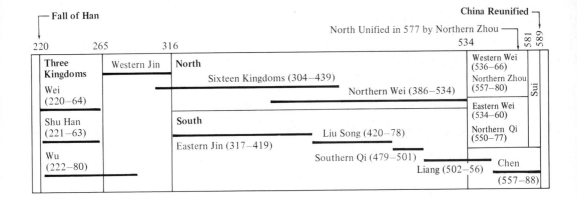

Fall of Han

China Reunified

North Unified in 577 by Northern Zhou

220   265   316   534   581 589

Three Kingdoms	Western Jin	North		Western Wei (536–66)	Sui
Wei (220–64)		Sixteen Kingdoms (304–439)	Northern Wei (386–534)	Northern Zhou (557–80)	
Shu Han (221–63)		South	Liu Song (420–78)	Eastern Wei (534–60)	
		Eastern Jin (317–419)		Northern Qi (550–77)	
Wu (222–80)			Southern Qi (479–501)		
			Liang (502–56)	Chen (557–88)	

G autama Siddhartha* (ca. 563–483 B.C.), the founder of Buddhism, was roughly contemporary with Confucius, but his teachings did not take hold in China until the collapse of the Han dynasty weakened faith in the imperial Confucian orthodoxy. By that time Buddhism, which had begun as a teaching directed at satisfying the spiritual quest of a small group, had developed into a universal faith. Considerable time passed before this religion from India sank its roots into Chinese soil; but once it had, Buddhism came to pervade the cosmopolitan culture of Tang China, which in turn left an enduring imprint on the societies of Korea and Japan.

Buddhism in India

Accounts of the Buddha's life were not committed to writing until centuries after his death. These narratives were the work, not of dispassionate scholars, but of faithful believers whose aim was to extol the great founder. Yet, despite the accretions of the mythical and the miraculous in these accounts, the Buddha they reveal is essentially a humane man, not a god. Only later was he deified.

Tradition has it that Gautama Siddhartha was born a prince and brought up in luxury. He was shocked into a search for religious understanding, however, when on three successive outings from the palace he encountered an old man, a sick man, and a dead man — and learned that such is the fate of humankind. He abandoned worldly pleasures to seek religious truth. Initially he became an ascetic and practiced austerities so severe that they almost cost him his life;

---

* Gautama refers to his clan, and Siddhartha was the name he received at birth. He is also known as Sakyamuni (sage of the Sakya tribe). After he attained enlightenment he was called the Buddha or the Tathagata.

ultimately he found a middle way between self-deprivation and gratification. His subsequent enlightenment under the bodhi (wisdom) tree (at which time he became the Buddha, or "Enlightened One") was achieved despite the efforts of Mara, the evil one, who first sent demons to assail him, and then sent his daughters (Discontent, Delight, and Desire) to tempt him, all equally in vain. The Buddha's success elicited a suitable cosmic response. The whole earth swayed, and blossoms rained from the heavens. After attaining enlightenment, he spent the remainder of his life teaching his disciples, a following whose growth led to the formation of communities of monks and nuns.

At the core of the Buddha's teachings are the Four Noble Truths. The first of these is that life is suffering. Like many religions throughout the world, Buddhism teaches that pain and unhappiness are unavoidable in life. The traditional response of Indian religions to this perception is to seek for ways to transcend life. Death is not the answer, for in the Indian view, living beings are subject to reincarnation in one painful life after another. According to the law of karma, for every action there is a moral reaction. A life of good deeds leads to reincarnation at a higher and more desirable level in the next cycle; evil deeds lead in the opposite direction. But the ultimate goal is not rebirth as an emperor or millionaire: it is to achieve Nirvana and never be born again. Legend has it that the Buddha himself gained merit in many reincarnations before his final rebirth, and stories of his previous lives have provided rich subject matter for the artist.

The second Truth explains the first, stating that the cause of human suffering is craving, or desire. This in turn leads to the third Truth: that to stop suffering, desire must be stopped. The cause of suffering must be completely understood and halted. This is accomplished by living the ethical life and practicing religious contemplation and the spiritual exercises set out in the last of the Four Truths.

The fourth Truth proclaims the Eightfold Path: right views, right intention, right speed, right action, right livelihood, right effort, right mindfulness, and right concentration. The religious life involves vegetarianism, celibacy, and abstinence from alcoholic beverages, as well as positive religious practices. Carried to perfection it leads to release from reincarnation and to Nirvana: that is, to the absolute, the infinite, the ineffable.

There is much that is subtle in the elaboration of these ideas and in their explication by the Buddha and his followers. The explanation of the doctrine that there is no ego provides an example. That which we think of as the self is merely a temporary assemblage of the five aggregates (material body, sensation, perception, predisposition, and consciousness). At any point in time an individual is a momentary cluster of qualities without any underlying unity. It is a dangerous delusion to think that these qualities pertain to some kind of permanent entity or soul: only by understanding that all is change can Buddhahood be achieved. Transmigration is likened to the passing of a flame from one lamp to another until it is finally extinguished. "Extinguished" is the literal meaning of Nirvana.

Many problems of a doctrinal interpretation were left unanswered by the

Buddha, for he was a religious teacher concerned with showing the way to salvation, not a philosopher interested in metaphysics for its own sake. The Buddha's concern for spreading the faith was carried on by later missionaries who undertook hazardous journeys to bring the message to distant lands. As in other religions, such as Christianity, later commentators worked out the philosophical implications of the founder's teachings, producing a mass of writings. These holy scriptures were compiled in the Tripitaka, or "three baskets," which consists of sermons attributed to the Buddha himself (sutras), later treatises (sastras), and monastic rules (vinayas). The enormity of this body of scripture indicates the vast breadth of Buddhism. It had no centralized organization or ecclesiastical hierarchy and developed in a generally tolerant atmosphere conducive to producing a rich variety of schools and sects.

The distinction between the Theravada sects, which still predominate in Sri Lanka and Southeast Asia, and the Mahayana schools, which played the major role in China and continue to do so in Japan, is the result of a major division in Buddhism that occurred early in its history. The word "Mahayana" literally means "greater vehicle," reflecting the claims of its followers to more inclusive and powerful teachings than those of their predecessors in the Hinayana, or "lesser vehicle" — a term generally resented by Theravada Buddhists. A branch of Mahayana Buddhism important for its development of doctrine was the Madhyamika (middle way) school, which taught that reality is empty or void (sunya). Emptiness became an absolute, underlying all phenomena. In innermost essence, everything, including the world of appearances, is Nirvana and empty. If everything is emptiness, then what is it that perceives the emptiness? The Yogacara (yoga practice) school held that the ultimate reality is consciousness, that everything is produced by mind.

Mahayana Buddhism developed not only a metaphysical literature whose richness and subtlety are barely hinted at here; it also broadened the appeal of Buddhism to draw in those people who did not have the time, training, or inclination for abstract speculation. A significant development was the growth of devotionalism directed at the Buddha, deifying him and placing him at the head of an expanding pantheon. Other Buddhas also appeared and had their following, especially Maitreya, the Buddha of the future, who exerted a messianic appeal and was often adopted as a symbol by Chinese rebel movements. The three-body doctrine helped to accommodate and justify new forms of Buddhism, for it taught that Buddhahood can be considered under three aspects: the "transformation body," that is, the historical personage of the Buddha, the "enjoyment body," that is, the celestial Buddha as beheld by the devout, and the "truth body" as understood in the abstractions of the metaphysicians.

In addition to the Buddhas, there were numerous lesser gods, but more important than these were the celestial Bodhisattvas, who postponed their own entry into Nirvana in order to help other beings. Somewhat like the Virgin Mary and the saints of Christianity, the Bodhisattvas themselves became objects of veneration and worship, none more than Avalokitesvara (Guanyin or Kuan-yin in Chinese, Kannon in Japanese), famed for the shining quality of his mercy. In China this embodiment of the gentle virtues was gradually transformed into a feminine figure. Sometimes depicted with multiple hands and arms, Avalokitesvara is a favorite subject of Buddhist sculpture. Buddhist art was itself a significant development, dating from the first images of the Buddha that were sculpted in India in the first century A.D. in what was at the time a daring departure from tradition.

Buddhism appealed to people in China, and later to people throughout East Asia, because it addressed itself to human suffering with a directness unmatched in their native traditions. It also provided a well-developed body of doctrine, art, magic and medicine, music and ritual, even heavens and hells for those bewildered by the abstract quality of Nirvana. Buddhism was spread by missionary monks who followed the caravan routes linking the northern part of India with western China. The new religion faced formidable cultural and linguistic barriers among the Chinese and might well have remained simply an exotic foreign faith had not the collapse of the Han dynasty set people to questioning the traditional verities. During the years of dislocation and confusion that followed, China was more open to the message of a foreign religion than ever before. The history of Buddhism in China cannot be understood, therefore, without reference to other aspects of Chinese history.

China Divided

The three states (Wei, Wu, and Shu Han) into which China was divided after the fall of the Han did not last long. One more effort to reunite the land was made under the Jin (Chin, 266–316), but when that short-lived dynasty fell, control over the North passed to non-Chinese peoples, some of whom had been settled within China during the Late Han and had increasingly participated in China's military struggles. The capture and devastation of Luoyang in 311 by the "barbarians" sent shock waves throughout the Chinese world.

After 316 China was effectively divided. During this period of division (316–589), while the "barbarians" ruled in the North, five dynasties succeeded each other in the South: Eastern Jin (Chin), Liu Song (Sung), Southern Qi (Ch'i), Liang, and Chen (Ch'en). Together with the preceding southern state of Wu, they are generally known as the Six Dynasties.

In the North, meanwhile, there were 16 regional, overlapping kingdoms between 304 and 439. These short-lived kingdoms, which generally barely managed to survive their founders; provide a contrast to the more substantial achievements of the Northern Wei (386–534). (See Figure 4-1.)

The Northern Wei

The nomadic peoples who established states in the North had already been exposed to Chinese civilization in varying degrees prior to their conquests.

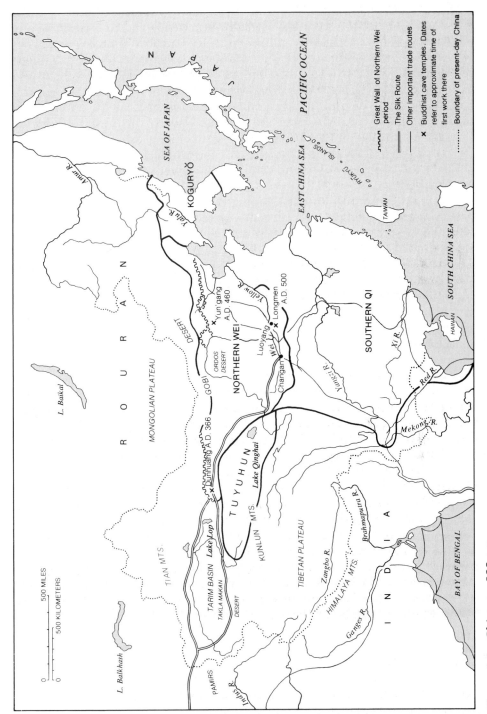

Figure 4-1   China ca. 500 A.D.

Typically, they possessed the military skills and resources required to carve out a state but lacked the administrative experience and trained personnel needed to govern a settled agricultural people. They could, to be sure, avoid this problem by turning their new possessions into pasture, but this would be self-defeating since it would destroy the wealth that had drawn them into China in the first place. If they were to enjoy China's wealth on a long-term basis, they had to devise a political system more sophisticated than the tribal organization they brought from the steppes. Usually this meant relying on Chinese administrators who knew how to operate a tax system, keep records, and run a government. But the ensuing Sinification had to be kept in check if the conquerors were to retain their power and something of their cultural heritage.

The problem of how to use Chinese personnel and techniques without becoming either Chinese or irrelevant was to face all major dynasties of foreign conquest, including the last of all the dynasties, that of the Manchus (1644–1911). The Northern Wei did not really solve this problem, but it was nevertheless the most successful state in East Asia during the fifth and early sixth centuries. A major shift took place in 493–94 when the regime moved its capital from Shanxi, close to its old tribal home, south to the old and venerated city of Luoyang, and then went on to gain control of all North China down to the Huai River. In Luoyang itself major changes and improvements were made. The Northern Wei organized the capital city into regular wards, an innovation that became the model for the great Tang capital of Changan, as well as for Tang Luoyang. The Northern Wei is also known as the Tuoba (T'o-pa) Wei after the Chinese name for the Xianbei (Hsien-pei) tribal group who founded it. The Xianbei are considered a proto-Mongolian people originally from Manchuria.

Long years of warfare and devastation in the North brought on large-scale migrations of Chinese to the South. This influx stimulated social and economic development in the South, but the exodus created a population shortage in the North, so that much arable land remained uncultivated for want of labor. The Northern Wei responded to this problem with massive forced relocations of populations, so that deserted lands could be reclaimed and government revenues increased. Also, in 486, it established the "equal field" system, which not only outlasted the dynasty but also influenced reformers in Japan. Based on the ancient principle that all land belongs to the emperor, this system provided for the allotment of agricultural holdings to each adult peasant for the duration of his or her working life. When a landholder reached old age or died, the land reverted to the state and could be reassigned. Exceptions were made, however, where the nature of cultivation required greater continuity of tenure. Silk culture, for example, involved permanent planting and continuous care of mulberry trees. Although this was not the original intent, such land came to be held in perpetuity by its proprietors. In return for land, cultivators were obliged to make certain tax payments and render labor-services such as road building and military service.

The implementation of the "equal field" system in devastated areas did not prevent the Northern Wei from cooperating with landed aristocrats entrenched elsewhere. From the outset, the Tuoba rulers employed Chinese advisers, and they early on gained support for their rule within the existing Chinese power structure by adopting the nine-rank system. This system, which had originated in 220 as a means for recruiting officials through local recommendation, had by the fourth century become a system for appointing men to office according to their inherited family rank. This emphasis on birth reflected the enduring power and prestige of great Chinese families, some of them descendants of those who had controlled the countryside during the Later Han. Their distinguished ancestry, their embodiment of Confucian traditions, and their aristocratic style and conduct created an aura of distinction that complemented their great landholdings and the strength they derived from a mutually supportive network of marriage relations. Their position was further strengthened by the fact that during the Northern Wei local officials, most of whom were members of great families, enjoyed considerable autonomy. Among other things they had the right to appoint their subordinate officials; thus, by appointing relatives they could perpetuate family power and status. What they lacked, however, was institutionalized military might.

Continuing Chinese influence proved a source of weakness to the Northern Wei. During the last half century of its reign, men from distinguished families were increasingly attracted into the Sinicized central government, in which Chinese was the official language. In Luoyang everyone wore Chinese dress, and even Tuoba nobles had to adopt Chinese names. Many married Chinese wives. This Sinification finally alienated those among the conquering tribes who had not adopted Chinese ways, including the troops stationed in frontier garrisons. They expressed their displeasure in the usual way; by taking up arms. The Northern Wei state was split and came to an end.

Later in the sixth century, the Northwest reemerged as a source of military power, for this was the base from which the Sui eventually reunified China. By that time, an aristocracy of mixed Chinese and Xianbei ancestry had developed. This new aristocracy, however, did not enjoy the prestige of the older northeastern families, some of which had moved to Luoyang, choosing government service even though it meant severing their local roots. It is of significance for the following Sui and Tang periods that some of the most distinguished aristocratic families were able to survive despite the turmoil and confusion of the times.

Buddhism in the North

Today the Northern Wei is perhaps best known for its legacy of Buddhist art, particularly the sculpture found in cave temples at Yungang (Yün-kang) in Shanxi and Longmen near Luoyang (See Figure 4-2). These works occupy an

Figure 4-2   Entrance to the Buddhist cave temples at Longmen.

important place in the history of Chinese art and also influenced the art of Korea and Japan. The Bodhisattva from the caves at Longmen (see Figure 4-3), for example, shows how by the late Northern Wei Chinese artists had assimilated and transformed an art which, like the concept of creating temples in caves, was Indian in origin. In contrast to the lovingly sensuous modeling of the naked body in three dimensions that is the glory of the Indian sculptor, the essentially linear style of the figure, with its geometric composition and frontal orientation, is characteristically Chinese. At its best, this art reproduced in metal and stone the simple piety and sweet spirituality of a religious age.

Such works of art are but one of the visual signs that mark the beginning of the complex process by which a foreign religion took hold in China and was, in turn, influenced by Chinese styles and viewpoints. When Buddhism first reached China during the first century A.D., it had been introduced as the religion of foreign merchants. Through the period of division the trade routes remained open, since trade was as advantageous to the nomadic peoples who controlled oases and taxed caravans as it was to the buyers and sellers in the

Figure 4-3
Seated Bodhisattva. Stone,
Longmen, Late Northern Wei.
Museum of Fine Arts, Boston.

more settled regions. As life became more difficult in China, Buddhism both acclimatized itself to Chinese circumstances and became more appealing to those who were disillusioned with the old ways, especially during the century between the collapse of the Han and the fall of Luoyang. It spread further during the subsequent period of "barbarian" conquest. Devoted missionaries won patronage from rough tribal leaders by using feats of magic to convince them that Buddhism was a more powerful religion than that of the shamans.

But Buddhism was powerful also in other ways. It enabled tribal chiefs to see themselves in new and grander roles, and it appealed to alien rulers. Through their patronage of this universalistic religion, which like themselves was foreign to China, such rulers could create a broad and venerable base for their claims to legitimacy as they attempted to create multiethnic states.

Political patronage was important, but to survive and prosper Buddhism also had to win a wide following among the Chinese people. In this endeavor its foreign origins were not an asset but a liability. Words and ideas, as well as artistic forms, had to be translated into Chinese terms.

Translating Buddhist texts into Chinese proved a formidable undertaking, since they were the products of a radically different culture and were written in a language totally unlike Chinese. The problems faced by the early Buddhist translators were similar to those which much later plagued Christian missionaries trying to render the Bible into Chinese. Particularly vexing was the need to introduce unfamiliar concepts at the very heart of Buddhism. Just as Christians were later to agonize over ways of translating "God" into Chinese, Buddhists racked their brains over words like "Nirvana." One early solution was to employ Daoist terminology. This had the advantage of sounding familiar. But it could also lead to a great deal of confusion, as when the Daoist term for "non-action" (wu-wei) was used to express the quite different concept of Nirvana.

Another possibility was not to translate at all but to transliterate, that is, to employ Chinese characters to approximate the sound rather than the meaning of the original word. Transliteration was most suitable for reproducing foreign proper names in Chinese, and this became the standard practice continued to this day. It was, and still is, also used for technical terms. In both cases the results were apt to be unwieldy and sometimes even misleading, since even in relatively modern times the Chinese reader has found it difficult to divorce the characters from their meanings.

Despite these handicaps scholar-monks made good progress in their work. The greatest of these translators was Kumārajīva, who, like many of his predecessors, was a Central Asian. Early in the fifth century he directed a translation project in Changan staffed by some thousand monks. In a vivid comment on the translator's art, he once compared his work to that of a man who chews rice in his mouth and then gives it to another to swallow. He and his staff produced good translations of basic Hinayana and Mahayana texts and were also responsible for the introduction of Madhyamika teachings, but the appeal of these abstract metaphysical theories was limited to a few intellectually inclined monks. Kumārajīva was only one of the many monks from Central Asia whose missionary zeal contributed greatly to the growth of Buddhism in China. But the traffic was not all one way: Chinese also undertook the long pilgrimage to India. The monk Fa Xian (Fa Hsien), who made the trip during 399–414, left a detailed account of his travels that serves as a prime source for the history of India during this period.

To overcome cultural barriers, early Buddhist apologists argued that their religion was basically compatible with the Chinese heritage and played down areas of potential conflict. That they enjoyed considerable success is shown by inscriptions at Yungang, Longmen, and elsewhere which reveal that the pious considered the donation of an image not only an expression of their religious faith but also a demonstration of their filial piety, and of reverence for ancestors whose souls were included in their prayers. (The idea of non-self, or non-soul, never had much currency in popular Buddhism nor was it generally taught even by well-educated Chinese monks.) Yet not everyone was convinced by this attempt to fuse Buddhism and filiality. After all, one of the prime dictates of the latter demanded the continuation of the family and thus conflicted with the celibate life of the monk and nun. Withdrawal from the secular world left Buddhists open to charges of antisocial behavior, and the growth of monastic wealth and influence made the Buddhist church vulnerable to political attack. Buddhism had its share of enemies; its progress was not all smooth, nor did it go unchallenged.

Challenges to Buddhist Influence

A strong competitor both for state patronage and popular support was the Daoist church. This had originated in the Later Han and now developed its own organization and priesthood along lines suggested by Buddhism. Frequent disputes arose between Buddhists and Daoists concerning various religious claims. For example, Daoists maintained that Lao Zi had traveled to India where he became the Buddha, while the Buddhist accounts depicted Lao Zi and Confucius as disciples of the Buddha, and even portrayed the semidivine founders of Chinese civilization as Bodhisattvas.

Since this rivalry involved power and patronage as well as matters of belief, it also had its fiercer aspects; it was a major factor in the persecution of Buddhism by the Northern Wei during 446–52 and again by another state in the North in 574–78. Instigated by Daoists and Confucians, both persecutions aimed at the destruction of Buddhist monasteries and the elimination of the Buddhist religious establishment, which had grown wealthy and powerful. (No attempt was made, however, either then or later, to suppress private Buddhist beliefs or ideas.) In both cases the persecution ended as soon as there was a change of ruler, and the new emperor made generous amends. Buddhism had grown too strong to be crushed by government fiat, and the persecutions appear to have done little permanent damage.

Religious persecution revealed considerable tension between church and state, but instead of suppressing the religion, the usual pattern, again exemplified by the Northern Wei, was for the state to place controls on the Buddhist church. This was done in order to prevent the monasteries from becoming havens for tax-dodgers or men escaping their labor obligations, to bar fraudulent transfers of land titles to tax-exempt religious institutions, and to enforce standards for ordination and for clerical conduct. Regulation was achieved by creating a clerical bureaucracy not unlike its secular counterpart. Northern Wei emperors appointed a monk to be Chief of Monks, and he presided over a network of Regional Chiefs of Monks, who in turn supervised the Buddhist orders while also looking after the interests of the religion. Thus the great Northern Wei cave temples were created through a combination of official support by the court and efforts of the Buddhist community itself. In the meantime Buddhism was also making gains under the very different political and social circumstances prevailing in the South.

The South

Spared the nomad incursions and warfare that plagued North China, the South during the period of division enjoyed relative tranquility, despite a series of political intrigues, palace coups, and the like which disturbed life at court. As in the North, here too a hereditary aristocracy of great families stood at the top of the social hierachy. But in the South the influence of the great families was not merely local — on the contrary, they dominated the courts of a succession of Southern dynasties. Not only did they enjoy exemption from taxation and labor-service, but they had ready access to office and set the whole tone of court life. In the fifth century, they even managed to obtain legislation prohibiting intermarriage between aristocrats and commoners. Their entrenched privileges seriously hampered government efficiency. Yet they were far from invincible. For one thing, their power was constantly being undermined by intense and recurrent conflicts among themselves. Friction between émigré families and those with deeper local roots was endemic. The influence of the aristocratic families was also weakened by their lack of military power and their inability to control military strongmen of nonaristocratic background.

Despite the turbulence of political conflict the South was making significant economic progress. Partly through migration from the disturbed North, partly through development of the land, the fertile area of the lower Yangzi saw a very substantial increase in population and productivity. Further south, Fujian now became truly Chinese for the first time as a result of increased Chinese settlement. As Chinese settlers moved in, the local aborigines were either pushed back into the hills or absorbed into the Chinese population.

Rice culture was the cornerstone of the agricultural economy of the South. Sophisticated wet-field cultivation of rice, much more productive than growing rice on dry land, took time to perfect. Not only did it involve experimentation with various strains of rice, it also entailed the construction of paddy fields and careful irrigation to keep the field wet and to maintain the water at an even temperature. When the fields were laid out on sloping ground or when terraces were constructed on hills, a complicated system of dams and reservoirs was necessary.

In the Han the Chinese developed a technique for raising seedlings in a nursery and transplanting them later in the paddies when the season was right. Such early planting in nurseries greatly increased the yield, but it also increased the demands for labor. Refugees from the North helped to augment the labor supply, and in that sense made a direct contribution to the growing prosperity of the South. The enlarged labor force was, in turn, sustained by the increased rice yields obtained from wet-field cultivation, which produced more calories per acre than did Northern dry-field agriculture. It is because rice has the ability to support high population density that the development of the South was to be of great consequence for the future history of China.

The South made great strides not only in the economic sphere but also in the development of secular culture. As we have seen, the South had already made important contributions to Chinese literature and the arts. Now its contributions formed the mainstream of Chinese cultural development, largely because the South fell heir to the lively cultural life that had accompanied the collapse of the Han.

Secular Culture and the Arts

When, with the fall of the Han, the old world disintegrated, intellectually as well as physically, thoughtful men were prompted to reexamine old assumptions and find new ways to give meaning to their lives. Whereas the collapse of the old Zhou (Chou) order gave rise to classical Chinese thought, the new civilizational crisis made men receptive to a new religiosity and stimulated a cultural flowering in which the aesthetic dimension of human experience and creativity was accorded full recognition and given free play.

Intellectually there was a turning away from Confucian scholasticism, although some of the most brilliant thinkers of this period, such as Wang Bi (Wang Pi, 226–249) and Guo Xiang (Kuo Hsiang, d. 312), continued to accept the validity of Confucian social values. Both these thinkers contributed to the development of what is known as Neo-Daoist philosophy. Wang Bi, writing on the *Daodejing (Tao Te Ching)* and the *Yi Jing (I Ching)*, gave new depth to the concept of non-being *(wu).* For him, original non-being *(benwu, pen-wu)* was the ultimate reality, the origin of all being. For Wang it was a source of metaphysical unity in a physical world that was disunited. He was also the first to introduce two complementary concepts that were to have a long history in Chinese philosophy: *ti (t'i)* and *yong (yung),* usually translated "substance" and "function," and understood by Wang Bi also in the sense of latent and manifest. In contrast to Wang Bi, Guo Xiang, author of a major commentary on the *Zhuangzi (Chuang Tzu)* denied the centrality of *wu.* He understood people to be composed of three elements which they must accept: "spontaneity (a universal, natural, and nonpersonal force that lies within each of us); limitations in time and society (their span of life, natural endowment and place in society); and daily renewal (an incessant state of change characteristic of all beings)." Doing so they will "enter into a 'marvelous coincidence' with themselves and with the oneness of the world, into the mystic fusion with the immanent force that produces everything and has no beginning or end."[1]

Many refined and sensitive men turned to mystical nihilism for an explanation of ultimate reality, and sought to attain it through spiritual contemplation, a "sitting in forgetfulness" so complete that forgetting is itself forgotten. Nor were other, less sublime, ways of forgetting neglected. A favorite pastime of the cultured gentleman was "pure talk." In contrast to the "pure criticism" *(qingyi, ch'ing-i)* directed against the government by Later Han Confucians, "pure talk" *(qingtan, ch'ing-t'an)* was clever repartee for its own sake. The highest honors went to the man who thought up the most adept and pithy characterization of his acquaintances. This witty, verbal game was far removed from the social and political concerns enjoined by Confucians.

Equally un-Confucian was the veneration of nature as an ultimate, and the search for naturalness in conduct even at the price of the social conventions and ideas of propriety prized by the Confucian tradition. The result was a burst of self-expression in the arts and in the lives of the sophisticated, who let themselves go in music, poetry, and personal attitudes. Most famous are the Seven Sages of the Bamboo Grove (third century), a group of gifted friends noted for their artistic accomplishments and their eccentricity. Wine flowed freely at their gatherings. One man was always followed by a servant carrying a bottle in one hand and a spade in the other — equipped for all eventualities in life or in death. Sometimes he drank stark naked at home. One startled visitor who found him in that state was promptly informed that his house was his pair of trousers; "What are you doing in my trousers?" the "sage" berated him. The men of this age did not invent eccentricity and unorthodox behavior, and they were certainly not the first to enjoy their cups. What was new was that they gave such conduct intellectual respectability.

It is in keeping with the spirit of the age that there was a strong interest in the study as well as in the appreciation of nature. Attempts were made to recreate and accelerate natural processes in alchemical furnaces, in an effort to create gold or the elixir of immortality. Advances in alchemy were matched by those made in medicine, where the object was to find new ways to prolong life, indefinitely if possible. The quest for immortality had long been pursued by followers of religious Daoism. One set of techniques to this end consisted of breathing exercises reminiscent of Indian yoga, but dating well before the appearance of Buddhism in China, and designed to nourish an embryo of immortality within the body in a process of internal alchemy. Refined diets, gymnastics, and sexual practices also formed part of the Daoist repertoire.

When Luoyang was captured by the "barbarians," its fall served to confirm the disillusionment and general pessimism felt by residents of the South. The continuing arrival of émigrés from the North reinforced this spirit. The more sophisticated turned to witty conversation, meditation, alchemy, and wine as a diversion from the depressing social and political problems of the day. It was this discontent and yearning for greater stability that made the society of southern China receptive to Buddhism. But it also served to liberate individual impulses to artistic expression, channeling energies that formerly had been devoted to philosophy and government into the secular arts. The result was an outburst of achievements in those arts which are the most highly prized and most closely identified with the Chinese gentleman: poetry, calligraphy, and painting.

Poetry

Many themes characteristic of the time found their expression in the poetry of Tao Jian (T'ao Chien, 365 – 427), also known as Tao Yuanming, regarded as one of China's greatest poets. After a short career in government, he retired to live the life of a country gentleman, although not without ambivalent feelings toward official life and its obligations. But there is in his verse much about wine, the simple country life, books, and nature. Poems such as this have an enduring appeal:

> I built my cottage among the habitations of men,
> And yet there is no clamor of carriages and horses.
> You ask: "Sir, how can this be done?"
> "A heart that is distant creates its own solitude."
> I pluck chrysanthemums under the eastern hedge,
> Then gaze afar toward the southern hills.
> The mountain air is fresh at the dusk of day;
> The flying birds in flocks return.
> In these things there lies a deep meaning;
> I want to tell it, but have forgotten the words.[2]

Tao especially loved chrysanthemums and wrote about them often; ever since, this "hermit among the flowers" has been associated with his name. The poem conveys a serene harmony with nature that is a lasting Chinese ideal and a common theme in much later Chinese poetry.

Other fine poets also wrote during this period. But there was at the same time a tendency for poets to indulge in increasingly artificial styles (for example, extreme parallelism in construction, with two lines matching each other word for word) and to exhibit their virtuosity in using an exotic vocabulary, as Han poets had in their rhapsodies. As a result spontaneity, creative freshness, was gradually lost, so that versification was already approaching a dead end when political unification from the North put an end both to the southern courts and their poetry.

More significant than poetic output, per se, was the development of a new attitude toward literature, which grew out of a deep concern with the process of poetic creation. Formerly the poetic art had been viewed as a vehicle for moral instruction, but in an era when the hold of old values was noticeably weakening, the old didacticism gave way to an appreciation of poetic creation in its own right. Hence increased emphasis was placed on stylistic devices, exotic language, and the like. When Xiao Tong (Hsiao T'ung) wrote the preface to his famous literary anthology, Wenxuan (Wen-hsüan, 530), he could frankly explain that his selection was based on purely aesthetic considerations. Two lines of Lu Ji (Lu Chi 261 – 303) give the flavor of the poetry of this period:

> Trying the empty Nothing, and demanding Something
> Banging the silent Zero, in search of Sound.[3]

They are from his famous rhapsody (fu) on literature, itself a work of high literary art.

Calligraphy

Of all the visual arts, Chinese scholars traditionally have given first place to calligraphy (see Figure 4-4). Behind this high esteem for calligraphy lies the aesthetic appeal and the mystique of the Chinese characters themselves, already noted in our discussion of the first inscriptions on oracle bones. It also

Figure 4-4   Basic forms of calligraphy, from the brush of Dr. Léon L. Y. Chang. The top two characters in the "dragon" column and the top characters in the "book" and "good" columns exemplify the Li form (clerical, or official); the third and fourth characters in the "dragon" column and the second characters in the "book" and "good" columns exemplify the Zheng (Cheng, also called Kai) form (regular, or standard); the fifth character in the "dragon" column and the third characters in the "book" and "good" columns exemplify the Xing (Hsing) form (longhand, or running); the bottom characters in each column exemplify the Cao (Ts'ao) form (cursive, or shorthand).

DRAGON   BOOK   GOOD

reflects the intensively literary nature of Chinese culture. Moreover, the development of cursive script during the Later Han turned writing into an intensely personal art, a vehicle for self-expression and a creative outlet, well suited to educated persons who had been wielding the brush and working with ink since childhood. Calligraphy came to be especially valued as a means for conveying the writer's deepest self, so that according to one Tang scholar one character was sufficient to reveal the writer. The flow of the lines and the rhythm of the brush creating the abstract beauty of the whole were now far more important than legibility. Thus Chinese appreciation of calligraphy as high art contained much of the pleasure and excitement associated with abstract art, as well as with graphology, in the West.

"In every terrible period of human history there is always a gentleman in a corner cultivating his calligraphy and stringing together a few pearls of expression."[4] Thus wrote Paul Valéry in 1915. If so, it is no wonder that calligraphy flourished during the years following the collapse of the Han, nor that the new emphasis on self-expression was particularly conducive to this art.

The greatest calligrapher of the age was Wang Xizhi (Wang Hsi-chih, 321 – 379), a fourth-century master whose art inspired, and served as a model for, generations. He, and two of his sons who also became famous calligraphers, drew inspiration from Daoism with its emphasis on the natural. They sought to express naturalism, itself an abstract quality, through what was in effect "artistic penmanship," except, of course, that they wrote with ink brushes, not pens. It was a magnificent challenge and typifies the artistic strivings of the age. The effort required years of practice. Wang Xizhi is said to have destroyed everything he had written before the age of 50 because he was dissatisfied with it. Unfortunately, none of his original work survives. Copies exist, but none is earlier than the Song. Reproduced here (see Figure 4-5) is a letter by a famous Song calligrapher and painter who drew inspiration from Wang Xizhi and one of his sons. The fourth line (reading right to left) is an example of the musical "continuous stroke" style for which they were famous.

Painting

In painting, the main subject continued to be the human figure, although the beginnings of China's great landscape tradition can also be traced back to this period. Preeminent among the painters was Gu Kaizhi (Ku K'ai-chih, ca. 344 – ca. 406) famed for capturing with his brush the essential character of his subjects, as when by adding three hairs to a chin he succeeded in depicting a man's wisdom. Among the most famous of his paintings still extant, although probably only a copy, is his hand-scroll illustrating a poem entitled "Admonitions of the Instructress to the Court Ladies" in which the painted panels alternate with lines of the text. The scene reproduced here (see Figure 4-6) illustrates the lines, "if the words you speak are good, men for a thousand *li*

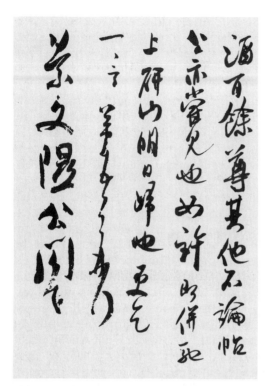

Figure 4-5
Portion of a letter by Mi Fei. (From
Gu Gung Fa Shu No. 11 [Taipei,
Taiwan: National Palace Museum,
1968], p. 11b). Selected and translated
by Dr. Léon L. Y. Chang.

The text may be translated as follows:
" . . . (sent) more than 100 vases of wine (from Yangzhou), not to mention the
other (gifts). Concerning the *tie** which you have seen previously, with your
permission, I shall have it brought to you, too. The *yenshan*† will be returned to
you by tomorrow.
Awaiting a word from you,
Fei salutes more than once at the Pavilion of
The Honorable Shi Jinwen."

*tie: a model of calligraphy, either an ink-rubbing or a handwritten original.
† *yenshan:* a rock of unusual or grotesque shape. Usually placed in front of
an ink-stone on a scholar's desk, *yenshan* were appreciated as objects of art
and valued as collectors' items.

will respond; but if you depart from this principle, even your bedfellow will
distrust you." Presumably it is the emperor who is mistrusting the lady, although this scene has sometimes been read the other way around. The other
panels also illustrate moral edicts basically Confucian in content, although the
artist himself was known for his Daoist eccentricity.
    The enhanced interest taken in painting led to the development of art criti-
cism and stimulated the classic formulation of the six rules, or principles, of

painting by Xie He (Hsieh Ho), an early sixth-century portrait painter. Most important, but also allowing for the widest latitude of interpretation, is his first principle, which calls on the artist to imbue his painting with a cosmic vitality and sense of life. These terms have been translated by Alexander Soper as "animation through spirit consonance" where "spirit" is a translation of "qi" ("ch'i") the vital force and stuff of man and the universe.[5] *Qi* is also a central concept in Chinese medicine; and we will encounter it again as a basic component of Neo-Confucian cosmology and metaphysics. The concept also figures in burial customs. The most eminent dead were fitted with suits of jade to prevent the *qi* from leaking out of their bodies; those who could not afford a complete outfit were equipped with stoppers for ears, nose, mouths, and so forth. In the context of aesthetics, it is the quality that causes a painting to reverberate with life.

Xie He's second law demands structural strength in the brushwork, demonstrating the vital link between painting and calligraphy, which used the same basic tools and techniques. It was largely in the quality of the artists' brushwork that the Chinese looked for an expression of their vital inspiration.

Figure 4-6 Gu Kaizhi, Scene 5 from *Admonitions of the Instructress to the Court Ladies.* Ink and color on silk. British Museum, London.

The next three laws require less explanation since they correspond to criteria familiar in the West. They are: fidelity to the object in portraying forms, conformity to kind in applying colors, and proper planning in placing of elements — what we would call composition. The sixth and final principle is very Chinese, for it enjoins the copying of old masters. This is one aspect of the old Chinese veneration for the past. It was a way of preserving old masterpieces and at the same time provided training and discipline for later artists, who by following the brushwork of a great predecessor would gain technical competence and an understanding of the medium, just as apprentice calligraphers today still begin by copying the great masters of their art, internalizing and making it their own. In neither case is there any intent to deceive.

Buddhism in the South

In the South as in the North, Buddhism made great headway, winning substantial support among the aristocracy and the personal patronage of rulers. In contrast to the North where Buddhist missionaries had to deal with "barbarian" rulers, in the South erudite and clever monks won favor by adopting the stance and displaying the skills of the sophisticated gentlemen who dominated society. Thus quick-witted Buddhists became experts in "pure talk" and engaged also in highly abstract metaphysical discussions in which they displayed their command of the Chinese as well as Buddhist intellectual heritage. Given new prominence as a model for the Buddhist as aristocrat was the figure of Vimalakīrti, a wealthy layman who enjoyed life to the full and displayed great powers of intellect and a pure and lofty personality. (See Figure 4-7. This depiction of Vimalakīrti is from a later period and from Japan, but it illustrates that Buddhism was not only for the poor and ignorant.) Moreover, monasteries erected in beautiful surroundings offered a life of scholarly retreat and contemplation, posing an attractive alternative to the requirements of life in the world.

An outstanding patron of Buddhism in the South was Emperor Wu of Liang (r. 502–49), sometimes called the Emperor Bodhisattva. A devout Buddhist, he banished meat and wine from the imperial table; wrote commentaries on holy texts; held great assemblies of monks and laymen, one of which had an attendance of 50,000; built temples; and otherwise generously supported Buddhism, which he made the official religion. This does not mean that Buddhism enjoyed universal approval in the South any more than it did in the North. Its opponents in the South not only attacked its alleged subversive effects on state and society but also attempted to refute some of its teachings. For example, Fan Zhen (Fan Chen) argued against the concept of the indestructibility of the soul, now a common tenet of Chinese Buddhism, the original teaching of the Buddha notwithstanding. Against Fan Zhen's argument that the soul was a passing function of the body, just as keenness is a temporary attribute of a

Figure 4-7   Vimalakīrti. Clay,
45.2 cm high.
Pagoda of the Hōryūji.

knife, Emperor Wu solicited counterarguments and received 58 refutations
and only two replies supporting Fan Zhen's anti-Buddhist views. Such arguments provided background for later attacks on Buddhism, but the time was
not yet ripe for a major anti-Buddhist reaction. On the contrary, the full
flowering of Buddhism in China was still to come, after China was once
more united.

In this process of reunification Buddhism too, as we shall see, played its
part; for toward the end of the period of division, the contrasts between
Buddhism in North and South were fading. Monks traveled between the two
areas, and the same texts were studied and recited North and South. Furthermore, Buddhism was better able to contribute to reunification because it had
gone far toward adapting itself to Chinese civilization. In architecture, for
example, individual Buddhist halls followed native secular prototypes, and
the only major difference between a Buddhist temple and a Han palace compound was the presence in the former of a pagoda. This characteristically East
Asian structure, however, owed as much to the Han watchtower as it did to the
Indian stupa.

China on the Eve of Reunification

The changes that occurred between the fall of the Han and the Sui reunification were far-reaching and profound. The division of China had brought with it foreign rulers and a new religion. It had stimulated a new consciousness, which found expression in literature and art. And it had accelerated the development of the South, thus altering China's economic geography. These events are comparable to what took place in the West after the fall of Rome, and in both civilizations, traditional scholarly attitudes toward the postimperial age have been disparaging. Anti-Buddhist to begin with, traditional Confucians considered the division of the empire a sure indication that something was drastically wrong with the world. But this political division also had its positive side, for, as in the Warring States period, it made for intellectual choice and diversity.

In contrast to the history of the West after the fall of Rome, in China the factors making for political integration were strong enough, under the right leadership, to triumph in the end. Buddhism was one such factor, and Confucianism as a family ethic and as a state rationale persisted even when Confucian philosophy was in eclipse. Nor was the ideal of political unity ever challenged. At the close of the period, the last of the Five Dynasties in the South, the Chen (Ch'en, 537–89), attempted to organize a more centralized and therefore more powerful state. Ultimately, however, unification came from the North (specifically the northwest), which was, as always, militarily the strongest area. Unification proved a great and difficult undertaking — and one which in the end succeeded brilliantly.

NOTES

1. Isabelle Robinet, "Kuo Hsiang," in *The Encyclopedia of Religion* (New York: Macmillan, 1987) with some elisions and rearrangement.

2. Liu Wu-chi, *An Introduction to Chinese Literature* (Bloomington: Indiana Univ. Press, 1966), p. 64.

3. Eric Sackheim, . . . *the silent Zero in search of Sound* . . . ; *An Anthology of Chinese Poems from the Beginning through the Sixth Century* (New York: Grossman Publishers, 1968), p. ii.

4. Quoted in Etienne Balazs, *Chinese Civilization and Bureaucracy* (New Haven: Yale Univ. Press, 1964), p. 226.

5. Alexander Soper, "The First Two Laws of Hsieh Ho," *The Far Eastern Quarterly* 8 (1949): 412-23.

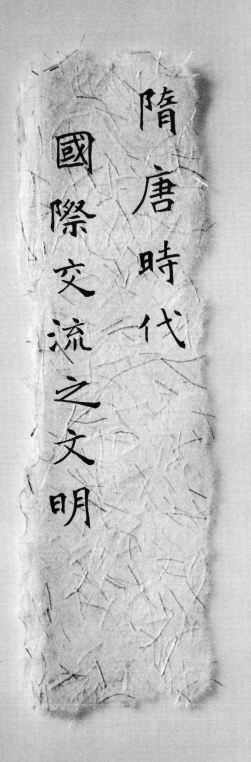

5

The Cosmopolitan Civilization of the Sui and Tang: 581–907

581	617		755 763		907
Sui (China Reunified in 589)	Tang			Late Tang	
			An Lushan Rebellion		

*C*hina was reunited in 589, and the second imperial period in Chinese history lasted approximately 300 years, until 907. It was during this period that China became the political model and cultural center for all East Asia. Buddhism flourished. Significant changes occurred in government and society. It was the classical period of Chinese poetry. Like the Han (in the first imperial period) the Tang dynasty followed a powerful but short-lived regime that had accomplished the task of reunification: the Sui. And like the Han, the Tang dynasty may be thought of as having an earlier and later phase, although there was no formal interruption of Tang rule. There are other ways, too, in which the two dynasties are comparable, but the differences between them are as instructive as their points of resemblance.

The Sui (581–617)

As we have seen in the previous chapter, the Northern Wei was unable to maintain a unified northern state after 534. In 577 another of the northern states, the Northern Zhou (Chou, 557–81), accomplished military reunification of the North. Four years later a Northern Zhou general unsurped the throne and founded his own dynasty, the Sui. In 589 the Sui defeated the last of the southern states and, thereafter, incorporated North and South into a single political system. The magnitude of this task has been compared to that facing Charlemagne (742–814) when he attempted to create a new Roman Empire in Europe. Indeed, in terms of land area, diversity of terrain, and variety of local cultures the two situations are quite comparable.

The Sui, unlike the Qin (Ch'in), did not attempt to impose a new pattern on China but adopted a policy of fusing various local traditions and amalgamating different elements. The contrast between the two unifying regimes is perhaps most striking in the area of ideology, for the Sui founder, although a convinced Buddhist, also made use of Confucian and Daoist traditions to legitimize his regime and gain acceptance and support. In formulating a legal code the Sui incorporated elements from different legal traditions, North and South. This was done so effectively that it provided the basis for the Tang and all subsequent legal codes. In other respects also there was a great deal of continuity between the Sui and the early Tang, which unlike the Han, did not repudiate the principles and policies of its immediate predecessor.

102

The Sui emperors, Wendi (Wen-ti, r. 581–604) and his son Yangdi (Yang-ti, r. 604–18), came from a northwestern aristocratic family of mixed Chinese and foreign ancestry. Politically, they sought through a combination of cultural policies and marriage alliances to reconcile the pretensions of the great aristocratic families of the Northeast and of the South. For example, Yangdi married a southern princess. The second emperor completed his father's ambitious project of building a canal linking China's two great rivers, the Yellow and the Yangzi, which enabled the political capital in the North to draw on the rich resources of the lower Yangzi. The completed Grand Canal went from Hangzhou to Kaifeng and was linked by extensions both to the area of modern Beijing (Peking) and to the Sui-Tang capital, the new Changan, which Wendi had built near the site of the old capital of the Former Han. The construction of official granaries further helped to establish a government economic network.

The Sui took equal care to further political consolidation and centralization. The state bureaucracy was reorganized, and a tier of local administration was eliminated to make local government more amenable to central direction. Furthermore, local officials were deprived of the authority to appoint their subordinates, a right they had enjoyed during the period of division. Other measures included the "rule of avoidance," which prohibited an official from serving in his native place, and the stipulation that no official could serve more than one tour of duty in the same locality. After this tour, usually of three years' duration, the official would be reassigned according to merit. Even more important, the Sui instituted a system of recruiting officials by examination. This deprived the hereditary high aristocracy of the monopoly of power they had enjoyed during the period of division, when appointments had been made by recommendation, and opened government service to a somewhat wider class of people, although service was still the prerogative of the well-born. These measures effectively reduced the ability of officials to establish a personal power base in the areas where they served, reduced the power of the great families to which they belonged, and made officials more responsive to the interests and direction of the central government.

As is to be expected of a unifying dynasty, the Sui was vigorous militarily. Expeditions were sent as far south as Central Vietnam and into Taiwan while, to the west, nomadic peoples were driven out of Gansu and eastern Turkestan. Colonies were established along the western trade routes, and further afield, in Central Asia, such states as Turfan became tributaries. Envoys were exchanged with Japan. The Sui also continued the militia system it had inherited from the northern dynasties and settled many troops in garrisons along the frontiers.

The dynasty's vigorous foreign policy demanded the organization and deployment of considerable military force. Most costly in terms of casualties and materiel were three unsuccessful campaigns against Koguryŏ, the state that controlled northern Korea and much of southern Manchuria. Successive defeats placed an unbearable strain on the dynasty's resources. Insurrection and rebellion became widespread, and the dynasty was doomed. It had overreached itself, trying to accomplish too much too rapidly. In the traditional Chinese view, however, the onus for its demise was assigned to Yangdi, who was cast as an archetypical bad last emperor, a self-indulgent tyrant — an image that was further embellished in popular literature, which depicts him as living in luxury while the people were starving, and frolicking with the numerous women of his harem, in a room lined with polished bronze screens to serve as mirrors, when he should have been minding the ship of state.

The Tang: Establishment and Consolidation

The Tang dynasty emerged from the struggles accompanying the disintegration of the Sui. Its founder was that dynasty's top general, a man related through his mother to the Sui ruling house. Many of his officials had also served the former dynasty. There was consequently no sharp break in the composition or the policy of the ruling group, but the fighting was hard and prolonged. It took up most of the reign of the founding emperor, known posthumously as Gaozu (Kao-tsu, r. 618–26). The emperor's second son won considerable success as a military commander. In 626 he killed the crown prince and another brother, apparently to forestall a plot against himself, and then he forced his father to abdicate. He is known as Taizong (T'ai-tsung, r. 626–49) and effected the political consolidation of the new dynasty.

Taizong's physical vigor and military prowess are suggested by the stone panels, over five feet high, showing in relief his favorite mount (see Figure 5-1). It was, however, his political abilities that caused him to become one of China's most admired and idealized rulers. He was particularly skillful in his selection of officials and wise in the knowledge of men. His most famous Confucian minister was Wei Zheng (Wei Cheng, 580–645), on whom he relied for ethical guidance. In a statement after Wei Zheng's death, Taizong compared his minister to a mirror in which to correct his judgment, just as a bronze mirror is used to correct one's dress and the past serves as a mirror for understanding the rise and fall of states. But although he sought Wei Zheng's counsel on moral issues, such as the punishment of officials, or the giving and receiving of gifts, he did not allow him to influence major policy decisions such as those concerning peace or war.

The emperor's policies generally followed and furthered those initiated by the Sui. He broadened the geographical composition of the bureaucracy by including men from areas other than his native Northwest, but government remained in the hands of aristocrats. The most pretentious of these were the high aristocrats of the Northeast, who looked down on the "semibarbarian" northwestern families, not excluding the imperial family. Taizong had a genealogy compiled to define the importance of various families throughout China and rejected the first draft in order to demote one of the great Hebei lineages and to promote the imperial clan to first place.

Figure 5-1   *General Qiu Xinggong of Emperor Tang Taizong's army removes an arrow from the Emperor's horse Autumn Dew.* Stone relief from tomb of Tang Taizong. Design attributed to Yan Liben (Yen Li-pen, d. 673). 147.4 cm × 152 cm. University of Pennsylvania Museum, Philadelphia.

Additional granaries and schools were built and a new law code promulgated. The code dealt with both criminal and administrative concerns and consisted of primary laws, meant to hold for all time, and secondary laws: regulations open to frequent adjustment to allow for changing conditions and local variations. There was also a refinement of the structure of government. The essential tasks of the central government were performed by Six Ministries (personnel, revenue, rites, war, justice, and public works), which were retained by later dynasties as their central administrative organs.

The early Tang emperors, like those of the Sui, drew on Buddhism and Daoism as well as Confucianism to legitimize their empire. As Howard Wechsler has shown, in contrast to earlier dynasties, they deemphasized rites centered on their own ancestors in favor of more public rituals performed by the emperor for the good of all. And they extended their own family to form a "political family" of ministers and high officials who were included in rites and granted "satellite tombs" on the vast grounds of the imperial tombs. Such tombs had also been granted in the Han, but not on anything like the Tang scale.[1] The fact that in China, unlike Japan, such tombs continued to be built even in a Buddhist age is not unconnected with issues of legitimation but beyond that also reveals deep-seated differences in attitudes toward burial and perhaps even death.

In foreign affairs Taizong pursued a strong, aggressive policy. He successfully pushed Chinese power even further west than had the Han, but, like the Sui, failed in Korea. With Chinese power extending all the way to the Pamirs and the land itself at peace, there was a resumption of foreign trade and influence that remained characteristic of the Tang period. Although many foreigners visited and dwelt in Chang 'an during Taizong's reign, the most famous traveler of the time was a Chinese monk. Xuanzang (Hsuan-tsang) who journeyed to India and returned with Buddhist texts and much information about foreign countries (see Figure 5-2). The emperor was more interested in the latter than the former and even tried to persuade the venerable

Figure 5-2   Xuanzang, a Tang Buddhist monk who traveled to India in search of Buddhist scriptures.

monk to return to lay life and become a foreign policy adviser. But Xuanzang declined, and Taizong financed the translation projects to which the monk devoted the rest of his life.

Taizong took care not to alienate the Buddhists, but like his predecessors he took measures to keep the Buddhist establishment under control. Furthermore, since the Tang ruling house claimed descent from Lao Zi, Daoism was also shown considerable favor. For example, Xuanzang was ordered to translate the *Daodejing (Tao Te Ching)* into Sanskrit for the benefit of the Indian world. This text and also the *Zhuang Zi (Chuang Tzu)* even found a place in the Tang system of civil service examinations, otherwise a major bastion of Confucian influence.

Taizong's last years were spoiled by disappointments in his sons and heirs. The crown prince became so infatuated with nomad ways, even living in a yurt, that he was finally deposed, and the emperor's favorite son was too deeply involved in intrigues over the succession to be trusted. In the end, the succession went to a weak young prince who, on Taizong's death, became Emperor Gaozong (Kao-tsung, r. 650–83).

Empress Wu and Emperor Xuanzong

The next emperor, Gaozong, began as quite a vigorous ruler, but the political history of the century between the death of Taizong and the outbreak of the devastating rebellion led by General An Lushan was dominated by two ruling personalities. The first of these was Wu Zhao (Wu Chao, 625?–706?), one of Taizong's concubines who won Gaozong's affection. She engineered the removal and often the murder of all rivals, and dominated government after Gaozong suffered a stroke in 660. After he died, in 683, two of her sons ruled in succession, but in 690, not satisfied to rule through puppets, she proclaimed herself "emperor" of a new dynasty, the Zhou, thereby becoming the only woman in Chinese history to rule in her own name. For legitimization Empress Wu turned mainly to Buddhism, proclaiming herself an incarnation of Maitreya and ordering temples set up in every province to expound a sutra, the *Dayunjing (Ta-yün-ching)*, which prophesied the appearance of a female world ruler 700 years after the passing of the Buddha. Her patronage of Buddhism also extended to other temples and sects, and much work was done in the Longmen caves during her reign. She was especially supportive of Huayan Buddhism, which conceived the world as centered on Vairocana Buddha, much as Empress Wu aspired to be the center of the political order.

The legitimacy of Empress Wu's power was also bolstered by a genealogy compiled in 659 that listed families according to the official rank attained by their members, rather than according to their traditional inherited social standing, with the Wu family placed first. Under her rule the bureaucracy was expanded, and many of the new positions were filled through the examination system. Although this opened government careers to a wider group than before, in the final stage of the process, candidates continued to be judged on their appearance and speech, criteria that inevitably favored the wellborn. It was also normal practice for candidates to try to win favor with an examiner prior to the tests. Those who could used their family connections for this purpose; others sent samples of their verse in the hope of impressing the men who held the keys to a government career. Under Empress Wu, men who entered government through the examinations were able for the first time to attain the highest office, even that of Chief Minister, although the Empress herself preferred to bypass this office and work through the "Scholars of the Northern Gate," who formed a kind of personal secretariat. Gradually, however, in the course of the first half of the Tang, examination graduates acquired great prestige and came to hold the highest offices, even though the majority of officials still entered government service through other means, making use of family connections. At the same time, government service gradually became the most desirable and prestigious career in the empire.

Under Empress Wu, Tang power reached its furthest geographic extent (see Figure 5-3). But this expansion was not achieved peacefully; constant fighting occurred, particularly against the Tibetans. In Korea Empress Wu supported the successful efforts of the state of Silla to unify the peninsula. Although China was unable to dominate the newly unified state, relations remained cordial throughout her reign. Until around 700 she remained a vigorous although ruthless ruler, but during her last years the empress, now in her seventies, came under the influence of sycophantic courtiers. She was deposed in 705, and the Tang was reestablished.

The second major ruler was Xuanzong (Hsüan-tsung, r. 713–56), also known as the "Brilliant Emperor" (Ming-huang). His reign is considered the high point of the Tang: economically, politically, and culturally. His court must have been truly splendid. The emperor, a horse lover, is said to have kept 40,000 horses in the royal stables, including a troupe of dancing horses. Poetry and painting flourished, and horses were a favorite theme for poets, painters, and potters. It is fitting that Han Gan (Han Kan), probably the greatest of the Tang horse painters, served at Xuanzong's court. This was also the time in which landscape painting came into its own. The most admired of all Tang painters, Wu Daozi (Wu Tao-tzu), also lived during this period. It is said of him that one day, after painting a scene on a wall, he walked into it — leaving only the empty wall behind. He must have been a remarkable master to have inspired this story; unfortunately, none of his work is known to have survived.

The political achievements of Xuanzong's government included reformation of the coinage, repair and extension of the Grand Canal, and the implementation of a land registration program. To carry out these measures, he employed special commissions headed by distinguished aristocrats. Men of equally imposing background also staffed the Censorate, the organ of the government charged with the surveillance of the bureaucracy. There was a tendency at this time for officials to polarize into two groups: members of the

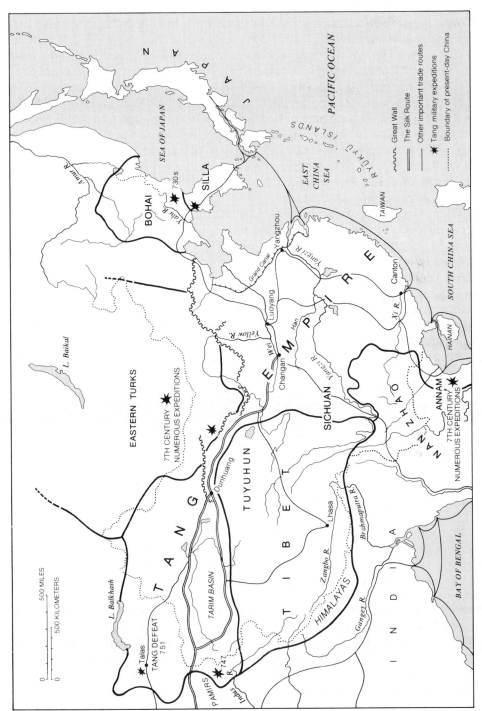

Figure 5-3   The Tang Empire

high aristocracy and those of less exhalted rank. Nevertheless, factors influencing political alignments were too complex to be reduced to simple family or regional patterns.

Important changes in the institution of government also occurred under Xuanzong. The power of the Chief Ministers increased, and a council, or cabinet, of Chief Ministers was established. This development was particularly significant because, near the middle of his reign, the emperor gradually withdrew from active participation in government. In 736 Chief Minister Li Linfu became a virtual dictator. He was of aristocratic stock, but he did not have an examination system degree and was often ridiculed by degree holders for his lack of scholarship. Nevertheless, he was an able administrator. When Li Linfu died in 752, his place was taken by Yang Guozhong (Yang Kuo-chung), a much less capable man.

Yang Guozhong owed his rise to the influence of his cousin, the royal concubine Yang Gueifei (Yang Kuei-fei). A beautiful woman, on the plump side in accord with the Tang ideal of female beauty, she so captivated the emperor that he neglected all else and was content to entrust the burdens of government to her relatives. The reign that had begun in such brilliance ended in disaster. In 755 General An Lushan rebelled, and the court was forced to flee to Sichuan. Along the way, loyal soldiers, blaming Yang Gueifei for the country's difficulties, forced the emperor to have her strangled. Xuanzong then abdicated.

City Life in the Capital: Chang'an

Even the most casual glance at a map of the Sui-Tang capital, Chang'an (see Figure 5-4), is enough to reveal that it was a planned city. Containing about 30 square miles, excluding the palace area, it was the largest planned city ever built, and also the largest city encompassed by walls. Its roughly one million inhabitants also made it the most populous city in the world, in its day. Roughly another million people lived in the greater metropolitan area outside the walls.

Many cities grow naturally in response to the social and economic needs of their inhabitants, but planned cities express the values and priorities of their builders. The essential feature of Chang'an is that it was built to be the capital of a great empire. In accord with ancient tradition, it was oriented so that both the city and the imperial palace faced south. The entire city was in a sense the home of the emperor. Its layout resembled that of a typical Tang house, with a service area in front and a garden in the rear. The imposing presence of the emperor and his government were further emphasized by the grand avenue that led from the main city gate to the palace and the government complex. Five hundred feet wide, it was well calculated to impress envoys from lesser lands with the might and grandeur of the great Chinese Empire.

The people of the city, including those employed in the government

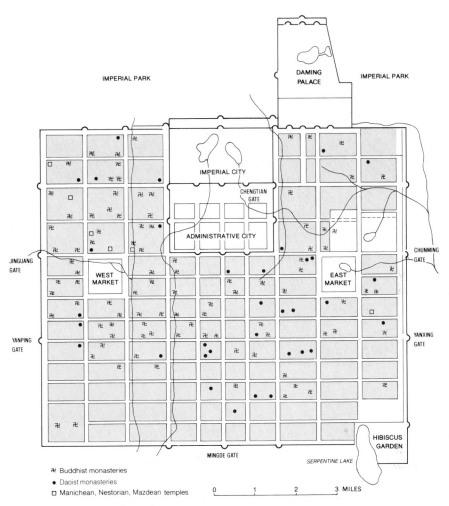

Figure 5-4   Tang Chang 'an.

complex, lived in rectangular wards. Each ward was a self-contained unit surrounded by walls, with entry provided through a gate that was closed each night. Two friends in adjacent wards might be able to see each other's houses but find it difficult to visit. Since it was the center of government, Chang 'an was hardly the place to escape government surveillance and interference. In contrast to medieval Europe, where the city became a refuge and a center of freedom, in China one sought freedom in remote mountains and hills. Not everyone wished to rusticate in a remote village however; there were many who bitterly bemoaned an enforced absence from the great capital — unless, perhaps, they were posted to the secondary capital of Luoyang or to the southern metropolis of Yangzhou.

Figure 5-5 *Armenoid Merchant
Holding Wine Skin.* Pottery
with three-color glaze, eighth
century, 37.2 cm × 25.4 cm.
Seattle Art Museum.

Tang culture was doubly cosmopolitan: first, in the sense that China was
open to cultural influences from India and the distant west; second, in the
sense that China, itself, was the cultural model for the other settled societies of
East Asia. Both aspects were reflected in the considerable number of foreigners who lived in Chang 'an. Some were students. Among these the most
numerous were the Koreans, of whom some 8,000 were said to be in Chang 'an
in 640. Other foreigners were engaged in commerce, coming from as far away
as India, Iran, Syria, and Arabia. The Armenoid wine-seller shown in Figure
5-5 probably sold his exotic beverage at the West Market, the center for foreign trade, where his customers could also enjoy other exotic foods and beverages and attend performances of foreign acrobats or magicians or see a foreign
play. Stylish Tang ladies sported foreign coiffures, while painters and potters
had a good time rendering the outlandish features of "barbarians" from distant lands. Images of foreigners from all over Central Asia and beyond to Iran
were prominent among the clay figurines manufactured in specialty shops to
be used for burial with the dead. Among the tomb figures are camel drivers and
grooms for the horses, examples of which can be found in almost all museum
collections of Chinese art. Information concerning foreign foods, music, and
customs can also be found in Tang writings, particularly poetry. It is characteristic of the robust and cosmopolitan spirit of the period that one of the

favorite pastimes of its aristocratic ladies and gentlemen was polo, a game which originated in Persia. The participation of women in such athletic activities and their fondness for riding (see Figure 5-6) are worth emphasizing in the light of the very different ethos that was to prevail in post-Tang times.

Among the amenities of the capital were the Serpentine Lake and the Hibiscus Garden in the southeast corner of the city, where newly granted degree holders celebrated their good fortune by floating wine cups on the water, and the emperor himself sometimes entered the Purple Cloud Pavilion to observe the festivities. Notably absent, however, were such public buildings as forums, baths, or stadiums found in cities inhabited by citizens rather than subjects. Nor did Chang 'an boast great, monumental structures of stone or brick. The men of Tang were under no illusion concerning the permanence of stone. In their view, it was the written word which endured.

As the map of Chang 'an (Figure 5-4) clearly shows, the city was also a religious center. Manichean, Nestorian, and Zoroastrian temples testify to Tang tolerance and cosmopolitanism, but their congregations, like those of Buddhist temples during the Han, were largely foreign. The opposite was true of the many Daoist and Buddhist establishments. Many of the latter were the

Figure 5-6 *Lady on Horseback.*
Painted clay, Tang, 38.1 cm ×
31.1 cm. Collection of Mr. and
Mrs. Ezekiel Schloss,
New York.

chief temples of flourishing sects, and some accommodated pilgrim monks from Korea and Japan. Just as Buddhist pagodas dominated the Chang 'an skyline, the Buddhist faith predominated on the intellectual and spiritual horizon. It was the time when Chinese Buddhism came of age.

The Flourishing of Buddhism

Although the state employed Confucian forms and learning, and Tang emperors often favored Daoism, this was the golden age of Chinese Buddhism. The early Tang state could restrict the number of monks and regulate monasteries but when the still vigorous Gaozong made a move to have monks pay obeisance to the throne, an eminent monk successfully countered that this went against monks' vows and that any ruler who forced them to do this would destroy his own chances for salvation and bring disaster on the country. In the end, the emperor had to give up even on a compromise to have them kneel in front of their parents. Buddhist monasteries flourished economically; they fulfilled important social roles; and their most outstanding monks had sufficient self-confidence to make their own formulations of doctrine and develop the teaching in new ways. For Buddhist art as well, it was an age of classic fulfillment.

Eight Buddhist sects appeared between 581 and 755, of which four enjoyed only temporary or limited success: the Disciplinary School (Lü), the Dharma Image (Faxiang, Fa-hsiang) the Sect of the Three Stages (Sanjie, San-chieh), the Esoteric School (Mi). The Disciplinary School restricted its concerns to monastic rules, rituals, and regulations. More deeply philosophical (but rejected after it lost imperial patronage) was Faxiang, propounded by the great pilgrim Xuanzang. It was basically a derivation of Yogacara Buddhism as interpreted by Xuanzang's teacher in India. As a school of metaphysical idealism it developed a subtle and complex psychology, but it departed from Mahayana universalism in its insistence on salvation through arduous meditation so that the *manas* (thought center), by attaining perfect wisdom, could restore the purity of *ālaya* (the storehouse) where are found the seeds of karma, some tainted and some pure. Faxiang taught that not all beings possess untainted seeds, and therefore not all were able to achieve salvation, a doctrine of limited appeal in China.

The Sect of the Three Stages (Sanjie) was particularly prone to government suppression. Its devotees divided time into the era of the true teaching, the era of the counterfeit teaching, and the era of the decay of the teaching. Although there was disagreement over exact periodization, the Tang was generally assigned to the period of decay, a view which Tang emperors naturally did not appreciate. Empress Wu and Emperor Xuanzong were particularly hostile. The latter, who had an abiding interest in Daoist magic, patronized Esoteric Buddhism (Mi) which was characterized by the use of mantras (mystic syllables), mudras (signs made by the position of the fingers and hands), and mandalas (pictorial representations of the cosmos — "cosmograms"). Although the Esoteric School influenced other sects, it did not flourish as an independent sect in China. It did flourish in Japan in the form of Shingon.

By contrast, the four major sects had considerable influence in China and in Japan. These were: Tiantai (T'ien-t'ai; Tendai, in Japanese), Huayan (Hua-yen; Kegon, in Japanese), Qingdu (Ch'ing-tu; Jōdo, in Japanese), and Chan (familiar to us from the Japanese name, Zen). The school that enjoyed the most official support under the Sui was Tiantai. Founded by Zhiyi (Chih-i, 538–97), it took its name from a mountain range in Zhejiang. Just as the Sui strove for political and economic integration, Tiantai developed doctrinal and metaphysical syncretism, that is, it combined elements of the various doctrines and practices. In particular it sought to combine the scholarly tradition of the South with northern pietism and meditation. Thus, a text esteemed in the North was considered Buddha's first sermon, but his last pronouncement, according to Tiantai was a sutra popular in the South. The complete Truth for Tiantai was contained in the Lotus Sutra, believed to have been preached by the Buddha to 12,000 arhats (saints), 6,000 nuns, 8,000 Bodhisattvas, and 60,000 gods. The great god Brahma attended, accompanied by 12,000 dragons, and there were hundreds of thousands of other supernatural beings. As he talked, a ray of light emanated from the Buddha's forehead revealing 18,000 worlds in each of which a Buddha is preaching. This text was enormously influential in East Asia, and its imagery inspired many artistic representations.

Tiantai doctrine centered on a tripartite truth: (1) the truth that all phenomena are empty, products of causation without a nature of their own; (2) the truth that they do, however, exist temporarily; (3) the truth that encompasses but transcends emptiness and temporariness. These three truths all involve and require each other — throughout Tiantai the whole and the parts are one. A rich but unified cosmology is built on this basis: temporariness consists of ten realms. Since each of these includes the other, a total of 1,000 results. Each of these in turn has three aspects — that of living beings, of aggregates, and of space. The result is 3,000 worlds interwoven so that all are present in each. Since, therefore, truth is immanent in everything, it follows that all beings contain the Buddha nature and can be saved. One eighth-century Tiantai patriarch taught that this includes inanimate things, down to the tiniest grain of dust.

Like Tiantai, Huayan taught the doctrine of emptiness and the interpenetration of all phenomena, but its teaching that all phenomena arise simultaneously in reciprocal causation was new. More interested in doctrinal subtleties than Tiantai, Huayan Buddhists distinguished between li, which can be translated as "principle" and is formless, and shi (shih) or phenomena. One of its greatest masters was Fazang (Fa-tsang, 643–712), who was generously patronized by Empress Wu. In a famous sermon Fazang once explained Huayan doctrine by setting up a Buddha figure surrounded by eight mirrors at the points of the compass. A ninth mirror was placed above the statue and a tenth below. When the Buddha figure was lit by a torch, each mirror reflected not only the Buddha but also all the other mirrors.

The remaining two sects emphasized practice more than doctrine. The

Jingtu (Ch'ing-t'u), or Pure Land sect, derived its name from the paradise in the West over which presides Amitābha (Amituofo, A-mi-t'o-fo in Chinese; Amida in Japanese), the Buddha of Infinite Light. Another great favorite of Pure Land Buddhists was Guanyin (Kuan-yin) the Bodhisattva of mercy. Drawing on a long Mahayana tradition, this school emphasized faith as the means for gaining rebirth in the land of bliss. The teaching of salvation by faith was often coupled with the idea that this was the appropriate means for a decadent age. A special practice of Pure Land Buddhism was the invocation of Amitābha's name. This, if done with wholehearted sincerity, would gain anyone rebirth in the Pure Land. The popular appeal of this sect was immense, and its spiritual dimensions probably received their furthest development in the teachings of the Japanese master Shinran (1173–1262).

The last school to be discussed was so influential in Japan that in the West it is generally known by its Japanese name, although Chan (Zen) was very much Chinese in origin and has affinities with Daoism. It taught meditation as the way for one to pierce through the world of illusion, recognize the Buddha nature within oneself, and obtain enlightenment. Whereas for other schools meditation was only one of many techniques, Chan rejected all other practices, such as the performance of meritorious deeds or the study of scriptures. The so-called Northern branch of Chan emphasized sitting in silent meditation and attaining enlightenment gradually. Southern Chan, founded by the man known as the Sixth Patriarch, Huineng (638–713), maintained that illumination comes in a sudden flash, although only after long searching. A Western analogy might be Newton's experience under the apple tree: he discovered the law of gravitation in a sudden flash, but he would never have done so had he not been constantly thinking about the problem, searching for a solution.

Southern Chan teachers often employed unorthodox methods to prod their disciples on the road to illumination. Their methods included irreverent or irrelevant answers to questions, contradictory remarks, nonsense syllables — anything to jar the mind out of its ordinary rut. Some masters would strike their disciples in the belief (as with Newton) that enlightenment might come as the result of a sudden physical shock. One widely practiced technique was for the master to assign his pupils a gongan (kung-an; kōan, in Japanese), an enigmatic statement to be pondered until the pupil attained an understanding that transcended everyday reasoning. One famous gongan asks: "what is the sound of one hand clapping?"

If the growth of sects illustrates the inner vigor of Buddhist religion, there were equally impressive outward manifestations of the strength of the Buddhist church. In the countryside, Buddhist temples performed important economic functions: operating mills and oil presses, maintaining vaults for safe-deposit, and performing other banking services including pawnbroking. The temples also held much land that they cultivated with semiservile labor, and they profited from their connections with wealthy patrons who sought to evade taxation by registering land under a temple name. Some temples provided medical care; still others entertainment. Much of their wealth was channeled into building and the arts.

Architecture and Art

Religious persecution and war have taken their toll on the architectural remains of Tang Buddhism. Remaining temples are limited to a very few pagodas and halls, the largest of which is located on Mt. Wu in Shanxi. This is similar in design to the Tōshōdaiji founded by a Chinese monk in Japan, a worthy expression of Tang self-confidence. Just as the message of the Buddha was considered universal in its appeal and application, the artistic styles of the Tang at its height were adopted beyond the seas in Japan. Built facing south, a hall such as this was oriented not to the topographic features of any particular location but to the cosmos that encompasses all.

Large scale Tang sculpture in wood and bronze has not survived, although the more than life-size bronzes at the Yakushiji in Nara, Japan, are fine representations of the Tang international style. In China there are a good many stone statues, including a very large Vairocana Buddha (the universal Buddha of Huayan and Esoteric Buddhism) just outside the caves at Longmen. More sculpture is preserved in other caves, with the best examples found at Tianlongshan (T'ien-lung Shan) in Shanxi. The Guanyin shown in Figure 5-7 is a Tang sculpture in the style seen in eighth-century Chang 'an. The sensuous quality of the body, clothed (not hidden) in diaphanous drapery, owes something to Indian influence, particularly that of the Gupta style (Gupta dynasty in India, 320–647). At their very best, Tang sculptures blend Indian delight in the corporality of mass with a Chinese sense of essentially linear rhythm. It is a combination most suitable for portraying Guanyin, combining the spiritual qualities of a supernatural being with merciful concern for earthly creatures. The balance between movement and restraint, like that between the worldly and the sacred, was difficult to maintain: in later Buddhist art, corporality degenerates into obesity, and the robes take on a wild, rococo life of their own.

Figure 5-7 Eleven-headed Guanyin. Limestone, eighth century, 100.8 cm × 31.7 cm. Freer Gallery, Washington, D.C.

We know that the temples at Chang 'an were decorated with great frescoes and that Wu Daozi (Wu Tao-tzu) did some of his best work for Buddhist establishments; a favorite scene was that of Amitābha presiding over his paradise. An important site for Tang painting is Dunhuang (Tun-huang), a major center for the caravan trade, famous not only for the art preserved in its grottoes but also for the many documents discovered there. Kumārajīva's translation of the Lotus Sutra is the most frequently found text, but administrative records, often written on the backs of religious works, make the Dunhuang material a major source for the study of Tang economic, social, and administrative history. Paintings dating from the Northern Wei and Tang also provide information on agricultural tools and techniques. Others depict major events in the Buddhist tradition, including scenes from Xuanzang's great journey.

In the ninth century (mid-Tang) an untrammeled, spontaneous style of painting, largely influenced by Chan Buddhism, developed in Sichuan. It is best represented by Wang Mò ("ink Wang") who made pictures by splashing ink on silk, usually while drunk. Chan painting flourished in Song China and will be discussed in the chapter on that period. A popular subject of the Chan painter in China was a pair of Tang recluses, wearing expressions of divine lunacy: Han Shan (Cold Mountain), named after the mountain in the Tiantai range where he made his home, and Shide (Shih Te, Foundling), who worked in a monastery kitchen on Cold Mountain and is usually holding a broom. Both men wrote poetry. The strong verse of Han Shan has been especially admired and is well represented in English translation.

Poetry

Buddhism influenced the work of other Tang poets. Foremost among them is Wang Wei (699–759), who is noted also for his landscape painting and his music, both now lost. His best poetry conveys the serenity and calm of the detached, enlightened man:

> I didn't know where the temple was,
> pushing mile on mile among cloudy peaks;
> old trees, peopleless paths,
> deep mountains, somewhere a bell.
> Brook voices choke over craggy boulders,
> sun rays turn cold in the green pines.
> At dusk by the bend of a deserted pond,
> a monk in meditation, taming poison dragons.[2]

The dragons are the passions; the scene is visual yet empty.

Buddhist serenity is but one theme in Tang poetry. Wang Wei, like other major poets, also wrote verses that reflect secular life. The following, celebrating the military exploits of a young horseman, suggests the period's military vigor:

> Alone, he can draw two carved bows at once!
> A thousand waves of enemy horsemen cannot daunt him.
> Astride his golden saddle, he strings his bow with white-feathered arrows,
> And ping! the plumed shower drops five khan dead![3]

Li Bo and Du Fu

During the Tang the ability to write at least passable poetry was one of the accomplishments expected of a gentleman, and it was usually a prerequisite for passing the civil service examinations. Consequently, the production of poetry was large: over 48,000 Tang poems by some 2,200 writers have been preserved. Their quality, however, is uneven, as would be the case if contemporary American politicians and business executives all were expected to write poetry. Furthermore, during the Tang, poetry was viewed not as a vocation, but as an avocation — and, sometimes, as a consolation.

Li Bo (Li Po, 701 – 63) and Du Fu (Tu Fu, 712 – 70), China's two most beloved and admired poets, experienced both the brilliance of Xuanzong's reign and the dark times of An Lushan's Rebellion. Li Bo was actually implicated in a secondary rebellion. Neither man was a political success, although Du Fu felt this more keenly than did the older poet. Both enjoyed friendship and wine and composed beautiful poetry with multidimensional meanings. They were personal friends, and Du Fu greatly admired Li Bo. Yet, despite all they shared, they differed greatly in personality and in their work. It is the contrasts between them that Chinese scholars and literary men have always stressed.

Like Wang Wei, Li Bo's subject matter included nature, but the nature described in poems such as "The Road to Shu Is Steep," which describes Xuanzong's flight to Sichuan during An Lushan's Rebellion (see Figure 5-8, in which this subject is treated pictorially) is much more exuberant than that of Wang Wei, more akin to the tradition represented by the Han rhapsodists. Li Bo's fondness for nature and for mountains blended well with his freedom of spirit. Although he wrote poems in many forms, he preferred old-style verse *gushi, (ku-shih)*, which was without the restrictions and limitations placed on verse in the new style *jintishi, (chin-t'i shih)* and left the poet free to devise his own rhythmic and verbal structure.

Li Bo was famous as the poet of wine:

> A pot of wine among the flowers:
> I drink alone, no kith or kin near.
> I raise my cup to invite the moon to join me;
> It and my shadow make a party of three.
> Alas, the moon is unconcerned about drinking,
> And my shadow merely follows me around.

Briefly I cavort with the moon and my shadow:
Pleasure must be sought while it is spring.
I sing and the moon goes back and forth,
I dance and my shadow falls at random.
While sober we seek pleasure in fellowship;
When drunk we go each our own way.
Then let us pledge a friendship without human ties
And meet again at the far end of the Milky Way.⁴

It is said that on one nocturnal drinking expedition on a lake, Li Bo fell into the water while trying to fish out the moon and died by drowning. This tale may be spurious! But it formed part of the traditional image, part of the legend of Li Bo. The Song painter Liang Kai captured this image of the slightly inebriated poet floating in space (see Chapter 6, Figure 6-6) with an economy of means that would have pleased Li Bo, for his own verse is deceptively simple. He knew that true art does not reveal its skill.

Both poets wrote highly compressed verse, but much of Du Fu's poetry, unlike that of Li Bo, is enriched by a patina of allusions that add weight and

Figure 5-8   Anonymous, *Ming Huang's* (that is, Xuanzong's) *Journey to Shu.* Hanging scroll, ink and color on silk, Tang in style but dates from Song or later, 55.9 cm × 81 cm. Palace Museum Collection, Taipei.

Detail Figure 5-8
Anonymous, *Ming
Huang's Journey to
Shu.*

majesty to the lines. Also in contrast to Li Bo, Du Fu was particularly effective in new-style poetry, especially the regulated verse *lushi, (lü-shih)* in eight lines with five or seven characters per line, and elaborate rules governing tone and rhyme as well as verbal parallelism. There are occasional poems, poems of friendship and wine, but Du Fu has perhaps been admired most for his social conscience and compassion. He can be biting in his commentary, as in two frequently quoted lines that form part of a longer poem written shortly before the An Lushan Rebellion:

> Inside the red gates wine and meat go bad;
> On the roads are bones of men who died of cold.[5]

Some of his most moving poems describe the suffering and hardships of ordinary people. One concerns the visit at night of a recruiting officer to the village of Shihao (Shih-hao). An old grandmother informs the officer that only two males are left at home: the old man who has fled and an infant son. She tells him to take her since she can at least cook — and in the morning she is gone.

Du Fu, like his contemporaries, frequently sent poems to those close to him. The following was written while he was living near the upper reaches of the Yangzi and is addressed to a brother living far away near the mouth of the river. The "wind in the dust" in the third line refers to the warfare that separates the two brothers:

To My Younger Brother

Rumors that you lodge in a mountain temple
In Hangzhou, or in Yuezhou for sure.
Wind in the dust prolongs our day of parting,
Yangzi and Han have wasted my clear autumn.
My shadow sticks to the trees where gibbons scream,
But my spirit whirls by the towers sea-serpents breathe.
Let me go down next year with the spring waters
And search for you to the end of the white clouds in the East.[6]

In other poems Du Fu tells of life in the thatched hut he inhabited during exile in Sichuan, and he often voices his dismay at the failure of his political ambitions. His aspirations and disappointments corresponded to the experiences of many of his readers, who admired his artistry and his humanism. Perhaps for all of these reasons, he was venerated as China's foremost poet.

The Rebellion of An Lushan (755–763)

The rebellion that drove the emperor into flight to Sichuan and created havoc in the country revealed underlying weakness in the Tang system. Only a strong emperor or an all-powerful chief minister like Li Linfu could prevent the friction between the aristocratic commissions and the regular bureaucracy from getting out of hand. Old institutions were revealed as inadequate under new conditions. The dynasty had adopted the "equal field" (*juntian, chün-t'ien*) system of land allotment developed by the Northern Wei as a way of bringing deserted land back under cultivation or opening up new lands, but this system proved unworkable when there was a shortage rather than a surplus of land. The breakdown of the land system brought in its train the failure of the taxation system, which was based on equal land allotments. Furthermore, most taxes were collected in kind, that is, goods rather than money, and this required a cumbersome system of transport and storage. The old militia system similarly proved inadequate for the dynasty's military requirements, which could only be met by large standing armies composed of professional soldiers.

In 747 a Tang army crossed the Pamirs, led by a Korean general who had opted for a career under the Tang rather than returning to his native land. The purpose of this expedition was to prevent Arabs and Tibetans from joining forces. The tactic succeeded, but four years later this same general suffered defeat on the banks of the Talas River near Samarkand. The loss of this battle not only put an end to Tang ambitions in the area but opened to Islam what had up to then been a Buddhist-oriented Central Asia. Earlier, Turkish peoples had caused conflict in the Northwest, but in 736 this area was stabilized when the pro-Tang Uighurs became the dominant power. In mid-century, however, the dynasty was challenged by an alliance between Tibet and Nan Zhao (Nan Chao), a southwestern state in the area of modern Yunnan Province. The government's response was to create military provinces along the frontiers. These were placed under the direction of military governors (*jiedushi, chieh-tu shih*) who were given logistic as well as military authority and gradually assumed other functions of government. Since the central army was in decline, a serious imbalance of power resulted between the home army and the powerful frontier forces. An Lushan, a general of Turkish extraction, began his rebellion in control of 160,000 troops in the Northeast.

An Lushan's forces seized both Luoyang and Chang 'an, and he proclaimed himself emperor of a new Yan (Yen) dynasty. But in 757 he was murdered by his son. The rebellion then continued, led first by another general of similar background, Shi Siming (Shih Ssu-ming), and then by his son. In the meantime, the court had taken refuge in Sichuan, the very large (75,000 square miles) and fertile province famed for its terraced hills, the flooded fields reflecting the light of the moon. (Fertile soil and a favorable climate make Sichuan perfect for rice cultivation, and for other crops as well, for it is said that anything that can be grown anywhere in China can be grown in Sichuan. Ringed by mountains, it is highly defensible. During the Second World War it served as a bastion for the Nationalist Chinese.)

In 763 the court was able to regain the capital, and the Tang was saved. However, the dynasty was able to accomplish its preservation only with the assistance of foreign, mostly Uighur, troops. Furthermore, it had to be content with purely nominal submission of the virtually independent "governors" in the Northeast, in the region west of the capital, in parts of Henan, and in Sichuan. Regional differences that before the rebellion had been worked out within the system now threatened to pull it apart.

The Late Tang

One long-term effect of the rebellion of An Lushan was the final abandonment of the "equal field" system and with it the practice of assessing taxes according to the number of individuals in a household. Instead, under Emperor Dezong (Te-tsung, 780–805), a new system was instituted that assessed households according to the size of their houses and the amount of land they held. Thus the government officially acknowledged the uneven distribution of land and tried to make the best of it. Since the new taxes were collected twice a year, the system is known as the Two Tax System. Another innovation provided that taxes be calculated in terms of money, although they were still collected in kind. The Two Tax System did not always operate effectively, but this basic approach to taxation persisted for 700 years.

Major economic support for the dynasty came from the South. A main source of revenue was the salt monopoly, for the government controlled all but one of China's major salt-producing areas. The government sold monopoly salt to merchants for distribution throughout China, thereby deriving income even from areas not under its political control.

Dezong strengthened the dynasty's finances and also built up a large palace army. The history of the Tang after An Lushan was thus not all downhill. Emperor Xianzong (Hsien-tsung, r. 806–20) was especially vigorous in fostering institutional renewal and in reasserting central control over some of the lost provinces. But both of these vigorous emperors relied on men directly dependent on them, the "inner court," rather than using the regular bureaucracy. The result, as in the Later Han, was the emergence of eunuch power. Eunuchs commanded the palace armies and once again formed self-perpetuating "families" through adoption. Xianzong was murdered by eunuchs, whose power grew greatly in the 820s and 830s — an attempted coup against them in 835 failed. Moreover, officialdom at the time was divided into bitterly hostile factions. A dispute that lasted half a century arose out of a disagreement over the results of a special civil service examination held in 808.

Both Dezong and Xianzong personally favored Daoism. This was also true of Wuzong (Wu-tsung, 840–46) who, among other things, built a Terrace for Immortals within the palace grounds so that he might "ascend into the mists and wander freely through the nine divisions of Heaven." Personally hostile to Buddhism, he further could not resist the temptation to meet great and pressing financial needs by seizing Buddhist riches. He is, consequently, best known for his persecution of the church: monastic lands and wealth were confiscated, monks and nuns were returned to lay life, slaves and dependents were released. The emperor himself claimed to have defrocked 260,500 monks and nuns and when it was all over the regulations allowed for only 49 monasteries with around 800 monks in all the empire. Irreparable damage was done to collections of sacred texts, to the bronze statues that had been the glory of Buddhist sculpture, and to religious buildings. The policy of persecution was promptly reversed by Wuzong's successor, but the Buddhist establishments were to suffer another devastating blow during the enormously destructive rebellion of Huang Chao. Particularly hard hit were sects such as Tiantai and Huayan, which focused on textual studies and were never to recover. Only two sects continued to flourish: Pure Land, grounded in the hearts of the people, and Chan, which took pride in its freedom from texts and patronage.

Late Tang Poetry and Culture

For about 20 years after Du Fu's death in 770 no great poetry appeared, but in the 790s Han Yu (768–824) and Bo Juyi (Po Chü-yi, 772–846) began to write in their own distinctive and widely imitated styles. The latter was not only a very prolific poet, author of some 2,800 pieces, but was also particularly beloved wherever Chinese influence reached. His "Everlasting Remorse" is the classic poetic rendition of the tragedy of Xuangzong and Yang Guifei. Unlike Du Fu, he wrote in simple and easy language. Like Du Fu he had a strong social conscience:

An Old Charcoal Seller

An old charcoal seller
Cuts firewood, burns coal by the southern mountain.
His face, all covered with dust and ash, the color of smoke,
The hair at his temples is gray, his ten fingers black.
The money he makes selling coal, what is it for?
To put clothes on his back and food in his mouth.
The rags on his poor body are thin and threadbare;
Distressed at the low price of coal, he hopes for colder weather.
Night comes, an inch of snow has fallen on the city,
In the morning, he rides his cart along the icy ruts,
His ox weary, he hungry, and the sun already high.
In the mud by the south gate, outside the market, he stops to rest.
All of a sudden, two dashing riders appear;
An imperial envoy, garbed in yellow (his attendant in white),
Holding an official dispatch, he reads a proclamation.
Then turns the cart around, curses the ox, and leads it north.
One cartload of coal — a thousand or more catties!
No use appealing to the official spiriting the cart away:
Half a length of red lace, a slip of damask
Dropped on the ox — is payment in full![7]

In other poems, he tells of his daily life, his family, and routines. He once described himself as addicted to poetry, bursting forth whenever he sees a fine landscape or meets a beloved friend: "madly singing in the mountains."[8]

Han Yu championed the Old Prose movement (which wanted to return to the style of writing found in the classics) in opposition to the elaborate parallelism and rhetorical flourishes of more recent prose. He is best known for an essay in which he reaffirmed the Confucian Way. Han Yu subsequently became one of the heroes of Song Confucians who considered him their precursor. In his poetry as in his prose, Han Yu preferred the old styles, writing long poems rich in original and daring similies. A common theme in his work is the classic complaint of the Tang gentleman–poet: lack of official recognition. A scholar is like a fine horse, in need of proper care if he is to flourish. The trouble with the world lies not in the lack of horses, but in the absence of a ruler who understands horses. Han Yu's works were not always serious; he also showed a lighter side. He wrote an essay admonishing a crocodile and a poem about losing one's teeth.

Other writers of the Late Tang include the historiographer Liu Zhiji (Liu Chih-chi, 661–722), the philosopher Li Ao (d. ca. 844), and the poets Li He (Li Ho, 791–817) and Li Shangyin (812?–58). Li He, a brilliant man who died young, was long neglected by later Chinese scholars. He had a penchant for quaint and even frankly odd language; as one Chinese critic put it: his verse has a demonic quality. Li Shangyin, on the other hand, wrote frequently of love — not a common theme in Chinese poetry.

Du Fu seems to have been the first poet, or at least one of the first, to write on or about paintings. He showed a keen awareness of the perishability of silk and ink. And he was right, for the poems have survived long after the paintings disappeared. The main sources for Tang landscape painting are literary descriptions and later copies. Long after the Tang, Wang Wei was credited with having established a gentleman's style of calligraphic painting in monotone, but none of his work has survived. It is said to have contrasted with the precision of line and decorative coloring of the court style, illustrated in Figure 5-8 by a copy made not earlier than the Song. The coloring, blue and green, is a hallmark of Tang art, but the pleasure the artist takes in the fantastic mountains is typical of all Chinese landscapists. Here, however, in contrast to later mountainscapes, nature does not overwhelm man. Instead, it provides a setting for his activities. The scene is Emperor Xuanzong's flight to Sichuan during the An Lushan Rebellion, although as Michael Sullivan has suggested it really looks more like a pleasure excursion than a precipitous retreat after tragedy and defeat.[9] Be that as it may, this painting is probably as close as we can now get to the style of the Tang, an important reference point for later Chinese painting as well as a delightful work in its own right.

Collapse of the Dynasty

During its last 50 years, the Tang dynasty was weakened by conflict and divided loyalties in the capital; mistrust between officials in the capital and their military commanders in the field; and by suspicions, manipulations, and falsifications of all kinds. Even reports concerning natural disasters were falsified, as when an official assured the emperor that a plague of locusts had proven harmless because they had "all impaled themselves on thorns and brambles and died.[10] The story makes a sad litany of mismanagement, corruption, and incompetence. Meanwhile, bandit gangs, a refuge for the desperately poor and dislocated, increased in number, size, and ambition. Forming themselves into confederations, they progressed from raiding to rebellion; what had once been a nuisance now became a threat. Power, whether bandit or "legitimate," went to the strong and ruthless. Ordinary people survived as best they could the depredations of bandits and soldiers alike. Even though the dynasty made occasional gains, each rally amounted to no more than one step forward followed by two steps backward.

The most serious rebellion was led by Wang Xianzhi (Wang Hsien-chih), who was succeeded after his death by Huang Chao. The latter destroyed Canton (879), killing many of its foreign as well as Chinese population. He is most notorious, however, for the brutality that he displayed after he captured Chang 'an in 880. Huang Chao failed in his ambition to create a new dynasty; after his rebellion, once-unified China was thoroughly fragmented (see Figure 5-9).

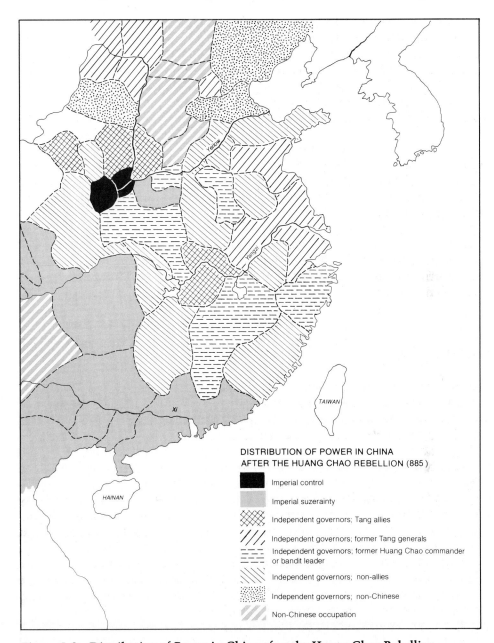

Figure 5-9   **Distribution of Power in China after the Huang Chao Rebellion**

SOURCE   Adapted from Robert M. Somers, "The Collapse of the T'ang Order," (Ph.D. dissertation, Yale University, 1975), pp. 204-05.

The survival of the court now depended on the tolerance of, and especially the competition among, its neighboring rivals. An important factor in the shifting military and political balance of North China were the policies of the foreign peoples who inhabited the northern borderlands. Among these the Shatuo Turks were now the most important. Their intervention on behalf of the dynasty rescued it from destruction several times and enabled the Tang to survive the Huang Chao Rebellion. In 905 the Shatuo Turks concluded an alliance with a people from Mongolia called the Khitan, an alliance that continued through the Five Dynasties period (907–60). Indeed the Shatuo Turks themselves formed the second of these dynasties. This was the Later Tang (923–34), which as its name implies tried to rule in the Tang tradition. They did not succeed in creating a lasting state, but a part of North China remained in foreign hands until the Ming.

The fighting at the end of the Tang was particularly severe in the Northwest, and it devastated Chang 'an. There was panic in the streets, people screaming, scrambling over walls, stampeding while "rebels rage like stamping beasts"; "blood flowing like boiling fountains," severed heads, houses in flames, people eating bark or human flesh; deserted palaces where brambles grow and fox and rabbit run wild. These are some of the images in "The Lament of Lady Qi (Ch'i)," a long ballad composed by Wei Zhong (Wei Chung, 836–910) after Huang Chao ruined the city. Its most famous lines capture the essence of the tragic contrast between past greatness and present disaster:

> The Inner Treasury is burnt down, its tapestries and
>   embroideries a heap of ashes;
> All along the Street of Heaven one treads to dust
>   the bones of State officials.[11]

Chang 'an, which the first Han emperor had made his chief city over a thousand years before, was never again to be China's capital.

The fall of the Tang brought to an end the story of a great city and a great dynasty. It also marked the end of the hereditary high aristocracy that had dominated the Period of Disunity and had accommodated itself to the Tang bureaucratic order even after an examination degree carried more weight than a pedigree. In broad terms, the fall of the Tang brought to a close a period of Chinese martial vigor and self-assertion vis-à-vis its nomadic and seminomadic neighbors. At the same time the foreign religion that had fascinated and comforted the Chinese people for centuries began to lose intellectual vigor.

This is not to deny that there were continuities, particularly between the Later Tang and the Song, for many of the characteristics of the later period, ranging from the tax system to intellectual developments, are easily traceable to the eighth century or even earlier. It is, therefore, useful to distinguish between the earlier and later parts of the Tang dynasty even as we turn our attention to the Song and the start of the late imperial age.

NOTES

1. Howard Wechsler, *Offerings of Jade and Silk: Ritual and Symbol in the Legitimation of the T'ang Dynasty* (New Haven: Yale Univ. Press, 1985),

2. Burton Watson, *Chinese Lyricism: Shih Poetry from the Second to the Twelfth Century* (New York: Columbia Univ. Press, 1971), p. 175.

3. Chang Yin-nan and Lewis C. Walmsley, *Poems by Wang Wei* (Rutland, Vt.: Charles E. Tuttle, 1959), p. 76.

4. Liu Wu-chi and Irving Yucheng Lo, eds., *Sunflower Splendor* (Garden City, N.Y.: Anchor Press/Doubleday, 1975), p. 109.

5. A. R. Davis, *Tu Fu* (New York: Twayne, 1971), p. 46.

6. A. C. Graham, *Poems of the Late T'ang* (Baltimore: Penguin Books, 1965), p. 47.

7. Liu and Lo, *Sunflower Splendor*, pp. 206–07.

8. Arthur Waley, trans., *One Hundred and Seventy Chinese Poems* (London: Constable & Co., Ltd., 1918; reprinted 1947), p. 144.

9. Michael Sullivan, *The Arts of China* (Berkeley Univ. of California Press, 1973), p. 293.

10. Robert M. Somers, "*The Collapse of the T'ang Order*," (Ph.D. dissertation, Yale Univ., 1975), p. 102.

11. *Ibid.*, p. 145.

PART THREE

Late Imperial China

Bottle Vase. Guan porcelain, Song, 16.8 cm high. Sir Percival David Foundation, London.

6
China During the Song: 960–1279

	Jin (Jurchen) 1115–1234	
Liao (Khitan) 907–1119		Mongols
Northern Song	Southern Song	

*T*he Song (Sung) period (960–1279) represents a new phase of Chinese history. This dynasty did not match the Tang in military power or geographic extent: indeed after 1127 North China was lost to the state of Jin (Chin) founded by the Jurchen people from Manchuria. But what makes the Song of crucial importance is the emergence of features that were to remain characteristic of traditional China. Foremost among them was the emergence of new elites in place of the old hereditary aristocracy. There were also dramatic and far-reaching changes in the economy. In philosophy, and also in painting, the Song achievement attained classic dimensions, creating a heritage that for centuries to come inspired and challenged thoughtful men throughout East Asia.

A New Elite

The old aristocratic families that had been so prominent under the Tang dynasty did not survive the turbulence that accompanied the decline and fall of the Tang. The way was thus cleared for the rise of new families who, ideally, based their prestige on literary learning, their power and formal status on office holding, and their wealth on land ownership. Although these attributes did not necessarily overlap, when all three were present they reinforced each other. Even though the spread of printing (a late Tang invention) made books cheaper and encouraged the diffusion of literacy, a certain economic level still had to be reached before a family could afford to dispense with the labor of a son in the fields and pay for his education. Education, in turn, was a prerequisite for an official career, while office holding provided opportunities for the acquisition and protection of wealth.

Song social structure was more complex than this, however. There were also the overeducated poor and the undereducated rich: the deeply learned scholar who lived a life of frugal obscurity, and the man of wealth who was not fully educated by elite standards and who was ineligible for political appointment and unwelcome in high society. The fact that learning, office, and wealth did not necessarily coincide made for considerable social variety, a variety further enhanced by the contrasts between urban and rural life and by major regional differences. Furthermore, status was a function of the social group. Even a   **133** criminal (say, a salt smuggler) might well enjoy high standing within his community although despised by the official elite. It is important to remember that in premodern times the web of government rested only lightly on society and that the world of officialdom was remote from most people's lives. The reminder is necessary, since most of the historical sources stem from that world of the scholar-official, which also supplied traditional China's historians. This scholar-official elite played a crucial role in maintaining Chinese unity, but unity should never be mistaken for uniformity.

During the Southern Song (1127–1269, the term for the period after the dynasty had lost the North), the tendency was for elite families to concentrate on securing the continued welfare and prosperity of their families by prudent management of their affairs and property. They strengthened their local roots by assuming leadership roles in the construction of public works such as bridges and waterworks, in social welfare measures, in temple building, and in defense. Marriage ties with similar families helped to confirm and perpetuate their influence. These leading local families acted as powerful intermediaries between their local communities and the central state.

In contrast to societies in which status is inherited, the Chinese system neither guaranteed continuity of status for these elite families nor were there laws barring the way for those trying to rise from below. Economically, also, movement up and down was made possible by the ready transferability of land and other forms of wealth, which was further facilitated by the custom of dividing estates among heirs rather than leaving them intact to a single son. Yet, once established, some local elite families could persist for generations.

To distinguish the new elite from the old, scholars have termed them the "gentry" and further distinguished between the relatively large local gentry and the more restricted upper gentry composed of those who held office or were eligible to do so by virtue of success in the civil service examinations. The men in both groups were educated. Although the examinations were open to almost all men, excluding only a small minority such as the sons of criminals and the like, most candidates came from the local gentry. However, obtaining an official degree was difficult, and the competition was intense.

The Examination System

The system of civil service examinations came into its own in the Song and (except in the Mongol period) remained the most prestigious means of government recruitment. Although during the Song many men continued to enter the civil service through other means, such as sponsorship by an official, in later dynasties the examination route represented the norm for entry into government service. The system was only abolished in the twentieth century. During this vast span of time, the system was refined and greatly elaborated, but its basic features were already clearly in evidence in the Song.

Structurally the system provided for an orderly progression through a series of tests (three during the Song, more later). These began at the local level, included a metropolitan examination given in the capital to candidates from the entire country, and culminated in a palace examination held under the personal auspices of the emperor. The practices of the Tang whereby candidates brought personal influence to bear on the examiners were now eliminated, and the government went to great lengths in its attempt to secure impartiality. The papers of candidates, who were identified only by number, were copied by clerks before being submitted for grading in order to prevent a reader from recognizing the author of any paper by its calligraphy. The battle of wits between would-be cheaters and the authorities seeking to enforce honesty lasted as long as the examinations themselves and was pursued with great ingenuity by both sides. Despite occasional scandals the examination system enjoyed a well-deserved reputation for honesty.

Success in the examinations required first of all a thorough command of the classics, which the candidates had to memorize. Candidates had to be able to identify not only well-known lines but also the most obscure passages, and even sequences of characters that made no sense to anyone who did not know the exact context in which they appeared in a classic text. Tests of memory and exercises demonstrating command over formal literary styles were favored by examiners, since they made grading easier and more objective. Thus formal criteria were stressed in judging the poems that candidates were usually required to compose as part of their examinations. There was a persistent tendency for the examinations to turn into mere technical exercises, testing skills that revealed little about either a man's character or his administrative competence. This remained true even though the candidates were also required to discuss the meaning of designated passages from the classics and to answer questions concerning statecraft that had some theoretical bearing on the policy problems of the day.

Competition was rough, and preparing for and taking the examinations became a way of life. It has been estimated that the average age of those who completed the entire process and received the coveted *jinshi (chin-shih,* "presented" or "advanced" scholar) degree was in the mid-30s. Since some areas, notably the southeast, were more advanced culturally and educationally than other, regional quotas were proposed, but, unlike during later dynasties they were largely not enacted. As a result men from the southeast predominated. Even with quotas, competition was bound to be more intense in some areas than others, but the most serious inequity was caused by the increasing importance of alternative examinations given to the relatives of officials. This, along with the special treatment accorded the numerous imperial clansmen, in effect signified the abandonment of fairness during the Southern Song.

Despite its shortcomings the examination system did facilitate the careers of China's greatest statesmen during the Song and later. And it graduated administrators who shared a common intellectual heritage and recognized a common set of values, men who were scholars as well as officials. It provided a measure of social mobility, largely determined the educational curriculum, and shaped the structure of the lives of those who aspired to a degree. It is no wonder, therefore, that the examinations themselves became a subject of profound concern and intense debate. The tradition of protest against its inadequacies is almost as old as the system itself. There were those who wished to see it abolished altogether, and many others who argued for reforms of various kinds. The examination system, therefore, remained a topic of political debate and scholarly controversy.

The Northern Song

"Northern Song" designates the period from 960 until 1126 when the dynasty had its capital in the North, at Kaifeng. During this period the Song government ruled over both North and South. However, from the time of the dynasty's founder, Emperor Taizu (T'ai-tsu, r. 960–76), and his brother, Taizong (T'ai-tsung, r. 976–97), who completed the establishment of the dynasty, the Song had to tolerate a non-Chinese presence in North China. This was the Liao dynasty (907–1119), which had been created by a tribal people known as the Khitan and included sixteen prefectures on the Chinese side of the Great Wall. Relations between the Song and the Liao were frequently hostile, but the two states came to terms in 1005 after the Song emperor, Zhenzong (Chen-tsung, r. 997–1022), had personally taken the field against the Khitan. Negotiations led to a treaty that included provisions for diplomatic exchanges, trade, and a Song agreement to send the Liao contributions in silk and silver. For the Song the cost was considerably less than would have been required to finance a military solution, and the dynasty would rather pay than fight.

The Liao were not the Song's only troublesome neighbors. In 1038 there was a challenge from the West as the leader of the Ordos-based Tangut peoples organized the Xi Xia (Hsi Hsia) state and invaded Shaanxi. In 1044, under Emperor Renzong (Jen-tsung, r. 1022–63), the Song signed a peace treaty with the Xi Xia along the lines of its earlier agreement with the Liao. The Xi Xia, however, remained a military problem for the Song until the Song lost all of North China to the Jin (1115–1234).

Initially the Song had welcomed the emergence of the Jin as an ally, but the dynasty's attempt to "use barbarians against barbarians" ended in disaster. The last two emperors of the Northern Song, Huizong (Hui-tsung, r. 1100–26), China's greatest imperial painter and calligrapher (see Figure 6-1) but not equally distinguished as a ruler, and his son, Emperor Qinzong (Ch'in-tsung, r. 1126–27), were taken to Manchuria as prisoners of the Jurchen and there lived out their lives. The dynasty was able to reestablish itself in the South, but the North, homeland of Chinese civilization, remained lost. Not until the founding of the Ming dynasty in the fourteenth century was the North to come again under Chinese rule (see Figure 6-2).

Figure 6-1   Song Huizong, *Five-Colored Parakeet.* Hanging scroll, colors on silk, 53 cm high. Museum of Fine Arts, Boston.

Government and Politics

Song government was basically organized along Tang lines, but Song statesmen, careful students of history, were determined to avoid past errors as well as to profit from past achievements. One precedent the dynasty was particularly anxious to avoid was the reemergence of warlords such as had eventually destroyed the Tang. The dynastic founder, himself a general, saw to it that power was placed in civilian hands, and his successors pursued the same policy. By such devices as the rotation of troops and frequent changes of command, the court prevented generals from developing personal power and succeeded in keeping commanders in line. Indeed, the military profession suffered a permanent loss of status, and it became a truism that good men are not turned into soldiers any more than good iron is wasted to make nails.

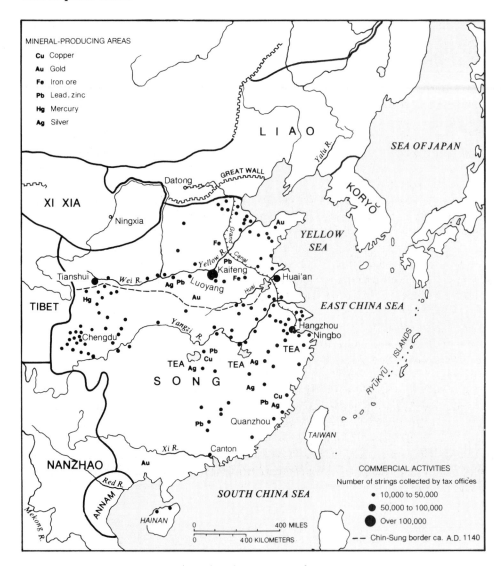

Figure 6-2   Song China — Political and Commercial

NOTE To suggest the scope of the Song economy, this map also indicates tea and metal production. Economic data taken from the map "Centres Commerciaux de la Chine des Sung" by Etienne Balazs, published in Françoise Aubin, ed., *Sung Studies — Etudes Song in Memoriam Etienne Balazs*, Series I, No. 3 (Paris: Mouton & Co. and Ecole des Hautes Etudes, 1976).

Nevertheless, with a huge army and sophisticated weapons, the Song managed to persevere for over 300 years against a formidable succession of enemies. Yet, the maintenance and support of the military establishment was expensive, as was the financing of an expanding civilian bureaucracy. Naturally, Song scholars and officials disagreed over economic and fiscal policies much as they did over the examinations and over the linked issues of foreign and military policy.

The political process during the Song was complicated by factionalism and infighting. Bureaucratic politics was conducted, not by stable and legitimized political parties united by a common program, but by factions whose members might share some common policy commitments but were more likely to be held together by personal relationships and temporary alliances. Characteristically, factions accused each other of narrow self-interest, and each held its opponents responsible for the development of factionalism itself, a phenomenon condemned by the court and by Confucian theory as inimical to the state.

Each faction sought to obtain the emperor's support for its members and policies. Such imperial support was as crucial in practice as it was in theory, for the disappearance of an aristocratic counterweight served to increase the power of the throne. Nevertheless, Song emperors were notable in using this power to manipulate rather than to intimidate their officials. Those who fell out of imperial favor usually suffered nothing worse than exile. It is perhaps indicative of the political tone of the dynasty that it had no counterpart to the imperious rulers of the past: no one comparable to Emperor Wu of the Han or Taizong (T'ai-tsung) of the Tang. Indeed, its most famous emperor was Huizong, already mentioned as an artistic success and political failure. The dynasty also produced China's greatest and most controversial reform minister, Wang Anshi (Wang An-shih), who was able to initiate new policies so long as he enjoyed the support of Emperor Shenzong (Shen-tsung, r. 1067–85). Wang's policies and career throw much light on state and society in eleventh-century China. They illustrate what government could do and could not do and how the system functioned.

Wang Anshi

Wang Anshi (1021–86) was not the first Song reformer. That honor went to Fan Zhongyan (Fan Chung-yen, 989–1052), famed for his definition of a true Confucian as "one who is first in worrying about the world's troubles and last in enjoying its pleasures." Fan and Wang's reforms were part of a Confucian revival that dominated eleventh-century intellectual life. Both men sought to bring government closer to the Confucian ideal, but Wang went far beyond his predecessor in initiating new programs, and in the process, he antagonized his most illustrious contemporaries, among them the dynasty's greatest historian, Sima Guang (Ssu-ma Kuang, 1019–86), the poet and theorist of culture,

Su Shi (Su Shih, also known as Su Dongpo, Su T'ung-p'o, 1037 – 1101), and its most creative philosophers.

One of Wang's first acts, signalling his economic activism, was to establish a finance planning commission (1069). This, like the establishment in 1072 of a state trade system was designed to save money for the government by breaking the monopoly on government procurement held by large merchants. The latter measure provided that the government should deal directly with small suppliers who now became eligible for government loans. Wang's willingness to innovate and readiness to delegate authority is exemplified by the "bureaucratic entrepreneurship"[1] he fostered in allowing the officials of the Tea and Horse Agency maximum discretion in operating the Sichuan tea monopoly.

A consistent feature of Wang's economic policies was a preference for dealing in money rather than in commodities. Tax payments in cash were substituted for the customary deliveries of supplies to the palace (1073). Similarly, Wang instituted a tax to finance the hiring of men to perform local government service (1071), a function previously assigned to well-off local families on a rotating basis. He also increased the amount of currency in circulation. Nevertheless, there was a currency shortage brought on by increased demand.

Wang Anshi did not neglect agriculture. To save small farmers from the ruinous short-term interest rates of 60 to 70 percent charged for carry-over loans during the hard months between spring sowing and autumn harvest, he instituted farming loans ("young shoots money") with a maximum interest rate of 20 percent for the season (1069), but pressures to make money soon eclipsed the social welfare aspect of the program. To deal with the perpetual problem of faulty tax rolls and fraudulent records, Wang also initiated a land survey in 1072, but that too ended in failure.

Another program organized people into groups of 10, 30, and 300 families to ensure collective responsibility for local policing, tax collections, and loan repayments, and to supply men for a local security force that could also function as a military reserve. Another measure designed to cut the dynasty's enormous military expenses provided for placing horses with farmers. In return for maintaining them, the farmers could use the horses in peacetime but were obligated to turn them over to the army in case of military need. This program was not well conceived, however, since farm horses do not make good military steeds.

A number of programs were rendered ineffective because they were sabotaged by officials or were used to oppress the very people they were intended to help. Thus reforms of personnel recruitment and of management were crucial to effective program implementation. Wang Anshi tried to obtain the men he needed by changing the examination system. He included law as a subject to be tested, assigned his own commentaries on the classics as official interpretations to be followed by the candidates in their papers, and stressed the classic known as *The Rites of Zhou (Zhou Li)*, since it provided justification for institutional reform. He also tried to circumvent the entire examination system by expanding the state university and ensuring its graduates direct entry into the civil service. Wang further realized that most of the actual work of government, particularly on the local level, was performed, not by the civil service officials who were sent out for a tour of duty to preside over a district or prefecture, but by a subbureaucracy of clerks, petty agents, and various underlings who remained permanently in place. These men shared neither the status nor the learning of the officials, and there was little to restrain them from squeezing maximum profit out of their jobs. Despised as notoriously corrupt, they tended to become still more corrupt to compensate themselves for being despised. Wang's policy was to reduce their number, improve their pay, place them under stricter supervision, and give the most capable among them an opportunity to rise into the regular bureaucracy.

Wang's personality as well as his measures made him many enemies; by 1076 he was out of office. In the middle and late seventies, his program lost momentum, but a full reaction did not set in until the death of his imperial patron, Emperor Shenzong. However, there was a partial revival of the reform program under Emperor Huizong. Still later, individual measures similar to those of Wang Anshi were reinstituted from time to time, but no minister again tried to do so much so rapidly. Nor did they share his vision of an activist government integrating state and society.

In China, as elsewhere, political and economic developments were closely intertwined. The economic history of the period is complex, and there is much still to be learned, but clearly the Song was a period of dramatic economic change.

The Economy

Qualitatively and quantitatively Song economic changes were so extensive that scholars have termed them revolutionary. Furthermore, they occurred in all three areas of primary economic activity: industry, agriculture, and commerce. (For commerce, metals, and tea see Figure 6-2.) Of this triad, industrial growth peaked during the Northern Song, whereas agricultural and commercial growth continued even after the loss of the North.

During the Song, important progress was made in the production of many commodities. Paper making and all the processes involved in book production advanced; there was progress in salt processing; and notable developments occurred in ceramics. Other kinds of economic activity, such as tea processing and shipbuilding, also gained new eminence, and China now developed a coal and iron industry that was the most advanced in the world. In North China, as later in Europe, deforestation provided the major incentive for coal production. Much of this coal found its way into furnaces used to smelt iron mined in an area stretching in an arc from southern Hebei to northern Jiangsu. Estimates for total annual pig iron production range from 35,000 to as much as 125,000 tons, with the actual figure probably closer to the upper end of this scale. Using coke in blast furnaces fanned by box bellows, the Chinese developed the technology for smelting iron and carbonizing it to produce steel.

Much of the iron and steel went to equip the Song army of well over one million men, providing them with swords, other weapons, and armor of various kinds. Even their arrows were tipped with steel. Other ferrous metal products included tools for farmers, carpenters, and other workmen; major consumer items such as stoves; and smaller items such as nails and needles. High-grade steel was used to produce bits for drilling wells and to make the chains used to support suspension bridges.

A good deal of the metal, as well as other products, was consumed in the Northern Song capital, Kaifeng (see Figure 6-3). Located near the junction of the Yellow River and the canal system leading to the prosperous southeast, this city had originated as a commercial center and continued to function as such after it also became the political capital. It housed not only government offices, garrisons, warehouses, and arsenals but also private textile concerns, drug and chemical shops, shipyards, building material suppliers, and so forth. There was also a thriving restaurant and hotel industry. In contrast to the symmetrical, planned layout of the Tang capital, Kaifeng grew organically, and in the process, it outgrew the old system of enclosed wards and spilled beyond its city walls as its inhabitants sought relief from urban congestion.

Some of the mining and manufacturing enterprises were large-scale operations employing hundreds of workers, while other concerns were confined to small workshops. Various kinds of brokers facilitated commercial transactions, and numerous lines of business were organized into guilds or associations that supervised the terms of trade and also served as intermediaries between their members and the government. As in medieval Europe, members of the same profession or guild frequently (but not always) set up shop in the same city street or district.

The growth of manufacturing and the development of Kaifeng and other cities were sustained by an increase in agricultural yields. At the same time, the opening of new markets for rural products stimulated the development of agriculture, now called upon to feed a population that had passed the 100 million mark. The size of harvests was increased by the use of improved farm tools, advances in water control, wider application of fertilizers, and the introduction of new strains of rice, most notably an early ripening variety native to central Vietnam. Different strains of rice (low or high in gluten, drought resistant, early or late ripening) were cultivated to suit local conditions. In the southeast it became common practice for a rice paddy to produce two crops a year, either two harvests of rice or one of rice followed by a crop of wheat or beans grown on the paddy after it was drained.

A major effect of increased agricultural yields was to confirm the South as China's richest and most productive region. In this respect, it left a more permanent influence on subsequent Chinese history than did the development of the coal and iron industries in the North. Economic growth in the North was disrupted by the Jurchen invasion in the twelfth century and by

Figure 6-3   The "Rainbow Bridge," Kaifeng. Detail of *Spring Festival on the River* by Zhang Zeduan (Chang Tse-tuan). Hand-scroll, ink and light color on silk, early twelfth century, 25.5 cm high. Palace Museum, Beijing.

that of the Mongols in the thirteenth, by a major shift of the Yellow River in 1194, and by the permanent decline of Kaifeng and its market. In the south, however, advanced agricultural practices continued to spread, enabling commerce and cities to continue to flourish during the Southern Song.

Before turning to these developments, it is well to recall that economic growth rarely benefits all people equally. It does not prevent corruption, with the price, in the end, being paid by those too poor to afford bribes and presents. Nor did it preclude the wealthy from increasing the size of their holdings by taking advantage of the numerous peasants who did not hold sufficient land to maintain themselves and had to work as tenant sharecroppers or as field servants in conditions of legal inferiority. Wang Anshi's reforms notwithstanding, peasants continued to suffer from inequitable taxation and exorbitant interest rates. Peasant uprisings during the dynasty were rare, but there was unrest and rebellion in the 1120s. Much of the good that Emperor Huizong accomplished by building schools and sponsoring charities was undone by the heavy burden of taxation and the exactions of government. Especially notorious were the emperor's demands for rare plants, stones, and novelties destined to decorate the imperial garden and collected from the people without compensation.

The Southern Song (1127–1279)

Despite the deployment of catapults, flamethrowers, and incendiary devices made with gunpowder (another Chinese invention), the Song lost the North. The dynasty carried on under a son of Emperor Huizong, Gaozong (Kao-tsung, r. 1127–62), who at the nadir of his career was forced to flee from the Jurchen troops by taking refuge on some islands off the southeast coast. Then, however, the tide of war turned. In 1138 Gaozong designated Hangzhou as a "temporary capital," and a peace agreement with the Jin was concluded in 1142. The previous year had brought the death in prison of Yue Fei (Yüeh Fei, 1103–41), one of China's most celebrated generals, subject of a novel and numerous stories and plays, still today extolled as a hero who had paid for his patriotism with his life. Conversely, Qin Guei (Ch'in Kuei, 1090–1155), the minister who effected the peace, came to be despised as the prototype of the traitor. Later, iron statues representing Qin Guei and his wife in chains were placed on the grounds of Yue Fei's tomb beside Hangzhou's West Lake. For a long time, visitors used to express their contempt by spitting at the statues, but that is now prohibited.

In the treaty of 1142 the Song accepted the Huai River as its northern boundary, agreed to make annual payments to the Jin, and recognized the Jin as its superior. Nevertheless, relations between the two states remained uneasy. Fighting broke out again between 1161 and 1165. After a period of unfriendly coexistence, cold war once again turned into active warfare, for the last time, from 1206 to 1208. This time the war came to an end only after the Song handed over to their enemy the severed head of the minister responsible for starting the war. The Jurchen state was gradually Sinified during the twelfth century, as indicated by its adoption of such institutions as the examination system, but this did not induce the Song to look any more kindly on its northern neighbor.

The Southern Song government was therefore by no means unhappy when the new Mongol power rose in the North to challenge the Jin. When the Mongols destroyed the Jin and occupied North China in 1234, the Song's situation became precarious. The dynasty continued to hold on for another 40 years, however, largely because of its maritime strength. When the end did come, it was hastened by naval treachery.

Among the reasons for the Southern Song's ability to sustain itself for a century and a half were the geographic defensibility and the prosperity of the South as well as the government's ability to command acceptance as the legitimate regime and to perform the traditional functions of government. However, it also suffered from internal ills: unstable imperial leadership (the first three emperors ended their reigns by abdicating), factional divisiveness in officialdom, and a general decline in government effectiveness. The government's monetary policies eventually produced rampant inflation and a shrinking tax base resulted from the decline of small landholders and tax evasion by those who held much land. To deal with the latter situation, an ambitious land reform program was launched by Chief Councilor Jia Sidao (Chia Ssu-tao, 1213–75) during the 1260s. Large landowners were required to sell to the government a portion of their holdings, which the government then managed itself. The economic gains thus realized, however, were counterbalanced by the disaffection of the wealthy and powerful at a time when the state required maximum unity against the Mongol threat.

The government had its troubles, but the dynasty continued to inspire loyal devotion to the end—and even beyond. Not only had men sacrificed their lives in its defense even after the cause was hopeless; there were also others who remained loyal even after its demise. This was a new phenomenon in Chinese history, and, as with so many Song innovations, set a precedent for later ages.

Southern Song Cities and Commerce

Politically and psychologically the loss of the North was a grave blow to the dynasty, but economically the loss was much less severe, since by this time a good two-thirds of China's population and wealth were in the South. As elsewhere in the world, the development of cities and commerce went hand in hand.

Commercial transactions were facilitated by the use of paper money, a Chinese innovation. This medium of exchange originated in Sichuan with the circulation of private certificates of deposit secured by funds placed in private shops. In the eleventh century, paper money was issued for the first time by the government. As long as these notes were adequately secured by goods or specie (hard money) they worked well. However, the government could not resist the temptation to issue more paper money than it could back with solid reserves. When this became generally known the notes depreciated in value.

A large part of China's internal as well as foreign trade was waterborne, for it was less expensive to transport goods on rivers and canals than to cart them overland. China's oceangoing ships were large, capable of carrying several hundred men. They were navigated with the aid of the compass, a product of China's traditional excellence in the study of magnetism. In other ways, too, the ships were technologically advanced. Their features included: "watertight bulkheads, buoyancy chambers, bamboo fenders at the waterline, floating anchors to hold them steady during storms, axial rudders in place of steering oars, outrigger and leeboard devices, oars for use in calm weather, scoops for taking samples off the sea floor, sounding lines for determining the depth, compasses for navigation, and small rockets propelled by gunpowder for self-defense."[2] Merchant ships could be converted to military use, and the superiority of its navy was crucial to the Southern Song's military security.

The trading cities of the South were known for their prosperity, the fast pace of life, and also for the reputed frivolity and shamelessness of their inhabitants. The greatest city was Hangzhou. Situated between the Yangzi (to which it was linked by canal) and the international ports of the southeast coast, it was a government and trade center, home of merchants and officials. Flanked by the Zhe (Che) River and the West Lake, Hangzhou, like Venice, was a city of bridges and canals; and it evoked the enthusiasm of that cosmopolitan Venetian Marco Polo, who described it as, "without doubt the finest and most splendid city in the world,"[3] even though by the time he visited it late in the thirteenth century, Hangzhou was no longer the capital and the South was generally disdained by China's new Mongol masters.

Hangzhou merchants, organized into guilds, offered their customers all kinds of merchandise ranging from the staples of life to exotic perfumes, fine jewelry, and other luxury items. There were bookstores and pet shops. Among the amenities offered by the city were exquisite restaurants, tea houses, cabarets, and baths. Entertainment was also provided by a host of popular performers, chess masters, fortunetellers, acrobats, storytellers, and puppeteers. There were also numerous practitioners of the world's oldest profession, ladies "highly proficient and accomplished in the use of endearments and caresses," who completely captivated Marco Polo and other foreign visitors.[4] Outside the city, the surrounding hills with their Buddhist temples provided opportunities for pleasure excursions, and a favorite pastime was boating and partying on West Lake, still today a favorite resort.

The inhabitants of Song cities did not escape the grimmer aspects of urban life. The threat of fire was ever present, and the government took various protective measures against this menace. In Kaifeng, the Northern Song capital, guard stations were placed at 50-yard intervals, and watchtowers were erected, each manned by 100 firefighting soldiers. In the case of Hangzhou, the city was divided into zones. Two thousand soldiers were responsible for the 14 zones within the city, and another 1,200 stood ready to combat fires in 8 suburban zones. These firefighters were equipped with buckets, ropes, hatchets, fireproof clothing, and other paraphernalia. Despite these precautions, there were frequent and destructive conflagrations. Crime, too, was a fact of urban life, and the cities and towns alike had their share of criminals: confidence men who passed lead off as gold, holdup specialists against whom merchants required special police protection, and other petty criminals who eked out a living as best they could. For those who could not make a decent living, honestly or dishonestly, the city still offered advantages not available in the village. On special occasions, public alms were distributed, and there were state hospitals and dispensaries, and houses for the aged, the decrepit, and the orphaned. If worst came to worst, those dying in poverty at least had the consolation of knowing that they would receive proper burial even if they had no relatives to pay for it.

Since the government derived considerable revenue from foreign trade (for example, through customs duties, licensing fees, sales and transit taxes, and so forth) this was one of the rare times in Chinese history when it actually encouraged overseas commerce. It maintained harbors and canals, built breakwaters, erected beacons, operated warehouses, and even set up hotels. Merchants who attracted foreign shipping to Chinese ports were rewarded. Among the major imports were aromatics and drugs, textiles, minerals, and miscellaneous luxury items, while the primary exports included silks, metals (especially copper coins exported to Japan), and ceramics. The export of the latter was actively encouraged by the government, and the discovery of Song shards not only throughout South and Southeast Asia but also in the Middle East and along the east coast of Africa attests to the wide popularity of the Song product. This was the precursor of the later export trade that was to make the word "china" a synonym for "porcelain."

The Confucian Revival

Even when Buddhism had prevailed as the major spiritual, intellectual, and aesthetic influence, the family ethic and political ideology of Confucianism had never been totally eclipsed. During the Song, Chan (Zen) and Pure Land Buddhism as well as religious Daoism flourished, but Confucianism was especially attractive to the new elite. The revitalized Confucianism of the Song took many forms. It stimulated a revival of classical scholarship, new achievements in historical studies, and fresh departures in Confucian speculative thought. And it prompted a more earnest devotion to Confucian principles.

Confucianism had always emphasized the study of history, and the Confucian revival brought with it a renewed interest in historiography. Outstanding among historians was Sima Guang, a bitter opponent of Wang Anshi who looked to the classics rather than history for guidance. Sima Guang had the confidence and vision to do something no scholar had attempted since the Han: a study of virtually the whole of Chinese history (taking up where the Zuo Zhuan (Tso Chuan) had left off) rather than confining himself to a single dynasty. Animating his work was the conviction that an accurate account of the past could teach moral and practical lessons for the present, and thus he gave his work the title A Comprehensive Mirror for Aid in Government (Zizhi Tongjian, Tzu-chih t'ung-chien). In a departure from tradition, he included in the finished work discussions of the discrepancies he had found in the sources and his reasons for choosing one version of events over another.

The Confucian emphasis on right understanding of the past as a guide to proper life and preparation for service to the state, implied a commitment to education. Confucius himself had become a teacher when he failed in his quest for a ruler to implement his ideas. Thus it is no accident that the Confucian revival under the Song was accompanied by the burgeoning of schools, both government schools during the Northern Song and private academies after the loss of the North. Famed among the latter was the White Deer Grotto Academy, which was run, for a time, by the renowned philosopher Zhu Xi (Chu Hsi, 1130–1200), and it was primarily through private academies that his Neo-Confucian philosophy was perpetuated.

At the White Deer Grotto Academy, students were exposed to a heavy mixture of moral exhortation and scholarship so that they might emerge both virtuous and erudite. Like dedicated teachers everywhere, the committed Confucian scholars were forever pleading with their students to forget such careerist considerations as passing examinations and to concentrate on the serious business of learning and self-improvement. To become truly educated, the guidance of a teacher was believed extremely important. But for the sake of those who lived in remote places without teachers, Zhu Xi and his friend Lu Zuqian (Lü Tsu-ch'ien, 1137–81) compiled an anthology of Song Confucianism for self-instruction, which became enormously influential in Korea and Japan as well as in China. It draws on the writings of the four Northern Song thinkers who came to be considered as the founders of the new Confucian philosophy, Zhou Dunyi (Chou Tun-i, 1017–73), the two brothers Cheng Hao (Ch'eng Hao, 1032–85) and Cheng Yi (Ch'eng Yi, 1033–1107), and Zhang Zai (Chang Tsai, 1020–77). Its title is *Reflections on Things at Hand (Jinsi lu, Chin-ssu lu)*.

Reflections deals with many matters of practical concern ranging from guidance on how to manage a family to advice on when to accept political office and when to decline. It includes discussions of political institutions and behavior. Its main emphasis, however, is on self-perfection, which alone makes all the rest possible.

The authors of *Reflections* were careful to distinguish their teachings from the doctrines of Buddhism and Daoism and attacked the teachings of the Buddha and Lao Zi. Yet, even the staunchest Confucian was not immune to the attractions of Chan Buddhism. Meanwhile, a continued interest in Daoism in the highest quarters was evidenced when in 1019 the state sponsored the printing of the Daoist Tripitaka *(Daozang, Tao-tsang)* resembling in length and scope its Buddhist prototype. Given this rich Buddhist and Daoist heritage, it should not come as a surprise to find that Song Confucian philosophers were influenced by these two traditions even as they sought to undermine them by creating a more sophisticated philosophy of their own.

Philosophy and Values

It was the great strength of the new Confucianism that it was at once a creed that gave meaning to the life of the individual, an ideology supporting state and society, and a philosophy that provided a convincing framework for understanding the world. It conceived of the world as an organic whole and itself constituted an organic system in which each aspect reinforced the other in theory as well as in practice.

This new philosophy, known in the West as Neo-Confucianism, received its classic formulation by Zhu Xi, but neither he nor the four philosophers whose work he excerpted in *Reflections* were accepted as orthodox in their own day. It was not until the second quarter of the thirteenth century that Zhu Xi's teachings received official recognition and his commentaries on the *Four Books* were officially accepted. Of these four books, considered repositories of fundamental truth, only the *Analects* had been universally revered by all Confucians throughout history. The other three, *The Mencius, The Great Learning,* and *The Doctrine of the Mean* (the last two are chapters from the *Records of Rites*) were subjects of controversy for most of the Song period.

It was characteristic of East Asian thinkers that they did not present their ideas in systematic philosophical treatises but as commentaries on the classics, in miscellaneous writings (including letters), and in conversations that were recorded by disciples. This made the study of their ideas very demanding but also encouraged successive generations of scholars to reinterpret Confucianism in their own way. Neither in the Song nor later was Neo-Confucianism a monolithic philosophy.

Song thinkers, like earlier Chinese philosophers, found it congenial and fruitful to think in terms of complementary opposites, interacting polarities such as inner and outer, substance (*ti, t'i*) and function (*yong, yung*), knowledge and action. Perhaps they were particularly attracted to this mode of thought because it enabled them to make distinctions without doing violence to what they perceived to be an ultimate organic unity. In their metaphysics they naturally employed the ancient *yin* and *yang,* but more central to their thought was the conceptual pair *li* and *qi (ch'i)*.

This *li,* not to be confused with the term meaning ritual (which is written with a different character), is usually translated as "principle." Since the Chinese word does not distinguish between singular and plural, *li* can also be understood as a network of principles. Indeed, the accepted Song etymology of the word was that it originally signified veins running through jade. Thus each individual *li* is part of the entire system, and in the philosophy of Cheng Yi and Zhu Xi, this system constitutes the underlying pattern of reality. In this view nothing can exist if there is no *li* for it. It is characteristic of the Confucian and Neo-Confucian cast of mind that this applies as much to the realm of human conduct as it does to the physical world. The *li* of fatherhood has the same ontological status (order of being or order of reality) as the *li* for mountains. No distinction is made between the former, which is defined in moral terms, and the latter, into which value judgments do not enter, for the world of moral action and that of physical objects is held to be one and the same. Both are comprehensible and both are equally "natural."

Qi is a more difficult word to render into English. It can be characterized as the vital force and substance of which man and the universe are made. It can also be conceived of as energy, but energy which occupies space. In its most refined form it occurs as a kind of rarefied ether, but condensed it becomes the most solid metal or rock. In his cosmology Zhu Xi envisioned the world as a sphere in constant rotation, so that the heaviest *qi* is held in the center by the centripetal force of the motion. The *qi* then becomes progressively lighter and thinner as one moves away from the center. This way he explained why, for instance, the air at high altitude is thinner than that at sea level.

It was theoretically possible to construct a philosophy based on either concept. Zhang Zai (Chang Tsai) based his theories entirely on *qi* whereas Zhu Xi's contemporary Lu Jiuyuan (Lu Chiu-yüan, 1139–93) asserted that *li* alone exists. Cheng Yi and Zhu Xi, however, accepted both as irreducible entities, although *li* had logical and ontological but not temporal priority over *qi*. Actually, in Zhu Xi's system *li* was further identified with the Supreme Ultimate *(taiji, t'ai-chi)*, which had formed the basis of Zhou Duni's metaphysics. In this way *li* was elevated to a level superior to *qi*. Nevertheless, in the actual world *li* never occurs without *qi*. This was a very important doctrine, for it enabled the Song philosophers to accept Mencius' theory of the essential goodness of humankind and to explain man's frequent departures from that goodness: people were composed of good *li* and more or less impure *qi*. The ancient sages were born with *qi* that was perfectly pure: they were born perfect. But ordinary folk have to cope with more or less turgid *qi:* they must work to attain perfection.

For ordinary people, the way to attain perfection is by truly grasping the *li*, but since these are found within everyone as well as out in the world, there was disagreement over the proper method of self-cultivation. Zhu Xi generally stressed the "investigation of things," by which he meant primarily the study of moral conduct and especially the timeless lessons contained in the classics. Consequently his school was associated with an emphasis on scholarly learning, even though it by no means ruled out more inner-directed endeavors such as silent meditation and reflection. Lu Jiuyuan, in contrast, foreshadowing the teachings of the major Ming dynasty philosopher Wang Yangming, stressed inner illumination. For him, without the reader's innate understanding, even the classics remain without meaning. The truth is within: he once went as far as to say, "the classics are all footnotes to me."

The intellectual atmosphere was further enlivened by other Confucians who rejected theoretical speculation and insisted that the true vocation of a scholar lay in concentrating on matters of practical statecraft. But by narrowing their intellectual focus these thinkers also narrowed their appeal, so that in the end they had less influence on the course of Chinese thought than did Zhu Xi or Lu Jiuyuan.

Associated with Song Neo-Confucianism was a moral seriousness that demanded vigilance against selfish desires and called for an ideal selflessness, but we must not exaggerate the influence of philosophers on people's actual behavior as they went about their daily affairs. Judging by the Southern Song degree-holder and official Yuan Cai (Yüan Ts'ai), author of *Precepts for Social*

Life, the propriety of devotion to family preservation was generally taken for granted. Yuan was no doubt in the majority in insisting on decency rather than theorizing about absolute virtue.

In theory widows should not remarry, and the woman who remained faithful to her betrothed even though he died before the marriage could be consummated took her place among the Confucian paragons, but even among the elite (though not among royalty) widow remarriage was not uncommon. It goes without saying that a woman's proper place remained in the home.

Information is scanty, but also traceable to the Song is the practice of footbinding,* a practice which caused agonizing pain to many generations of Chinese girls. In a convergence of ethics and aesthetics, tiny feet were thought to enhance a girl's attractiveness and, at the same time, to deter her from straying into mischief. We should note, however, that the practice was apparently rare in Song times and that it was not part of a Confucian social program. It is worth mentioning that Li Qingzhao (Li Ch'ing-chao, 1094–ca. 1152), the dynasty's and China's most famous female poet never mentioned footbinding. She did leave an attractive description of her early married life when her husband was a university student and used to pawn some of his clothes to buy rubbings and fruit. Afterwards, "we would sit facing each other, then unfold and enjoy the scrolls of rubbings while munching the fruit." [5] The stone portraits of two Song ladies in Figure 6-4 suggest self-assured grace.

The Song philosophers gave the old concept of *ren* (*jen*, humaneness) a new metaphysical dimension. Zhang Zai proclaimed, "all people are my brothers and sisters, and all things are my companions." [6] It is in keeping with this ideal that the age saw a new growth in secular charities sponsored by eminent Confucians, their lineages, or the state. In Song poetry, too, there was a continuation of the old tradition of employing verse to protest political and economic conditions and also a new interest in ordinary things and in rendering scenes from everyday life.

Song Poetry

The Song was a prolific period for poetry. (One eighteenth-century scholar listed 3,812 Song poets.) There are, for example, a great many poems depicting the hardships of life in the country and the disastrous effects of bad officials and/or bad weather. But it would be wrong to view rural life as just one

---

* A procedure used to restrict the growth of the feet. The feet of young female children were wrapped tightly in bandages (about two inches wide and ten feet long). Over a period of time, the four toes of each foot were bent into the sole, and the sole and heel were brought as close together as possible. The great toe was left unbound. This practice probably originated during the Five Dynasties period. It later became more widespread among the upper classes until, in the later dynasties, it not only was prevalent among the high Chinese elite but was also widely practiced in other social strata. It continued well into the twentieth century.

Figure 6-4   Two Song ladies. Cave 165, Maijishan, Gansu.

unrelieved misery. The following is one of four poems in which a Late Northern Song poet describes life in his native village:

> At cock crow the whole village rouses.
> Gets ready to set off for the middle fields:
> Remind the wife to be sure to fix some millet,
> Shout to the children to shut the gate behind us.
> Spade and hoe catch the morning light;
> Laughter and hubbub mingle on the road.
> Puddles from the night before wet our straw sandals;
> Here's a wild flower to stick in the bun of your hair!
> Clear light breaks through the distant haze;
> Spring skies now are fresh and gay.
> Magnolia covers the wandering hills;
> In the empty field, a brocaded pheasant preens.
> The young people have come like racing clouds;
> Owl-like, an old man squats on his heels alone.
> The yellow earth glistens from the rain that passed;
> Clouds of dust race before the wind.
> Little by little, the whole village gathers,
> Calling greetings from field to field.
> The omens say it will be a good month;
> Let's keep on working, down to sundown![7]

The poetry of this time provides many pictures of daily life and personal
routines, glimpses into people's private inner lives, and their responses to
misfortunes and joy. And it reflects their broader concerns, as when a Southern Song patriot, disgusted by his government's peace policy, complains:
"Stabled horses die of obesity; strings unstrung break on the bow."[8] At the
same time poetry was an art with its own technical demands.

The Northern Song poem quoted above is in the form of five-character
old-style verse, and many fine Song poems were written in the old forms.
These include poems by Su Shi, a versatile exponent of the centrality of cultural creativity. Su is also famous for expanding the *ci (tz'u)* form of poetry.
Written to tunes, of which the titles are all that now remains, the *ci* required
great skill in fitting the words to the musical pattern. But it allowed the poet
unusual freedom in diction, since he was permitted to incorporate colloquial
expressions. Actually Su Shi's genius was not bound by any set form. Perhaps
his most famous works are two rhapsodies *(fu)* on the Red Cliff, site of a
famous battle fought during the Three Kingdoms period. Su Shi also wrote
many poems on friendship, drinking, and nature. Like other Song poets he
knew and loved the literature of the past. But he also brought to it a critical
spirit. For example, his view of the highly respected and beloved Tang poet
Meng Jiao (Meng Chiao) was by no means representative of his time. The
following poem surely will strike a responsive chord in anyone who has ever
labored over a poem only to discover that the reward gained was not worth the
effort expended.

Reading the Poetry of Meng Jiao — First of Two Poems

> Night: reading Meng Jiao's poems,
> Characters fine as cow's hair.
> By the cold lamp, my eyes blur and swim.
> Good passages I rarely find —
> Lone flowers poking up through the mud —
> But more hard words than the *Odes* and *Li sao* —
> Jumbled rocks clogging the clear stream,
> Making rapids too swift for poling.
> My first impression is of eating little fishes —
> What you get's not worth the trouble;
> Or of boiling tiny mud crabs
> And ending up with empty claws.
> For refinement he might compete with monks
> But he'll never match his master Han Yu.
> Man's life is like morning dew,
> A flame eating up the oil night by night.
> Why should I strain my ears
> Listening to the squeaks of this autumn insect?
> Better lay aside the book
> And drink my cup of jade-white wine.[9]

Su Shi was at the center of a circle of talented friends who not only wrote fine poetry but also excelled in calligraphy and painting, for these were the three arts of the gentleman-scholar. Su and others frequently wrote their poems on a painting, thus combining the three arts in a single work, and Su himself saw a close relationship between poetry, "pictures without form," and paintings, "unspoken poems."[10] For Mei Yaochen (Mei Yao-ch'en, 1002–60), poetry itself must go beyond words and "express inexhaustible meaning which exists beyond the words themselves."[11] Su Shi's views on painting were in advance of his time in that he rejected representationalism as childish. For Su, a painting such as the bamboo by his friend Wen Tong (Wen T'ung, 1018–60), China's first great bamboo painter, was practically a self-portrait, revealing the noble character of the painter (see Figure 6-5).

Painting and the Arts

The bamboo branch attributed to Wen Tong and reproduced here illustrates what the painter can accomplish employing the ink and brush of the calligrapher. Roger Goepper's analysis is worth quoting in full:

All the elements have been drawn with a single confident brush stroke: the sections of the stem and the branches with a firm and elastic writing brush *(ganbi, kan-pi)*, the counter-pressure of whose springy tip can be felt in the hand; the leaves with a softer and limper brush *(shuibi, shui-pi)*, which submits obediently to the slightest pressure of the hand. The interaction of the graphic forms resulting

Figure 6-5   *A Broken Branch of Bamboo*, attributed to Wen Tong. Album leaf, ink on paper, 31 cm × 48.3 cm. Palace Museum Collection, Taipei.

from these two techniques largely determines the general impression created by the painting, the individual elements becoming fused in a composition filled with tension and vitality. The diagonal upward movement of the stem is answered contrapuntally by the smaller twigs, while the sudden break diverts the thrust from the top left-hand corner and causes it to fade out into the largest blank space in the composition. At the same time this break introduces an element of the unexpected and exciting into the picture; it disturbs the harmonious sequence of its construction and hints at the outside forces that affect the bamboo and determine its fate, as they do with man. The fixed points of the composition lie on the one hand in the knots of the stem, accentuated by small brush dashes, and on the other in the areas of radiation formed by the rhythmic play of the overlapping leaf spears.[12]

Expressiveness and spontaneity were prized by Chan painters, some of whom worked in the ink-splash technique of "ink Wang" (see Chapter 5), dashing off their work, destroying what did not come out right, but never laboring over their art, confident that artistic inspiration, like religious enlightenment, comes in a flash. The finest Chan painters lived during the Southern Song and were as unrestricted in subject matter as in style. Thus for

Mu Qi (Mu-ch'i), one of the greatest masters of the genre, six persimmons could mirror the truth as faithfully as any portrait of the Buddha. Liang Kai's (Liang K'ai) famous portrait of Li Bo (Li Po, see Figure 6-6) suggests that he and the Tang poet were kindred spirits. This art was not highly regarded by later Chinese connoisseurs, but it was prized in Japan.

There was also less iconoclastic Buddhist art. Particularly notable were gilded wooden figures of Guanyin (Kuan-yin) seated in a position of "Royal Ease," with one leg raised supporting an arm. Housed in temples more delicate and refined than their Tang predecessors and now more generally capped by gracefully curved roofs, such figures were among the best products of the last phase of Buddhist art.

A new age demanded a new means of artistic expression. The towering achievement of Song art was in landscape painting. Developing styles which first appeared during the Five Dynasties period shortly before the Song, Song painters produced classic works of art strikingly different from the paintings of earlier times.

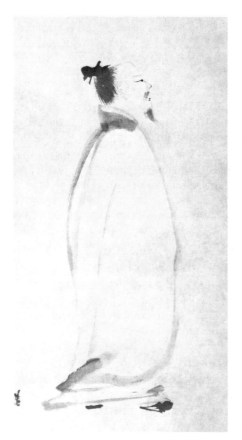

Figure 6-6   Liang Kai, *Li Bo*. Ink on paper, mid-thirteenth century, 79 cm high. Tokyo National Museum.

Just as Sima Guang sought to encompass all of history in his *Zihi Tongjian*, and Neo-Confucian philosophers sought to develop a universal philosophy, the great landscape painters sought to encompass the whole of nature in their work. Thus they produced works of unparalleled monumentality such as Fan Kuan's (Fan K'uan d. ca. 1023) *Traveling among Streams and Mountains* (see Figure 6-7). Impressive scope, strength, and dark tones have replaced the rich colors, the clarity of line, and the decorative charm of earlier landscape paintings (compare Figure 5-8). The principles of composition have also changed. For the first time we find the classic Chinese perspective in which the picture surface is divided into three planes, one near and one distant, with the middle plane occupied by water or mist. Whereas nature in earlier paintings provided a setting for man, here man is reduced to his proper dimensions, and a road invites the viewer to enter the painting and contemplate the grandeur of nature, the *li* of the universe.

Fan Kuan was a northerner. In the South, other masters like Dong Yuan (Tung Yüan, d. 962) and his disciple Juran (Chü-jan, fl. ca. 975) depicted the softer and more atmospheric mountainscapes of their region and founded another influential tradition. The difference between the southern and northern painters was not only a matter of tone and technique, but as Richard M. Barnhart has suggested of Dong Yuan, "The southern master appears to have wished to meditate upon the land, as a poet; the northern masters to dramatize it." [13]

This was also an age which produced fine hand-scrolls through which the viewer could travel at leisure as the painting was gradually unrolled, an effect recaptured only with difficulty by the modern museum visitor who sees such a painting completely spread out in a glass case. Frequently in such works the viewer follows a river, and might even, as in the famed Qinming (Ch'ing-ming) Festival Scroll, visit the capital itself. Today this painting provides valuable material for the student of Song urbanization as well as delight to the lover of art (see Figure 6-3).

The world of the Song painter, northerner and southerner, gentleman-amateur, monk, or professional, was as varied as was the intellectual and literary life of the period. It serves little purpose to list names and styles, but a few more works may illustrate something of the range of Song art as well as its general direction. The first, by Emperor Huizong, is a classic in its own, much practiced genre. The carefully studied, realistic yet idealized, five-colored parakeet (see Figure 6-1) well meets the standards demanded by the emperor in a famous edict: "Painters are not to imitate their predecessors, but to depict objects as they exist, true to color and form. Simplicity and nobility of line is to be their aim." [14]

Artists who lived after the period of the monumental masters such as Fan Kuan knew that the classical achievement could not be repeated and sought modes of expression more fitting for their own times. Frequently they chose to paint a part of nature rather than the whole, a branch to represent the tree.

Figure 6-7 Fan Kuan, *Traveling among Streams and Mountains.* Hanging scroll, ink and light color on silk, 129.6 cm × 74.9 cm. Palace Museum Collection, Taipei.

Detail Figure 6-7   Fan Kuan, *Traveling among Streams and Mountains.*

Figure 6-8   Ma Yuan, *On a Mountain Path.* Album leaf, ink and light color on silk, 27.4 cm × 43.1 cm. Palace Museum Collection, Taipei.

Figure 6-9   Xia Guei, *A Pure and Remote View of Rivers and Mountains.* Section of handscroll, ink on paper, 46.4 cm high. Palace Museum Collection, Taipei.

One painter who did this was Ma Yuan (ca. 1160 – ca. 1225), often known as "One-cornered Ma" because of his tendency to concentrate his compositions in one corner of the surface. One of his themes (see Figure 6-8) is that of the scholar quietly contemplating and enjoying nature. Both the scene and its vision of nature are full of charm. Another favorite Southern Song painter, along with Ma greatly appreciated in Japan, was Xia Guei (Hsia Kuei, fl. ca. 1190 – 1230). Figure 6-9 reproduces a section of his hand-scroll *A Pure and Remote View of Rivers and Mountains,* a masterpiece in which the artist made the most of the musicality of the medium. Many have imitated his style, but very few were able to achieve the subtlety and strength of his brushwork animating the austerity of his composition.

In one other art form the Song represents a classic achievement: Song ceramics have long been admired as combining the vigor of earlier work in this medium with the grace of the ware that was to be produced later. As in painting, there were major differences between northern and southern styles, reflecting in this case not only different tastes and a varied clientele but also differences in the chemical composition of the clays used by potters. Song wares include stoneware and porcelain, vessels covered with a slip (clay coating) that has been carved away to produce a design, others covered with enamel or decorated with a painting. Colors run from white through grays to black, as well as various hues from lavender to olive. Perhaps most prized are the celadons, blue-green ware often decorated with a crackle (network of fine cracks) formed by the glaze cooling more rapidly than the vessel (see page 183, left). Some of this exquisite ware was made especially for the imperial household, and such pieces are fitting representatives of the refinement and elegance which were not least among the Song's achievements.

NOTES

 1. Terms coined by Paul J. Smith. Cf. his "Taxing Heaven's Storehouse: The Szechwan Tea Monopoly and the Tsinghai Horse Trade, 1074–1224" PhD. dissertation, Univ. of Pennsylvania, 1983.

 2. Mark Elvin, *The Pattern of the Chinese Past* (Stanford: Stanford Univ. Press, 1973), p. 137.

 3. R. E. Latham, trans., *The Travels of Marco Polo* (Baltimore: Penguin Books, 1958), p. 184.

 4. *Ibid.*, p. 187.

 5. Quoted in J. Y. Liu, *Essentials of Chinese Literary Art* (North Scituate, MA: Duxbury Press, 1979), p. 37.

 6. Wing-tsit Chan, *A Source Book in Chinese Philosophy* (Princeton: Princeton Univ. Press, 1963), p. 497.

 7. Qin Guan (Ch'in Kuan), in Kojiro Yoshikawa, *An Introduction to Sung Poetry*, trans. Burton Watson (Cambridge: Harvard Univ. Press, 1967), pp. 16–17.

 8. Liu Wu-chi, *An Introduction to Chinese Literature* (Bloomington: Indiana Univ. Press, 1966), p. 119.

 9. Burton Watson, trans., *Su Tung-p'o* (New York: Columbia Univ. Press, 1965), p. 59.

10. Susan Bush, *The Chinese Literati on Painting: Su Shih (1037–1101) to Tung Ch'i-ch'ang (1156–1636)* (Cambridge: Harvard Univ. Press, 1971), p. 25.

11. Jonathan Chaves, *Mei Yao-ch'en and the Development of Early Sung Poetry* (New York: Columbia Univ. Press, 1976), p. 110.

12. Roger Goepper, *The Essence of Chinese Painting* (Boston: Boston Book and Art Shop, 1963), p. 134.

13. Richard M. Barnhart, "Tung Yüan," in Herbert Franke, ed., *Sung Biographies—Painters*, Münchener Ostasiatische Studien, vol. 17 (Wiesbaden: Franz Steiner Verlag, 1976), p. 141.

14. Arthur Waley, quoted in Goepper, *The Essence of Chinese Painting*, p. 106.

蒙古帝國與元代

7

The Mongol Empire and the Yuan Dynasty

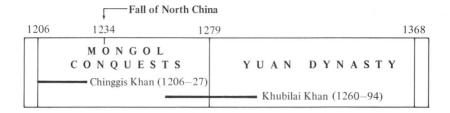

The Mongols are famed as the world's foremost conquerors, creators of the largest empire in the history of the planet (See Figure 7-1). They established their supremacy over most of Eurasia, including Russia and Persia, all of Central Asia, China, and Korea. Mongol armies reached as far West as the Adriatic; in the East they took to ships to attack Japan and Java. Even those lands that, like Japan, preserved their independence were affected by the Mongol challenge. For a time, communication between East and West was facilitated by Mongol domination and encouragement of trade. But the Mongol territory was too vast, local cultures too various and deeply rooted, the centrifugal forces too strong for the Mongol Empire to last very long. Ultimately the empire disintegrated.

Chinggis Khan: Founding of the Mongol Empire

Temüjin, the man known to the West as Chinggis (Genghis, Jenghis) Khan (ca. 1167 – 1227), was the son of a Mongolian tribal chieftain. When his father was killed, the boy was forced to flee and spent a number of years wandering. Eventually he returned to his tribe, and began his career as a world conqueror by avenging the murder of his father. Gradually he gained ascendency in the hierarchy of Mongol tribal chiefs. He was almost 40 by the time he established his leadership over all the Mongol tribes, which, at a great meeting held in 1206, recognized him as the supreme ruler, the Chinggis Khan. As the supreme ruler he unified the tribes, organized them into a superb fighting force, and started them on the road to conquest and far-flung empire.

Unifying the tribes was a difficult task, not only because they were widely dispersed but also because of the nature of tribal life. The tribesmen were excellent fighters, jealous of their independence. It required great determination, political skill, knowledge of men, and a manifest ability to lead, to weld these tribal groups into a people. It also required ruthlessness, drive, military skill, and personal courage. Apparently Chinggis Khan had these qualities. He was able to obtain the support of the hardy tribesmen. Equally significant, both as a testament to his leadership qualities and as an indication of his   **163** personal power, was his ability to attract a following of *nökhör*. These were men who renounced all other ties to clan or tribe and gave their patron their sole and complete loyalty. Many of Chinggis Khan's best generals were *nökhör*.

It does not detract from Chinggis Khan's personal achievement to note that more impersonal forces were also at work inducing the Mongols to unify and attack the settled peoples who sometimes broke off trade vital to the steppe nomads. Particularly serious was a drop in climactic temperature that reduced the amount of grass available to feed the animals vital for Mongol subsistence.

Clans and tribes remained the basic units of Mongol organization, but at a higher level the people were also bound together by loyalty to the Great Khan and by a law code *(jasagh)* first promulgated in 1206 and later expanded. Also transcending tribal divisions was the army, which was organized on a decimal system in units of tens, hundreds, and thousands. An elite corps, which grew to 10,000 men, formed its core. At the height of the campaigns, the total army may have numbered nearly 130,000 men. It was joined in those campaigns by almost an equal number of non-Mongol warriors, the forces of other peoples who joined the Mongols rather than attempt to resist the whirlwind.

The Mongol army was a superb force in terms of overall direction, organization, and the toughness and ability of its individual fighting men. These fighters lived in the saddle: they could even sleep on horseback while their horses marched. When necessary they withstood great privation and endured all kinds of hardship. They were able to cover enormous distances at great speed, changing mounts several times in the process. The Mongol horses too were very hardy, able to endure extremes of climate, and in winter to find food by digging it out from under the snow or stripping twigs and bark from trees. Moreover, on the command level, the Mongols achieved masterly feats of planning and carrying out their operations. Their enemies were defeated as much by the Mongols' rapid movements and the precise coordination of their far-flung armies as they were by their ferocity and superb tactical discipline.

Whatever the Mongols could not use they destroyed. That was the fate of cities that resisted. As for their inhabitants, the women and children were enslaved, the men either killed or used as living shields in the next battle or assault on a city. Mongol brutality left terror in its wake. Even for Europeans, who lived in a far more military culture than that of China, the encounter with Mongol arms was an overwhelming experience that could only be explained in supernatural terms. According to *The Chronicle of Novgorod*, "God alone knows who they are and whence they came."[1] In Russia, Poland, and Hungary the merciless Mongols appeared as manifestations of God's wrath; their cruelties, acts of divine punishment meted out to sinners.

By the time of his death in 1227, Chinggis Khan had established Mongol supremacy in Central Asia, begun the offensive against Russia, destroyed the Xi Xia (Hsi Hsia) state, fought the Jin (Chin), and captured Beijing (Peking). His headquarters remained in Mongolia, where Karakorum served as the capital city, although it did not take on the appearance of a major city with a city wall and permanent buildings until 1235. This was the work of Ögödei (r. 1229–41), who as Great Khan had inherited the richest part of his father's empire. According to Mongol custom, however, other portions had been assigned to Ögödei's brothers, who ruled over three major khanates in Turkestan, Russia, and Persia.

The death of Chinggis Khan and the division of his patrimony did not diminish the momentum of Mongol conquests: in 1231 Mongol troops crossed the Yalu River into Korea and continued their advance in North China, taking Kaifeng in 1233 and Luoyang in 1234. Also in 1234 they completed the destruction of the Jurchen Jin dynasty. Mongol armies were equally successful in the West, where Kiev fell in 1240, Baghdad in 1258. In 1241 a Mongol army was on the Adriatic. And then they turned back. Western Europe was spared, not because the Mongols were beaten in battle or had been awed by the Western defense, but by a command decision of the Mongol general. The exact reason for the turnabout is not known, but geography most probably played a role. The vast number of horses required by the Mongol army needed great open plains on which to graze.

The Mongols developed a courier system to link their empire; couriers could cover up to 200 miles a day. They also had a written language based on that of another tribal people, the Uighurs, and Chinggis Khan created a body of written law, the *jasagh*. However, the Mongols lacked an organized political system capable of molding their vast and diverse conquests into a lasting unity. Particularly grave was the absence of a formalized system of succession. Where complex political institutions did exist, as in China and Persia, they were grafted on to a local culture; otherwise, there was simply the old tribal system that had been unified by Temüjin's character and thus could not long survive his death, despite his attempt to create a legal system in the *jasagh*. That he created *jasagh*, coming from a tribal culture, is a mark of his genius; that he so greatly underestimated the task of institutionalizing his rule is a mark both of the limits of his genius and of the gulf between the tribal and settled cultures.

Under Chinggis Khan's grandson Khubilai (1215–94), who became Great Khan in 1260, the capital was transferred from Mongolia to Beijing (1264). In doing so Khubilai tacitly relinquished the Mongol claim to rule the entire world. Once again the political balance of East Asia was dominated by China, although this time not by Chinese.

China under the Mongols: The Early Years (1211–1260)

Almost half a century passed between Chinggis Khan's first attack on Chinese territory (1211) and the beginning of Khubilai's reign. It was a period that helped to set much of the pattern for later Mongol rule in China. In both the military operations against the Jurchen Jin and the subsequent civil administration of North China, the Mongols made use of non-Mongols, particularly

Khitan leaders who had a tradition of hostility toward the Jin and Chinese who felt no great loyalty toward the Jurchen. The services of such men were essential to the Mongols, operating as they were in unfamiliar terrain and outnumbered by their enemy. Indeed, their ability to use men of non-Mongol background was essential, as the Mongols themselves numbered only around one and a half million people. Thus non-Mongol military leaders were accepted as *nökhör* by the Khan and granted the privileges that went with that status, including the receipt of lands to rule.

Among the non-Mongols in the service of the Khan, Yelü Chucai (Yeh-lü Ch'u-ts'ai, 1189–1243) was the most outstanding. As a Sinicized Khitan of royal Liao lineage, and a first place examination graduate under the Jin, Yelü was well equipped to mediate between the Mongols and their Chinese subjects. Summoned to Mongolia by Chinggis Khan in 1218, he became influential as the court astrologer and is said to have played a role in the Mongol decision to stay out of India. But his real prominence came under Ögödei when he was able to persuade the Khan to reject the proposal by a group of Mongols that all the territory conquered in North China be turned into pasturage. This was a serious proposal consistent with the Mongol way of life and, especially, with the crucial need for great quantities of horses if the Mongols were to retain their power. Other nomadic peoples, most recently the Jurchen, although much less involved than the Mongols in maintaining power outside China, had pondered the same alternatives. But in the end, Yelü's position prevailed. He persuaded the Khan, not by appealing to Chinese theories of government, but by demonstrating the profits to be gained through an orderly exploitation of a settled and productive population. Yelü was thereupon, in 1229, placed in charge of taxation and created a tax system staffed by civilian officials.

Rising eventually to highest office, he worked hard to fashion a centralized administration along Chinese lines but achieved only partial success. For example, he failed in his attempt to subject privileged non-Chinese in North China to the same taxes imposed on the Chinese population. He did obtain enactment of a census, but he could not disuade Ögödei from granting lands to supporters, which were beyond the government's fiscal control. In this case his proposal would have affected Chinese as well as non-Chinese leaders whose self-interest was at stake. The division of China into large-scale and loosely controlled military commands continued throughout the Mongol period; these commands later evolved into the large provinces into which China was divided during the Ming and Qing (Ch'ing).

Yelü rescued Chinese scholars from captivity and found positions for them, including posts as tutors to Mongol nobles, but his revival of the civil service examinations was very short lived. Toward the end of his life he suffered increasing setbacks. Throughout his career he appealed to Mongol greed. In the end he was outbid by Central Asian merchants who argued that they could extract more wealth for the Mongols from China through tax farming than Yelü could through a centralized state tax system. Tax farming was a system by which interested individuals bid against each other for the right to collect the taxes from a certain area for a specified period of time. The bidder who offered to raise the largest amount for the Mongol rulers was awarded the contract. Any amount he could raise over the amount to be given to the government he could keep for himself. Obviously this system appealed to the rapaciousness of both the government and the tax farmer, and the most ruthless measures were used to exact ruinously high taxes. Despite Yelü's protests that this was ultimately a short-sighted policy harmful to the people who produced the wealth, a Muslim businessman was, in 1239, granted the right to collect taxes in North China.

At the time of Yelü Chucai's death in 1243, it looked as though his work was coming undone. His career demonstrated the difficulties involved in creating a Sino-Mongolian state.

Khubilai Khan and the Early Yuan

Khubilai Khan (r. 1260–94), who in 1264 had transferred the capital to Beijing, followed this, in 1271, by the adoption of a Chinese dynastic name, Yuan, as well as Chinese court ceremonials. Chinggis Khan now received a posthumous Chinese title (Taizu, T'ai-tsu), and Khubilai himself appears in the Chinese histories under the name of Shizu (Shih-tsu). Previous khans had preferred, as was their tradition, to live among their herds and tents instead of taking up permanent residence in the capital; they spent as much time hunting as they did looking after government operations. Khubilai, in contrast, spent most of his time in Beijing or in his summer capital at Shangdu, in Inner Mongolia. He was careful to give at least an appearance of ruling in a Chinese manner while engaged in "a delicate balancing act between ruling the sedentary civilization of China and preserving the cultural identity and values of the Mongols."[2] Among measures designed to accomplish the latter were a prohibition against Mongols marrying Chinese, his own practice of taking only Mongol women into the palace, and a policy of discouraging Mongols from associating with Chinese. That he also saw himself as a universal ruler is indicated by an unsuccessful attempt to propagate a new alphabet that he hoped could become a universal script. On the other hand, he did not try to devise a uniform code of law applicable to all the different peoples under his rule, and the Yuan remained the only Chinese dynasty lacking such a code.

His first concern was to make himself truly master of all China, completing the military conquest initiated by his grandfather and continued by Chinggis Khan's successors. The subjugation of the Southern Song was difficult, for resistance was stiff, and the Mongols had to learn new techniques to operate successfully in the South. They were finally victorious, assisted by the defection of much of the Song navy. When the Southern Song fell in 1279, the Mongols became the first nomadic conquerors to rule all of China (see Figure 7-1).

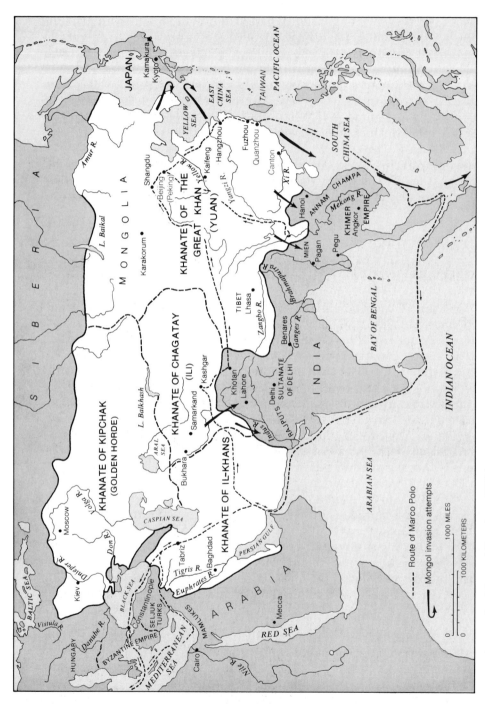

Figure 7-1   The Mongol Empire   1294

This did not bring an end to warfare. Although Khubilai's empire was China based, his ambitions were not confined to China. He sent an expedition against Japan in 1274 and, after he was master of all of China, organized a second, more massive attack in 1281. Both attacks failed. Plans for a third attempt were never carried out. This was largely because in the 1280s Mongol forces were occupied with operations in Southeast Asia where repeated attacks were made on Vietnam and Burma. In 1281 and again in 1292 the Khan's fleet attacked Java. These expeditions forced local rulers into ritual submission but did not expand the territory under actual Yuan control. At the same time Khubilai could not afford to neglect China's inner Asian frontier, where he was repeatedly challenged by Ögödei's grandson, Khaidu. There, Khubilai and his successors concentrated on securing Mongolia. This they accomplished but at the cost of giving up their ambition to dominate Central Asia as well.

Within China the long and bitter struggle against the Southern Song left lasting wounds. Chinese hatred and bitterness were matched by Mongol suspicion and distrust of the southerners. A significant number of Chinese remained loyal to the old dynasty, continued to employ Song terminology, and dreamed of a Song restoration while refusing to serve the new power. On the other hand, the Mongols relegated southerners to the lowest category in their fourfold division of society along ethnic lines. Highest status in this system was accorded to the Mongols. Next came persons with special status (se-muren, se-mu jen). These were Mongol allies, largely from Central Asia and the Near East, such as Turks, Persians, and Syrians. They played an important role in government financial administration, often served as managers for Mongol aristocrats, and enjoyed special privileges as financiers. Organized into special guilds, they financed the caravan trade and loaned out money at usurious rates. The third status group, although termed "hanren, han-jen," which usually means "Chinese," included all inhabitants of North China: those of Khitan, Jurchen, or Korean family background as well as native Chinese. Finally, at the bottom, were the 80 percent of the Chinese population that lived in the South, the "nanren, nan-jen" or "southerners," also referred to by the less neutral term "manzi, man-tzu," that is, "southern barbarians." This fourfold division of society deeply affected the Yuan's treatment of its subjects. It was expressed in the recruitment and appointment of government officials, in the conduct of legal cases, and in taxation.

Actually, as we have seen, the most cultivated scholars lived in the South. Most resigned themselves to the new order and accepted the Yuan as the recipient of the Heavenly Mandate, but others remained unreconciled even though Khubilai had placed Chinese Confucians in high posts and had shown himself so receptive to their advice that he even had his son and heir educated in the Confucian manner. The emperor was also a generous patron of Chinese arts and letters, but he refused to reinstitute the civil service examinations and continued to give top priority to expensive military campaigns. To avoid dependence on Chinese officials, Khubilai continued to employ foreigners, including Muslims, Tibetans, Uighurs, and other Central Asians, and even men from the Far West such as the Persian astronomer Jamal al-Din and the Venitian Marco Polo.

Religion

The Mongol tolerance of foreigners also extended to foreign religions. The early khans liked to sponsor religious debates at their courts, and under the Mongols all religions were granted tax exemption. Nestorians and Muslims, Christians and Jews were welcome. After the Daoist master Qiu Chuji (Ch'iu Ch'u-chi, d. 1227) visited Chinggis Khan in Central Asia, Daoism was particularly favored, but the competition for official patronage was finally won by the proponents of Tibetan Buddhism. After gaining the submission of Tibet, the Mongols used a prominent Tibetan abbot to rule on their behalf over this mountainous land, where the dominant religion was an amalgam of Indian Buddhism and the native Bon religion. Known as Lamaism, after the Tibetan word designating a monk, this religion was more sophisticated and universal than the native shamanism of the Mongols. The Mongol rulers were impressed by the Lamaist formulae and charms infused with magic power to cure or harm; and they were attracted to the Tibetan religion as a form of Buddhism practiced by a hardy, nonagricultural people like themselves. In 1260 a Mongol lama was established as State Preceptor and in 1261 he was given responsibility for the entire Buddhist clergy. Khubilai's successor continued to favor Lamaism, and as a result of imperial munificence, there was a proliferation of Buddhist art. Much of this art showed Tibetan or Nepalese influence, but it never won the esteem of students of Chinese art. A very different expression of official favor took the form of an edict, issued in 1309, stipulating that anyone striking a lama would have his hand cut off, and that an offender would lose his tongue for insulting a lama. Lamaism, however, made little impact on the Chinese population. Even the conversion of the Mongol people who had remained on the steppe did not take place until the sixteenth century.

The Economy

The Mongol conquerors did not disturb the class structure of South China, nor did the conquerors inflict permanent damage on the economy of the South. Khubilai made a start in the reconstruction of the shattered economy of the North, but the South remained the main economic region. There the ceramics and silk industries continued to flourish and a new cotton industry also developed. (Cotton culture may have been borrowed from the aboriginal inhabitants of China's southern provinces; a species of cotton was cultivated in Western Yunnan by the third century A.D. However, cotton did not become important economically until the Yuan.) One of the financial policies that the

Mongols adopted from their Jin and Song predecessors was the use of paper money. Concerned not to disrupt the economic life of the South, Khubilai even provided for conversion of Southern Song paper money into that of the Yuan, and he also made paper money the sole legal currency. As long as the paper currency was well backed, this policy was a success despite the slow inflation that set in after 1280. In other areas too, including the rehabilitation and extension of the Grand Canal, Khubilai's regime accomplished much. He displayed an ability to learn and to adjust to new circumstances in administrative as well as in military matters. What he could not do was to construct a system that would run smoothly of itself, and, unfortunately for the dynasty, there was not to be another Khubilai Khan.

The Yuan after Khubilai Khan

Although the Yuan after Khubilai accomplished more than traditionally hostile Chinese historians would later admit, it never achieved the strength and longevity of a major Chinese dynasty. Lacking a tradition of orderly succession to rulership, the Yuan was troubled by numerous succession disputes. During the 40 years after Khubilai's death, seven emperors came to the throne, often to the accompaniment of bloodshed and murder. The last time men from the Mongolian steppe played a major role in these struggles was 1328. Even earlier, in 1307, the Mongolian homeland had been reduced to a province under civil administration. But the elimination of the steppe as a power base did not alleviate internal tensions. Nor was the dynasty able to devise a lasting formula for balancing the diverse elements in government and society.

Court politics were dominated by factionalism, which found expression in fluctuating government policies. Personnel policies were a particularly sensitive area. Not until 1313 was an imperial edict issued reviving the civil service examinations based on the Confucian classics and the commentaries of Zhu Xi (Chu Hsi). The first tests were given in 1315. Although this was a major concession to the Confucian literati, the system favored the Mongols and their non-Chinese allies, who were given simplified examinations and occupied 30 percent of all government posts. Under these circumstances some Chinese, hungry for office, could not resist the temptation to assume foreign names. In 1335 the Chancellor, Bayan (Chancellor 1335 – 40), obtained an imperial decree to cancel the examinations and thereby gained the enmity of all Confucians, who viewed the reinstitution of the examinations both as a step toward the normalization of government and as an opportunity for personal advancement. Bayan was overthrown by the Mongol leader, Toghto (d. 1356), who served as Chancellor from 1340 to 1344 and again from 1349 to 1355. Toghto revived the examination in 1342. Although degree holders enjoyed great prestige, the examinations did not regain the prominence they had enjoyed during the Song, nor did they become the prime method of government recruitment.

Still worse from the Chinese scholar's point of view was the persistent Yuan policy of according military officials supremacy over the civilian.

A major cause for concern during the 1340s was the Yellow River, which broke its dikes, flooded, and, most disastrously, began to change its course. One part of the river flowed north of the Shandong Peninsula; another emptied into the Grand Canal, putting it out of commission. Not only did this cause great dislocation and suffering to the inhabitants of the affected areas, it also threatened the economic survival of the dynasty by interrupting shipments of grain from the South. The only alternative to the Grand Canal route was by sea, but the maritime route was in constant danger from an increasingly bold and assertive pirate, Fan Guozhen (Fang Kuo-chen). Clearly a massive effort was required for the government to reestablish control over the river or over the sea route, and it lacked the resources to do both. Given the choice, Toghto decided to concentrate on the more immediately threatening and more manageable inland problem. Furthermore, rather than settle for a superficial and temporary solution, he proposed the digging of a new channel for the Yellow River south of the Shandong Peninsula. Although his plan ran into political opposition, this great feat of hydraulic engineering was successfully carried out during Toghto's second administration. Under the direction of a Chinese engineer it was completed with the labor of 150,000 civilians and 20,000 troops.

Rebellion

The Yellow River problem was solved, but the cost was high, for it strained to the utmost the economic resources of the government and the people. An excessive issue of inadequately backed paper money produced growing inflation, which added its toll to the hardships of the population already suffering from government exactions. The seemingly hopeless situation prompted people to turn to religious salvationism, and the messianic teachings of the White Lotus Society found a responsive audience, as countless people placed their faith in the coming of Maitreya, who would put an end to all suffering and injustice. Under a leader who claimed descent from the Song imperial line, the society attracted the miserable: dismissed clerks, deserters from the Yellow River project, peddlers, outlaws, the idle, and the displaced. Known as the Red Turbans after their headdresses, these people turned to open rebellion in 1352, and for the next three years much of Central and South China was lost to the Yuan. However, under Toghto's leadership, the dynasty was able for the time being to put down this challenge, ultimately employing forces composed mainly of Chinese soldiers. Yet when Toghto, after the defeat of the Red Turbans, turned his attention to eliminating a rebellious salt smuggler who had seized a town on the Grand Canal and proclaimed a new dynasty, the Mongol Chancellor would not allow a Chinese general to have the glory of applying the *coup de grâce*.

While Toghto was in power, the government maintained control over its military forces by taking great care in the making of appointments, by separating command and supply functions, and by generally exercising central leadership, but after his fall no other political strongman appeared to prevent the formation of regional power centers. These developed when the government made concessions to various commanders combatting a renewed rebellion, which proclaimed itself a revival of the Song. During the last twelve years of the Yuan, the issue at stake was not so much the survival of the dynasty as the determination of its successor.

It turned out that the future belonged neither to the regional commanders nor to the rebel Song regime in the North, but to an organization led by Zhu Yuanzhang (Chu Yüan-chang, 1328–98) in the South. Zhu had been born into a poor family and as a youth served as a novice in a Buddhist monastery. Later he became a beggar and eventually was drawn into the Red Turbans, where he rose to become a military commander. After the defeat of the Red Turbans, he became a leader of his own rebel organization. In contrast to the Red Turbans, who had directed their animosity as much against local landlords as against the dynasty, Zhu undertook to reconcile the local elite. By abandoning the messianic radicalism of the earlier rebels and by demonstrating his intention to reconstruct the traditional kind of imperial government, he was able to gain valuable support among the gentry. Although some of the Chinese elite remained faithful to the Yuan and one of the most valiant and loyal defenders of the dynasty was a Chinese general, Zhu Yuanzhang could not be stopped. By 1368 it was all over: The Mongol court fled to Mongolia, and a new dynasty, the Ming, was established with its capital at Nanjing. Early in his reign Zhu Yuanzhang, known posthumously as Taizu (T'ai-tsu), issued an order proscribing unorthodox religious sects, foremost among them the same White Lotus sect that had inspired his own campaign to power.

Although the Mongols enacted social policies, such as creating hereditary families of artisans, they do not appear to have had a lasting effect on Chinese social structure. The effect of the Mongol period on Chinese political culture is generally considered more important. It is to this period that scholars have looked to explain the contrast between the rather benign government of the Song and the more authoritarian rule of the Ming. The Mongols had set an example of strong imperial rule and, in their declining years, had provided a lesson of what could happen in the absence of strong central direction. The lesson was not lost on the Ming founder.

Cultural Life

Although earnest scholars saw it as their mission to serve the Way by serving (and civilizing) the Mongols, others, especially at the beginning of the dynasty, found withdrawal from active politics more compelling or fulfilling. Private academies with their Neo-Confucian curriculum offered an attractive alternative to government service and, along with official sponsorship, helped to assure the perpetuation of Neo-Confucianism as the prevalent orthodoxy.

Meanwhile, a good number of talented men, who in more normal times would have taken up a political career, made a living by pursuing occupations that brought them into close daily contact with ordinary, common people. Some became doctors, others took up fortune telling, still others turned to the theater for their livelihood. The result was the creation of great drama and art.

Yuan Drama

The theater arts had a long history in China before drama reached its classic form during the reign of Khubilai Khan. Early shamanistic religious dances, performances of music and acting staged for the amusement of the imperial court, "ballets" such as the Tang poet Bo Juyi's (Po Chü-yi) favorite, "Rainbow Skirts and Feather Jackets," all form part of the background of the mature Yuan music drama. Equally important was the heritage of popular entertainment, including the various theatricals staged for the benefit of the inhabitants of Song Kaifeng and Hangzhou (both of which had thriving theater districts), featuring not only performances by live actors but also puppet shows and shadow plays. Both these arts have a long pre-Song history. In the puppet theater some puppets were on strings, others on sticks, still others were controlled by explosive charges, and some productions featured "live puppets," that is, children manipulated by a "puppeteer." In the shadow plays, the audience observed silhouettes of figures manipulated behind a screen and in front of lights. Among the precursors of the Yuan drama, none are more important than the storytellers who had enlivened the urban scene ever since the Song. Already in Song Hangzhou they were numerous enough to form "guilds." Set up in their stalls, they recited their stories, sometimes to the accompaniment of musical instruments. Each man had his specialty: realistic stories, stories of ghosts and the miraculous, religious tales, stories based on historical episodes. Their art consisted not in simply relating an old story but in making it come vividly alive by dramatic modulations of the voice and other dramatic devices. Cyril Birch tells of a fairly recent practitioner of the art who, " 'in one breath' could produce seven distinct sounds to represent in realistic fashion the screams of a pig in the successive stages of its slaughter." [3] Thus the development of the theater did not inhibit the continuing flourishing of the art of the storyteller, but this art did leave its mark on the formal conventions not only of the theater but also of the novel, and it influenced the content as well as the form of both of these popular genres.

It is therefore not surprising that the plots of many of the 171 Yuan plays still extant are based on earlier materials. Historical episodes such as the marriage of the Han palace beauty Wang Zhaojun (Wang Chao-chün) to a

Xiongnu (Hsiung-nu) chieftain, the political and military ploys devised by Zhuge Liang (Chu-ko Liang) and his contemporaries of the Three Kingdom period, the tragedy brought on by East Asia's most famed *femme fatale*, Yang Gueifei (Yang Kuei-fei), the story of Xuanzang's (Hsüan-tsang) pilgrimage to India, and other historical and semihistorical events provided the Yuan dramatists with some of their most effective and popular themes. And the plays for their part did much to fix in the popular mind colorful, larger-than-life images of these personages, creations of the poetic imagination at work embellishing the more prosaic historical accounts.

The Yuan theatergoers also enjoyed dramatic renditions of old love stories, such as that of the beautiful Ying-ying and a student named Zhang (Chang) recounted in the highly celebrated thirteenth-century play *The Romance of the Western Chamber* by Wang Shifu (Wang Shih-fu). In adapting the old tale to the stage, Wang did not hesitate to rework his materials for greater theatrical and literary effect. Thus, in the play, skillful use is made of the refusal of Ying-ying's mother to honor her promise to marry her daughter to whomever will rescue them when they are surrounded by rebels. Ying-ying, already greatly attracted to the young rescuer, now gives him her heart. And the injustice of the mother's act also transforms Nurse Huaining from an obstacle into a highly resourceful ally. To please his audience, the playwright departs from the Tang version of the story and has the drama end with the couple overcoming all obstacles to their happiness, including Ying-ying's mother. After Zhang passes his examinations, they are united in marriage. Love triumphs in the end. This happy resolution is characteristic of the genre, for these plays were designed to appeal to an audience not only of connoisseurs but also of ordinary people with little or no formal education, who desired happy endings.

The repertoire of the Yuan theater included many plays expressing a longing for justice. Some featured that model of official rectitude and wisdom Judge Bao (based on a real official, Bao Zheng (Pao Cheng, 999 – 1062), a champion of justice who repeatedly uncovers even the most ingenious deceptions of the wicked. Prominent among the villains of such plays are greedy and unscrupulous officials who subvert the moral order they are theoretically committed to uphold. Among the heroes are Robin Hood-like figures, outlaws who have right on their side even as they defy the state and its laws. (Many of these heroes also appear in the Ming novel *The Water Margin*; see Chapter 8). No doubt many members of the audience derived vicarious pleasure from witnessing the punishment of venal and corrupt officials resembling those who in real life went uncorrected. The plays do not deal with contemporary events in any obvious way nor do they directly cast aspersions on the regime. Yet one wonders what a Mongol spectator would have made of the scene in *Autumn in the Palace of Han* where the playwright described the hardships facing Wang Zhaojun (Wang Chao-chün) among the "barbarians" when she will have only "tasteless salted flesh" to eat, and for drink "clabbered milk and gruel."[4]

The plays were written for standard actors' roles: leading man, leading lady, villain, and so on. The characters too can be classified into easily recognizable types such as the faithful lovers of *The Romance of the Western Chamber;* the corrupt officials and wise judges of the courtroom dramas; the uncouth but virtuous outlaws; and the beautiful, talented, and strong-minded courtesans. Most plays consisted of four acts between which short interludes, or "wedges," could be inserted. Since stage props were few, characters regularly made speeches of self-identification. The playwrights also used occasional recapitulations, carry-overs from the tradition of the storyteller.

Music played an important part in the theater. The songs or song sequences in each act were in a single mode or key. The lute and zither were the standard instruments of the Yuan northern drama. In contrast to the mellow, refined music of the southern drama that reached its height under the Ming, the Yuan sound was vigorous and spirited. The Yuan drama's roots in the tradition of oral narrative are also revealed in the assignment of all arias to a single performer. Thus in *Autumn in the Palace of Han,* only the emperor sings.

The products of the Yuan playwright frequently achieved high literary excellence. Dialogue written in the spoken language of the time lent an earthy freshness to texts, which at times included bawdy vulgarisms such as no respectable Confucian scholar of later times would have allowed to flow from his brush. Such language contributed to the bad repute in which the Yuan drama was held in polite circles under later dynasties, until it was appreciatively rediscovered in the twentieth century. What was valued by the critics were the plays' poetic passages, particularly the lyric songs (*sanju, san-ch'ü*), which rank with other major forms of Chinese poetry in their technical intricacy, musical subtlety, and employment of various poetic devices, including the effective use of imagery. Just as connoisseurs judged paintings by the quality of their brushwork, critics focused on the merits of the poetry in the plays. Thus a fifteenth-century critic praised the poetry of Ma Zhiyuan (Ma Chih-yüan), author of *Autumn in the Palace of Han,* as resembling "a phoenix gliding and singing in the highest clouds."[5]

The Romance of the Western Chamber is beloved for its poetry. In it Yingying herself is deeply moved when Zhang sings to her of love, and "word follows word like the endless dripping of a water-clock."[6] Here Zhang's song was accompanied by his zither, but the sanju were sung without accompaniment. In the great plays the poetry is an integral part of the work, contributing to dramatic development. Thus the recurrent image of the moon, which appears more than 50 times in the poetry of *The Romance of the Western Chamber,* helps to give the drama unity and depth. It is present, of course, when after long courtship, the lovers are united. Then, "the bright moon, like water, floods the pavilion and terrace."[7]

The lovers have to suffer through a long period of separation and uncertainty before their union is made permanent at last, but they are fitting representatives of an essentially optimistic and life-affirming theater that combined high art with wide appeal to all classes.

Yuan Painting

In contrast to the theater, in which individuals from all kinds of backgrounds participated and which had something for everyone, the painting for which the Yuan is famous was a much more esoteric pursuit. But whereas literary men later disdained the drama as plebeian, the achievements of the great Yuan painters were admired by all later connoisseurs.

The distinction between the professional who sells his wares to the aesthetically naive and the amateur who paints for himself and his friends did not originate in the Yuan but was confirmed by those critical of the taste of the Mongol court. Professional artists continued to take pride in the perfection of their techniques and the excellence of their craftsmanship. Gentlemen-amateurs, no less serious about their art, found in brush and ink a vehicle for self-expression and for the cultivation of self. Yuan painting, therefore, often contains an element of self-portraiture, although rarely was this as explicit as in *Emaciated Horse* (Figure 7-2) by the Song loyalist Gong Kai (Kung K'ai, 1222–1307), who belonged to the generation that experienced the change of dynasties. His painting expresses the self-image of the Chinese scholars who found themselves condemned to live in a world that did not respect their talents or prize their values; a world in which, as indicated in the poem Gong added to his painting, the stables of the former dynasty remained empty. The horse had long been a symbol of the scholar-official, and was perhaps an

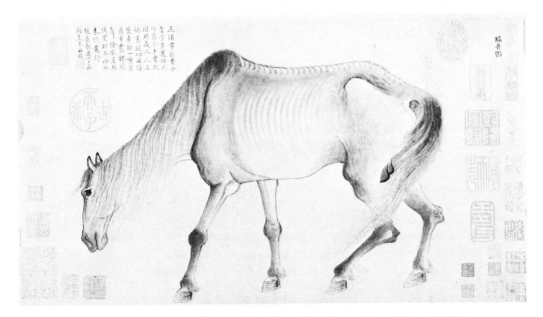

Figure 7-2   Gong Kai, *Emaciated Horse*. Hand-scroll, ink on paper, 30 cm × 57 cm. Abe Collection, Osaka Municipal Museum of Fine Arts.

especially fitting symbol for the neglected Confucian living under a conqueror who prided himself on his horsemanship. The very gauntness of Gong's haggard horse brings out the essential strength of its splendid physique. To those who understood its meaning, the painting was an eloquent, proud, and poignant statement of a bitter shared fate.

The most famous Yuan horse painter was also the outstanding exception to the rule that the gentleman-artist avoided the imperial stable. Zhao Mengfu (Chao Meng-fu, 1254–1322) held high office under the Mongols and paid the price in lost friendships and inner suffering. Later Chinese scholars, although not approving of his career, were compelled to recognize the force of his genius as a major painter and one of China's truly great calligraphers. Indeed, his paintings of horses were so prized that forgeries abound. Zhao's work is illustrated here not by a horse but by *Autumn Colors on the Qiao (Ch'iao) and Hua Mountains* (see Figure 7-3), which exemplifies a deliberate archaism that greatly appealed to the Yuan literati.

As *Autumn Colors* shows, Zhao's archaism demanded the complete rejection of the aesthetics of his immediate predecessors. No trace can be found here of the styles of Ma Yuan and Xia Guei (Hsia Kuei), and there is a deliberate, consistent avoidance of prettiness. Beyond that, Zhao had discarded developments in perspective and ignored size relationships in his attempt to recapture an earlier noble simplicity. Zhao and his contemporaries, somewhat like the Pre-Raphaelites of nineteenth-century England, tried to return to the rugged honesty of an earlier age and to unlearn the lessons of the classic period of their art. The Chinese painters, however, were more ready than the

Figure 7-3
Zhao Mengfu.
Autumn Colors on the Qiao (Ch'iao) and Hua Mountains. Hand-scroll, ink and colors on paper, dated 1296, 28.4 cm × 93.2 cm. National Palace Museum, Taipei.

Figure 7-4　Ni Zan, *The Rongxi (Jung-hsi)
Studio.* Hanging scroll, ink on paper,
dated 1372, 74.7 cm × 35.5 cm.
National Palace Museum, Taipei.

Pre-Raphaelites to sacrifice surface beauty for the sake of attaining what Zhao
called "a sense of antiquity" (*guyi, ku-i*). They also differed in that they conceived of their art in terms of calligraphy: both painting and calligraphy served
the purpose of writing down on paper or silk the ideas the gentlemen had in
their minds. In the two paintings reproduced in Figures 7-2 and 7-3, the
unused space does not serve as a horizon, nor does it contribute to the overall
composition. Therefore, the use of this space for calligraphy does not disturb
the painting. In a sense the painting, too, is calligraphy just as, in another
sense, the calligraphy is painting.

　　Now, as earlier, calligraphy was prized as a revelation of the lofty character
of its cultivated practitioner, an emphasis which made for variety in style, in

Figure 7-5   Wang Meng,
*The Forest Grotto at
Juqu (Chü-ch'ü)*. Hanging scroll,
ink and colors on paper,
68.7 cm × 42.5 cm.
National Palace Museum,
Taipei.

painting as well as in writing. The master painters of the Yuan did not share a uniform style, nor did individual artists necessarily limit themselves to a single style. There is, for example, a famous anecdote concerning the painter Ni Zan (Ni Tsan, 1301–74), who one night, while inebriated, painted bamboos that a friend next day criticized for not looking like bamboos. Exemplifying the Yuan painter's disdain for representation, Ni replied that he was delighted: few indeed can paint bamboos so that they do not resemble bamboos in the least! Yet, Ni often painted ordinary bamboos. Bamboos which, like the gentleman-scholar, bend before the wind but do not break were a favorite subject of the literati-painters, who could also find Daoist significance in the fact that the center of this plant is hollow, that is, empty. Reproduced in Figure 7-4 is Ni's *The Rongxi (Jung-hsi) Studio*, which exemplifies not only Ni's calligraphic talents but also the cool restraint of his unpeopled landscapes. Like Zhao Mengfu, he has avoided all painterly tricks. He achieved a calm, bland poetry. This aesthetic of the cool and clean is also found in the white and also in the blue-and-white ceramics of the age.

At the opposite stylistic pole from Ni Zan are the paintings of Wang Meng (ca. 1309–85), especially his later work which employs "unraveled hemp fiber" and S-shaped strokes (see Figure 7-5). Where Ni Zan works in monochrome, Wang delights in bright colors. In Ni, nature is stable and empty, but Wang fills his space with natural forces surging around the abodes of his recluses and threatening to burst forth beyond the borders of the painting. Perhaps this was an appropriate statement for a period when social and political forces in China were about to burst through the Yuan dynastic framework.

In considering the cultural achievements of the Yuan, it is worth noting that foreign influence did not enter the world of the literati-painter. Conversely, no appreciation or even an awareness of their art is to be found in the literature of the European visitors, such as Marco Polo and his successors of the fourteenth century. Although there was a Catholic archbishop in Beijing and relations across the great Eurasian land mass were often cordial, these relations had a low priority on both sides of the world, for the distances were enormous, and Europe as well as China was faced with far more immediate challenges and opportunities in politics, economics, art, and thought closer to home. In many respects China was ahead of Europe at the time. Literati painting of the type prized in the Yuan was not even considered worthy of note by Europeans prior to the nineteenth century, and it was not until the twentieth century that people in the West learned how to see and value these paintings.

NOTES

1. R. Mitchell and N. Forbes, trans., *The Chronicle of Novgorod 1016-1471* (London: Camden Society, 3rd Series, Vol. 25, 1914), p. 64.

2. Morris Rossabi, *Khubilai Khan: His Life and Times* (Berkeley: Univ. of California Press, 1987), p. 115.

3. Cyril Birch, trans., *Stories from a Ming Collection: The Art of the Chinese Story-Teller* (New York: Grove Press, 1958), pp. 10–11.

4. Cyril Birch, ed., *Anthology of Chinese Literature* (New York: Grove Press, 1965), 1: 483.

5. Chung-wen Shih, *The Golden Age of Chinese Drama: Yüan Tsa-chü* (Princeton: Princeton Univ. Press, 1976), p. 160.

6. *Ibid.*, p. 192.

7. *Ibid.*, p. 159.

8

The Ming Dynasty: 1368-1644

1368	1424	1505	1590	1644
EARLY MING	EARLY MIDDLE PERIOD	LATE MIDDLE PERIOD	LATE MING	

T he Ming was the last Chinese dynasty to rule China. The stability of the regime and the general prosperity of the people, as well as notable achievements in literature, philosophy, and the arts, demonstrated the continued vitality of the Chinese tradition and its capacity for growth and transformation. When, toward the end of the Ming period, the first modern Europeans arrived in China, they found much to admire (see Chapter 9). The Ming's Manchu successor, the Qing (Ch'ing) dynasty, owed much of its success to the solidity of its Ming foundations.

Chinese Society during the Ming

Traditional accounts of the Ming, as of other dynasties, present Chinese history from the perspective of the capital. This is certainly understandable, for this is where the official records were maintained and the great dynastic histories were commissioned and compiled. Moreover, there is considerable merit in looking at things from this point of view. Not only was the capital the center of government and the residence of the emperor, it was also a primary center of political power, scholarship, and the arts. Decisions and innovations made in the capital shaped the history of China.

But the student of Chinese history must also bear in mind that China is an immense country, highly varied in population, culture, climate, and terrain, and, as observed earlier, one in which the direct impact of government on people living outside the capital was (until very recently) limited. At the local level the central government was represented by the magistrate, who in theory was responsible for everything that happened in his district. He was supposed to supervise tax collection, provide public security, administer justice, and see to the economic as well as moral needs of the population. Since, however, his staff was small and the average Ming district had a registered population of over 50,000, the magistrate's control and influence were restricted.

Local society operated according to its own rhythms, its patterns influenced and affected by government to be sure, but not determined by it. Indeed, the history of China suggests that occurrences in the provinces had as much influence on the center as acts of the central government had on the provinces. Thus the view from the center needs to be complemented by the study of local history.

183

Particularly important was the role of the local gentry who had great influence on local government officials. Gentry and officials moved in the same social and cultural circles, were of the same class, and usually had close social ties. Even if uninfluenced by personal associations, officials could hardly disregard the gentry, the magnitude of whose influence has induced a Japanese scholar to write of "gentry rule," that is "indirect regional rule that went beyond the boundary of mere tenant-landlord relations" and included political rule (administering justice, mediating quarrels, maintaining public order, administering relief, etc.), cultural rule (education, culture, guidance of public opinion, etc.), and economic rule (control of the market, etc.).[1] This no doubt needs qualification, but the gentry did preside over provincial life and gave it much of its tone. The continuance of their prominence in local affairs from the Ming on contributed greatly to the general stability of Chinese society.

There is no reason to believe that regional variations in social structure and economic relationships were of lesser magnitude in the Ming than later since they reflect differences between ecosystems as well as local traditions. For example, whether early (say in the Song) or late (twentieth century) all "descent groups" (groups larger than a family descended from a common ancestor) were not organized into "lineages" (descent groups with shared assets, usually land), and social organization varied not only over time but also over space. The general trend was for the strongest lineages to develop in the southeast, but the present state of research is not sufficient to attempt a social/historical map or timeline. Similarly, though we know that there were bondservants on landed estates in the sixteenth century as well as tenants and hired workers, the situation was complex (for example, bondservants could also be landlords), and geographic parameters are as yet unclear.

In her exemplary study of a county in Anhui, Hilary J. Beattie found that the local gentry dated back to the early Ming, that gentry lineages were formally organized in the sixteenth century, and that they were able to survive the rebellions and upheavals of the late years of the dynasty and even the great nineteenth-century Taiping Rebellion.[2] They were able to accomplish this by maintaining solid economic roots in local land ownership and by investing their income in education. Education, in turn, secured their local status, in addition to providing the requisites for competing in the civil service examinations. Members of the gentry who succeeded in becoming officials used their political influence and their economic assets to benefit the lineage, but the gentry were able to sustain themselves even during periods lean in examination success. This suggests that local social and economic status was the primary source of their power and that there was greater continuity in the family background of the local elite than there was among those capable and fortunate enough to gain access to a career in the imperial bureaucracy.

Among the means used to secure lineage cohesion were the periodic compilations of genealogies. These not only fostered a sense of historic continuity among lineage members but also identified the individuals belonging to the lineage. Prominent gentry lineages also maintained ancestral halls and graveyards and conducted ceremonial sacrifices to lineage ancestors. Not infrequently, the income from lineage land was used for these purposes. Lineage solidarity was also maintained by general guides for the conduct of their members and by formal lineage rules. One penalty for severe infractions of these rules was expulsion. The contrast in status between the local elite and the government underlings who served in the subbureaucracy (see Chapter 6) is revealed by the stipulation found in many lineage rules that any member sinking to the occupation of government clerk or runner be promptly expelled. The individual gentry lineages also profited from participation in a complicated network of marriage relationships.

As we shall see, the socioeconomic conditions changed during the two and three-quarter centuries of the Ming. Particularly intriguing are regional variations in the pace and direction of change and the reasons for variation from one district or province to another. Concerning the general relationship between the center and local communities, the theories of G. William Skinner are especially fruitful. Skinner has suggested that by the middle of the nineteenth century there were in China some 45,000 market towns, each the nucleus of an "autonomous economic system . . . structured spatially according to the principle of centrality and temporally by the periodicity of its market days."[3] He further suggests that in times of dynastic decline and during the insecurity accompanying a change of dynasty, these cells closed themselves off from the larger body politic and that they gradually reopened as peace and stability were reestablished. Although this theory has not been applied to the analysis of the history of specific events in the Ming or any other dynasty, it suggests one way to explain how the local gentry were able to retain their position despite dynastic upheaval.

The Early Ming (1368–1424)

The early Ming was a period of vigorous Chinese military resurgence after the period of Mongol domination. The founder of the dynasty, Zhu Yuanzhang (Chu Yüan-chang) is known posthumuously as Taizu (see Table 8-1), ruled for 30 years (1368–98) and left his imprint on the reigns that followed. His was a martial spirit. For his era name he chose Hongwu, which means "grand military achievement," and his military accomplishments were certainly impressive. By the end of his reign, the Ming had won control of all China and dominated the frontier region from Hami, in Xinjiang, north through Inner Mongolia and into northern Manchuria. Beyond that, the Ming had won the subjugation of Korea as well as various Central and Southeast Asian states which sent tribute (see Figure 8-1.) Chengzu (r. 1402–24), the third Ming emperor, often referred to by his reign name, Yongle, continued his father's expansionist policy, leading five expeditions against the Mongols, intervening in Annam and then incorporating it into the empire, and sending out great maritime expeditions, which established China as a naval power. The early

Table 8-1   Ming Emperors

Temple Name		Era Name		
Pinyin	*Wade-Giles*	*Pinyin*	*Wade-Giles*	*Era Dates*
Taizu	T'ai-tsu	Hongwu	Hung-wu	1368–1399
Huizong	Hui-ts'ung	Jianwen	Chien-wen	1399–1402
Chengzu	Ch'eng-tsu	Yongle	Yung-lo	1403–1425
Renzong	Jen-tsung	Hongxi	Hung-hsi	1425–1426
Xuanzong	Hsüan-tsung	Xuande	Hsüan-te	1426–1436
Yingzong	Ying-tsung	Zhengtong	Cheng-t'ung	1436–1450
Taizong	T'ai-tsung	Jingtai	Ching-t'ai	1450–1457
Yingzong (restored)		Tianshun	T'ien-shun	1457–1465
Xianzong	Hsien-tsung	Chenghua	Ch'eng-hua	1465–1488
Xiaozong	Hsiao-tsung	Hongzhi	Hung-chih	1488–1506
Wuzong	Wu-tsung	Zhengde	Cheng-te	1506–1522
Shizong	Shih-tsung	Jiajing	Chia-ching	1522–1567
Muzong	Mu-tsung	Longqing	Lung-ch'ing	1567–1573
Shenzong	Shen-tsung	Wanli	Wan-li	1573–1620
Guangzong	Kuang-tsung	Taichang	T'ai-ch'ang	1620–1621
Xizong	Hsi-tsung	Tianqi	T'ien-ch'i	1621–1628
Sizong	Ssu-tsung	Chongzhen	Ch'ung-chen	1628–1645

NOTE   The Ming founder initiated the practice followed by all subsequent emperors of retaining a single era name (*nianhao*, literally "year designation") throughout his reign. Normally the era name remained in use until the end of the Chinese lunar year in which the emperor died. Transposing the Chinese dates into the Western calendar, it turns out that all except three Ming emperors (Chengzu, Muzong, and Shenzong) died during the year preceding the change in reign name. (For example, Taizu died on June 24, 1398 but *Hongwu* was used through January 5, 1399; Huizong was enthroned on June 30, 1398 but Taizu's era name remained in effect for the remainder of that lunar year.

   Ming emperors are often known by their era names rather than by their posthumous temple names. In order to comply with the style of most English language materials, we will refer to Ming emperors by their temple names but use era names for the emperors of the Qing (1644–1911).

Ming was thus a period of vigorous Chinese military resurgence coming after the period of Mongol domination.

   Taizu was a harsh and autocratic ruler. The position of Chancellor was abolished, and ministers now had to kneel in front of the emperor whereas in the Song they had stood and in the Tang they had sat in the imperial presence. Taizu insisted on deciding personally even matters of secondary importance. A very hard worker, he went through stacks of memorials: in one period of ten days he is reported to have perused 1,660 memorials dealing with 3,391 separate matters. In 1382 he appointed four Grand Secretaries to help him with this workload, but it was not until later in the dynasty that the Grand Secretariat developed into an institution. Merciless in exterminating those who stood in his way or were suspected of doing so, he obtained information

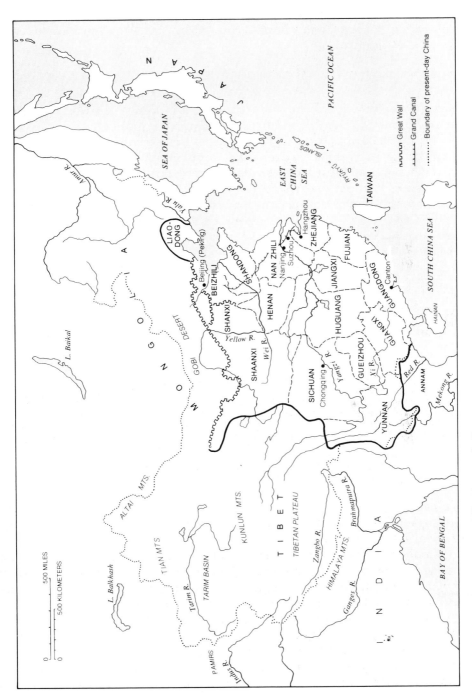

Figure 8-1   Ming China, Middle Sixteenth Century

through a secret service provided with its own prison and torturing apparatus. Officials who displease the emperor were subjected to beating in open court. Always painful and terribly humiliating, the beating was sometimes so severe that the victim died.

Although harsh and suspicious, Taizu was also a strong and capable leader. A major objective was to assure control of the countryside. To do this he established the *li-jia (li-chia)* system as a basis for labor-service and local security. Under this system, every ten families in an area constituted a *jia*, and ten *jia* formed a *li*. Each household was required to post a notice on its door indicating the names, ages, and occupations of its members, and all members of a *li* were responsible for each other's conduct. At the same time, the emperor energetically furthered the work of reconstruction and of relief for the poor, some of whom were resettled, and he established an effective tax system. Furthermore, he reestablished the imperial university, founded many schools, and reinstituted the civil service examinations. Confucianism again became the official state doctrine. But the emperor rejected the antiauthoritarian aspects of the thought of Mencius and had 85 sections (about one-third of the text) expurgated from *The Mencius* before accepting it as a legitimate book.

Chengzu (or Yongle) was as politically and militarily vigorous as his father but did not follow the first emperor's example in all respects. After defeating his nephew, the second emperor, in a massive civil war, Chengzu moved the capital from Nanjing to Beijing, which he largely rebuilt. To assure supplies for the capital, he also reconstructed the Grand Canal. Just as severe as his father when it came to purging real or suspected opponents, he was better educated than Taizu and more generous in his patronage of Confucianism. Not only did he hold more frequent civil service examinations, he also sponsored major scholarly projects. The most grandiose of these was the compilation of a huge literary treasury, which employed more than 2,000 scholars and when completed in 1408 resulted in a compendium of 22,877 rolls, or chapters. Under Chengzu the complete, unexpurgated *Mencius* was also once more made available.

It is sometimes said that the Ming reaction against the hated Mongols led to an overreaction against all things foreign, but this is not entirely true. For example, Chengzu not only sponsored a great compendium of Song Neo-Confucianism but also patronized the publication of Buddhist works, including a new edition of the Tripitaka. After the death of his wife, he had a Buddhist monastery near Nanjing repaired and built there an octagonal porcelain pagoda nine stories tall, more than 276 feet high. It remained standing until destroyed in 1854 during the Taiping Rebellion.

Maritime Expeditions (1405–1433)

The vigor of the early Ming was spectacularly demonstrated by seven great maritime expeditions sent out by imperial command under a Muslim eunuch named Zheng He (Cheng Ho, 1371–1433). The first of these voyages included 27,800 men, 62 or 63 large ships, and 255 smaller vessels, and the third was of similar dimensions. Their destinations included not only various areas of Southeast Asia but also the Indian Ocean, Arabia, and the east coast of Africa. The voyages were unique in their scope and official sponsorship, but the technology which made them possible had previously been employed in private ventures not considered worth recording by official historians. Thus it is interesting to observe that on their first voyage the expedition had dealings with Chinese settlers in Sumatra. Reportedly they also defeated a Chinese "pirate" in those waters, killing 5000 men and bringing the leader back for execution in Beijing.

The Chinese sources emphasize that the reason for launching these expeditions was Chengzu's desire to locate the nephew from whom he had seized the throne but who had eluded capture. More broadly they may be viewed as an aspect of early Ming military and political assertiveness, for they effectively demonstrated Chinese power and brought tributary envoys to the Ming court, for example, the King of Borneo who died in China in 1408 and was buried outside Nanjing, where his grave can still be seen. It is recorded that as a result of the fourth voyage, 19 countries sent tribute.

Foreign envoys coming to render submission enhanced the court's glory and prestige. Also forthcoming from foreign lands were exotic objects and animals. The emperor was particularly delighted by giraffes, represented in Beijing as auspicious "qilin" ("ch'i-lin")," or "unicorns." Most probably trade was also a motive for the voyages; we know that ships of the first voyage carried silk and embroideries on board. And trade was a major factor in inducing foreign lands to send envoys to China. On the Chinese side, however, the Ming never looked upon trade as something intrinsically worthwhile.

From the official Chinese point of view, these expeditions did not have an economic rationale. Furthermore, their eunuch leadership did not win them friends among Confucian officials. When Chengzu died, they lost an enthusiastic supporter, although his successor Xuanzong (r. 1426–35) did send out one last expedition. Just as the expeditions can be seen as part of a general early Ming assertiveness toward the rest of the world, their abandonment forms part of a broader pattern as the dynasty trimmed its ambitions and abandoned an attempt to subdue Vietnam (1426). Another incentive for maintaining an ocean navy was removed with the completion, in 1417, of a system of locks which maintained a waterlevel sufficiently high to allow the grain vessels supplying the capital to use the Grand Canal throughout the year. No longer was the capital dependent on sea transport about six months a year. Furthermore, the crucial land frontier once again demanded military attention: fighting Mongols was a vital enterprise, whereas ocean expeditions were a luxury.

In the absence of a strong naval effort, Chinese waters became the domain of pirates and smugglers, a situation not ameliorated by the dynasty's regulations to control and curb maritime trade. For example, already during the Yongle period, the Japanese had been officially limited to one tribute mission every ten years, composed of only two ships with a maximum of 200 men (later raised to 300) to call at Ningbo (Zhejiang province). These regulations were not always enforced, for private Chinese interests as well as the Japanese stood to profit by the trade conducted on these occasions. But the regulations illustrate the dynasty's negative attitude toward relations with maritime countries.

The Early Middle Period (1425–1505)

The 75 years of the Early Middle Ming were generally a period of peace, stability, and prosperity, under emperors less ambitious for military glory and personal power than Taizu and Chengzu. It was Xuanzong who abandoned the Ming effort to control Annam. However, he did lead one expedition against Mongol raiders in the North. The Mongols were particularly troublesome under his successor, Yingzong (Ying-tsung) whom they actually captured and held prisoner for a year. As a result Yingzong had two reign periods (Zhengtong 1436–49, and Tianshun, 1457–64) — after his release from the Mongols, he spent six and a half years in confinement in a palace in the capital while his brother held the throne. In the 1460s and 1470s there was a revival of Chinese military strength. The Great Wall was strengthened and extended for 600 miles to protect the northern border of Shaanxi. Although it goes back to the third century B.C., the wall as it stands today owes much of its imposing mass and extent to the Ming.

Domestically, eunuch influence increased. Taizu had warned against giving eunuchs positions of responsibility, but under the third emperor Zheng He was but one of a number of capable eunuchs in the emperor's service. Xuanzong went a step further when he established a school for eunuchs, but this did not prevent the continuing hostility of Confucian officials, who seem to have criticized even honest and able eunuchs as a matter of principle. Eunuchs enjoyed unique opportunities for informal, relaxed conversation with emperors who often turned to them for advice or, as in the case of Zheng He, entrusted them with important missions.

To preserve himself from drowning in the flood of official business, Xuanzong also selected certain ministers to screen memorials, draft edicts, and the like. This informal group of two to six officials became increasingly influential during the last quarter of the fifteenth century and became known as the Grand Secretariat.

Ming emperors generally believed in doing things on a grand scale. For example, in 1425 the court reportedly had 6,300 cooks in its employ, preparing meals not only for the considerable palace population but also for government officials on set occasions. Xuanzong had a special taste for Korean food and sent eunuchs to Korea to bring back, among other things, virgins, eunuchs, and female cooks. He also took an active interest in the arts and was probably the only emperor after Huizong (Hui-tsung) of the Song to be a gifted painter and poet. Among the noted painters who served for a time at his court was the flower and bird specialist Bian Wenzhi (Pien Wen-chih, ca. 1356–1428). Another famous painter was Dai Jin (Tai Chin, 1388–1462), who worked in the Ma-Xia tradition of the Southern Song. His artistic talents did not, however, save him from dismissal when he painted the coat of a fisherman red, a color reserved for the garments of officials. Returning to his native Zhejiang, he became a leader in what was known as the Zhe (Che) school of painting.

Xuanzong's reign is also known for its bronzes and especially for its porcelain. Under the Ming, private kilns continued to produce ceramics in traditional styles, but it was the imperial kilns, turning out vast quantities of vessels in many different shapes, which stood at the forefront of technical and artistic development. Whereas the Yongle period of Emperor Chengzu is noted for its white porcelain, by Xuanzong's reign blue-and-white ware had come into vogue and reached its classic peak (see Figure 8-2). During the following reign the imperial kilns enjoyed a monopoly of blue-and-white porcelain, protected by an order prohibiting its private sale. But this could not be maintained for very long. Ming blue-and-white had such appeal that it soon stimulated imitation, and it went on to win admiration not only in East Asia but in such distant lands as Persia and Holland. The porcelain of each reign had its own characteristics. During the fifteenth century, its color range was broadened when white porcelains were decorated by painting them with various enamel colors. The five-colored enamels made during the reign of Emperor Xianzong (Hsien-tsung, r. 1465–88) are particularly prized.

Figure 8-2   Plate with bird decoration. Blue-and-white porcelain, Early Ming, probably Xuande, diam. 50.2 cm.

The Early Middle period came to an end with the death of Xiaozong (Hsiao-tsung, r. 1488–1505), a model of Confucian propriety and a rare monogamist among the Ming emperors. His was generally a calm reign, but after more than 130 years, the dynasty was beginning to show signs of deterioration. The trends which would trouble government during the sixteenth century were already at work beneath the surface.

The Later Middle Period (1506–1590)

This period covers three reigns and the beginnings of a fourth. It was a time when government suffered from inadequate imperial leadership, but the political system still showed a capacity for reform. The first of these emperors, reigning from 1506 to 1521, paid no attention to government but devoted his time and energy to sports, entertainments, sex, and drink. Under the second (1522–67), the arts flourished but government did not. The emperor became engrossed in increasingly longer Daoist ceremonies. By the end of his reign, there were ceremonies which continued for twelve or thirteen days and nights. The third emperor, Muzong (Mu-tsung, r. 1567–72), reigned for only five years, during which he paid more attention to private pleasures than to public business. The fourth emperor, Shenzong (Shen-tsung, r. 1573–1620), was a minor during the period under consideration here. Throughout the Later Middle period Grand Secretaries and eunuchs wielded great power.

A decline in government honesty and efficiency was apparent both in the capital and in local government. On the district level, the gentry increasingly abused their local power and influence even as they absented themselves from their holdings, for many had moved to cities and towns. Then, as now, the lure of social, cultural, political, and economic opportunities was a major attraction of urban life. As absentee landlords, they often succumbed to the temptation to charge high rents, allocate taxes unfairly, charge exhorbitant interest on mortgage loans, and so on. Class differentiation increased, and a dangerous cleavage developed between those who owned and those who worked the land. Hostilities built up, hostilities which found expression in market disturbances, riots, tenant uprisings, and finally rebellions. Yet, some gentry lineages, sobered by these events, mended their ways, and returning to the frugality enjoined on them by ancestral admonitions, and were able to survive the dynasty and prosper.

Inequities in taxation hurt the government as well as small peasants, but there were also reformers. Most notable was Hai Rui (Hai Jui, 1513–87) who had a reputation for uprightness, courage, and concern for the common people. As a magistrate he reassessed the land to make taxes more equitable, wiped out corruption so effectively that government clerks were reduced to poverty, and himself led a life of exemplary frugality. His refusal to toady to his superiors earned him powerful enemies, and he came close to losing his life when he submitted a scathing memorial that, among other things, charged the emperor with neglect of government and excessive indulgence in Daoist ceremonies. During the Ming one did not denounce an emperor with impunity: in prison Hai Rui was tortured and condemned to death by strangulation. He was saved only by the death of the emperor. On his release from prison he resumed his career but was forced into retirement when he offended powerful families by forcing them to return lands they had seized illegally. Late in life, in 1585, he was recalled to office, and after he died he was idealized as the perfect official incarnate. About four centuries later, in the 1960s, Hai Rui became the focus of a major controversy (see Chapter 16).

A very different kind of reformer was Zhang Juzheng (Chang Chü-cheng, 1525–82), who dominated government during the reign of Muzong and for another ten years during Shenzong's minority. He has been described as a Confucian Legalist, for he was convinced that strong and strict government was ultimately for the people's benefit. Efficiency and control were the hallmarks of his policy. Among his achievements were a repair of the Grand Canal, reform of the courier system, new regulations designed to strengthen central control over provincial officials, and a reduction in the total number of officials. He eliminated eunuch influence from the Six Ministries, prevented censors from abusing their authority, and tried to reform the provincial schools.

Zhang was also troubled by what was happening in the civil service examinations. Ever since Taizu had lent imperial favor to an essay form composed of eight rigidly stipulated sections and known as the "eight-legged essay," the tendency had increasingly been to judge papers on the basis of form rather than content. This eased the task of the examination readers but threatened to turn the examinations into mechanical exercises. Zhang, who served as an examiner in 1571, wanted the questions to emphasize current problems and the answers to be graded on content. But in his contempt for "empty" theorizing, he went beyond this and ordered the suppression of private academies. These he also considered undesirable, as potential breeding grounds for political associations and as holders of tax-exempt land. However, the decree banning academies (1579) did little permanent damage to these institutions.

To improve government finances, Zhang directed an all-China land survey and also extended to the whole country the "single whip method of taxation," previously tried out in Zhejiang and Fujian. This replaced the Two Tax System first instituted during the Tang. Implementation remained incomplete, but, in principle, the new method provided for the consolidation of tax obligations into a single annual bill. Another important innovation was the use of silver as the value base for tax assessment. The silver tael (ounce) remained the standard monetary unit into the twentieth century.

Zhang Juzheng made many enemies. They had their revenge after his death, when his family property was confiscated and his sons were tortured. But he left the regime in sound financial condition at a time when it was sustaining heavy military expenditures, fighting Mongol invasions between 1550 and 1570 and maintaining military preparedness thereafter. The government's fiscal health at this time reflected the general economic strength of sixteenth-century China.

The Economy

Peace and stability made for prosperity. During the first century of the Ming, northern agriculture was rehabilitated, but the South remained the most populous and prosperous region. The gradual spread of superior strains of rice, which had begun during the Song, permitted a steady increase in China's population, which rose from 65–80 million in the fourteenth century to about 150 million by the end of the sixteenth. At the same time the introduction in the sixteenth century of new crops from the Americas laid a foundation for still further population increases which were to follow in the Qing.

Ming economic developments may have been less dramatic than those of the Song. It is difficult to find major breakthroughs or radically new technologies or types of industries, but change was so substantial that scholars speak of a "second commercial revolution." Notably there was an increase in interregional trade in staples as well as an increase in the growing of cash crops, most notably cotton in the Yangzi Delta, which now became an importer of grains. There was increased use of money, and participation in an impersonal market influenced the behavior of rich and poor even as the growth of commerce increased class differentiation. Nourished by trade, such great lower Yangzi cities as Nanjing, Suzhou, and Hangzhou prospered. Among the important industries of the period were the porcelain and ceramic kilns centered in Jiangxi, the cotton manufacture of Nanjing, and the silk weaving in Suzhou. Hebei remained the center of iron manufacture, and Anhui was known for its dye works. Indigo and sugar cane, along with cotton, were important cash crops grown for the market. A well-known seventeenth-century technical manual, *Creations of Man and Nature*, offers impressive evidence of the inventiveness of Chinese craftsmen within the parameters of their technical and intellectual tradition.

Literacy

Another indication of prosperity was an increase in literacy, not only among the well-educated and ambitious but also among the more humble and less sophisticated. Bookshops did a brisk business. Among the best sellers were collections of model examination papers used by candidates to cram for tests. They also sold encyclopedias, colored prints, novels, collections of short stories, guides that explained the classics in simple language, and books of moral instruction illustrated with tales of wrong-doing and retribution.

The audience for wood block prints was even wider than that for books. Although it was the Japanese who developed the colored wood block print to its highest aesthetic form, the colored print was originated in China and achieved its greatest excellence there in the seventeenth century. The first colored print formed the frontispiece of a Chinese Buddhist sutra and is dated 1346. More colorful and less spiritual were the five-color illustrations of Ming erotica.

There were also, during the Ming, educated men who had failed to advance through the examination system and who, turning to literary careers, helped preserve the popular arts. Two such men were Feng Menglong (Feng Meng-lung, 1574–1646) and Ling Mengqi (Ling Meng-ch'i, 1580–1664), authors of widely read anthologies of short stories. Both men were also dramatists and scholars. Feng's interests ranged particularly wide; for instance, he wrote books on gambling as well as on Confucianism. But he is most famous for publishing *Stories, Old and New*, three collections of colloquial short stories based on the promptbooks of the storytellers, who had formed part of the urban entertainment scene at least as far back as Southern Song Hangzhou. Liu Wu-chi's description of the subject matter of Feng's stories reveals their diversity:

> Their range includes: quasi-historical tales of kings and generals, faithful friends and filial sons; romantic yarns of strange lands and peoples; supernatural stories of marvels and prodigies, spirits and ghosts, Buddhist monks and Daoist immortals; realistic stories of scandals in monastic establishments; daring exploits of brigands and thieves; murders, lawsuits, and court trials; domestic tragedies and bloody revenges; social comedies and family reunions.[4]

Ling, son of a noted publisher and scholar, rewrote and retold the stories in the two collections he published, both entitled *Striking the Table in Amazement at the Wonders*.

The Novel

The novel, like the short story, only gradually freed itself from its antecedents in the oral tradition of storytelling, eliminating extraneous material and refining crudities. In composition it remained essentially episodic, and Chinese novels often include poems. Despite the literary excellence and subtlety of works written by and for the educated elite and the interest they stimulated among late Ming scholars, in the end even the greatest novels did not gain Confucian legitimacy as high literature. In Japan the novel was an honored part of literary culture, but in China reading a novel was a surreptitious pleasure indulged in by students when their teacher was not looking — or vice versa. Many novels of the Ming period retold old stories or embellished historical episodes; others were adventure stories, serious or comic; and still others were pornographic. The four major novels that have come down to us from the Ming are *The Romance of the Three Kingdoms*, *The Water Margin* (translated also as *All Men Are Brothers*), *Journey to the West*, and *The Golden Lotus*.

The Romance of the Three Kingdoms (Sanguozhi yenyi, San kuo chih yen i) was first published in 1522, although it may have been written in the late Yuan. It is a fictionalized account of the conflict between Wei, Wu, and Shu, the three states which divided China in the third century A.D. In its pages the gifted but badly flawed character of Cao Cao (Ts'ao Ts'ao), the martial heroics of Guan Yu (Kuan Yü), and the strategic genius and devoted loyalty of Zhuge Liang (Chu-ko Liang) come vividly alive. It is no wonder that ordinary people in China formed many of their perceptions of historical figures from this and other novels. This literature was also popular in Korea and Japan where *The Romance of the Three Kingdoms* was widely read and much loved.

A different kind of history supplied the materials for *The Water Margin (Shuihuzhuan, Shui-hu chuan)*, which was based on a Yuan play. It is set in the closing years of the Northern Song and recounts the deeds of 108 bandit heroes, men driven by the cruel corruption of a decadent government to take justice into their own hands, outlaws who champion the oppressed and avenge the wronged. Numerous episodes, rendered in everyday speech, tell of feats of strength and daring, clever stratagems, and acts of savage but righteous vengeance. The novel's theme did not endear it to the political authorities, and during the Qing dynasty it was officially proscribed. However, it continued to be sold under the counter and enjoyed a broad readership. Among the eminent twentieth-century leaders who read it with profit as well as delight was the young Mao Zedong (Mao Tse-tung).

The third major Ming novel, *Journey to the West (Xiyuji, Hsi-yu chi, translated also as Monkey)*, first published in 1592, describes the trip to India of the Tang monk Xuanzang (Hsüan-tsang). The trip is transformed into a fantastic journey, a heroic pilgrimage, and a tale of delightful satire and high comedy. Monkey is one of three supernatural disciples assigned by Buddha to accompany the priest and protect him from the monsters and demons that threaten him along the way. Many times Monkey saves the day, for he is endowed with penetrating, although mischievous and restless, intelligence and has acquired many magical gifts: he can somersault through the air for leagues with the greatest of ease, has the power to change into all kinds of shapes, and can transform his body hairs into a myriad of monkeys. Over his ear he wears a pin, which becomes an enormous iron cudgel when needed. The novel can be enjoyed as sheer fantasy, or for its satirical accounts of the bureaucratic organization of Heaven and the underworld, or as a religious allegory.

Although the authors of these novels are believed known, the men named are either obscure or the attribution itself is in doubt. The question of authorship of the fourth great Ming novel, *Qinpingmei (Chin p'ing mei)*, translated as *The Golden Lotus*, is even more obscure, and for good reason, since no respectable gentleman would have wanted his name linked to an erotic novel condemned by the Chinese as pornographic. In its 100 chapters, *Qinpingmei* gives a detailed account of the dissipations of a wealthy lecher. It offers a naturalistic tableau of amorous intrigues within the household and beyond, of drinking parties and sumptuous feasts, and portraits of go-betweens and fortunetellers, doctors and mendicants, singing girls and venal officials, and so on. After a life of sex without love, the hero, reduced to an empty shell, meets a fitting death, and the novel rolls on for another 20 chapters to recount the unraveling of the household.

Ming Drama

In the Ming, drama in the Southern style reached its peak. It differed from the Northern drama (discussed in the preceding chapter) in language, form, and music. Southern plays were much longer, running to forty and more scenes, and the songs, accompanied by the bamboo flute, were assigned to choruses as well as to the leading players. The result has been described as an "undulating cavalcade"[5] composed of scenes varying in length, number of players, and importance. Because of the length of the plays and the familiarity of the audience with their plots, performances of Ming drama, as of Japanese Nō., came to feature selected scenes from a number of plays rather than playing one all the way through. The authors were often sophisticated literary men, writing as much for their peers as for the wider public, at times more concerned to achieve literary excellence than to create effective theater. Ming playwrights were prolific: some 1,200 titles are still known.

Acknowledged as the greatest Ming playwright was Tang Xienzu (T'ang Hsien-tsu, 1550–1616), who earned a jinshi (chin-shih) degree but had a frustrating official career. In his *The Dream of Han Tan* a young man falls asleep as he is trying to prepare a meal of millet grain. He then sees his whole life in a dream: he comes in first in the *jinshi* examination, performs great deeds, is slandered and condemned to death, cleared and promoted. As he is about to die, he wakes up to discover that the millet on the stove is nearly ready to eat. This makes him realize that life itself passes as rapidly as a dream. Tang wrote three other dream plays, and a dream also features importantly in his most admired work, *The Peony Pavilion*. This long play of fifty-five scenes centers on a love so strong that it is able to bring the dead back to life.

Other well-known Ming dreams were written on the theme of love. A perennial favorite was the disastrous love of the Tang emperor Xuanzong (Hsüan-tsung) for Yang Gueifei (Yang Kuei-fei). The repertoire also contained plays on more contemporary matters. One of the last Southern masterpieces was *The Peach Blossom Fan*, completed in 1699 and depicting the end of the Ming half a century earlier. In it the conflict between traitorous villains and loyal heroes is intertwined with the story of the love shared by a loyal young scholar and a virtuous courtesan. Southern dramas continued to be performed and written, but toward the end of the eighteenth century there arose a new form of theater, based more broadly on popular taste. This was Peking Drama, famed for its actors and singers more than for its writers. Its repertoire consists largely of adaptations of older works.

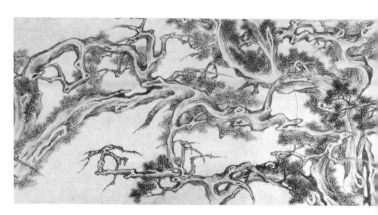

Figure 8-3   Wen Zhengming, *The Seven Junipers of Changshu.* Section of hand-scroll, ink on paper, 28.8 cm high; total length, 362 cm.

Painting

The most notable center for painting in the Later Middle Ming was Suzhou, where the Wu school flourished ca. 1460–1560. Suzhou was a prosperous city, a financial and commercial community located near the juncture of the Grand Canal and the Yangzi River. A great cultural center famed for its poetry, painting, calligraphy, and drama, it became a place of refuge for sophisticated people fleeing the uncertainties of political life, a place where the literati could pursue their own interests in peace, the home of the gentleman cultivating his artistic talents without regard for money or career. It was famous, too, for its gardens, conceived and designed as miniature replicas of vast nature.

Designations like "Zhe school" and "Wu school" are Chinese classifications based on the artist's residence, style, and/or social status. Unfortunately for the modern student, these three categories did not always coincide: not all amateurs resided in Suzhou; some professionals adopted "amateur" styles, and so forth. However, in stylistic terms, the Zhe school declined in the sixteenth century. Its most characteristic contribution to Chinese art was the continuation of Southern Song academic painting. For fresh departures one must turn to Suzhou.

The man who stood at the beginning of the Wu tradition was Shen Zhou (Shen Chou, 1427–1509), who was also a talented poet and calligrapher. He lived in comfort on an estate about ten miles out of town and loved to paint the landscape of Suzhou. Although deeply influenced by Yuan painting, he gradually developed a style of his own that conveyed a genial warmth and a sense of ease and naturalness.

Wen Zhengming (Wen Cheng-ming, 1470–1559) studied painting under Shen Zhou and, like his master, was a versatile scholar. He admired and frequently followed the model of Zhao Mengfu, the great Yuan painter, but he was too talented an artist to follow one model only. Nor did he spend a lifetime perfecting a single style or refining a single vision. Instead he worked in many different manners during his long and productive life. Some of his paintings

contain references to painting styles going back to the Tang, styles previously revived during the Southern Song and the Yuan. Such multiple historical references were among the qualities most admired in his work by Ming and later connoisseurs.

It is not possible to illustrate the work of an artist like Wen Zhengming with a single "representative" painting, but *The Seven Junipers of Changshu* is one of his most distinctive and powerful (see Figure 8-3). Wen's inscription states that he was copying Zhao Mengfu, but this is "copying" at its most creative, for what it shares with the Yuan painter is the power of its abstraction and the expressiveness of its brushwork. It also shares a love for the old: the trees were originally planted in A.D. 500, and four were replaced in the eleventh century. But here the accent is not on venerable age, but on strength and an explosive vitality that cannot be contained by the edges of the paper. In the artist's own rhapsody *(fu)*, which he added to his painting, he invites the viewer on a flight of the imagination:

> Like creaking ropes the junipers dance to the wail of the wind, conjuring up a thousand images: split horns and blunted claws, the wrestling of the dragon with the tiger, great whales rolling in the deep, and giant birds who swoop down on their prey. And now, like ghosts, they vanish, now reappear, vast entangled forms.[6]

Ming Thought: Wang Yangming and Others

Like Wen Zhengming's junipers, Ming thought could not be confined within the framework intended for it, and it was a contemporary of Wen's by the name of Wang Yangming (Wang Shouren or Wang Shou-jen, 1472–1529) who opened up new intellectual vistas within Neo-Confucianism. Unlike the gentlemen-painters of Suzhou, Wang had a very active official career. At its low point he suffered two months in prison and a beating of 40 strokes followed by exile in Gueizhou, but he subsequently served with great courage and distinction not only as a civil administrator but also as a military commander rendering outstanding service by suppressing rebels.

Ming thinkers had to cope with the problems of living a Confucian life in a world which remained stubbornly un-Confucian. Despite the state's official support for Confucianism, Chinese government and society were as far from resembling the Confucian ideal as ever. How was one to live a proper life in a society that was not right and proper, amid the venality of officials, the social changes induced by economic expansion, and the continuing politicization of government administration?

Ming intellectuals also had to redefine the role of the educated scholar-official-literati in Chinese society. The growth of commerce created a new prosperity, new sources of power, and, de facto, new value systems. At the same time, the spread of literacy undercut the monopoly of classical thought, classical culture, and the status of those with a classical education. Moreover, there was a sense that in a postclassical age perhaps the only way the scholar could make a personal contribution was through specialization—a marked departure from the traditional aim of universal knowledge.

In an effort to define their personal and social roles, the educated were forced to question the nature of their own nature:

> Was is static or dynamic, metaphysical or physical, an abstract ideal or an active force, a moral norm or a trans-moral perfection? . . . How was the individual to understand that nature in relation to his actual self and his society? [7]

The issue at stake was not purely intellectual. It involved a quest not only for knowledge but also for wisdom and a striving for sagehood. For Wang Yangming the essential insight came suddenly, at the age of 36 after a period of intense thought while he was in exile in Gueizhou. His experience has often been likened to the sudden enlightenment sought by Chan Buddhists.

Like Lu Jiuyuan (Lu Chiu-yüan), Wang Yangming identified human nature with the mind-heart (xin, hsin), which he in turn identified with principle (li). For Wang, as for Lu, li alone exists. Everyone is endowed with goodness and has an innate capacity to know good (liangzhi, liang-chih). Self-perfection consists in "extending" this capacity to the utmost. Everyone can attain perfection because all are endowed with the gold of sagehood. People may differ quantitatively in their abilities, but qualitatively they are the same, just as the gold in a small coin is in no way inferior to that in a large one. Thus Wang Yangming took it very calmly when a disciple reported that he had gone out for a walk and found the street full of sages. That was only to be expected. However, there is need for strenuous effort to refine the gold by eliminating the dross, that is, "selfish desires." Sagehood does not come easily.

External sources of doctrinal authority, including the classics and the words of the sages, have only a secondary, accessory function. According to Wang Yangming, "If words are examined in the mind and found to be wrong, although they have come from the mouth of Confucius, I dare not accept them as correct." [8] Conversely, if the mind finds them correct, it does not matter if the words have been uttered by ordinary folk. The truth is in and of the mind. It remains one whole because the mind and *li* are universal.

As is the case for all Neo-Confucians, the truth that concerns Wang Yangming is at once metaphysical and moral. Furthermore, it is not to be grasped by abstract intellectualization but must be lived. What is true of sensory knowledge holds for all knowledge: a person can no more know filial piety without practicing it than he can know the smell of an odor or understand pain without experiencing them. Knowing and acting are not only inseparable, they are two dimensions of a single process: "Knowledge in its genuine and earnest aspect is action, and action in its intelligent and discriminating aspect is knowledge." [9] A man may discourse with great erudition and subtlety on filiality, but it is his conduct which will reveal his depth of understanding. To employ a modern example, a person who "knows" smoking is bad for him but persists in the habit reveals that he does not really "know" this with his whole being. A perfectly integrated personality is, of course, one of the marks of the sage.

Wang Yangming had an abiding influence because he spoke to some of the persistent concerns of East Asian thinkers and activists. One may, for example, detect in Mao Zedong's discussions of the relationship between theory and practice overtones of the Ming philosopher's insistence on the unity of knowledge and action. Another reason for his influence is that he was the kind of thinker who opens many doors rather than being a rigid systematizer. The thought of the Late Ming can best be understood as developing out of some of the ideas present in his own teachings as well as in reaction to some of his views.

Ming Thought after Wang Yangming

Some of Wang Yangming's followers and disciples led courageous but quite conventional lives of public service, self-cultivation, and teaching, but others developed the more radical implications of his thought. Thus Wang Yangming taught that the mind in itself is above distinctions of good and evil, an idea with a strong Buddhist flavor and compatible with Daoist ideas. The tendency to combine Confucianism, Buddhism, and Daoism was a very old one and attracted a good many Ming intellectuals. It was present in Wang Yangming but was carried further by Wang Ji (Wang Chi, 1498–1585), who freely employed Buddhist and Daoist terms and valued Daoist techniques of breath control. However, he remained a Confucian in his rejection of empty abstract speculation and in his moral values.

Wang Ji and Wang Gen (Wang Ken, 1483–1541) are considered the founders of the Taizhou branch of Wang Yangming's teaching, named after Wang Gen's native prefecture where he established a school. Wang Gen was born into a family of salt producers and remained a commoner throughout his life. In 1552 his enthusiasm for the teachings of the sage prompted him to build himself a cart such as he imagined Confucius to have used. He then rode in it to Beijing to present a memorial. He attracted much attention in the capital until persuaded by embarrassed fellow disciples of Wang Yangming to return south. He remained a vigorous and fervent popular teacher, attracting a good many commoners as students.

In their personal conduct as well as in their teachings, the more radical followers of Wang Yangming stretched the parameters of Confucianism to the utmost and went beyond the limits tolerated by the state. He Xinyin (Ho Hsin-yin, 1517–79) was a courageous defender of free discussion in the academies and so devoted to all humanity that he turned against the family as a restrictive, selfish, exclusive institution. His unorthodox ideas, courageous personal conduct, and reputation as a troublemaker eventually helped land him in prison, where he died after being beaten. Another controversial figure was Li Zhi (Li Chih, 1527–1602), who carried the individualism implicit in Wang Yangming's philosophy to the point of defending selfishness. A thorough nonconformist, he denounced conventional scholars who, he claimed, lacked an authentic commitment to the core values of Confucianism. In 1588 Li Zhi shaved his head and became (at least in appearance) a Buddhist monk. But he continued to offend the literati; in 1590 local gentry organized a mob that demolished the temple where Li was staying. Imprisoned in 1602, he committed suicide. Until a modern revival of interest in his ideas, he was best known as an editor of The Water Margin, and the novel's opposition to the establishment accords very well with Li's own attitudes.

An important trend in the Late Ming was toward syncrecism both in religious movements and in scholarly writings. For example, Jiao Hong (Chiao Hung, ca. 1548–1620) went beyond earlier theorists who had considered Confucianism, Buddhism, and Daoism as independent and complementary. Instead he saw the three teachings as forming a single teaching so that each could help explain the others.

The significance of He, Li, and Jiao may lie not so much in their intellectual influence, which was limited, but rather in demonstrating the limits to which Ming thought could be stretched. Li Zhi shocked not only members of the official establishment but also activist Confucians, who were dismayed by the radical subjectivism of this line of thought and appalled by the Buddhistic notion that human nature was beyond good and evil. Such earnest Confucians also saw it as their duty to protest forcefully against political abuses and to object against such un-Confucian conduct as the refusal of Zhang Juzheng (Chang Chü-cheng) to retire from office to observe mourning on the death of his father. Early in the seventeenth century, the Donglin (Tung-lin) Academy, founded in 1604 in Wu Xi northwest of Suzhou, became a center for such "pure criticism," which cost many Donglin men their lives. Conflict between pro-Donglin and anti-Donglin factions lasted through the final 30 years of the dynasty, but before considering these political events, it is appropriate to turn to another area of activity where Wang Yangming's dictum concerning the unity of knowledge and action was applied: the world of art.

Dong Qichang and Late Ming Painting

Dong Qichang (Tung Ch'i-ch'ang, 1555 – 1636) was a major painter and callig-rapher, the leading connoisseur of his generation, and China's foremost art historian. Many of the ideas of Dong and his circle were not new, but he gave them their final authoritative expression. The key to his analysis was the division of painters into Northern and Southern schools resembling the Northern and Southern branches of Chan Buddhism. The assignment of a painter into one group or the other was not based on geography but on the man's social standing and on his style. A "Northern" painter was defined as a professional who stressed technical excellence and fine craftsmanship to pro-duce handsome paintings of maximum visual appeal. In contrast "Southern" painters were literati, men of wide reading and profound learning for whom painting was an experience of self-expression, a chance to allow their genius and sensibility free play, much as in calligraphy. Dong traced these two lines all the way back to the Tang and cast Wang Wei as the founder of the "South-ern" tradition. He also included painters of his own dynasty in his analysis. Furthermore, Dong and his friends affirmed their affiliation with the "South-ern" tradition.

Self-indentification with a tradition of amateurism did not preclude the study of earlier masters. Dong himself was influenced in calligraphy by Zhao Mengfu and Wen Zhengming, and in painting he greatly admired the great masters of the Yuan. But he emphasized the need to "unlearn," and a painting such as his picture of the Qingbian (Ch'ing-pien) Mountains (see Figure 8-4) has only a faint resemblance to its purported tenth-century model. Nor is there in this painting any desire to represent mountains as they actually appear to the eye or to define the depth relationships between them by clearly placing them one behind the other. Natural forms are tilted, compressed, and juxta-posed, not to represent nature but to emphasize the painting's formal organi-zation and the interplay of light and dark. The effect of Dong's theories and art on seventeenth-century painting is suggested by Wang Yuanqi (Wang Yüan-ch'i, see Chapter 10), who described Dong as having "cleansed the cobwebs from landscape painting in one sweep.[10]

In the final years of the Ming there were artists painting in a number of different styles, many playing on earlier modes. A painter who took as his point of departure the classic Song landscape but turned it into an expression of his own fantastic imagination was Wu Bin (Wu Pin, ca. 1568 – 1626): Figure 8-5 shows a landscape such as never was nor ever could be. As James Cahill has observed, "Solids evaporate into space, ambiguous definitions of surface unsettle the eye as it moves over them, and the towering construction of spires and cliffs, like the creation of some titanic, demented sculptor, balances on an absurdly narrow base."[11] Paintings such as this suggest both some of the potentialities and some of the dangers inherent in Ming individualism. In the seventeenth century the dynasty, like the painting, found itself balanced on too narrow a base.

Figure 8-4   Dong Qichang,
The Qingbian Mountain.
Hanging scroll, ink on paper,
dated 1617, 225 cm × 67 cm.

Figure 8-5   Wu Bin,
Landscape. Hanging scroll,
ink and light colors on paper,
306.5 cm × 98.5 cm.

Late Ming Government (1590–1644)

A conspicuous feature of the last 50 years of the dynasty was the inadequacy of its emperors. When Zhang Juzheng died in 1582, Emperor Shenzong, then not quite 19, saw to it that during his reign no minister would again dominate the government, but soon the emperor himself ceased to bother very much with government. From 1589 to 1615, a period of more than 25 years, he did not hold a single general audience, and from 1590 to his death in 1620, he only conducted personal interviews with Grand Secretaries five times. Nor, except on matters of taxation and defense, did he respond to memorials. As a result much government business was left undone. He was particularly remiss in personnel matters. By the end of his reign, not only were the offices in the capital seriously understaffed, but it has been estimated that as many as half of the prefectural and district posts were also unfilled. Whereas at the start he had punished officials who criticized him in their memorials, during the last 20 years he largely ignored even them. Some high officials withdrew from their posts without authorization — they too were ignored.

The emperor did take an interest in military matters. From the 1580s on there was fighting in the southwest against various tribal peoples as well as against the Thais and especially against the Burmese. In the 1590s there were campaigns in Inner Mongolia, and large Ming armies fought a Japanese invasion of Korea. These military actions were generally successful but enormously expensive. Also costly but not as successful was the Ming military effort in Manchuria, where the Manchu chief Nurhaci founded a state and fought the Ming to a draw (see Chapter 10).

Emperor Xizong (Hsi-tsung, r. 1620–27) was peculiar even by Late Ming standards. He "did not have sufficient leisure to learn to write" [12] but spent all his time on carpentry, creating many pieces of fine furniture, which he lacquered himself. Factionalism, which in the absence of strong imperial leadership had flourished under Shenzong, now turned vicious, as a very capable and equally unscrupulous eunuch, Wei Zhongxian (Wei Chung-hsien, 1568–1627), gained power due to his influence over the emperor. Wei purged all opponents, foremost among them the members of the Donglin faction, six of whom died in prison after torture. One of these men, Zuo Guangdou (Tso Kuang-tou), in his notes to his sons left vivid descriptions of agonizing pain and suffering, which he interlaced with exclamations of his fervent devotion to the emperor, for example, "my body belongs to my ruler-father." [13] Like He Xinyin and Li Zhi, Zuo demonstrated his Confucian selflessness even to the point of death, but his martyrdom, unlike theirs, testifies to the persuasiveness of a kind of Confucian authoritarianism in which even a carpenter-emperor could command the loyalty others might think due, if at all, only to a sage. To the end, the dynasty retained the loyalty of most of its officials. A remarkable group of men, comparable to the Song loyalists, remained faithful to the dynasty even after it had come to an end.

Wei Zhongxian was not content with the realities of power but was also hungry for public recognition. He heaped honors on himself and even had a nephew take the emperor's place in performing sacrifices in the imperial temple. He also encouraged a movement to have temples housing his image built throughout China. But he did not survive Emperor Xizong for long, and the temples perished shortly after the man. The succeeding emperor, Sizong (Ssu-tsung, r. 1627–44), attempted reform during his reign, but the lack of a consistent policy is suggested by the high turnover of the regime's highest officials: from 1621 to 1644 the presidents of the Six Ministries were changed 116 times.

Bureaucratic infighting and corruption was something the dynasty could no longer afford, for during the reign of Shenzong the earlier fiscal surplus had been turned into a mounting deficit. But the trouble went deeper:

> The Ming fiscal administration was in essence built on the foundation of a grain economy. With its diversified rates and measurements, self-supporting institutions, regional and departmental self-sufficiency, divided budget, separate channels of cash flow, numerous material and *corvée* labor impositions, and local tax captains, the fiscal machinery was grossly unfit for a new monetary economy. . . . However, [these unsatisfactory features of the Ming fiscal administration] would not have been so appallingly evident had not the wide circulation of silver thoroughly changed the nation's economic outlook. The archaic fiscal structure became more outdated than ever because it was set against the background of a mobile and expanding economy.[14]

The wide circulation of silver also left China vulnerable to inflation when silver imports, largely from Manila, were interrupted.

Furthermore, the delicate balance between the central government and the local elite was upset when the dynasty made too many concessions to the gentry. Too much was given away, too many fields were removed from the tax rolls. Large landowners were able to find tax-shelters through various manipulations, and only peasant freeholders remained to pay taxes. Locally resentment against the gentry grew, while the shortage of funds forced the dynasty to neglect vital public works. Grain stored for emergency use was sold off. Even the postal system was shut down. Finally, the regime failed to pay even its most strategically placed troops: when the end came, the capital garrison had not been paid for five months.

Military deserters and dismissed postal employees were among those who took the lead in forming the outlaw gangs that appeared first in Northern Shaanxi and then spread from there. As they grew in size and strength, they progressed from disorganized raiding to more ambitious objectives. Two groups emerged as most powerful. One established itself in Sichuan and was led by Zhang Xianzhong (Chang Hsien-chung, ca. 1605–47), a leader notorious for his brutality. The other was led by Li Zicheng (Li Tzu-ch'eng, ca. 1605–45), a former postal attendant, whom the official sources depict as a cruel but dedicated leader, and who is celebrated in the People's Republic as a hero.

In 1644 Li Zicheng seized Beijing, and the Ming emperor committed suicide; but Li proved unable to found a new dynasty, for he had not taken the necessary ideological and administrative steps to win over the members of the scholar-official elite. For them he represented at best an unknown force, but no one could rule China without their cooperation. This was understood by Li's most powerful and capable competitors even though they came from Manchuria. When they came to build their dynasty, they made extensive use of Ming precedents.

NOTES

1. Shigeta Atsushi as discussed in Mori Masao, "The Gentry in the Ming: An Outline of the Relations Between the *Shih-ta fu* and Local Society," *Acta Asiatica* 38 (1980): 31–53.

2. Hilary J. Beattie, *Land and Lineage in China: A Study of T'ung-ch'eng County, Anhwei, in the Ming and Ch'ing Dynasties* (Cambridge: Cambridge Univ. Press, 1979).

3. G. William Skinner, "Chinese Peasants and the Closed Community: An Open and Shut Case," in *Comparative Studies in Society and History* 13 (1971): 272.

4. Liu Wu-chi, *An Introduction to Chinese Literature* (Bloomington: Indiana Univ. Press, 1966), pp. 216–17.

5. K'ung Shang-jen, *The Peach Blossom Fan*, trans. Chen Shih-hsiang and Harold Acton (Berkeley: Univ. of California Press, 1970), p. xiv.

6. Tseng Yu-ho, in Richard Edwards, *The Art of Wen Cheng-ming (1470–1559)* (Ann Arbor: The Univ. of Michigan Museum of Art, 1976), p. 122.

7. Wm. Theodore de Bary and the Conference on Ming Thought, *Self and Society in Ming Thought* (New York: Columbia Univ. Press, 1970), p. 12.

8. Wing-tsit Chan, trans., *Instructions for Practical Living and Other Neo-Confucian Writings* (New York: Columbia Univ. Press, 1963), p. 159.

9. Wing-tsit Chan, *A Source Book in Chinese Philosophy* (Princeton: Princeton Univ. Press, 1963), p. 681.

10. Quoted in James Cahill, *Fantastics and Eccentrics in Chinese Painting* (New York: The Asia Society, 1967), p. 22.

11. James Cahill, *Fantastics and Eccentrics*, p. 36.

12. Quoted in Arthur W. Hummel, ed., *Eminent Chinese of the Ch'ing Period* (Washington, D.C.: GPO, 1943), 1: 190.

13. Quoted in Charles O. Hucker, "Confucianism and the Chinese Censorial System," in David S. Nivison and Arthur F. Wright, eds., *Confucianism in Action* (Stanford: Stanford Univ. Press, 1959), p. 208.

14. Ray Huang, "Fiscal Administration During the Ming Dynasty," in Charles O. Hucker, ed., *Chinese Government in Ming Times* (New York: Columbia Univ. Press, 1969), pp. 124–25.

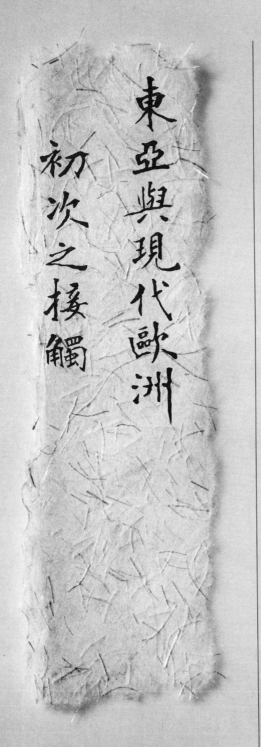

東亞與現代歐洲
初次之接觸

9

East Asia and Modern Europe: First Encounters

1514 – Portuguese Reach China	1614 – Persecution of Christians in Japan
1543 – Portuguese Reach Japan (Shipwreck)	1630 – Japan Closed to Foreigners
1549 – St. Francis Xavier Lands in Kyūshū	1700 – 300,000 Christian Converts in China
1571 – Spanish Conquest of Philippines	1742 – Pope Decides against Jesuits in Rites
1601 – Matteo Ricci Received by Emperor of China	Controversy

*T*he early contacts between post-Renaissance Europe and China had nothing like the impact of those which were to follow in the nineteenth century. The story of these early relations can be conceived as an overture setting the tone, introducing basic themes, and establishing the harmonics of the history to come. At the same time these contacts helped set the stage for that history, because the failure of the early intermediaries to build viable bridges of mutual understanding made it all the harder to do so later when China and Japan had to deal with a Europe transformed by the French and Industrial revolutions.

As in more modern times, there were interconnections between Western encounters with China and with Japan. For example, the experience of the Jesuits in Japan influenced their approach to China. In this respect what happened in Japan can help us understand this period of Chinese history. In both cases the story begins with the Portuguese.

The Portuguese in East Asia

The pioneers of European global expansion were the Portuguese, who reached India in 1498, China in 1514, and Japan in 1543. Having wrested control of the seas from their Arab rivals, they established their Asian headquarters at Goa (1510), a small island off the coast of West India. They then went on to capture Malacca (1511), a vital center for the lucrative spice trade, located on the straits which separate the Malay Peninsula from Sumatra (see Figure 9-1). It was the desire to break the Arab spice monopoly that supplied the economic motive for this initial European expansion. Spices were highly valuable relative to their bulk and weight. Easily transported and fetching a high price, they formed an attractive cargo. And there was an assured market for them in Europe, where they added flavor to an otherwise dull diet and made meat palatable in an age when animals were slaughtered in the fall for want of sufficient fodder to sustain them through the winter. They were also used in medicine and in religious ceremonies.

Prospects for trade were hampered, however, by the fact that Europe, needing pepper and other spices from Asia, had no European commodities of equal

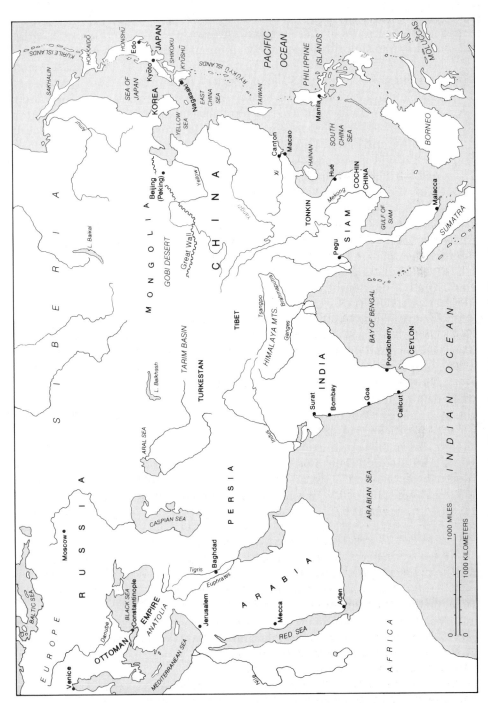

Figure 9-1   Eastern Europe and Asia in the Sixteenth and Seventeenth Centuries

importance to offer in return. Initially, therefore, Portuguese adventurers in East Asia supported themselves by a mixture of trade and piracy — like their Japanese predecessors in these waters. They were able to do this successfully because they had superior ships and weapons and were better seamen. Eventually, however, they became the primary carriers of goods in the East Asian trade, taking goods from one Asian country to another — Southeast Asian wares to China, Chinese silk to Japan, and Japanese silver to China. Their profits from this trade were used to purchase spices and other products for European markets. But before this trade could prosper, they had to secure entry to China and Japan. This posed problems quite different from those they had encountered in seizing a small island off the coast of politically divided India or in driving the Arabs from Malacca.

In China they got off to a very bad start. Not waiting for official permission to trade, they engaged in illegal commerce and even built a fort on Lintin Island, located at the mouth of the river that connects Canton to the sea. Their unruly behavior did not endear them to the Ming authorities and served to confirm the opinion that these "ocean devils" were a new kind of barbarian. The outrageous behavior of the Portuguese traders was further embellished by the Chinese imagination. When the Portuguese bought kidnapped Chinese children as slaves, the Chinese concluded that their purpose was to eat them. They long continued in the firm belief that they were dealing with barbarous child eaters. Not just a popular rumor held by the ignorant, this belief found its way into the official history of the Ming dynasty.

The first Portuguese envoy to China not only failed to obtain commercial concessions; he ended his life in a Cantonese prison. It was a most inauspicious beginning. But the Portuguese would not leave, and their superiority on the seas made it impossible for the Chinese to drive them out. A *modus vivendi* was reached in 1557 when the Portuguese were permitted to establish themselves in Macao in exchange for an annual payment. There the Portuguese administered their own affairs, but the territory remained under Chinese jurisdiction until Macao was ceded to Portugal in 1887. Macao and nearby Hong Kong still remain under European control but are scheduled to revert to China in 1997.

The Jesuits in Japan

Trade and booty were not the only objectives of the Europeans who ventured into Asian waters. Missionary work was also important: mid-sixteenth-century Goa boasted some 80 churches and convents. From the beginning, the missionary impulse provided a strong incentive as well as religious sanction for European expansion; and it was the missionary rather than the trader who served as prime intermediary between the civilizations of East Asia and the West from the sixteenth to the twentieth centuries.

Among the early missionaries, the great pioneers and the most impressive leaders were members of the Society of Jesus (Jesuits). Founded in 1540, this tightly organized and rigorously disciplined religious order formed the vanguard of the Catholic Counter-Reformation. They were the "cavalry of the church," prepared to do battle with Protestant heretics in Europe or the heathen in the world beyond. Along with its stress on martial discipline and intensive religious training, the Society was noted for its insistence on intellectual vigor and depth of learning. The latter included secular as well as sacred studies, and the ideal Jesuit was as learned as he was disciplined and devout.

In 1549, less than ten years after the founding of the Jesuit order, St. Francis Xavier (1506–52), one of the original members of the Society, landed in Kyūshū This was just six years after the Japanese had encountered their first Europeans, some shipwrecked Portuguese who landed on the island of Tanegashima. Xavier was well received and was soon able to establish cordial relations with important men in Kyūshū. First impressions on both sides were favorable. The Japanese were impressed by the strong character and dignified bearing of the European priests. The Jesuit combination of martial pride, stern self-discipline, and religious piety fitted well with the ethos of sixteenth-century Japan. Nor did the Christian religion seem altogether strange. On the contrary, initially Christianity, brought to Japan from Goa, seemed just another type of Buddhism. It was similar in some of its ceremonies to those found in Buddhism, and it was difficult for the early priests to convey the subtleties of theology, to explain the difference between God and the cosmic Buddha, for example, or to distinguish Paradise from the Pure Land. At last, the Jesuit fathers concluded that the devil, in all of his malicious cleverness, had deliberately fashioned Buddhism to resemble the true faith so as to confound and confuse the people.

The initial meeting of the Jesuits and the Japanese was facilitated by the similarities in their feudal backgrounds. In Japan, Xavier and other Europeans found a society that resembled their own far more than did any other outside Europe. "The people," wrote Alessandro Valignano (1539–1606), "are all white, courteous and highly civilized, so much so that they surpass all the other known races of the world."[1] Only the Chinese were to receive similar praise — and, indeed, to be regarded as "white." Donald Lach has summarized the qualities the Jesuits found to admire in the Japanese: "their courtesy, propriety, dignity, endurance, frugality, equanimity, industriousness, sagaciousness, cleanliness, simplicity, discipline, and rationality."[2] On the negative side, besides paganism, the Jesuits were appalled at the prevalence of sodomy among the military aristocracy and the monks. They criticized the Japanese propensity to suicide and also found fault with the "disloyalty of vassal to master, their dissimulation, ambiguity, and lack of openness in their dealings, their bellicose nature, their inhuman treatment of enemies and unwanted children, their failure to respect the rule of law, and finally their unwillingness to give up the system of concubinage."[3] Nevertheless, the similarities between Japanese culture and their own gave the Jesuits high hopes for the success of their mission.

In their everyday behavior the Jesuits tried to win acceptance by adapting themselves to local manners and customs, as long as these did not run counter to their own creed. "Thus," Valignano observed, "we who come hither from Europe find ourselves as veritable children who have to learn to eat, sit, converse, dress, act politely, and so on."[4] They learned how to squat Japanese style, learned to employ the Japanese language with its various levels of politeness, and mastered the art of tea — the Jesuit dwelling was usually equipped with a tea room so that their guests could be properly entertained. C. R. Boxer has pointed out that the Christian monks came from a land with rather different standards of personal cleanliness: "Physical dirt and religious poverty tended to be closely associated in Catholic Europe where lice were regarded as the inseparable companions of monks and soldiers."[5] But in Japan the devoted monks even learned to wash, a major concession to Japanese sensibilities. Still there were limits: Valignano could not bring himself to endorse the Japanese custom of taking a hot bath every day. That would really be going too far!

Careful attention to the niceties of etiquette was required of the Jesuit fathers in their strategy of working from the top down. It was their hope to transform Japan into a Christian land by first converting the rulers and then allowing the faith to seep down to the populace at large. The purpose of their labors was not to Europeanize Japan or China, but to save souls. They realized that the enthusiastic support of the ruling authority would be an invaluable asset, while without at least the ruler's tacit approval they could do nothing.

This approach met with considerable success in Kyūshū, where they converted important local lords, who ordered their people to adopt the foreign faith. Although there were numerous cases of genuine conversion, some lords simply saw the light of commerce, adopting a Christian stance in the hope of attracting the Portuguese trade to their ports. On at least one occasion it happened that when the great Portuguese ship did not appear, they promptly turned their backs on the new faith. The Jesuits themselves became involved in this trade and also in politics. For seven years they even held the overlordship of Nagasaki, granted to them by a Christian lord.

Xavier and the monks who came after him realized that real progress for their mission depended on the will not only of local Kyūshū lords but of the central government. Xavier's initial trip to Kyōto came at an unpropitious time — the city was in disorder. But Nobunaga (1532–84), the first of Japan's three great unifiers, soon became a friend of the Jesuits. Attracted by their character and interested in hearing about foreign lands, perhaps he was also happy to talk with someone not part of the hierarchical order which he himself headed. This personal predilection also coincided nicely with reasons of state. It was consistent with his hostility toward the Buddhist orders and with his desire to keep the trading ships coming in. Hideyoshi (1536–98), Nobunaga's successor, was at first similarly well disposed toward the foreign religion. He liked dressing up in Portuguese clothes, complete with rosary, and he once said that the only thing that kept him from converting was the Christian insistence on monogamy.

Figure 9-2   Namban screen. Section of a sixfold screen, 164 cm × 365.6 cm, Kano Mitsonobu school, ca. 1610. Namban-Bunka-Kan, Ōsaka.

The political and economic success of the Jesuits helped the spread of Christianity, but power, or the semblance of power, always entails risks. There was the danger that the ruler might perceive the activities of the monks not as assets bolstering his own position but as liabilities, actual or potential threats to his authority. A portent of future disaster came in 1587 when Hideyoshi issued an order expelling the monks. Eager to encourage trade and not really feeling seriously threatened, Hideyoshi did not enforce the decree, but it foreshadowed the persecutions that were to begin in earnest 36 years later, in 1614.

There was a surge of popularity for things Western, for instance, "Southern Barbarian Screens," showing the giant black ships of the foreigners. The barbarians themselves were depicted as exceedingly tall and rather ungainly, with sharp, long noses and red hair, wearing the ballooning pantaloons which formed the standard fashion in the Portuguese empire (see Figure 9-2). Other scenes, based on paintings from Europe, depicted various barbarian topics: the battle of Lepanto, an Italian court, European cities, maps of the world, not to mention religious subjects. While some artists painted European subjects in Japanese style, others experimented with Western perspective and techniques of shading to produce three-dimensional effects. Nor were Western motifs limited to painting. Western symbols were widely used in decoration: a cross on a bowl, a few words of Latin on a saddle, and so forth.

The Impact of Other Europeans

Despite the order of 1587, Western influences continued to enter Japan. The situation was further complicated when the Portuguese were followed by other Europeans. The first of these to reach Japan were the Spanish, whose conquest of the Philippines (named after Philip II) was completed in 1571. To the Japanese, Manila presented a new source of profitable trade, but the colonization of the Philippines also alerted them to the imperialist ambitions of the Europeans and revealed connections between Christian evangelism and colonialism. With the arrival of the Dutch and English Protestants in the early 1600s, there were also Europeans in Japan who broke the link between trade and missionary activity and did their best to fan Japanese suspicions of their Catholic rivals. Now, as later, the "West" did not represent a single interest nor did it speak with a single voice.

The Spanish empire differed from that of Portugal in kind as it did in scale. Whereas the Portuguese maintained themselves by the proceeds from the inter-Asia trade, the Spanish commanded the precious metals of the New World. Indeed, silver from Spanish America became a major factor not only in the economy of Spain and Europe but also in China. Vast quantities of the precious metal reached China by way of Manila to pay for Chinese silks. In China this silver helped to finance late Ming military expenses, pay for costly public works, and made possible court extravagance that left the government all the more vulnerable when silver imports decreased drastically in the 1630s. The disruption of the inflow of silver aggravated China's economic distress, helped to undermine the Ming dynasty, contributed to its collapse, and continued during the difficult years of consolidating the new dynasty.

Conversely, the resumption of the silver flow in the 1680s helped to fuel China's subsequent prosperity. Lloyd Eastman put it pungently when he wrote, "By the late sixteenth and early seventeenth centuries, therefore, China (or sizeable regions thereof) had become a silver 'junkie,' addicted to large and steady fixes of the precious metal to maintain an economic high."[6] As the parenthetical remark suggests, the extent to which the availability of silver affected China's individual regions remains unclear, but what is clear even in this early period is that participation in the world system could bring new wealth but also entailed new risks.

The immediate effect on Japan of the coming of the Spaniards was to complicate the situation of the Jesuits. The Spanish were every bit as committed to the missionary enterprise as were the Portuguese, but they patronized Franciscan monks rather than Jesuits. The first Franciscan arrived in Japan from Manila in 1587. Much less well informed about conditions in Japan than the Jesuits, the Franciscans were less discrete in their work. They rejected the

Jesuit strategy of working from the top down, and, instead of associating with the samurai, worked among the poor and forgotten, the sick and miserable, those at the very bottom of society. The Jesuits did not disguise their contempt for the ignorance and poverty of the Franciscans, the "crazy friars" (*frailes idiotas*) as they called them, and these sentiments were heartily reciprocated by the friars, who scoffed at Jesuit pretensions.

The "Closing" of Japan

It was an omen of things to come when Hideyoshi, in 1597, crucified six Franciscan missionaries and 18 of their Japanese converts after the pilot of a Spanish ship driven ashore in Japan reportedly boasted about the power and ambitions of his king. Like his two predecessors, Tokugawa Ieyasu (1542–1616), founder of the shogunate that finally brought peace and stability to Japan, was at first friendly to the Christians, but he too turned against them. In 1606 Christianity was declared illegal, and in 1614 he undertook a serious campaign to expel the missionaries.

By 1614 there were over 300,000 converts in Japan. The destruction of Christianity was long and painful. Tortures, such as hanging a man upside down with his head in a pit filled with excrement, were used to induce people to renounce their faith. Before it was all over, there were more than 3,000 recognized martyrs, of whom less than 70 were Europeans. Others died without achieving martyrdom. In 1637–38 there was a rebellion in Shimabara, near Nagasaki, against a lord who combined merciless taxation with cruel suppression of Christianity. Fought under banners on which Christian slogans were written in Portuguese, and led by some masterless samurai, it was a Christian version of the rural uprisings characteristic of the century of warfare before Nobunaga. In its suppression, some 37,000 Christians lost their lives.

Persuasion as well as violence was employed in the campaign against Christianity. Opponents of Christian dogma argued that the idea of a personal creator was absurd and asked why, if God was both omnipotent and good, he should have tempted Adam and Eve and devised eternal punishment in Hell for non-Christians even though they led exemplary lives. According to Christian teaching, even the sage emperors Yao and Shun would end in hell. The First Commandment was attacked as leading to disobedience of parents and lord; a loyal retainer should accompany his lord even into hell.

Such arguments suggest that the Japanese saw Christianity as potentially subversive, not only of the political order, but of the basic social structure, for it challenged accepted values and beliefs and demanded a radical reappraisal of long-revered traditions. Its association with European expansionism posed a threat from abroad, and, as exemplified by the Shimabara Rebellion, it also harbored the seeds of radical disruption at home. Thus the motivation for the government's suppression of Christianity was secular not religious. The shogunate was not worried over the state of its subjects' souls, but it was determined to wipe out a dangerous doctrine.

Not only Christianity but all foreign influences were potentially subversive, including trade that would tend to the advantage of the Kyūshū lords rather than the Tokugawa. Gradually the shogun further restricted foreign contacts. The Spaniards were expelled in 1624, one year after the English had left voluntarily. In 1630 Japanese were forbidden to go overseas or to return from there or to build ships capable of long voyages. The Portuguese were expelled after the Shimabara Rebellion on the grounds of complicity with that uprising. When they sent an embassy in 1640, its members were executed. The only Europeans left were the Dutch (see Figure 9-3), who kept other Europeans from trying their luck in Japan until the English and Russians challenged Dutch naval supremacy in the late eighteenth and early nineteenth centuries. The Dutch themselves were, in 1641, moved to a tiny artificial island of Deshima in Nagasaki Harbor, where they were virtually confined as in a prison. The annual Dutch vessel to Deshima was all that remained of Japan's contact with Europe, but an annual average of almost 26 Chinese ships came to Nagasaki, and Japan also maintained indirect diplomatic links with Korea. The "closing" was not complete, but relations with the West were greatly diminished.

Figure 9-3 *A Dutch Dinner Party.* Nagasaki color print, 22 cm × 33 cm.

The Jesuits in China

The beginnings of the Jesuit missions in China and Japan were closely linked. Xavier himself hoped to begin the work in China. He realized this was not only a great project in itself but also a major step in the Christianization of Japan, providing an answer to the question he was constantly asked there: "If yours is the true faith why have not the Chinese, from whom comes all wisdom, heard of it?"[7] But Xavier died before he could reach his goal. Three further Jesuit attempts to enter China also failed. Then Valignano established a special training center in Macao so that missionaries could study the Chinese language and culture in preparation for work in China. As in Japan, it was Jesuit policy in China to concentrate on gaining the support and, if possible, conversion of the upper classes. To this end, they once more went as far as possible to accommodate themselves to native sensibilities and ways of doing things.

Again, as in Japan, the strong character and attractive personalities of the first missionaries were of great importance in gaining them entree. The outstanding pioneer was Matteo Ricci (1551 – 1610). A student of law, mathematics, and science, he also knew a good deal about cartography and something of practical mechanics. Once in the East, he was also able to master the Chinese language and the classics. Slowly Ricci made his way in Chinese officialdom, impressing scholars and officials by his knowledge of mathematics, astronomy, and cartography, his command of Chinese classical learning, and his prodigious memory. At last in 1601, after 18 strenuous years, Ricci was received in an imperial audience and won permission for himself and his colleagues to reside in the capital. (By this time they had discarded the Buddhist robes worn by Jesuits in Japan and had adopted Confucian dress as more acceptable to the Chinese.) In Beijing (Peking) he was able to win over and convert a number of prominent men. By the time Ricci died in 1610, the mission was well established in the capital and accepted by the government. Ricci's body was laid to rest in a plot donated by the emperor.

During the period when the Japanese were persecuting Christians with increasing ferocity, the Jesuits in China labored fruitfully, building on the foundations laid by Ricci. They were particularly successful in demonstrating the superior accuracy of European astronomical predictions. Thereby they succeeded in displacing their Muslim and Chinese competitors and established themselves in the Bureau of Astronomy. This was an important and prestigious office, reflecting the importance of the heavenly bodies in Chinese thought. Jesuit gains in this area were solidified by the work of Adam Schall von Bell (1591 – 1666), a German Jesuit who was a trained astronomer and served as chief government astronomer. Schall von Bell also assisted in casting cannon for the Ming, although it did not save the dynasty.

The Jesuits made some notable converts among the literati, particularly during the troubled years of the declining Ming. Most notable was Xu Guangqi (Hsü Kuang-ch'i, or Paul Hsü, 1562 – 1633), who translated Euclid's *Elements* and other works on mathematics, hydraulics, astronomy and geography, thereby becoming the first Chinese translator of European books. With the help of such men, Western science and geography were made available to China, but European influence remained limited. Thus, when Li Zhi (Li Chih), one of the most forceful and independent Late Ming thinkers, met Ricci, he was impressed with the Jesuit's personality but saw no merit in his proselytizing mission.

The triumph of the Manchus (see Chapter 10) did not seriously disrupt Jesuit activity. Schall von Bell was retained by the new dynasty as their astronomer, and he was followed by the Belgian Jesuit, Ferdinant Verbiest (1633 – 88), the last of the trio of great and learned missionary fathers. Verbiest, like Schall von Bell, cast cannon and in other ways won the favor of the great Manchu emperor, Kangxi (K'ang-hsi, r. 1662 – 1722). A good account of Jesuit activities at court comes from the emperor's own brush:

> With Verbiest I had examined each stage of the forging of cannons, and made him build a water fountain that operated in conjunction with an organ, and erect a windmill in the court; with the new group . . . I worked on clocks and mechanics. Pereira taught me to play the tune *"Puyanzhou"* on the harpsichord and the structure of the eight-note-scale, Pedrini taught my sons musical theory, and Gheradini painted portraits at the Court. I also learned to calculate the weight and volume of spheres, cubes, and cones. . . .[8]

The Emperor accepted the Jesuits' science with alacrity and took their quinine for the sake of his health. He also discussed religion with them, but here they were less successful: "I had asked Verbiest why God had not forgiven his son without making him die, but though he had tried hard to answer I had not understood him."[9] In China, as in Japan, the fathers found it most difficult to explain the central tenants of their faith to people with very different ideas about the nature of the universe and of the divine.

The highpoint for early Catholicism in China came in the middle years of Kangxi's reign, but by 1700 there were no more than 300,000 Christians in China, roughly the same number as in much smaller Japan a century earlier. In both cases the missionaries were there on sufferance, dependent on the good will of the authorities. And in China, as earlier in Japan, divisions between the Europeans themselves strongly contributed to their undoing.

The Rites Controversy

The controversy that brought an end to the missionary activity in China centered on the Jesuit policy of accommodation, which was opposed by the rival orders, particularly and vigorously by the Dominicans. It revolved around the question of the proper attitude a Christian should adopt toward Confucianism, its doctrines, and practices. This kind of dispute had not arisen in Japan, where Catholic fathers of all orders agreed in their condemnation of Buddhism and Shinto and in their absolute refusal to allow their converts to have anything to do with such heathen religions.

In China, however, the basic strategy used by Ricci and followed by his successors was to accept the teachings of Confucius, "the prince of philosophers." They argued that they had come, not to destroy Confucius, but to make his teachings complete, capping his doctrines with the truths of revealed religion. Like Chinese thinkers intent on using Confucius in new ways, the Jesuits also discarded and condemned previous interpretations and commentaries on the classics. They attacked Neo-Confucianism and developed new theories of their own. In their enthusiasm for the classics, the Jesuits turned Confucius into a religious teacher. Some members of the order went as far as to trace the origin of the Chinese people to the eldest son of Noah. The most extreme even claimed to find Christian prophecies in the Yi Jing. Meanwhile, the Dominicans held that the ancient Chinese were atheists and argued against the Jesuit portrayal of Confucius as a deist. The resulting literature greatly influenced Western understanding of Chinese philosophy. At its best it was a serious effort by Europeans to understand Chinese thought in what they believed to be universally valid terms.

The status of Confucius and the acceptability of the classics were major issues for missionaries operating in a society dominated by the Confucian examination system. Even more troublesome, however, was the related problem posed by Confucian observances. Were the ceremonies in veneration of Confucius, held in the temples of Confucius throughout the land, acts of religious devotion and therefore anathema to a Christian? Or were they social and political in character, secular expressions of respect for China's greatest teacher? Even more important, what about the rites performed by every family in front of the tablets representing its ancestors? Was this a worship of the departed spirits and thus the most iniquitous idolatry? Or did these acts of commemoration to one's forebears merely convey a deep sense of filial piety? Were the two kinds of ceremonials civic and moral in nature, or were they religious, and therefore sacrilegious? Consistent with their stand on Confucianism, the Jesuits claimed the ceremonies were nonreligious and therefore permissible. The Dominicans disagreed.

The issue was fiercely debated, for much was at stake. Theology aside, it is easy to see the practical reasons for the Jesuit standpoint. To exclude Christians from performing the ceremonies for Confucius would be to exclude them from participation in Chinese political life. Worse still, to prohibit the ritual veneration of ancestors would not only deprive Chinese Christians of their sense of family but would make them appear as unfilial, immoral monsters in the eyes of their non-Christian fellows. If Christianity rejected the classics and advocated this kind of nonconformist behavior, it would be turned into a religion subversive of the Chinese state and society. Persecuted and condemned, Christianity would be unable to reach many souls, who would thus be deprived of their chance for salvation.

But the Dominicans could muster strong counterarguments. Why should a church that condemned Protestant Christianity condone Confucian Christianity? The issue was not the acceptability of Christianity to the Chinese but whether the salvation of souls would be fatally jeopardized by tolerating false

Confucian doctrines. In their eyes, nothing could be allowed to interfere with the Christian's sacred duty to maintain the purity of the faith.

The Decline of Christianity in China

The question, "when does Christianity cease to be Christianity" was to reappear in the nineteenth century and is not all that different from the question, "when does Marxism cease to be Marxism," which agitates some thinkers today. Such questions are never easy to resolve, and perhaps only true believers need grapple with them. Be that as it may, in the papacy, the church had a source of authority that could rule on what was acceptable and what was not. The process of reaching a decision was complicated and involved. What is important here is that the outcome went against the Jesuits. In 1704 the pope condemned Chinese rituals, and in 1742 a decree was issued that settled all points against the Jesuits. This remained the position of the Catholic Church until 1939. Grand and powerful emperors like Kangxi, however, saw no reason to abide by the judgment of Rome as to what was fitting for their realm. They naturally favored the Jesuit point of view. In the end, the pope would send only those missionaries the emperor of China would not accept.

One major difference between the course of events in China and Japan was that in China neither a desire for trade nor fear of its possible consequences influenced decisions concerning missionary policies, for the trade conducted sporadically by European ships was of only peripheral concern to the Chinese government.

Some missionaries remained in China after the break, including the Jesuit Guiseppe Castiglione, who served as court painter for half a century, 1715–66. Among other things, he designed a miniature Versailles for the Summer Palace, destroyed in the nineteenth century. Michael Sullivan has described his fusion of artistic traditions as a "synthetic style in which with taste and skill and the utmost discretion, Western perspective and shading, with even an occasional hint of chiaroscuro, were blended to give an added touch of realism to painting otherwise entirely Chinese in manner."[10] Figure 9-4 shows a painting in the European manner done at the Chinese court. It is an anonymous portrait of an imperial concubine playing at being a European peasant girl. Just as Louis XV of France sometimes amused himself by having his courtiers and their ladies assume Chinese dress, the Qing emperor Qianlong enjoyed exotic Western costume on occasion.

Regardless of the Rites Controversy, the Christians also had opponents in China itself, motivated by the usual combination of self-interest and conviction. There was no Chinese counterpart to Nagasaki: instead, Canton and the surrounding area, the part of China most exposed to the Europeans, already at this time took a negative view of the foreigners. Christianity was proscribed in 1724. Some churches were seized and other acts of persecution occurred, but the suppression of Christianity was not as thorough as that which had taken

Figure 9-4 Anonymous, *Portrait of Xiang Fei.* Mid-eighteenth century. Palace Museum, Beijing.

place in Japan. This was probably because there was no Chinese equivalent to the Shimabara Rebellion — at least not yet. Not until the nineteenth century did the potential of Christianity as an ideology of peasant revolt become evident in China. By the end of the eighteenth century, the number of Chinese converts had been reduced to about half their number at the beginning of the century.

Much research remains to be done on the influence of this period of early Western contact on Chinese thought and civilization. There was certainly some stimulus from the West, but more frequently the Western influence seems not to have progressed much beyond the appreciation of European exotica, such as clocks and other mechanical devices. Ricci himself lived on as the patron saint of clockmakers. The influence was much stronger the other way, for the Jesuit reports on China were well received in Europe and helped to create the image of an ideal China dear to the *philosophes* of the European Enlightenment. In the arts there was an enthusiasm for things "Chinesy" — *chinoiserie*. Neither *chinoiserie* in Europe nor *namban* ("Southern Barbarian") art in Japan may have reached great aesthetic heights, but in their relative openness to foreign stimulus, there is a certain resemblance between early modern Europe and Japan (but missing in China) in this period of first encounters.

NOTES

1. C. R. Boxer, *The Christian Century in Japan* (Berkeley: Univ. of California Press, 1951), p. 74.
2. Donald F. Lach, *Asia in the Making of Europe*, Vol. I, *The Century of Discovery* (Chicago: Univ. of Chicago Press, 1965, p. 728.
3. *Ibid.*
4. Quoted in Boxer, *The Christian Century in Japan*, p. 214.
5. *Ibid.*
6. Lloyd E. Eastman, *Family, Fields, and Ancestors* (New York: Oxford Univ. Press, 1988), p. 126–27).
7. A. H. Rowbotham, *Missionary and Mandarin* (Berkeley: Univ. of California Press, 1942), p. 46.
8. Quoted in Jonathan Spence, *Emperor of China* (New York: Alfred A. Knopf, 1974), pp. 72–73.
9. *Ibid.*, p. 84.
10. Michael Sullivan, *The Meeting of Eastern and Western Art* (New York: New York Graphic Society, 1973), pp. 66–67.

滿人治下之中國

10
China under the Manchus

Rise of Manchu Power	Q I N G D Y N A S T Y		Late Qing
Later Jin (1616–36)	Kangxi (1662–1722)	Qianlong (1736–95)	Opium War (1839–42)

I n this chapter we will consider Qing (Ch'ing) China (1644–1911) during the seventeenth and eighteenth centuries, when they did not yet have to confront the full onslaught of the modern world, and challenges from abroad could be contained and even disregarded. The study of this period not only affords a last look at the internal dynamics of traditional China's state and society but is also crucial for an understanding of what was to follow in modern times.

The Ming dynasty collapsed primarily for internal reasons, and for a short time a Chinese rebel even controlled Beijing (Peking), but it was rulers from beyond the Great Wall in Manchuria who became the Ming's true heirs. Establishing the Qing, the Manchus became only the second dynasty of conquest to rule over all of China, and the Qing emperors ruled much longer and with greater success than had their Mongol predecessors in the Yuan. In fact, they were able to expand the empire to its greatest size ever, and for a time China achieved remarkable stability and prosperity (see Figure 10-1).

Formation of the Manchu State

The Ming dynasty, always sensitive to dangers from the North, maintained peace and order in Manchuria partly by diplomacy and partly by establishing "commanderies" under the hereditary control of tribal clients. To provide for the security of Chinese settlers in the Liao River basin, it also maintained the "Willow Palisades," a line of willows and a deep trench along which checkpoints were maintained. As long as the Ming was strong and the local Jurchen tribes divided, the frontier area was reasonably stable. However, the concurrent decline of the Ming and the emergence of tribal unity changed all that.

The Manchu state was founded by Nurhaci (1559–1626), who fought, married, and negotiated his way to leadership and power. Originally supported by the Ming, he continued to send tribute to Beijing until 1609. But he was powerful enough also to defy the Chinese dynasty when he wished, and in 1616 declared himself emperor of the Later Jin (Chin) thereby identifying his regime with the Jurchen Jin dynasty established in North China from 1115

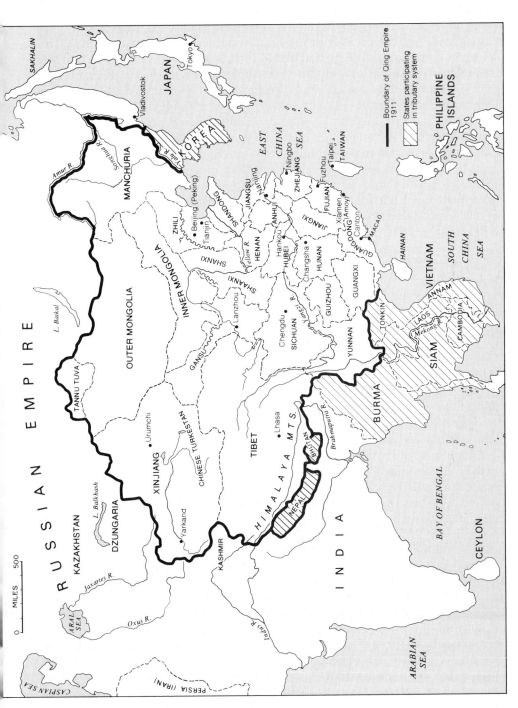

Figure 10-1   The Qing Empire   1775

to 1234. There had long been Chinese frontiersmen among the Manchus, but Nurhachi's conquest of the agricultural lands in Liaodong and southern Manchuria increased the number of his Chinese subjects including both free Chinese adherents, who were treated like Manchus, and others treated as captives and turned into bondservants to serve the Manchus in their homes, estates, and workshops. Expansion increased the state's economic and human resources and made Chinese expertise and models available to the new state. But Nurhachi, like his successors, was also concerned to preserve his people's tradition. When it came to developing a script for the Manchu language, he had his experts turn to Mongolian, not Chinese, as a base.

In 1625 Nurhaci established his capital at Shengyuan (Mukden), but the following year he suffered his first major defeat at the hands of a Ming general who made effective use of Portuguese cannon. Nurhachi died that same year and was succeeded by his son, Hung Taiji (also known as Abahai and after 1636 as Taizong, r. 1626–43), who continued to build on his father's foundations. The most important of these was the banner system. This was devised by Nurhaci in 1601 when he formed his troops into companies of 300 men, organized under four large banners, colored yellow, white, blue, and red. In 1615 he added four more banners using the original colors but adding borders to the flags. Each banner was headed by one of Nurhaci's sons who was responsible for the civil as well as military administration of all his troops and their families. In 1621 the first Mongol company was organized, and in 1636 Hung Taiji created the first Chinese company. By the time of the conquest, there were eight Mongol and eight Chinese banners along with the eight Manchu banners. In terms of the number of companies involved, the breakdown was 278 Manchu, 120 Mongol, and 165 Chinese. These formidable troops now also enjoyed artillery support, for the Manchus made good use of Chinese experts to cast cannon.

Even before the conquest not only were there more Chinese than Manchus in the Manchu state, but Chinese collaborators contributed enormously to the success of military campaigns. The Manchu rulers thus needed to create a political system that would gain the approval and participation of Chinese officials without sacrificing Manchu control. On the one hand, they created an Assembly of Princes and High Officials composed almost exclusively of Manchus, but Hung Taiji also adopted the Six Ministries (personnel, revenue, rites, war, justice, and public works), the Censorate, and other Ming institutions. Each of the ministries was headed by a Manchu prince and initially provided with four presidents, two Manchu, one Mongol, and one Chinese. The formula was soon changed, but what was established was the principle of ethnic balance in the central government under Manchu supervision.

An unequivocal indication that Hung Taiji cherished ambitions beyond Manchuria came in 1636 when he altered the name of his regime from Later Jin to Qing (Ch'ing, meaning "pure") while changing the name of his people to Manchu. At the same time he sought to preserve their identity and their fighting traditions by retaining traditional tribal customs and dress. By the time of his death Hung Taiji had reduced Inner Mongolia to vassalage, forced Korea into submission, and won control of the Amur River regions in the North, but the conquest of North China was achieved after his death by Dorgon (1612–50), acting as regent for the 6-year-old second Qing emperor. (See Table 10-1 for a list of Qing emperors.)

The Conquest

On April 25, 1644, when the last Ming emperor hanged himself even as his soldiers were laying down their arms and opening the gates of Beijing to the rebels, the immediate key to the military situation lay in the hands of the Ming general Wu Sangui (Wu San-kuei) whose army controlled access into China. When Wu decided to cooperate with the Manchus, the fate of the rebels in Beijing was sealed. The Qing troops entered the city in June. Most important of all, the new dynasty continued to gain the adherence of trained and experienced officials who preferred the Qing to the unruly and unreliable rebels. Not only their military success but their readiness to rule in a Chinese manner gave credibility to the new dynasty whose attitude toward the institutions it inherited was one of "adjustments, not replacements; overhaul, not wholesale substitution."[1]

The subjugation of the rest of the country, especially of the south, was not easy and would have been impossible without the cooperation of Chinese generals like Wu Sangui. Ming loyalists tried, sometimes with desperate heroism, to keep their cause alive in the South but were too divided and weak to mount a serious challenge. Sometimes the Manchu forces advanced peacefully aided by turncoats, but others sacrificed their lives in loyalty to the former dynasty. Beyond the normal carnage of warfare there was a terrible ten-day massacre in Yangzhou that left the city's gutters filled with corpses. After the capture of Nanjing, the loyalist capital, in June 1645, Dorgon enforced the demand that all men wear their hair in a queue (pigtail) and shave their heads in the Manchu fashion, an order which ordinary men as well as members of the elite found particularly humiliating.

After the fall of Nanjing, the Qing was not in full control of the South. Prolonged resistance came along the southeast coast, much of which was controlled from 1646 to 1658 by Zheng Chenggong (Coxinga, 1624–62), the son of a Chinese pirate-adventurer and a Japanese mother. The father had been baptized by the Portuguese at Macao but became a Ming supporter, and the son too was honored by the beleaguered Ming house. Originally based in the Xiamen (Amoy) region, he later moved to Taiwan (or Formosa, to use the Portuguese name). In 1662 Zheng expelled the Dutch from Taiwan where they had maintained posts since 1624. He died the same year, but his son continued to defy the Manchus, who did not subdue the island until 1683. It then was placed under the administration of Fujian Province thus bringing it under mainland control.

Table 10-1 Qing Emperors

| ERA NAME | | ERA DATES | Temple Name | |
Pinyin	Wade-Giles		Pinyin	Wade-Giles
Shunzhi	Shun-chih	1644–1661	Shizu Zhang huangdi	Shih-tsu Chang huang-ti
Kangxi	K'ang-hsi	1662–1722	Shengzu Ren huangdi	Sheng-tsu Jen huang-ti
Yongzheng	Yung-cheng	1723–1735	Shizong Xian huangdi	Shih-tsung Hsien huang-ti
Qienlong	Ch'ien-lung	1736–1795	Gaozong Chun huangdi	Kao-tsung Ch'un huang-ti
Jiaqing	Chia-ch'ing	1796–1820	Renzong Jui huangdi	Jen-tsung Jui huang-ti
Daoguang	Tao-kuang	1821–1850	Xuanzong Cheng huangdi	Hsüan-tsung Ch'eng huang-ti
Xianfeng	Hsien-feng	1851–1861	Wenzong Xian hunagdi	Wen-tsung Hsien huang-ti
Tongzhi	T'ung-chih	1862–1874	Muzong Yi huangdi	Mu-tsung Yi huang-ti
Guangxu	Kuang-hsü	1875–1908	Dezong Jing huangdi	Te-tsung Ching huang-ti
Xuantong	Hsüan-t'ung	1909–1912	none	

The final stage of pacification was the War of the Three Feudatories (1673–81) fought against Wu Sangui who had created a practically autonomous state for himself in Yunnan and Guizhou. Two other generals long associated with the Manchu cause also carved out states for themselves, one in Guangdong and the other in Fujian. An indication of the extent to which the Qing had by then won Chinese acceptance was that, in the war against these three satraps, the Qing dynasty acquired its own loyalist Confucian martyrs.

The elimination of this last obstacle to full domination was undertaken by Emperor Kangxi (K'ang-hsi, r. 1662–1722), who was only 15 years old at the time. He went on to become the dynasty's greatest ruler and, among other things, took measures to cement the loyalty of the Confucian literati. However, some of the most original and provocative thinkers of the seventeenth century refused to serve the new dynasty. Three men in particular stand out as intellectual giants. The youngest of these, Wang Fuzhi (Wang Fu-chih, 1619–1704) was 50 at the time Emperor Kangxi dismissed the regent who had been governing in his name and began ruling on his own. Thus all three men belong to the generation whose crucial life experience was the collapse of the Ming.

Three Thinkers

Wang Fuzhi, Huang Zongxi (Huang Tsung-hsi, 1610–95), and Gu Yanwu (Ku Yen-wu, 1613–82) all fought for the Ming while they could and when that was no longer possible refused to serve the new dynasty. Both Huang's teacher, Liu Zongzhou (Liu Tsung-chou, 1578–1645) and Gu Yanwu's mother refused to live under the Manchus. Instead they manifested their deep loyalty to the old dynasty by starving themselves to death, a form of suicide consistent with the injunction of filial piety, which prohibits a person from defacing the body he received from his parents. All three men were as independent in their thought as they were in their lives, but they were deeply influenced by Late Ming thought, even though rejecting some of its ideas. Indeed, a strong case can be made for treating the intellectual history of the seventeenth century as a single topic, since the Manchu conquest brought no abrupt break in intellectual continuity. This needs to be stressed, partly because it is frequently overlooked, partly because any brief discussion of a man's ideas tends to focus on his own original contributions rather than on that part of his mental universe which he inherits and accepts relatively unaltered.

Of the three, Wang Fuzhi was the least influential in his own day, despite the fact that his intellectual range, depth, and sophistication were immense. As it was, his work had to wait for some 200 years before it was published. Then his anti-Manchu views were welcomed by new, modern-minded opponents of the dynasty.

Philosophically, Wang is interesting for having developed a metaphysical monism based on qi (ch'i) drawing on ideas first advanced during the Song (Sung) by Zhang Zai (Chang Tsai). The primacy of qi did not entail a rejection of *li* (principle), but it did deny *li* ontological independence. The view that in the last analysis only *qi* exists represents the polar opposite of the elevation of *li* by Wang Yangming. In this respect, and in his views on human nature and the desires, Wang Fuzhi represents the intellectual tendency that was given its fullest expression by the eighteenth-century thinker Dai Zhen (Tai Chen).

None of the three men was interested in abstract theorizing for its own sake. Wang, like the others, was stimulated by the critical problems of his time to undertake a careful study of history, developing analyses and insights still stimulating to modern students. Combining a deep study of *The Classic of Change* with his historical investigations, Wang emphasized the need for people to suit their actions to the exigencies of historical circumstance, recognizing that the policies and institutions of one age are not necessarily suitable for another. This was hardly a new idea, although Wang gave it new emphasis. More radical was his rejection of cultural as well as temporal universalism. Wang regarded culture as molded by a people's environment, with the result that he considered Chinese and "barbarian" cultures equally valid, each in its own place. Wang believed they should be kept apart: Chinese should no more "civilize" foreign peoples than "barbarians" should interfere with China. Ideally Chinese and "barbarians" should resemble fish: passing by each other without taking the least notice. This position contrasted sharply with the facts, of course: "barbarian" Manchu domination over China in the name of universalistic Confucianism.

Like Wang Fuzhi, Huang Zongxi had an abiding interest in the study of history. A great historian, he authored a compendium of Ming thought but did not live to complete a similar undertaking for the Song and Yuan, which were left to a disciple to finish. Both remain invaluable for the study of Chinese philosophy and intellectual history. Of the three thinkers, Huang was the least hostile to Late Ming thinkers in the tradition of Wang Yangming, whose emphasis on the mind was frequently cited by early Qing critics as a cause for the weakness and even collapse of the old dynasty.

Huang's study of history and politics led him to formulate a stringent critique of imperial despotism. This is contained in his *Plan for the Prince*, a wide-ranging critical study of government, its measures and institutions. In a scathing attack on the selfishness of imperial despots, he wrote:

> In ancient times the people were considered hosts and the prince was the guest. All of his life the prince spent working for the sake of the people. Now the prince is the host and the people are guests. Because of the prince the people can find peace and happiness nowhere.[2]

Among the policies advocated by Huang were the restoration of a strong chief ministership and tax and land reforms; for a Confucian he was unusually well disposed toward law. But he placed his ultimate faith in education, stressing the importance of schools and reaffirming the Confucian insistence that the emperor and his highest officials attentively listen to the lectures of the wisest in the land. Huang was attracted to the old preimperial system of

decentralized government because he felt it provided local officials with maximum authority to exercise their moral and political wisdom.

Gu Yenwu was in substantial agreement with the ideas Huang expressed in
his *Plan for the Prince*, including the need for decentralization, but, unlike
Huang, he was bitterly critical of Wang Yangming and Late Ming thinkers
whose "empty words" he likened to the "pure talk" *(qingtan, ch'ing-t'an)* of
the Chinese scholars during the transition from Late Han to barbarian rule (see
Chapter 4). Instead, Gu insisted on real and practical learning, solidly based on
scholarship. This meant going back to the original sources to reconstruct their

Figure 10-2   Hongren, *The
Coming of Autumn*. Hanging
scroll, ink on paper, 122.4 cm
high.

Figure 10-3   Zhu Da (Bada Shanren), *Fish and Rocks.* Section of hand-scroll, ink on paper, 29.2 cm × 157 cm. The Cleveland Museum of Art.

meaning rather than relying on Song and later commentaries. Gu himself wrote important studies in historical geography and inscriptions, but he is especially famous for his work in historical phonetics. His essays, collected under the title *Records of Daily Knowledge,* show the range and critical spirit also found in the work of his two great contemporaries. But Gu was far more influential than they, for he became the virtual founder of Qing philological scholarship and what was termed "Han Learning," as distinguished from the metaphysical speculation associated with "Song Learning."

Textual scholarship was a field in which Qing scholars subsequently made great contributions. It was a field encouraged by Kangxi and later emperors.

Early Qing Painting

In painting as in thought the most original work was done by men who refused to serve the new dynasty. Among those who found tranquility in a Buddhist monastery was Hongren (Hung-jen, 1610–63) who "represented the world in a dematerialized, cleansed vision . . . revealing his personal peace through the liberating form of geometric abstraction."[3] His masterpiece, *The Coming of Autumn* (see Figure 10-2) displays a marvelous sense of structural depth.

Although Hongren had his followers, other seventeenth-century painters were too highly individualistic to found schools or perpetuate styles. One of the most eccentric was Zhu Da (Chu Ta, ca. 1626–1705), also called Bada Shanren (Pa-ta Shan-jen), who was distantly related to the Ming imperial house. His personal behavior was distinctly odd: he sang and laughed frequently but refused to speak. His painting was equally unusual: surging landscapes, huge lotuses, and birds and fish with the eyes of a Zen patriarch. His hand-scroll *Fish and Rocks* (see Figure 10-3) begins with a section (not shown here) done with a dry brush, and the brushwork becomes wetter as the painting proceeds — note the water plants and lotuses on the left. Poems and painting remain cryptic in meaning. The strange rock invites speculation, or perhaps it is "simply the outpouring of the artist's passing mood that has condensed into the picture of a rock."[4] Another strong individualist was Gong Xian (Kung Hsien, ca. 1618 – 89). Although his manner of building up his strokes to render light and shade suggests Western influence, his brooding landscapes are the products of his personal vision (see Figure 10-4).

Daoji (Tao-chi, ca. 1641 – 1717) was another descendant of the Ming imperial house who became a Buddhist monk, but in name only. In addition to his paintings he is known for his *Notes on Painting* in which he writes of the single line from which the whole painting grows. Like all post-Song painters he is keenly aware of himself as living and working in a postclassical age under the long shadows of the old masters. But he insists on the autonomy of his art, proclaiming that his paintings are as much a part of himself as are his beard and eyebrows, his lungs and bowels. His was a forceful vision, and he had an original technique, particularly in his use of color. Daoji eventually became reconciled to the Manchu dynasty and was twice received by Emperor Kangxi. In the more relaxed political atmosphere which followed, he felt free to acknowledge his royal Ming lineage in his seal (the equivalent of a Western artist's signature).

Figure 10-4   Gong Xian, *A Thousand Peaks and Myriad Valleys.* Hanging scroll, ink on paper, 102 cm × 62 cm. Rietberg Museum, Zurich, C. A. Drenowatz Collection.

Not all painters of the early Qing were eccentrics or individualists. There were also more orthodox painters. Outstanding were four artists all named Wang. Wang Shimin (Wang Shih-min, 1592–1680) was a student of Dong Qichang (Tung Ch'i-ch'ang), the great Ming master whose influence on the idea as well as the practice of painting can be seen even in the works of the individualists. Both Wang Shimin and his friend and second cousin Wang Jian (Wang Chien, 1598–1677) were influenced by Yuan painting. Their most gifted student was Wang Hui (1632–1717). His "Landscape in the Style of Juran" (Figure 10-5) is typical in that he uses the style of the Song master as his point of departure to create a painting very much his own. The overall composition may not be new, but as Wen Fong has pointed out, his originality lies in the vitality of his brushwork, which infuses his painting with kinetic energy.[5]

In 1691 Wang Hui received an imperial commission to supervise the painting of a series of scrolls commemorating Kangxi's southern tour. Shown even more favor by the emperor was Wang Yuanqi (Wang Yüan-ch'i, 1642–1715), who became Kangxi's chief artistic adviser in 1700. His fascination with form and structure and his concentration on surface space have been compared with Cézanne. Both "seem to have occupied a comparable position in their respective painting traditions; each in his way representing the rejection of a traditional, rationalized spatial organization in favor of a formal construction in abstract space."[6] They differ in that the art of Wang Yuanqi, like that of Wang Hui, was at heart calligraphic. Another difference was that the Chinese artist had the good fortune to be understood and appreciated by the political and artistic establishment of his day.

The Reign of Kangxi

Emperor Kangxi was on the throne from 1662 to 1722 and actually ruled from 1668 on. As already noted, he was able to complete the Manchu conquest of China in campaigns fought largely by Chinese troops under Chinese generals. After the incorporation of Taiwan, Kangxi turned his attention to China's borders in the North and West. In the Amur River region his army destroyed a Russian Cossack base. This success was followed by the Treaty of Nerchinsk signed with Russia in 1689, which settled frontier problems between the two great empires and regularized relations between them. It also removed the threat of a possible alliance between the Russians and a confederation of Western Mongols. Against the latter, Kangxi personally led his troops in 1696–97 and won a great victory. Around the middle of the seventeenth century, Western Mongols had intervened in the politico-religious struggles taking place in Tibet and had remained as conquerors. Under Kangxi, the Qing too became deeply involved. In 1720 Qing armies entered Tibet and installed a pro-Chinese Dalai Lama (the spiritual and secular ruler of Tibet). This was to be the first but not the last Qing intervention in Tibet.

山川渾厚
草木華滋
甲辰春倣巨然筆意
偹翁老先生壽　王翬

Figure 10-5   Wang Hui,
*Landscape in the Style of
Juran (Chü-jan)*. Hanging
scroll, ink on paper, dated
1664, 131 cm × 65.5 cm.
Collection of Mr. and Mrs.
Earl Morse.

Kangxi's martial exploits were, in part, a reflection of a conscious sense of identification with his Manchu forebears and his desire to preserve the traditional Manchu way of life, which he saw as essential to maintaining Manchu supremacy. Another expression of this feeling was the organization of great hunting expeditions, in which he took considerable delight. To help preserve Manchu distinctiveness, one of the first acts of Kangxi's reign was the closing of Manchuria to Chinese immigration. During the Qing, Manchus were not allowed to marry Chinese, and Manchu women were not allowed to bind their feet. Kangxi was very much the Manchu, but he was not anti-Chinese. Like previous non-Chinese invaders, however, he felt impelled to take steps to avoid being submerged in the larger Chinese population and more sophisticated Chinese culture.

Under Kangxi a strict balance was maintained between Manchus and Chinese in the top metropolitan administrative posts, and in the provinces, generally, a Chinese governor was counterbalanced by a governor-general, usually placed over two provinces, who was a Manchu, a Mongol, or a Chinese bannerman. Military security was provided first of all by hereditary banner forces garrisoned in strategic locations throughout China. They lived apart from the general population in their own communities and were commanded by a general responsible directly to Beijing. Another group used by the emperor were his Chinese bondservants, who managed the imperial household and could be used for confidential tasks. Like eunuchs, they were dependent on imperial favor, but unlike eunuchs, they did not offend Chinese feelings. Bondservants were used by Kangxi to submit secret memorials on conditions in the provinces and also managed the emperor's personal treasury and the monopolies, including the maritime customs.

Kangxi was a very vigorous man. He rose well before dawn each day to go through a great stack of memorials before receiving officials, beginning at 5 A.M. (later changed to 7 A.M. to accommodate officials not living near the palace). His tours of personal inspection in the South are famous. To show his benevolence, he reduced taxes and forced Manchu aristocrats to desist from seizing Chinese lands. He was also a man of wide intellectual interests, including, as we have seen, Western learning. He won the affection of many of the Chinese literati by holding a special examination in 1679, and not only patronized artists but sponsored the compilation of the official Ming history, a great phrase dictionary, a giant encyclopedia, and an exhaustive dictionary of Chinese characters. The philosophy of Zhu Xi (Chu Hsi) received his special support.

Yongzheng

Kangxi was one of the most successful emperors in all of Chinese history, but he was unable to provide for a smooth succession. After his death, the throne was seized in a military coup by a prince who became Emperor Yongzheng

(Yung-cheng, r. 1723–35). After he became emperor, Yongzheng censored the record of his accession to the throne and also suppressed other writings he deemed inimical to his regime, particularly those with an anti-Manchu bias. Like his father, he used military force to preserve the dynasty's position in Mongolia, and when Tibet was torn by civil war during 1717–28, he intervened militarily, leaving a Qing resident backed by a military garrison to pursue the dynasty's interests.

Yongzheng was a tough, hard-working ruler bent on effective government. Seeing the need to restructure the financing of local government in order to free magistrates from dependence on private and informal funding, he accomplished a great deal by way of fiscal rationalization, though in the long run effective reform below the district level proved unattainable. In carrying out such reforms, the emperor made effective use of the secret palace memorial system and also increased government efficiency by forming a five-man Grand Council to supersede the Grand Secretariat as the chief body concerned with high policy.

Yongzheng's reign was despotic, efficient, vigorous and brief. By the simple device of sealing the name of the heir-apparent in a box kept in the throne room, Yongzheng was able to assure that on his death there would be no struggle over the succession. Thus he prepared the way for what was to be the Qing's most splendid reign, that of Qianlong (Ch'ien-lung).

Qianlong

During Qianlong's reign (1736–95), the Qing achieved its greatest prosperity, and geographic expansion into Central Asia reached its greatest extent (see Figure 10-1, p. 227). This was made possible not only by Chinese strength but also by the disunity and declining strength of the Inner Asian peoples. The declining vitality of these peoples has been subject to various interpretations. As summarized by Morris Rossabi, the most plausible explanations include the diminishing importance of the international caravan trade in an age of developing maritime commerce, a trend toward the development of sedentary societies marked by urbanization, and Russian expansion that reduced the area to which tribes could flee in retreat, thereby reducing their mobility.[7]

Under Qianlong, Chinese Turkestan was incorporated into the Qing dynasty's rule and renamed Xinjiang, while to the West, Ili was conquered and garrisoned. The Qing also dominated Outer Mongolia after inflicting a final defeat on the Western Mongols. Its policy there was to preserve Mongol institutions, but it allowed Chinese merchants to enter and exploit the people, thus reinforcing the anti-Chinese animosities of the animal-herding Mongols. It is no accident that when the Qing fell in the twentieth century, the Mongols promptly declared their independence. Throughout this period there were continued Mongol interventions in Tibet and a reciprocal spread of Tibetan Lamaism in Mongolia. Qianlong again sent armies into Tibet and firmly established the Dalai Lama as ruler, with a Qing resident and garrison to preserve Chinese suzereinty. Other than that, no attempt was made to integrate Tibet into the empire after the manner of Xinjiang. Further afield, military campaigns against Annamese, Burmese, Nepalese, and Gurkhas forced these peoples to submit and send tribute.

This expansion involved millions of square miles and brought into the empire non-Chinese peoples (such as Uighurs, Kazakhs, Kirghiz, and Mongols) who were at least potentially hostile. It was also a very expensive enterprise. The dynasty enjoyed unprecedented prosperity and managed in the mid-1780s to accumulate a healthy financial reserve, but its resources were not inexhaustible. Yet the emperor delighted in the glory and wealth. He built a sumptuous summer residence, partly of Western design, and undertook grand tours of the empire, including six tours of the South. In his policy toward the literati, he combined Kangxi's generous patronage of scholarship with Yongzheng's suspiciousness of anti-Manchu writings. The greatest project sponsored by him was the Complete Library of Four Treasuries (Siku quanshu, Ssu k'u ch'üan-shu) of 3,000 volumes. This "final affirmation of the unity of knowledge and power in Chinese history"[8] preserved many books but also merged into a campaign to ferret out and suppress writings offensive to Manchu susceptibilities.

Decorative Arts

The splendor and opulence of the age was reflected in its ceramics and decorative arts. In this respect also the Qianlong period built on the achievements of the two preceding reigns. Under Kangxi, the royal kilns produced great numbers of bowls, vases, plates, and vessels, many of them manufactured especially for the growing foreign market. Among the most admired are oxblood vases, although more common were pieces whose basic color was green (famille verte). The plate shown in Figure 10-6 is painted to show a scene with six ladies sitting on a terrace. Along with their artistic qualities, such decorated ceramics provide much information about dress, architecture, and upper-class life and leisure.

In the Yongzheng period a pinkish rose color (famille rose) became the favorite. Fine copies of Song ware were produced during the Qianlong period, but there was no return to Song tastes. Among the most exquisite and finely crafted products of the Qianlong kilns were porcelains produced at the imperial kilns.

Bright colors were an important feature of interior decoration. The use of colored tiles as well as paint helped to produce a vibrant effect. Enamelware (especially cloisonné—that is, ware on which the enameled areas are separated by thin strips of metal), intricately carved lacquers and ivories, ornate embroideries, highly decorated furniture all testify to the era's taste for fine craftsmanship and rich detail. The entire style of this era evoked the

Figure 10-6 Dish
painting in *famille verte*
enamels. Kangxi period,
diam. 61 cm.

enthusiasm of European visitors and helped to encourage the eighteenth-century European craze for "chinoiserie" and the manufacture, both in China and in Europe, of highly commercial Sino-European products for the Western market. At their best, Chinese art objects of the eighteenth century are impressive in their high craftsmanship. Yet, to borrow a term used by early eighteenth-century Chinese scholars in their discussions of painting, the art was rather "overripe."

During the last years of the Qianlong era there were definite indications that the dynasty had passed its peak and that there was trouble ahead. Before discussing these, however, it is well to consider some of the other aspects of the century when the Qing was strong and seemed well.

Culture of the Literati in the Eighteenth Century

Scholarship, known as "evidential research" continued to flourish. At the beginning of the dynasty, Gu Yenwu, as already noted, wrote extensively on both statecraft and philology. Modern readers know him best for the former, but his immediate successors were more interested in his contributions to the latter. As a result, Qing scholars made important, even iconoclastic, discoveries concerning the questionable historicity of parts of such venerated classics as *The Classic of Change*, *The Classic of History*, and the *Records of Rites*. However, the concentration on philology easily led to the view that textual studies alone were truly "solid" (in the sense that they avoided abstract speculation) and "practical" (in the sense that this seemed the best way to uncover the meaning of the classics). The resulting narrowing of intellectual interest is exemplified by the contrast between Yan Yuan (1635–1704) and his chief disciple, Li Gong (Li Kung, 1659–1733). Although Yan Yuan was born too late to be a Ming loyalist, he shared the concerns of the generation that lived through the Ming-Qing transition. Accordingly, Yan condemned quiet sitting and book learning as standing in the way of true self-cultivation capable of "changing the world"; and he studied military science and medicine. But Li Gong expounded his teachings in the form of commentaries on the classics.

A major scholar and theorist was Dai Zhen (Tai Chen, 1723–77), who made important contributions to linguistics, astronomy, mathematics, and geography as well as philosophy. Like most of the creative seventeenth-century thinkers, he rejected the metaphysical existence of *li*, which he considered simply the pattern of things. Similarly he disputed Zhu Xi's dualistic theory of human nature, insisting that this went against the teachings of Mencius, that human nature is one whole and all good, and that moral perfection consists in the fulfillment of one's natural inclinations.

Dai Zhen shared his age's faith in philology, but this was not true of his contemporary Zhang Xuecheng (Chang Hsüeh-ch'eng, 1738–1801), who strongly disliked philological studies and sought for meaning in the study and writing of history. Zhang is perhaps most famous for his thesis that "the six classics are all history," by which he meant that they were not "empty" theoretical discussions but that they document antiquity and illustrate the Dao. A scholar must not stop at the facts but get at the meaning. Zhang once compared a work of history to a living organism: its facts are like bones, the writing is like the skin, and its meaning corresponds to the organism's vital spirit.

Along with history and philosophy, another subject of perennial concern to Chinese scholars was the function and evaluation of literature. The poet Yuan Mei (1716–97) held that the purpose of poetry is to express emotion, that it must give pleasure, and rejected the didactic view, held, among others, by Zhang Xuecheng, that it must convey moral instruction. Yuan's poetry and prose reflect the life of a talented, refined eighteenth-century hedonist, unconventional within the bounds of good taste, and marginally aware of the exotic West. One of his prize possessions was a large Western mirror much admired by his lady pupils. Among Yuan's less conventional works are a cookbook and a collection of ghost stories. His interest in the latter was shared by his friend, the painter Le Ping (Lo P'ing, 1735–99), the youngest, and last, of the so-called "Eight Eccentrics of Yangzhou," a man who claimed actually to have seen the apparitions he painted.

In the eighteenth century, painters of various schools were at work: professionals working in the meticulous and mannered "northern" style, eclectics drawing on diverse traditions and models, and individualists striving, sometimes excessively, for originality. An unusually interesting and prolific artist was the painter Gao Qipei (Kao Ch'i-p'ei, 1660–1734). Even in the Song and earlier, artists had experimented with unconventional materials instead of using a brush, but none had gone as far as Gao who painted with the balls of his fingers, the side of his hand, and a long fingernail split like a pen for drawing lines. Some 600 years separate Gao's *Young Crane under a Wutong Tree* (see Figure 10-7) and Emperor Huizong's parakeet (see Figure 6-1, p. 163). In that time not only the means but the purpose of art, and the artist's self-conception, had changed.

Qing painters and scholars generally perceived themselves as latecomers in a long and revered tradition. As such they faced a dilemma similar to that of painters, poets, and composers of our own time who no longer feel they can contribute to the traditional lines of development in their arts, that is, be another Rembrandt, Beethoven, and so forth. The classical masters had said what needed to be said, and the creative opportunities available to those who would imitate or compete with them were limited. Moreover, what had been valid for one age could not serve another. But if the time for classical achievements was past, future directions were by no means clear.

Figure 10-7   Gao Qipei, *Young Crane under a Wutong Tree*. Hanging scroll, ink on paper, 95 cm × 44 cm.

It was characteristic of the age — and here the analogy to our own times is also instructive — that old canons of art were rejected. Thus some artists cultivated the notion that the epitome of art was non-art, that is, the deliberate cultivation of innocent awkwardness. Similarly, it was now quite acceptable for an eccentric to display his eccentricity by selling his paintings. Both Gao and Le did so without jeopardizing their "amateur" status. The favorite place for such men was Yangzhou, where wealthy salt merchants derived prestige as well as pleasure from supporting a world of painting, poetry, and calligraphy. Including, but extending beyond, the circle of such sophisticates was the audience for popular drama and vernacular literature. The latter in particular reached new heights.

Qing Fiction

Many of the dynasty's best writers and thinkers were men who had failed in the examination route to success, an experience which perhaps helped them to view society with a measure of critical and even satiric detachment. The examinations themselves were a favorite target. Pu Songling (1640–1715), a short story writer, wrote this account of the seven transformations of a candidate in the provincial examination:

> When he first enters the examination compound and walks along, panting under his heavy load of luggage, he is just like a beggar. Next, while undergoing the personal body search and being scolded by the clerks and shouted at by the soldiers, he is just like a prisoner. When he finally enters his cell and, along with the other candidates, stretches his neck to peer out, he is just like the larva of a bee. When the examination is finished at last and he leaves, his mind in a haze and his legs tottering, he is just like a sick bird that has been released from a cage. While he is wondering when the results will be announced and waiting to learn whether he passed or failed, so nervous that he is startled even by the rustling of the trees and the grass and is unable to sit or stand still, his restlessness is like that of a monkey on a leash. When at last the results are announced and he has definitely failed, he loses his vitality like one dead, rolls over on his side, and lies without moving, like a poisoned fly. Then, when he pulls himself together and stands up, he is provoked by every sight and sound, gradually flings away everything within his reach, and complains of the illiteracy of the examiners. When he calms down at last, he finds everything in the room broken. At this time he is like a pigeon smashing its own precious eggs. These are the seven transformations of a candidate.[9]

This examination was held in a labyrinthine compound, with the candidates housed in individual cells where they had to spend the night. It was an eerie place sealed off from the rest of the world, for during an examination session the great gates could not be opened for any reason whatsoever. (If a man died during the examination, his body was wrapped in straw matting and thrown over the wall.) Thus it was a perfect setting for numerous tales of ghosts, usually the spirits of jilted maidens come to wreak their vengeance on the men who had done them wrong.

One of the two outstanding novels of the Qing was *The Scholars (Rulin waishi, Ju-lin wai-shih)*, by Wu Jingzi (Wu Ching-tzu, 1701 – 54). It is primarily a satire on the examination system but also catches in its net an assortment of other human follies, and presents vignettes of the pompous and the ignorant, the unworldly scholar and those who cheat him, the intricacies of social and political life, and so on. Although it is episodic in organization and somewhat uneven in quality, it incorporates certain technical advances in the art of storytelling, notably in the way it allows its characters to reveal their personalities gradually rather than labeling them at the very start. It is a fine work of literature as well as a treasure house for the social historian.

China's most beloved and greatest novel is *The Dream of the Red Chamber (Honglou meng)*, also translated as *The Story of the Stone*. Like *The Scholars* it offers priceless insights into Qing society, this time from the vantage point of a large, eminent family in decline. With rich detail embedded in its narrative fabric and a cast of hundreds, it reveals how such a family was organized and functioned, the relationship between the generations and the sexes, the lives of women, the status of servants, and so on, and it does this with fine psychological characterization based on the personal experience of the author Cao Xuehqin (Ts'ao Hsüeh-ch'in, 1715 – 63). But it is not only a novel of manners, for Cao's Buddhist/Daoist view of life gives it a metaphysical dimension and philosophical depth; C. T. Hsia has written that "it embodies the supreme tragic expression in Chinese literature,"[10] and that for its main protagonist, "the ultimate tragic conflict lies in a tug of war between the opposing claims of compassion and detachment."[11]

Economy and Society

So many lives were lost during the fighting and disorder that ravaged China during the Ming-Qing transition that after peace was restored, it took until late in the seventeenth century for the population to reach its previous high. A favorable land-peasant ratio as well as government policy favored free labor and a small-farm economy. On the other hand, the resumption of commercialization made for increased social stratification since market crops such as cotton generally entailed more risk as well as greater potential reward than did the growing of grains. Generalization about China's local social and economic foundations remains difficult and potentially misleading because conditions varied greatly from area to area. The most striking contrast remained that between the commercially advanced, rice-growing Yangzi Delta region with its well-organized lineages and the Northern Plain where the village, not the lineage, was the essential socioeconomic unit. Again, on the Chengdu (Ch'eng-tu) Plain in Sichuan, a commercialized region of dispersed settlements, the local marketing region formed the social as well as economic base. Nor should we forget that while China was predominantly rural, many people lived in its many urban places including Beijing, the world's largest city until surpassed by London around 1800.

A major development was an increase in agricultural production. This was partly the result of the maximum geographical spread of known products and techniques: superior strains of rice, improved irrigation methods, and better fertilizers, such as soybean cakes. However, production was also increased through the introduction of new crops originally native to America: corn, the sweet potato, and the peanut. The sweet potato and the peanut were of special importance because they did not require the same quality soil or climatic conditions as other products of Chinese agriculture and thus could be grown on land not previously cultivated. One beneficial result of increased output was tax reduction: with agricultural production up, tax rates could be lowered without reducing revenues. Emperor Yongzheng's reform of the tax system particularly benefited poor peasant farmers. The century saw an increase in Chinese life expectancy and an all-around improvement in the standard of living. These, in turn, undoubtedly made further contributions to agricultural production and to economic development generally.

Agriculture provided a foundation for the development of trade and manufacturing. Of the latter, the pottery kilns have already been mentioned. Another industry that now flourished was the cotton trade. Silk and hemp, brewing and paper, mining and metal working deserve mention as areas of strong activity, as do the spread of tea and sugar production. Accompanying increased internal trade was a growth of market towns linked by empire-wide merchant groups and serviced by a sophisticated banking system. As William T. Rowe has concluded, "the uniquely efficient water-transport system and marketing mechanism of preindustrial China allowed it to overcome the barriers of long distance and low technology, and to develop a national market by the mid-Qing, even though in Europe and elsewhere such a development may have been conditional upon the advent of steam-powered transportation."[12] Although the total value of internal trade far outweighed that of foreign commerce, the latter, too, contributed to Chinese well-being. Throughout the century the balance of overseas trade was in China's favor, and there was a strong inflow of gold and silver.

A major result of agricultural growth, peace, and prosperity was an increase in the size of China's population. By the end of the eighteenth century more people lived in China than in Europe; the Chinese population was in the neighborhood of 300 million, about double what it had been two centuries earlier. One result was the filling up of previously marginal areas within China and increased emigration of Chinese people into Southeast Asia. Meanwhile, at home growth in production failed to keep up with an expanding population, and the first to suffer were the poor who had to live by their labor at a time when labor was cheap and land was dear. State and society as well as the economy came under increasing pressure. As in Europe, the stresses resulting from population growth did much to destabilize the traditional order.

The challenge of population growth did not go completely unnoticed: Hong Liangji (Hung Liang-chi, 1748–1809) first wrote about the dangers inherent in this process in 1793. But, by and large, the state did nothing. The civil service was not expanded to meet the needs of society nor to accommodate the growing number of candidates, many of them superbly qualified. Even in the Song there were cases of men who spent a lifetime taking examinations — when the emperor asked his age, one such man replied, "fifty years ago twenty-three." Now the aged candidate became a stock figure in literature. The government even relaxed standards for men over 70 so that, past retirement age, they could at least enjoy the psychological satisfaction of receiving a degree. In an effort to weed out candidates, new examinations were introduced. Thus in 1788 the reexamination of provincial and metropolitan graduates was introduced. That brought the total minimum number of examinations required for the final degree to eight, not counting a final placement examination. By this time the criteria for judging papers had become exceedingly formalistic. Candidates spent years practicing eight-legged essays, and bookshops did a thriving business selling model answers. In the meantime, the old battle of wits between examiners and cheaters remained a draw (see the "cheating shirt," Figure 10-8).

The unsatisfactory state of the examination system, and the tendency of the

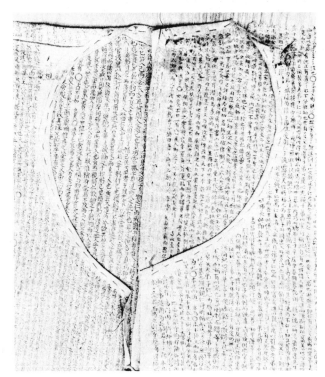

Figure 10-8 Cheating shirt. Fujii Museum (Fujii Saiseikai Yurinkan), Kyōto.

government to tinker and elaborate rather than reform and innovate, suggests a dangerous hardening of the institutional arteries, and during the last 20 years of Qianlong's reign there were other signs of trouble. One institution Qing statesmen were not worried about because it seemed to be working well was the system for dealing with European trade. Yet the mission of Lord Macartney to Beijing in 1793 (the same year Hong Liangji set down his thoughts concerning the population problem) indicated that the British did not share the Qing satisfaction with the status quo.

Overseas Trade and the Canton System

The Qing, early on recognizing that the flourishing maritime trade with Southeast Asia was of great economic importance to coastal communities and posed no security problems for the empire, basically left its management to local authorities. Though Kangxi instituted some restrictions on foreigners trying out the Chinese market, it was Qianlong who restricted them to Canton where a special area was set aside for the warehouses (called "factories") of the foreign traders who were allowed to reside there but not to bring their wives and settle down.

There were other restrictions under this Canton System (1760–1842). In all their transactions foreign traders were required to deal with a group of Chinese merchants who had been granted a monopoly of foreign trade. These merchants belonged to the Cohong, an association of firms (or hong) established for that purpose. In theory the Cohong was composed of a maximum of thirteen hong, but in practice there were only seven or eight such establishments, supervised by an imperial official who usually squeezed a good deal of personal profit out of his position. Each foreign ship was placed under the responsibility of a particular hong, which handled not only commercial matters but also saw to it that duties were paid and that the foreigners conducted themselves properly. Under this system, the foreigners were not granted direct access to Chinese officials, nor was allowance made for government-to-government relations. On the British side the prime agent was the East India Company, which enjoyed a monopoly of trade between England and China.

As Jane Leonard has pointed out, these arrangements separated maritime trade from the tributary system of conducting foreign relations.[13] Consequently when Macartney and later in 1816 Lord Amherst tried to expand trade and open European-style diplomatic relations, they ran head on against a well-established dynastic practice. The system continued to operate until China faced a Europe which could no longer be contained.

Internal Decay

As the expense of military campaigns far beyond the bounds of China proper mounted, the resources of even the prosperous Qianlong regime were strained to the utmost, while administrative laxity and corruption were rendering the government less efficient and more expensive. The worst offender was a Manchu favorite of Emperor Qianlong, a man named Heshen (Ho-shen, 1750–99), who rode high for 23 years. Assured of imperial support, he built up a network of corruption and amassed a huge fortune, leaving the enormous sum of 20 million taels when he died. Although bitterly detested he could not be removed, for he never lost Qianlong's confidence and affection. An attack on Heshen implied an attack on the aging emperor's own judgment and, furthermore, suggested the presence of the disease of factionalism. Perhaps Qianlong was especially sensitive to any signs of factionalism since his father, Emperor Yongzheng, had written a very strong critique on this subject. Like his political authority, the moral and intellectual authority of the emperor were now beyond question. Emperor Qianlong abdicated after his 60-year rule in order not to rule longer than his illustrious grandfather, but he continued to dominate the government until his death in 1799. Only then was Heshen removed and, in lieu of execution, allowed to take his own life.

As always, the burden of extravagance and corruption was borne by the common people. As a result many of them joined in the White Lotus Rebellion, which broke out in 1796 and was not completely suppressed until 1804. At its height it affected Sichuan, Hubei, Henan, Gansu, and Shaanxi. The rebellion drew its following by promising the coming of Maitreya, a restoration of the Ming, and the rescue of the people from all suffering. It gained momentum as it attracted the destitute and displaced and proved the power of its cause. It was also assisted by the ineffectiveness of the dynasty's response: government generals used the occasion to line their own pockets and bannermen proved their total incompetence. Not until after Heshan's fall did the government make real headway. A new, very capable commander was appointed, disaffected areas were slowly taken from the rebels, and militia bands organized by the local elite, whose members had the most to lose from radical social change, proved effective in putting down insurgency.

Heshan and the rebellion were both destroyed in the end, but corruption in government and misery in the countryside remained to plague the dynasty in the nineteenth century. On the surface, the problems faced by government and society seemed familiar and therefore capable of solution well within the boundaries of existing values and institutions, but later history was to suggest that the dynasty had succeeded better in dealing with problems of the past than in recognizing, let alone coping with, those just looming on the horizon. China was ill prepared for the onslaught that came later from a Europe which, during the last years of the Qianlong's reign, was being refashioned by the French and Industrial Revolutions. Despite economic growth and population pressures, political ills, and social disaffection, the fact that there was no indication of comparable revolution about to erupt in China suggests (for better or worse) the resilience of China's social structure and the continuing compatability between that structure and the political system.

NOTES

1. Frederick Wakeman, Jr. *The Great Enterprise: The Manchu Reconstruction of Imperial Order in Seventeenth-Century China* (Berkeley: Univ. of California Press 1985), Vol. I, 456–57.

2. Wm. Theodore de Bary, Wing-tsit Chan, and Burton Watson, comps., *Sources of Chinese Tradition* (New York: Columbia Univ. Press, 1960), pp. 387–88.

3. James Cahill, *The Compelling Image: Nature and Style in Seventeenth Century Chinese Painting* (Cambridge, Mass: Harvard Univ. Press 1982), p. 183.

4. Roger Goepper, *The Essence of Chinese Painting* (Boston: Boston Book and Art Shop, 1963), p. 138.

5. Wen Fong, quoted in Roderick Whitfield, *In Pursuit of Antiquity: Chinese Paintings of the Ming and Ch'ing Dynasties from the Collection of Mr. and Mrs. Earl Morse* (Princeton: The Art Museum, Princeton Univ., 1969), p. 41.

6. *Ibid.*, p. 183.

7. Morris Rossabi, *China and Inner Asia—From 1368 to the Present Day* (New York: Pica Press, 1975), pp. 139–40. Rossabi does not think Buddhism was a major factor, although it may have contributed to the decline. *Ibid.*, pp. 140–41.

8. R. Kent Guy, *The Emperor's Four Treasures: Scholars and the State in the Late Ch'ien-lung Era* (Cambridge, Mass.: Harvard Univ. Press, 1987), p. 37.

9. Quoted in Ichisada Miyazaki, *China's Examination Hell*, trans. Conrad Schirokauer (Tokyo and New York: John Weatherhill, 1976), pp. 57–58.

10. C. T. Hsia, *The Classic Chinese Novel* (New York: Columbia Univ. Press, 1968), p. 246.

11. *Ibid.*, p. 264.

12. William T. Rowe, *Hankow: Commerce and Society in a Chinese City, 1796–1889* (Stanford: Stanford Univ. Press, 1984), p. 62.

13. Jane Kate Leonard, *Wei Yuan and China's Rediscovery of the Maritime World* (Cambridge, Mass.: Harvard Univ. Press, 1984), Chapter 3.

PART FOUR

China
in the
Modern
World

Self-Portrait. Ren Xiong. Hanging scroll,
ink and color on paper. 177.5 × 78.8 cm.
Private Collection.

西方之入侵
中國

11
The Intrusion of the West: China

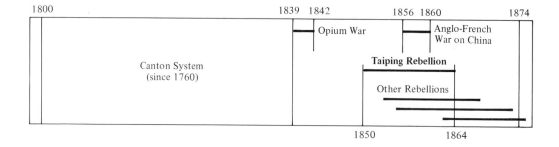

*I*n the nineteenth century Europe was supreme. Intellectual, political, and economic forces at work since the Renaissance had transformed European civilization and produced unprecedented wealth and power. The process was accelerated in the late eighteenth century by industrialization and the French Revolution, explosions that set off tremors reaching eventually all around the globe. During the century, the economic revolution created new wealth, new technology, new appetites, and new problems, first in England and then in other countries of Western Europe. The nation-state offered its citizens more, but it also made greater demands on them than had the old empires in Europe or elsewhere. It was also a tumultuous period of intense economic competition, stringent national rivalries, bitter class conflicts, and sharp clashes between old values and ideas and new. Yet few Europeans questioned the superiority — moral, intellectual, economic, and political — of their civilization.

The new Europe, powerful and aggressive, challenged all other civilizations and ultimately left its mark everywhere. That its impact on China and Japan was and remains intense can hardly be denied, but modern Chinese and Japanese history is also a product of the internal dynamics of their own history. One of the most interesting questions debated by scholars is the extent to which these dynamics were moving in the same direction as in the West. For example, both China and Japan experienced the development before 1800 of a national trade network serviced by large cities with strong mercantile communities employing sophisticated business methods. In contrast to their colleagues in Japanese studies, students of China tend to emphasize the barriers to further development explained variously by demographic pressures, an indifferent or hostile state, or a "high level equilibrium trap" (a self-regulating balance between production and consumption bereft of incentive for technological innovation), but they too recognize elements in the traditional civilization conducive to a modern transformation.

For both China and Japan, the impact of the modern world has thus partly been very destructive (as it was also in the West), and this aspect has been all too obvious. But modern forces also partly fused with older tendencies, strengthening some, distorting others, and at times even creating something new and original.

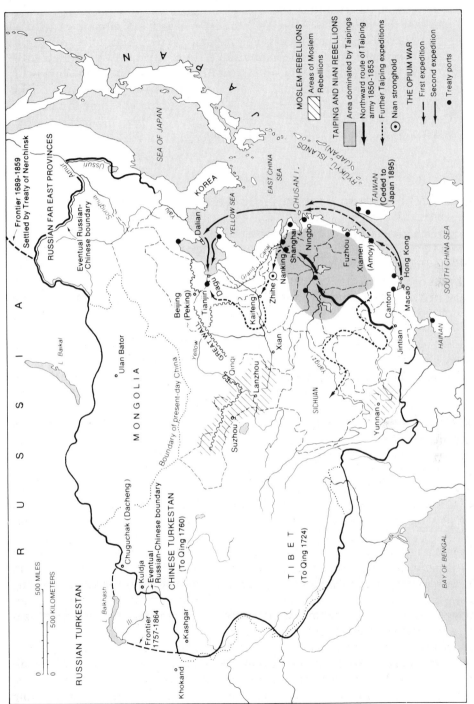

Figure 11-1   China in the Nineteenth Century

Terms such as "intrusion of the West" must also not be allowed to obscure the fact that the "West" was itself a pluralistic as well as a changing civilization. To understand developments in East Asia, it is necessary to bear in mind what was happening in Europe at the same time. Militarily the nineteenth century was the age of sea power, and Great Britain was the major sea power of the age. Thus Britain created the largest of the European overseas empires, and it was Britain that was most involved with China and forced China to abandon the Canton System and to open her doors to the West (see Figure 11-1). The pivotal event was the Opium War (1839–42).

Breakdown of the Canton System: Sino-British Tensions

As noted earlier, Chinese contact with the West in the eighteenth century was limited to commerce; there were no diplomatic relations. Even commerce was strictly limited as all Western commerce with China was carried out through the port of Canton (see Figure 11-2), Western residence in Canton was strictly regulated, and the terms of trade allowed Western merchants to deal with only

Figure 11-2 *Canton, ca. 1760.* Artist unknown. Gouache on silk, 47.7 cm × 73.7 cm. One of four creating a panorama of the waterfront. Peabody Museum, Salem.

a small group of Chinese firms (the Cohong), which had a monopoly on foreign trade. Western traders, used to more open commercial dealing in other parts of the globe became increasingly resentful. Thus, well before the actual outbreak of war, the limitations imposed by the Canton System seemed likely to lead to a clash between the increasingly aggressive Europeans and a Manchu-Chinese Empire past its prime.

Exacerbating political and economic tensions was the incompatibility of the Chinese and English views of themselves and the world. Both were supremely self-confident and proud of their own civilizations. Both were narrowly culture-bound. Thus when the Macartney mission arrived in Beijing (Peking) in 1793 in the hope of broadening the terms of trade and initiating treaty relations with China, the presents sent to Emperor Qianlong (Ch'ien-lung)* by England's George III were promptly labeled as "tribute" by the Chinese. Qianlong responded to the English monarch by praising his "respectful spirit of submission"[1] and, in the gracious but condescending language appropriate for addressing a barbarian king residing in the outer reaches of the world, turned down all his requests, political and economic. He saw no merit in the English request for representation in Beijing nor did he favor increased trade, "As your Ambassador can see for himself, we possess all things. I set no value on objects strange or ingenious, and have no use for your country's manufactures."[2]

On the English side, Lord Macartney refused to perform the ceremonial kowtow expected of barbarian envoys and performed by the Chinese themselves toward their superiors and by the emperor toward Heaven. Macartney was confident that the Chinese would perceive "that superiority which Englishmen, wherever they go, cannot conceal."[3] In the end, the Chinese allowed an informal audience that did not require the full kowtow (three kneelings and nine prostrations), but in their self-assessments the Chinese and the English remained as far apart as two peoples have ever been. The English sent another mission to China in 1816 headed by Lord Amherst, but he did not even get an audience at court.

The British motive for coming to China was and continued to be primarily economic. In contrast to China's self-sufficiency and Emperor Qianlong's disdain for foreign products, there was a Chinese product in great demand in Britain. This was tea. First imported in tiny quantities in the late seventeenth century, tea was initially taken up as an exotic beverage with medicinal properties, then popularized as a benign alternative to gin, and finally was considered a necessity of English life, with the East India Company required by Act of Parliament to keep a year's supply in stock at all times. Tea imports reached 15 million pounds in 1785 and double that amount in the decade preceding the Opium War. Not only did the East India Company depend on the income from the tea trade, the British government also had a direct stake in tea, since about one-tenth of its entire revenue came from a tax on Chinese tea. Not until the

---

* For both temple and era names of Qing emperors see Table 10-1, p. 230.

1820s did the Company begin experimenting with tea growing in India, and it was many years before Indian tea provided an alternative to the tea of China. The importance of Chinese tea extended even to American history: it was Chinese tea that was dumped from East India Company ships in the famous Boston Tea Party (1773).

The British problem was how to pay for this tea. There was no market for British woolens in China, and the "sing-song" trade in clocks, music boxes, and curios was insufficient to strike a balance of trade. Until the last third of the century, the sale of British imports covered 10 percent or less of the cost of exports, with the rest paid for in cash and precious metals. Unable to find anything European that the Chinese wanted in sufficient quantity, the English turned toward India and the "country trade." This was the term for trade between India and various places from the Indian Ocean to the China seas conducted under East India Company license by the private firms of British subjects. Money obtained in Canton by the "country traders" was put on deposit there for the Company against bills of exchange on London. In this way, England, India, and China were connected by a trade and payments triangle.

The Opium Trade

Until 1823 the largest commodity imported to China from India was cotton, but this never reached the volume necessary to balance the trade. That was accomplished by opium. Opium had long been used for medicinal purposes, but the smoking, or more accurately, the inhaling of opium fumes through a pipe, began in the seventeenth century. The spread of the practice was sufficient to provoke an imperial edict of prohibition in 1729, but this and subsequent efforts to suppress the drug were unsuccessful and opium consumption continued to increase. Distributed partly through older salt smuggling networks and protected by the connivance of corrupt officials, it spread steadily and proved particularly attractive to soldiers and government underlings. The drug was debilitating and habit forming (see Figure 11-3). Withdrawal was excruciatingly painful. Over time the addict developed a tolerance for opium and needed more and more of the drug to achieve a "high." The addict became a slave to opium. Thus, to pay for tea the Chinese were sold a poison. Since the opium was brought to China by country traders, the East India Company disclaimed responsibility for the illegal traffic in China. At the same time, however, it profited from the sale of opium in India where it monopolized the Bengal crop (Patna) and did what it could to control West Indian production (Malwa). In India itself, where the British as the paramount power felt a certain sense of responsibility, consumption of opium for nonmedicinal purposes was strictly prohibited.

The Chinese market for opium developed at such a pace that the balance of trade was reversed. During the 1820s and 1830s silver to pay for opium

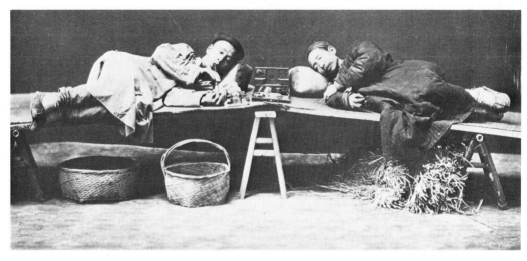

Figure 11-3   Opium Smokers.

imports seems to have left China in large quantities. This, in turn, helped cause a decline in the exchange rate between copper coinage and silver, which upset the basis of the Chinese monetary system. Thus, what began as a public health problem now became a fiscal problem as well. In 1834, the Company's monopoly of the China trade was abolished by the British government. This opened the gates of trade still wider on the British side, resulting in an increased flow of opium to China, and an increased flow of silver out of China. Thus abolition of the Company's monopoly made the problem worse.

Abolition of the Company's trade monopoly was a victory for English advocates of free trade, who were as antagonistic to restraints on trade abroad as they were at home. The immediate effect in China was to put an end to the system of Cohong-Company relations in Canton. Now in place of the Select Committee of the East India Company, the British side was represented by an official of the crown. To initiate the new relations, Britain sent out Lord Napier as First Superintendent of Trade with instructions to establish direct contact with the Qing viceroy, to protect British rights, and to assert jurisdiction over Englishmen in Canton. To accomplish these aims, he was ordered to use a moderate and conciliatory approach. Napier, however, more ambitious than diplomatic, immediately took an adamant stand on the issue of direct communication with the viceroy. He violated Chinese regulations by not waiting in Macao for permission to proceed to Canton and by sending a letter rather than petitioning through the hong merchants. With neither side willing to back down, the impasse developed into a showdown. All Chinese employees were withdrawn from the British community, food was cut off, and trade was stopped. Napier finally withdrew to Macao, where he died. This all took place in 1834. Unfortunately, in the ensuing lull no progress was made toward finding a new *modus vivendi* between the two sides.

For a brief moment the Chinese considered legalizing opium, but in 1836 the government decided on suppression instead. Dealers and addicts were prosecuted with great vigor, and imprisonments and executions were widespread, with the result that the price of opium dropped precipitously. This program was well under way when Lin Zexu (Lin Tse-hsü, 1785–1850), a man of excellent reputation and demonstrated intellect and ability, arrived in Canton in March 1839. As imperial commissioner, he was charged with stamping out the drug trade once and for all.

In Canton, Lin conducted a highly successful campaign against Chinese dealers and consumers. He also severely punished the corrupt officials who had connived at the trade. To deal with the foreign source of the opium, he appealed to Queen Victoria: "Suppose there were people from another country who carried opium for sale to England and seduced your people into buying and smoking it; certainly your honorable ruler would deeply hate it and be bitterly aroused." [4] He also admonished the foreign merchants, and he backed moral suasion with force.

What Lin demanded was that the foreigners surrender all their opium and sign a pledge to refrain from importing the drug in the future at the risk of confiscation and death. To effect compliance, he used the same weapons of isolating the foreign traders employed successfully in 1834 against Napier. Elliot, the British Superintendent of Trade, took a fateful step in response when he ordered the British merchants to turn their opium over to him for delivery to the Chinese authorities. By this act Elliot relieved the merchants of large amounts of opium they had been unable to sell because of the efficacy of the Chinese prohibitions, and he further made the British government responsible for eventual compensation. No wonder that the merchants enthusiastically dumped their opium: 21,306 chests were delivered to Lin Zexu. It took the Chinese 23 days to destroy it all.

In England great pressures were exerted on the government by firms interested in the China trade demanding prompt and vigorous military action. Lin meanwhile, pleased with his victory, continued to press Elliot on the issue of the bonds or pledges, but here he did not succeed. The Superintendent of Trade argued that it was against British law to compel the merchants to sign the bonds and that the imposition of the death penalty without the benefits of English judicial procedure was also contrary to British law. What was at stake here was the issue of British jurisdiction over British subjects, a source of Anglo-Chinese friction since 1784, when the British had refused to submit to Chinese justice. The issue came to the fore again in the summer of 1839 when a group of English sailors killed a Chinese villager in the Canton hinterland. Refusing to turn the men over to Lin Zexu, Elliot tried them himself, but when they were returned to England the men were freed, since the home court ruled that Elliot had exceeded his authority.

The first clash of the war took place in November 1839, when the Chinese tried to protect one of the only two ships whose captains had signed the bond despite Elliot's stand and now wanted to trade. When a British ship fired a shot across the bow of the offending vessel, the Chinese intervened with 21 war junks, which, however, were no match for the foreign ships. In December trade with the British was stopped, and on January 31, 1840, a formal declaration of war was announced by the governor-general of India acting in the name of the home government.

The Opium War (1839–1842)

In June 1840, the British force, consisting of 16 warships, 4 armed steamers, 27 transports, a troop ship, and 4,000 Irish, Scottish, and Indian soldiers, arrived in China. First the British blockaded Canton and then they moved north. They were fired on at Xiamen (Amoy) while trying to deliver a letter from Prime Minister Palmerston under a white flag of truce, a symbol the Chinese did not understand. They then seized Chusan Island, south of the Yangzi estuary, and Dinghai, the chief city there. The main body of the fleet sailed another 800 miles north to Beihe, near Tianjin, where Palmerston's letter was accepted. By this time the emperor had lost confidence in Lin Zexu whose tough policy had led to military retaliation. Lin was dismissed, disgraced, and exiled to Ili in Central Asia. His place was taken by the Manchu prince Qishan (Ch'i-shan, d. 1854), who pursued a policy of flattery and accommodation to get the British to return to Canton for further negotiations. This they did in September 1840.

Figure 11-4   *Foreign Devil.*
A Chinese sketch, ca. 1839.

When the negotiations with Qishan in Canton turned out unsatisfactorily from the British point of view, they resumed military operations, with the result that in January 1841 Qishan was forced to sign the Convention of Chuanbi, which provided for the cession of Hong Kong, an indemnity payable to Britain, equality of diplomatic relations, and the reopening of Canton. Both Qishan for the Qing and Elliot for the British thought they had done very well, but neither government accepted their work. The Chinese emperor was indignant at how much had been conceded while Palmerston fumed that Elliot had demanded too little. The reactions of the Chinese and British governments showed all too clearly how far apart they still were in their appraisal of the situation. Caught in the middle were the negotiators. Like Lin Zexu earlier, now Qishan came to feel the imperial displeasure: his property was confiscated and he was sent to exile on the Amur. Elliot too was dismissed; his next position was as consul-general in Texas.

In the renewed fighting Canton was besieged in February 1841, but the siege was lifted on payment of a ransom of 6 million Spanish silver dollars. However, before their departure the British experienced the growing hostility of the local population. They were attacked by a body of troops organized by the local gentry. Although militarily ineffective, the attack was an indication of popular sentiment (see Figure 11-4).

In August Elliot was relieved by Pottinger, and the last phase of the war began when the British moved north, occupying Xiamen in August and Dinghai in October. Reinforcements were sent from India, increasing the naval force and bringing troop strength up to 10,000. With this force Pottinger continued the campaign, advancing up the Yangzi until his guns threatened Nanjing. In Nanjing on August 29, 1842, the treaty was signed that brought the war to a close. It was a dictated peace imposed by the Western victor on the vanquished Chinese.

The Treaty System

The Treaty of Nanjing (together with the supplementary Treaty of the Bogue, October 1843) set the pattern for treaties China later signed with the United States and France in 1844, established the basic pattern for China's relations with the West for the next century, and supplied the model for similar treaties imposed on Japan. The Treaty of Nanjing marked the end of the Canton System. The Cohong monopoly was abolished. Five ports — Canton, Xiamen, Fuzhou, Ningbo, and Shanghai — were opened to Western trade. Britain received the right to appoint consuls to these cities, where British merchants were now allowed to trade and to reside together with their families. The treaty also stipulated that henceforth official communications were to be made on a basis of equality.

The Chinese were forced to pay an indemnity of 21 million Spanish silver dollars. Of this amount 12 million was for war expenses, in keeping with the normal European practice of forcing the loser to pay for the cost of a war. Another 6 million was paid as reparations for the opium handed over to Commissioner Lin, while the remaining 3 million went to settle the debts owed by the hong merchants to British merchants, thus liquidating another aspect of the old Canton System.

An important provision of the treaty established a moderate Chinese tariff of from 4 to 13 percent on imports, with an average rate of 5 percent. The Chinese, whose statutory customs levies had been even lower, did not realize that by agreeing to this provision they were relinquishing the freedom to set their own tariffs. On the British side there was the conviction that, as Adam Smith had taught, the removal of constraints on trade would benefit all by allowing everyone to concentrate on what he did best.

The British, having acquired an empire in India, with all the burdens of government that it entailed, did not seek to create another in China. Trade not territory was their aim. But they did demand and obtain a Chinese base. Hong Kong Island, at that time the site of a tiny fishing village, was ceded to them in perpetuity. Well-located and with an excellent harbor, it developed into a major international port.

The issue of legal jurisdiction over British subjects was settled by the Treaty of the Bogue, which provided for extraterritoriality, that is, the right of British subjects to be tried according to British law in British consular courts. The British, having only recently reformed their own legal system, were convinced of its superiority. There were precedents in Chinese history for allowing "barbarians" to manage their own affairs, but in modern terms extraterritoriality amounted to a limitation on Chinese sovereignty.

The Treaty of the Bogue also provided for most-favored-nation treatment. This obliged China to grant to Britain any rights China conceded in the future to any other power. Its effect was to prevent China from playing the powers off against each other. It meant that once a nation had obtained a concession it automatically was enjoyed by all the other states enjoying most-favored-nation status.

In the 1844 treaties the United States and France also received this status. In the American treaty China agreed to allow for the maintenance of churches and hospitals in the treaty ports, and to treaty revision in twelve years, while the French won the right to propagate Catholicism.

The status of the opium trade was left unsettled in the original treaties, and American agreement to outlaw smuggling did not slow down the growth of opium traffic, which was legalized under the next round of treaty settlements, 1858–60, and opium even functioned as a kind of money. From the annual 30,000 chests prior to the Opium War it expanded to reach a high of 87,000 chests in 1879. It then declined as native Chinese production of opium increased. British opium imports were down to about 50,000 chests when in 1906 the Qing took strong measures against the drug. British imports finally came to a stop in 1917, but opium smoking remained a serious social problem until the early 1950s.

For China the treaties solved nothing. A particularly ominous development was the permission granted foreign gunboats to anchor at the treaty ports, for when additional ports were opened it gave foreign powers the right to navigate China's inland waterways. Today, with the benefit of hindsight, it is apparent that the cumulative effect of the treaties was to reduce China to a status of inequality unacceptable to any modern nation.

China and the West (1842–1860)

Although it is now universally regarded as a milestone, the treaty settlement did not seem so to the Qing authorities who, as John Fletcher has shown, had made many of the same concessions as recently as 1835 in reaching a settlement with the tiny Central Asian state of Kokand involving an indemnity, a tariff settlement, the abolition of a merchant monopoly, and a special position exceeding that of most-favored-nation status seen as simply a case of "impartial benevolence."[5] It is therefore not surprising that very few men had any inkling of the dimensions of the challenge facing the empire. Thus even a perceptive scholar like Wei Yuan (1794–1857), author of the influential *Illustrated Treatise on the Sea Kingdoms* (first version, 1844) incorporated new information into old categories and did not feel compelled to break with tradition. And despite his geopolitical orientation, Wei underestimated the British threat.

Under the circumstances, the best that "experts" could suggest was for China to acquire "barbarian" arms and to employ the old diplomacy of playing off one "barbarian" against another. Less well-informed officials suggested that future military operations take advantage of the supposed physical peculiarities of the "barbarians," for example, their stiff waists and straight legs, which made them dependent on horses and ships, or their poor night vision.

Negotiations with the foreign powers were handled by the viceroy of Guangdong and Gwangxi. The first viceroy managed the English by charm and conciliation, "sharing their cup and spoon to hold their hearts,"[6] but he was later replaced by a more hard-line, intransigent official. Frustrated in attempts at local negotiation, the British demanded direct representation in Beijing. They also pressed for treaty revision because the opening of the new ports had not led to the anticipated increase in trade. Behind the demands for freer trade was the persistent belief that only artificial restrictions prevented the development of a giant market in China for British textiles and other products.

One cause for friction between the English and the Chinese was the repeated postponement of the opening of Canton in view of the strong antiforeign feeling of its people. The continuation of the opium trade did not help matters, and Chinese antagonism toward Europeans was reinforced by the development of a new commerce in Chinese laborers. These men were often procured against their will, crowded into dismal "coolie" vessels, and transported as contract laborers to work the plantations of Cuba and Peru. The boom set off by the discovery of gold in California in 1848 also brought Chinese immigrants to the United States, but they came as free laborers, their passage organized by Chinese merchants. By 1852 there were 25,000 Chinese in the American West, and by 1887 there were twice that number in California.

There were some efforts at cooperation during these years. With Chinese consent, the British set about suppressing piracy. More important was the establishment of the Foreign Inspectorate of Customs in Shanghai in 1854, after the Qing officials had been ejected by rebels. The Inspectorate became responsible for the collection of tariffs and the prevention of smuggling. By the new treaties of 1858, its authority was extended to all treaty ports, and it became an important source of support for the dynasty.

Despite such collaboration, however, there remained more discord than harmony, and in 1856 war broke out once more. The immediate cause of the war was the Arrow Affair. The Arrow was a Chinese-owned but Hong Kong-registered lorcha, a vessel with a Western hull but Chinese rigging, which although flying the British flag was boarded by Chinese officials, who seized twelve Chinese men whom they charged with piracy. When the viceroy returned the men but refused to apologize and guarantee there would be no repetition of the event, the British responded by seizing Canton. Then they withdrew, and there was a lull in the fighting while the British were occupied fighting a war in India set off by the Mutiny of 1857. When the war in China was resumed in December 1857, the English were joined by the French.

As in the first war, the Europeans again moved north, and again the first attempt at peace failed, since the Qing emperor refused to ratify the British and French Treaties of Tianjin negotiated in 1858. Hostilities then recommenced. This time the allies entered Beijing itself in 1860, and Elgin, the British commander, vented his anger by burning down the imperial summer palace. In October the Conventions of Beijing were signed to supplement the Treaties of Tianjin, which now also took effect. In addition to the usual indemnity, China was forced to open eleven new ports, to grant rights to travel in the interior, and to allow foreign envoys to reside in Beijing. In 1860 the French also surreptitiously inserted into the Chinese text a provision granting missionaries the right to buy land and erect buildings in all parts of China.

Russian Gains

The peace agreements were secured through the mediation of the Russian ambassador to Beijing, who used the opportunity to consolidate the gains Russia had made to date and to obtain new concessions for his country. Under Peter the Great and Catherine the Great, Russia's land empire had expanded into the area west of the Pamirs known as Russian Turkestan, and in 1851 Russia obtained trading privileges and the right to station consuls at Kuldja and Chuguchak (Dacheng) in the Ili region of Chinese Turkestan east of the

Pamirs. Now Kashgar, southwest of Kuldja, and Urga (Ulan Bator) in Outer Mongolia were also opened to them.

The most massive Russian gains, however, were in the Northeast. In the Amur region Nikolai Muraviev, governor-general of Siberia, had been putting pressure on the Qing since 1847. Now, in 1860, the entire area north of the Amur was ceded to the Russians, who also received the lands east of the Ussuri River, which were incorporated into the Russian Empire as the Amur and Maritime Provinces. In the latter Muraviev founded Vladivostok ("Ruler of the East," in Russian). Russia also now received most-favored-nation status. The gains Russia made at this time remain a source of conflict between the Russians and Chinese today.

Internal Crisis

The encroachments of the foreign powers, serious as they were, constituted only one of the threats facing the dynasty. An even greater danger to the regime developed internally as the government proved unable to deal with long-term problems that would have taxed the ingenuity and energy even of an honest and effective government. Foremost were the problems created by population pressures, for the population continued to increase in the nineteenth century as it had in the eighteenth. By 1850 the number of inhabitants in China had risen to about 430 million, without any comparable increase in productivity or resources. As the pressures of the struggle for survival strained old humanistic values to the breaking point, it all too often left little room for honesty, let alone charity. Life became brutish and hard. As ever, the poor suffered most, and they were legion, for the uneven distribution of land left many people landless, destitute, and despairing. The situation was made worse by government neglect of public works. The opium trade also contributed to the economic crisis, for silver continued to leave China, further disrupting the silver-copper ratio and thereby increasing the farmer's tax burden, which was calculated in scarce silver but paid in copper cash.

Government leadership was totally inadequate. Emperor Jiaqing (Chiach'ing, 1796–1820) tried to remedy the government's financial problems by cutting expenses but was unable to solve the underlying fiscal and economic problems. Sale of official posts and titles helped the treasury but did not raise the quality of the bureaucracy nor help the people who ultimately supplied the funds.

Emperor Daoguang (Tao-kuang, 1821–50) continued his father's policy of frugality. It is said that he himself wore old and patched clothes. His partial success in reforming the official salt monopoly system did not compensate for his failure to reinvigorate the Grand Canal or Yellow River managements, however. The former was impassible by 1849, after which tax grain had to be shipped by sea. The abandonment of the canal cost thousands their jobs. Emperor Daoguang did not live to see the Yellow River disaster of 1852. Since

1194 the great river had flown into the sea south of Shandong Peninsula but now, silted up, it shifted to the north, spreading flood and devastation over a wide area.

The next emperor, Xianfeng (Hsien-feng, 1851–61), was 19 when he inherited the throne and proved equally incapable of dealing with an increasingly menacing situation. Even while rebellion threatened the dynasty, a major scandal involving bribery and cheating shook the examination system.

Famine, poverty, and corruption gave rise to banditry and armed uprisings, as had so often happened in the past. The most formidable threat to the dynasty came from the Taiping revolutionaries. To aggravate the crisis even further, the dynasty also had to contend with rebellions elsewhere. In the border regions of Anhui, Jiangsu, Henan, and Shandong, there was the Nian Rebellion (1853–68) led by secret societies, probably related to the White Lotus Society. There was also a Muslim rebellion in Yunnan (1855–73) and the Dongan Rebellion in the Northwest (1862–75). Yet it was the Taipings who came closest to destroying the Qing in a civil war that in terms of bloodshed and devastation was the costliest in human history. It is estimated that more than 20 million people lost their lives.

The Taiping Rebellion (1850–1864)

The founder of the Taiping movement was a village school teacher named Hong Xiuquan (Hung Hsiu-ch'üan, 1814–64) who belonged to the Hakka minority, which many centuries earlier had migrated from the North to the Southeast, where they remained a distinct ethnic group. Originally Hong hoped for a conventional civil service career and four times went to Canton to participate in the examination for the licentiate, only to fail each time. Shocked by his third failure he became seriously ill and for 40 days was subject to fits of delirium during which he experienced visions. These visions he later interpreted with the aid of a Christian tract he picked up in Canton, where Protestant missionaries had made a beginning in their effort to bring their faith to China. He also received some instruction from an American Southern Baptist missionary. On the basis of his limited knowledge of the Bible and Christianity, he proceeded to work out his own form of Sinicized Christianity.

Central to Hong's faith was his conviction that in his visions he had seen God, who had bestowed on Hong the divine mission to save mankind and exterminate demons. He had also met Jesus and was given to understand that Christ was his own elder brother. This recasting of Christianity into a familiar familistic mode had its appeal for Hong's Chinese audience but dismayed Western Christian missionaries, who were further appalled by Hong's claims that he himself was a source of new revelation.

The emphasis in Taiping Christianity was on the Old Testament rather than the New Testament, on the Ten Commandments not on the Sermon on the Mount. Hong's militant zeal in obeying the first commandment by destroying

Buddhist and Daoist "idols" and even Confucian tablets soon cost him his position as a village teacher. He became an itinerant preacher among the Hakka communities in Guangxi, gaining converts and disciples as he went about spreading the word among the downtrodden and dispossessed, whom he recruited into the Association of God Worshippers. To the poor and miserable, he held out a vision of the "Heavenly Kingdom of Great Peace" (Taiping tianguo or T'ai-p'ing t'ien-kuo), an egalitarian, God-ordained utopia.

In keeping with both Christianity and native traditions, Hong and his disciples laid great stress on a strict, even puritanical, morality. Opium, tobacco, gambling, alcohol, prostitution, sexual misconduct, and foot binding were all strictly prohibited. Women were made equal to men in theory and, to a remarkable extent, also in practice. Also, consonant with both the Christian belief in the brotherhood of man and native Chinese utopian ideas was a strong strain of economic egalitarianism, a kind of simple communism. Property was to be shared in common, and in 1850 the members of the Association were asked to turn over their funds to a public treasury that would provide for everyone's future needs.

What stood in the way of realizing this utopia were the demons, mostly Manchus. By July 1850 the Association had attracted 10,000 adherents, primarily in Guangxi province. In defiance of the Qing they now cut off their queues, the long braids of hair hanging down from the back of the head, which had been introduced by the Manchus as a sign of Chinese subjugation. Since they also refused to shave the forepart of their heads, the government called them the "long-haired rebels."

Millenarian religious beliefs, utopian egalitarianism, moral righteousness, and hatred of the Manchus proved a potent combination when fused into a program of organized armed resistance. At this stage the Taipings also enjoyed good leadership. One of the outstanding secondary leaders was Yang Xiuqing (Yang Hsiu-ch'ing), originally a charcoal burner, who was a talented organizer and strategist. Starting from their base in Guangxi, the Taiping forces made rapid military progress. One of their favorite tactics in attacking cities was to use their contingent of coal miners to dig tunnels to undermine the defending walls. The incompetence of the government forces was also a help. As the Taiping armies advanced, they picked up strength. It has been estimated that their number reached over one million by the time they took Nanjing in 1853.

After such a quick advance, with their ranks swollen by new adherents only partially versed in Taiping tenets, the leadership decided it was time to call a halt and consolidate. The "Heavenly Kingdom of Great Peace" had formally been proclaimed in 1851. Now, with its capital at Nanjing, the attempt was made to turn it into a solid regime. To continue military operations, two expeditions were sent out. A small force was dispatched north and reached within 20 miles of Tianjin before suffering reverses and defeat. Large forces were sent west and enjoyed considerable success until 1856, but also were eventually defeated. The future of the rebellion depended in large part on the success of its planned consolidation.

Taiping Programs and Policies

The Taipings proclaimed a revolutionary program of political and economic reorganization. They did not want simply to establish a new regime on the old pattern but to change the pattern itself. The source for their official terminology and many of their ideas was *The Rites of Zhou (Zhou Li* or *Chou Li)*, long a source of radical thought in China.

The Taiping land program was based on a system of land classification according to nine grades found in *The Rites of Zhou*. The idea was that everyone would receive an equal amount of land, measured in terms of productivity of the soil, so that all their personal needs would be met. Any production over and above what was needed by the assignees was to be contributed to common granaries and treasuries. The system did not recognize private property.

The basic political structure was a unit of 25 families consisting of 5 groups of 5 families each. The leaders of these and larger units were to combine civil and military duties and also to look after the spiritual welfare of their people by conducting Sunday religious services. The Taipings developed their own hymns and literature including *The Three Character Classic* written in the vernacular. Taiping writings also served as the subject matter for a new examination system open to women as well as to men. In other respects, too, women were made equal to men, and there were female military units. Marriages took place in church and were monogamous.

Taiping treatment of Westerners was cordial but clumsy. They lost much good will by employing condescending language and expressions of superiority not unlike those used by Beijing. After the British failed to obtain Taiping recognition of their treaty rights, they decided on a policy of neutrality, and the other powers soon followed suit. This remained the policy of the foreign powers through the 1850s.

Dissension and Weakness

A turning point for the Taiping regime came in 1856 in the form of a leadership crisis they could ill afford. Yang Xiuqing, more ambitious than devout, had increased his power to the point of reducing Hong to a mere figurehead. To legitimize his position, Yang went into trances and claimed to be acting on God's orders, but he was unable to convince the other leaders. When he overreached himself, they turned on him. Yang, along with his family and thousands of followers, was killed, but no strong successor appeared to take his place. Meanwhile Hong Xiuquan was preoccupied with his religious visions. By the time Hong's cousin Hong Rengan (Hung Jen-kan, 1822–64) came into prominence in 1859, it was too late to restructure the regime. Hong Rengan was the most Westernized of the Taiping leaders but had neither the time nor the power to build the centralized and modern state he had in mind. His leadership lasted only until 1861.

Failure of the leadership was one source of Taiping weakness. Inadequate implementation of stated policies was another. Practice did not conform to theory. For example, Hong Xiuquan and the other leaders kept numerous concubines despite the Taiping call for monogamy. Moreover, there were many missed opportunities: the failure to strike before the dynasty could regroup; the failure to cooperate with secret societies and other opponents of the regime who did not share the Taiping faith; the failure to cultivate good relations with the foreign powers.

To make matters worse, Taiping revolutionary ideas repelled all those Chinese who identified with the basic Confucian way of life and understood that the Taiping program was not merely anti-Manchu but anti-Confucian, and thus subversive to the traditional social order. Consequently the Taipings not only failed to recruit gentry support, but they antagonized this key element in Chinese society. To the literati, rule by "civilized" Manchus was preferable to rule by "barbarized" Chinese.

Zeng Guofan and the Defeat of the Taipings

What ultimately saved the dynasty was a new kind of military force organized by Zeng Guofan (Tseng Kuo-fan, 1811 – 72), a dedicated Confucian and a product of the examination system. Unlike the old armies organized under the Qing banner system (see p. 228), Zeng's army was a strictly regional force from Hunan, staffed by officers of similar regional and ideological background personally selected by him. They, in turn, recruited soldiers from their own home areas or from members of their own clans. A paternalistic attitude of officers toward their men, a generous pay scale honestly administered, careful moral indoctrination, and common regional ties all helped to produce a well-disciplined force high in morale.

Qing statesmen were aware that strong regional armies such as Zeng's threatened the balance of power between the central government and the regions, and were ultimately dangerous to the authority of the dynasty. But the traditional armies of the regime had proved hopelessly inadequate, and the Manchu rulers had no choice but to trust their defense to Zeng. Although organized in Hunan, where it began its operations, the army also fought the Taipings in other provinces. It was not always victorious: twice Zeng suffered such serious reverses that he attempted suicide. But in the long run a well-led and highly motivated army, honestly administered and true to its purpose, proved superior to the Taiping forces.

The dynasty also benefited from the services of two other remarkable leaders. Zuo Zongtang (Tso Tsung-t'ang, 1812 – 85) and especially Li Hong-zhang (Li Hung-chang, 1823 – 1901) whose Anhui Army became the strongest anti-Taiping force. After the treaties of 1860 the Western powers sided with the regime that had made such extensive concessions to them, and Western arms were of great assistance particularly to the Anhui Army. A Western commander and Western officers led a force of four or five thousand Chinese troops in the Shanghai area. An American adventurer, Frederick T. Ward, was its first commander, and he was succeeded by the English officer Charles George Gordon ("Chinese" Gordon) as leader of the "Ever Victorious Army." Customs revenues helped loyalists purchase foreign arms and steamers and to establish arsenals.

After a series of victories the loyalist armies laid siege to Nanjing, and when the situation became hopeless in the Taiping capital Hong Xiuquan committed suicide. Shortly thereafter, on July 19, 1864, the city fell to an army commanded by Zeng Guofan's brother. As had happened often in this bitter war on both sides, the fall of Nanjing was followed by a bloodbath. Hong's son managed to flee but was discovered in Guangxi and executed. The Taipings, once so close to victory, were completely eradicated. Their example was to inspire future revolutionaries while conservatives continued to admire Zeng Guofan. But, at the time, many no doubt shared the ambivalence of Ren Xiong (Jen Hsiung, 1820 – 57), who served for a time in a military headquarters and portrayed himself with a military haircut but did not rest easily with his choice. (See page 251.) This original, unsettling work of art mirrors the stress of the times.

Although the other uprisings against the dynasty did not threaten the Qing as severely as had the Taipings, it still took considerable fighting to suppress them. In the campaigns against the highly mobile mounted Nian bands and the Muslim rebellions, Zeng Guofan, Li Hongzhang and Zuo Zongtang again played a prominent part.

According to Chinese political theory, force was merely an adjunct of government. The suppression of the Taipings, the Nians, and other rebels was only one aspect of the general effort to revitalize the dynasty.

The Qing Restoration

The leading statesmen and scholars of the Tongzhi period (1862 – 74) thought of themselves as engaged in a restoration (zhongxing, chung-hsing*), that is, a dynastic revival similar to the revival of the Han dynasty by the founder of the Later Han, or to the resurgence of the Tang after the rebellion of An Lushan. From this sense of historical precedent they derived the confidence to initiate a broad program, which they hoped would revitalize the dynasty.

To cope with the dislocations wrought by warfare, the Tongzhi leaders applied old remedies: relief projects were instituted, public works projects initiated, land reclaimed and water controlled, granaries set up, expenses cut, taxes reduced in the ravaged lower Yangzi Valley. As always, priority was placed on agriculture.

---

* A different term (weixin, wei-hsin in Chinese, ishin in Japanese) was used by the Japanese to designate their Meiji Restoration. Although the Japanese term comes from the Chinese Book of Songs and has the meaning of "making new," or "renovation," it lacks the historical referents and programmatic content of the Chinese term.

An aspect of the revival dear to the hearts of its Confucian sponsors was a strengthening of scholarship by reprinting old texts, founding new academies, opening libraries, and the like. Examination system reform was similarly high on the list of priorities, as was the elimination of corruption from the bureaucracy. In the examinations, questions dealing with practical problems of statecraft were introduced, and attempts were made to limit the sale of degrees and offices. By such measures, the reformers sought to raise the level of honesty.

However, the reforms did not penetrate to the crucial lower level of the bureaucracy as many county magistrates continued to gain office through purchase, and nothing effective was done to curb the rapacity of the solidly entrenched and notoriously corrupt sub-bureaucracy of clerks and underlings. Kwang-Ching Liu has concluded that in the early 1870s the old abuses were returning in at least three major provinces and that the absence of major new rebellions was largely due to the superior weaponry of the provincial and imperial armies.[7]

Furthermore, the dynasty was powerless to reverse the trend toward regionalism, which ultimately had grave consequences for the center and the provinces alike. In the latter, the disruption of old bonds with the central government removed many of the political constraints on local wealth and power. It thus set in motion a restructuring of local society that ultimately was to prove dangerous both to the state and to the social order.

Tongzhi was only six when he came to the throne, and the real leadership was in the hands of his uncle Prince Gong (Kung, 1833–98) and his young mother, the Empress Dowager Ci Xi (Tz'u Hsi, 1835–1908). Foreign policy was largely under the direction of Prince Gong, who expressed the regime's order of priorities thus:

> The situation today may be compared (to the diseases of a human body). Both the Taiping and the Nian bandits are gaining victories and constitute an organic disease. Russia, with her territory adjoining ours, aiming to nibble away our territory like a silk worm, may be considered a threat at our bosom. As to England, her purpose is to trade, but she acts violently, without any regard for human decency. If she is not kept within limits, we shall not be able to stand on our feet. Hence she may be compared to an affliction of our limbs. Therefore we should suppress the Taipings and the Nian bandits first, get the Russians under control next, and attend to the British last.[8]

It was apparent to Prince Gong that new approaches to foreign policy would be required if these objectives were to be met. In 1861 he sponsored the establishment of a new agency to deal with the foreign powers and related matters. This was the Zongli (Tsungli) Yamen (Office of General Management), not an independent ministry but a subcommittee of the Grand Council supervising a number of offices (see Figure 11-5). As such its influence depended on that of its presiding officer and his associates. It was, accordingly, most influential during the 1860s, when Prince Gong was at the height of his authority. An important innovation introduced by the Zongli Yamen was its

Figure 11-5   Three members of the Zongli Yamen and statesmen of the Tongzhi period. LEFT TO RIGHT, Shen Guifen, President of the Ministry of War; Dong Xun, President of the Ministry of Finance; Mao Changxi, President of the Ministry of Works.

appeal to international law, using Henry Wheaton's *Elements of International Law*, a standard text translated by the American missionary W. A. P. Martin.

Prince Gong, recognizing that Chinese officials would be at a disadvantage in dealing with foreigners unless they had a better understanding of foreign languages and learning, was instrumental in having the Zongli Yamen establish a school for foreign languages and other nontraditional subjects in 1862. The foreign language staff was foreign and included Martin, who became the school's president in 1869. By that time astronomy and mathematics had also been introduced, despite the objections of the distinguished Mongol scholar, General Secretary Woren (Wo-jen, d. 1871) who said: "From ancient down to modern times your slave has never heard of anyone who could use mathematics to raise the nation from a state of decline or to strengthen it in time of weakness." [9] Woren was not alone in his objections to this extension of "barbarian" influence.

Nevertheless, similar schools were established at Shanghai, Canton, and Fuzhou in association with arsenals and shipyards sponsored by Zeng Guofan, Zuo Zongtang, and Li Hongzhang (see Figure 11-6). Foreigners were relied on to run both the military and the educational establishments. In this way the foundations of "self-strengthening" and of modernization were laid, but the emphasis remained heavily military. This was true even of Feng Guifen (Feng Kuei-fen, 1809–74), an advocate of learning from the barbarians, who had the audacity to propose that examination degrees, including the *jinshi*, be presented to men demonstrating accomplishment in Western mechanical skills.

During the 1860s, following the close of hostilities, Chinese cooperation with the foreign powers brought certain advantages to the Qing, although there were some on both sides who were opposed to cooperation. (For example, Woren and men of similar views felt that China should resist all foreign influence and seek the expulsion of all foreigners; while the British mercantile community frowned on the efforts of Rutherford Alcock, English minister in Beijing, to work amicably with the government.)

An important area of cooperation was the Maritime Customs Service. The first director of the service, Horatio Nelson Lay, had acquired a fleet of eight gunboats for the Chinese in England. But although these were paid for by the Chinese, he arranged that the captain of the fleet should receive all his orders through and at the discretion of Lay himself! This was unacceptable to the Qing. There were protests. China's first effort to acquire a modern navy ended

Figure 11-6   Scene at the Nanjing Arsenal.

with disbandment of the little fleet (known as the Lay-Osborn flotilla), and Lay was pensioned off.

Matters improved, however, when Robert Hart succeeded Lay in 1863. Hart's attitude was the opposite of Lay's. He insisted that the customs was a Chinese service, that Chinese officials were to be treated as "brother officers," and he gave the Qing government well intentioned and frequently helpful advice on modernization while building the service into an important source of support for the dynasty.

Cooperation between the Qing and the powers was further exemplified by the first Chinese diplomatic mission to the West, which was headed by the retiring American minister to Beijing, Anson Burlingame. Accompanied by a Manchu and a Chinese official, Burlingame left China in 1867 for a trip to Washington, several European capitals, and St. Petersburg, where he died. Somewhat carried away by his own eloquence he told Americans that China was ready to extend "her arms toward the shining banners of Western civilization." [10] In Washington he concluded a treaty rather favorable to China.

The most important negotiations for treaty revision, however, were conducted in Beijing by the British. These culminated in the Alcock Convention of 1869, which included some concessions to the Chinese, among them the provision that British subjects under the most-favored-nation clause would enjoy privileges extended to other nationals only if they accepted the conditions under which those privileges were granted. It also allowed China to open a consulate in Hong Kong and contained provisions concerning duties and taxes. These concessions may not appear very far reaching, but the English merchant community felt threatened by them, and their opposition proved strong enough to prevent the ratification of the convention.

A fatal blow to the policy of cooperation came in 1870 in Tianjin. A Catholic nunnery there had made the mistake of offering small payments for orphans brought to the mission, and rumors spread that the children had been kidnapped and that the sisters removed the children's hearts and eyes to make medicine. The tense situation erupted into violence, and a mob took the lives of the French consul and 20 other foreigners, including 10 nuns, in what came to be known as the Tianjin Massacre. The powers mobilized their gunboats. Diplomacy finally settled the issue, largely because France's defeat in the Franco-Prussian War the same year deprived France of military power and forced the French to concentrate on domestic problems. But the decade ended with demonstrations of the gap between the two civilizations and with feelings of mutual bitterness and disdain.

Thirty years after the Opium War the dynasty had survived despite the maladies attacking it from within and without. The progress of the disease had been halted. But time was to show that there had been no genuine cure and that, in the long run, the medicine itself had potentially lethal side effects. In Japan, in contrast, the old regime had fallen, and work had begun on the creation of a new state and society.

NOTES

1. John K. Fairbank, Edwin O. Reischauer, and Albert Craig, *East Asia: Tradition and Transformation* (Boston: Houghton Mifflin, 1973), p. 257.

2. Franz Schurmann and Orville Schell, *The China Reader: Imperial China* (New York: Vintage Books, 1967), pp. 105 – 13, which reproduces Harley F. MacNair, *Modern Chinese History, Selected Readings* (Shanghai: Commercial Press Ltd., 1923), pp. 2 – 9.

3. John K. Fairbank, *Trade and Diplomacy on the China Coast: The Opening of the Treaty Ports, 1842 – 1854* (Cambridge: Harvard Univ. Press, 1953), p. 59, which quotes H. B. Morse, *The Chronicles of the East India Company Trading to China, 1635 – 1834*, 5 vols. (Oxford, 1926, 1929), 2: 247 – 52.

4. Ssu-yü Teng and John K. Fairbank, *China's Response to the West: A Documentary Survey, 1839 – 1923* (Cambridge: Harvard Univ. Press, 1954), p. 26.

5. John K. Fairbank, ed. *The Cambridge History of China*, vol. 10 (Cambridge: Cambridge Univ. Press, 1978), pp. 375 – 85.

6. Teng and Fairbank, *China's Response*, p. 38.

7. *The Cambridge History of China*, vol. 10, pp. 489 – 90.

8. Teng and Fairbank, *China's Response*, p. 76.

9. *Ibid.*, p. 76.

10. Quoted in Immanuel C. Y. Hsü, *China's Entrance into the Family of Nations: The Diplomatic Phase, 1858 – 1880* (Cambridge: Harvard Univ. Press, 1960), p. 168.

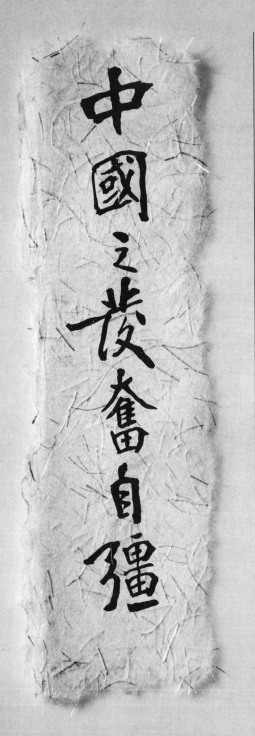

中國之發奮自彊

12
Self-Strengthening: 1874 – 1894

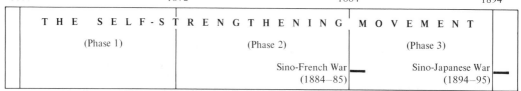

THE   SELF-STRENGTHENING   MOVEMENT

(Phase 1)   (Phase 2)   (Phase 3)

Sino-French War ___   Sino-Japanese War ___
(1884—85)   (1894—95)

The defeat of rebellion and the restoration of the Qing had given the dynasty a new lease on life and demonstrated the superiority of Western arms, prompting some leaders, notably Li Hongzhang (Li Hung-chang), to attempt selective modernization in order to strengthen and preserve state and society in the face of continued foreign pressure. This effort is known as the Self-Strengthening movement. Less ambitious and far-reaching than the Japanese modernization program, it was also less successful for a number of reasons — contrasts in geographical scale, in historical traditions, and in the structure and dynamics of society. The political situation, too, was very different.

The Empress Dowager and the Government

The dominant figure at court during the last phase of the Qing dynasty (which outlasted her by only three years) was the Dowager Empress Ci Xi (Tz'u Hsi, 1835–1908). (See Figure 13-1.) The intelligent and educated daughter of a minor Manchu official, she entered the palace as a low-ranking concubine but had the good fortune to bear the Xianfeng emperor his only son. After the Xianfeng emperor died, she became co-regent for her son, the Tongzhi emperor. Skillfully using her position to increase her power, she dominated her son and, it is rumored, encouraged him in the debaucheries that weakened his constitution and brought him to the grave at the youthful age of nineteen (1875). She then manipulated the succession in order to place on the throne her 4-year-old nephew, the Guangxu emperor (r. 1875–1908), and continued to make the decisions even when he ostensibly assumed the imperial duties in 1889. At first Prince Gong (Kung) had provided a counterforce at court, but his power declined in the seventies, and in 1884 he was removed from government altogether.

The Empress Dowager was a strong-willed woman, an expert at the arts of political infighting and manipulation. One of her most reliable supporters was the Manchu bannerman Ronglu (Jung-lu, 1836–1903), to whom she gave important military commands. Yet, it was an anomaly to have a woman in control of the court, and her prestige was not enhanced by rumors that she was

278

responsible for the murder of her rivals. Corruption in very high places also took its toll. The very powerful eunuch Li Lianying (Li Lien-ying, d. 1911) was totally loyal to his mistress but also totally corrupt, using his influence to amass a fortune. Ci Xi herself accepted payments from officials and misspent government funds. The most notorious case of financial abuse was her use of money intended for the navy to rebuild the summer palace destroyed in 1860 by Elgin and his troops during the second war between Britain and China. Eventually the navy department, established in 1885, became a branch of the imperial household, and China's most famous and magnificent "ship" was made of marble (see Figure 12-1).

Ci Xi's prime political aim was to continue in power. She had no profound aversion, but neither did she have any commitment, to the policy of selective modernization advocated by the champions of self-strengthening, and her understanding of the West was very limited. It was to her immediate political advantage to avoid dependence on any single group of officials and to manipulate a number of strong governors-general who had gained in power as a result

Figure 12-1   Marble Pavilion in the shape of a ship. Summer Palace, Beijing.

of the Taiping Rebellion. These indispensable provincial administrators could no longer be controlled by the court at will, but fortunately for Beijing (Peking), they remained absolutely loyal to the dynasty. The governors-general operated their own political and financial machines and commanded substantial military forces, but they were still dependent on Beijing's power of appointment. Major policy decisions continued to be made in Beijing. During this period, the central government was also strengthened financially by the receipts from the Maritime Customs. Thus the West helped to preserve the dynasty even as it was undermining its foundations.

Most powerful of the governors-general was Li Hongzhang, who from 1870 was firmly established in Tianjin, where he commanded an army, sponsored self-strengthening efforts, and successfully avoided transfer. A protégé of Zeng Guofan (Tseng Kuo-fan), he shared his master's devotion to the dynasty but not his Confucian probity. From his headquarters, not far from Beijing, Li dominated China's policy toward Korea, but he could not control its foreign policy elsewhere. Arguing for the priority of maritime defense, he had unsuccessfully opposed the emphasis on inner Asia, which produced Zuo Zongtang's (Tso Tsung-t'ang's) campaigns of the 1870s, and in the eighties he failed again when he tried to prevent war with France (1884–85). His opposition earned him the denunciations of his enemies, who castigated him as an arch traitor comparable to Qin Guei (Ch'in Kuei), always blamed for the Song's failure to regain the North from the Jurchen. The war, along with other developments in foreign relations, is discussed below; but first, consideration of the Self-Strengthening movement is in order. It was a movement in which Li played a major part.

Self-Strengthening

The Self-Strengthening movement began in the Tongzhi period when it was strongly military in orientation. Then, in its middle phase (1872–85), it expanded to include projects in transportation (shipping and railways), communications (telegraph), and mining. Finally, after China's defeat by France in 1885 until war broke out with Japan in 1894, it was broadened to include light industry. But throughout, it remained within traditional bounds.

Confucian pragmatism was nothing new. Willingness to adopt new means to strengthen and reform the state had animated a long line of Confucian scholars from the Song on, and, as it became clear during the early years of the nineteenth century that the Qing was in serious trouble, some scholars turned against philology to focus on what today would be called policy studies. *Huangchao jingshi wenpian (Huang-ch'ao ching-shih wen-p'ien, A Compilation of Essays on Statecraft)*, published in 1827, is a case in point. It is a collection of essays on social, political, and economic matters written by various Qing officials and compiled by He Changlin (Ho Ch'ang-lin, 1785–1841). Concern for reform and willingness to take a hard, critical look at financial and political institutions characterized the writings of leading intellectuals and, in the work of Wei Yuan began to merge with an interest in the West. First to see the West as a source for solving the dangerous problems it had created was Feng Gueifen (Feng Kuei-fen) who urged China to use "barbarian techniques" against the "barbarians," the hallmark of the Self-Strengthening movement.

Although self-strengthening was well established by the 1870s, its classic theoretical formulation came in 1898 from the brush of Zhang Zhidong (Chang Chih-tung, 1837–1909), a governor-general and practitioner of self-strengthening. Like Sakuma Shozan earlier in Japan, Zhang wanted to preserve traditional values while adopting Western science and technology. The idea was that Chinese learning would remain the heart of Chinese civilization, while Western learning would have a subordinate supporting and technical role. This was expressed in terms of the traditional Neo-Confucian dichotomy of *ti* (*t'i*, substance) and *yong* (*yung*, function): Western means for Chinese ends. The basic pattern of Chinese civilization was to remain sacrosanct, but it was to be protected by Western techniques.

Conservative opponents of self-strengthening feared that Chinese civilization would be contaminated by borrowing from the West, since, as they well knew, ends are affected by means. In the Confucian formulation, *ti* and *yong* are aspects of a single whole. The Confucian tradition had always been concerned with means as well as ends, and generations of scholars had insisted that the Way did not consist merely of "empty" abstractions but was concerned with practical realities. There was no essence apart from application. And there was a great deal more to the West than mere techniques. It was fallacious to believe that China could merely borrow the techniques of the West without becoming entangled in manifestations of Western culture. If China went ahead with efforts to adopt Western techniques while preserving traditional culture, the best that could be hoped for would be an uneasy compartmentalization. To preserve tradition in a period of modernization, the country would have to be protected from the kind of radical social reappraisal hailed in Japan by champions of "reason" like Fukuzawa Yukichi. The contrast with Japan is instructive, for there social change was sanctioned by an appeal to nationalism as symbolized by the throne, whereas in China Confucianism was much too closely associated with the social structure to allow for a similar development. Meiji Japan demonstrated that elements of Confucianism were compatible with modernization but also that modernization involved changes reaching into the very heart of a civilization.

An indication of the inadequacy of self-strengthening theory was China's failure to educate a new leadership, both fully Confucian and modern.

Education

The Self-Strengthening movement was led by impressive and capable men, such as Li Hongzhang, but there was a lack of competent middle-echelon officers and managers, as well as technical personnel such as scientists and engineers. The fastest way to make up this deficit was to send students overseas for training, which the Chinese did. However, this approach had only mixed success. The most extensive effort of this sort was made between 1872 and 1881, when 120 students were sent to the United States under the supervision of Yung Wing (in Mandarin Rong Hong, Jung Hung, 1828–1912), Yale class of 1854, and the first Chinese to graduate from an American university. The boys were between 15 and 17 years old, young enough to master new subjects, but also immature and easily swayed by their foreign environment. To assure continued Confucian training, they were accompanied by a traditional Confucian mentor. Nevertheless, they soon adopted American ways: participating in American sports, dating and in some cases eventually marrying American girls, and in a few instances even converting to Christianity. Yung Wing himself married an American and ended up making his home in Hartford, Connecticut.

The mission had been launched with the backing of Zeng Guofan and Li Hongzhang, but Li withdrew his support when the students were denied admission to West Point and when they were fiercely attacked by Beijing officials for neglecting their Confucian studies. The mission, poorly managed from the beginning, was abandoned. Among its participants were some of the first, but by no means the last, Chinese students who in the course of their overseas stay became alienated from their culture.

The obvious alternative to study abroad was to supply instruction in modern subjects at home. As we have seen, the advocates of self-strengthening were active from the start in doing just that, establishing a school in the capital and other schools in conjunction with several arsenals and the Fuzhou dockyard. By 1894 the government also operated a telegraph school, a naval and military medical school, and a mining school. These schools typically offered a curriculum encompassing both the classical studies required for success in the examination system and the new subjects for which they were established. Since command of traditional learning remained the key to entry into the civil service, students naturally tended to concentrate on that, for without an examination degree career opportunities were limited. The most famous graduate of the Fuzhou dockyard school was Yan Fu (Yen Fu, 1853–1921), who was sent to England to continue his studies at the naval college in Greenwich but after returning home to China was unable to pass the provincial examination. He became famous not as an admiral but as a writer and translator.

It did occur to some reformers to broaden the content of the examinations to allow candidates credit for mastering modern subjects, but suggestions along these lines encountered formidable opposition, since they were likely to affect the Confucian core of the civilization. A minor concession was finally made in 1887, which provided that 3 out of some 1500 provincial examination graduates might be granted that degree after being examined in Western along with (not in place of) traditional subjects. They would then be eligible for the *jinshi (chinshih)* examination on the same terms as the other candidates.

Creation of a leadership versed in modern subjects would have required major changes in the content and function of the examination system or its elimination altogether.

Economic Self-Strengthening

In China, as in Japan, there were those who wished to adopt Western technology so as to build up their country's economic strength. In Japan a strong central government took the lead in modernizing crucial sectors of the economy and successfully involved members of the upper classes in this undertaking. In China on the other hand, the government had neither the fiscal means nor the political will to lead a major sustained national effort. Instead, to quote John K. Fairbank, modernization "became a game played by a few high officials who realized its necessity and tried to raise funds, fund personnel, and set up projects in a generally lethargic if not unfriendly environment." [1]

In the first phase of the Self-Strengthening movement, the focus was military. Early projects included gun factories in Shanghai and Suzhou, the Jiangnan Arsenal in Shanghai and another arsenal in Nanjing, the Fuzhou dockyard, and a machine factory in Tianjin. These enterprises, partly due, perhaps, to their political sponsorship and operation under official control, suffered from bureaucratic corruption and poor management. Furthermore, they depended on foreigners for expertise and supervision of operations, but the individuals hired to perform these crucial tasks were frequently unqualified.

The accomplishments of the next phase of Self-Strengthening included a shipping company, textile mills, the beginnings of a telegraph service, and the Kaiping Coal Mines. Li Hongzhang took the lead in sponsoring and protecting new ventures under his policy of "government supervision and merchant operation," changed by Zhang Zhidong to "joint official and merchant operation." Capital came from both the public and private sectors. Private financing was very much desired, but capital was scarce and other forms of investment were more lucrative and prestigious. Private investment came primarily from Chinese businessmen resident in the treaty ports who were familiar with modern-style business ventures and techniques.

The overall records of such companies was mixed. The China Merchants Steam Navigation Company, as analyzed by Albert Feuerwerker,[2] provides a good example of how these concerns operated and of what was and what was not accomplished. When private capital proved insufficient to finance the company, Li Hongzhang put up the rest from public funds. To help the company make a go of it, Li secured the shipping line a monopoly on the transportation of tax grain and official freight bound for Tianjin. He obtained tariff concessions for the company and protected it from its domestic critics and enemies. In exchange, Li exercised a large measure of control, appointing and dismissing its managers, employing its ships to transport his troops, and using its payroll to provide sinecures for political followers. He also used its earnings to buy warships. To advance his policy in Korea, Li had the company lend money to the Korean government.

In the end, the overall record of this and similar companies was mixed. The investors made money and their political sponsors benefited. But after an initial spurt, the companies failed to establish a pattern of sustained growth. Instead, they stagnated. Moreover, they failed to train Chinese technical personnel. They were plagued by incompetent managers, by nepotism and corruption. Even their political sponsors, high officials in the areas where the enterprises operated, exploited the companies, regarding them as sources of patronage and revenue along the lines of the traditional salt administration, rather than as key investments for the modernization of the country. By the mid-nineties, there was a modern sector in the Chinese economy, but it was largely limited to the periphery of the empire (for example, the treaty ports and Hong Kong), where Chinese merchants were able to hold their own quite successfully against foreign competition.

The Traditional Economic Sector

While the new Western-style enterprises proved disappointing, developments in the traditional sector were hardly encouraging. Chinese tea merchants, despite sophisticated institutions and techniques adequate to sustain their dominance of the domestic market, found it increasingly difficult to compete internationally against tea grown in India and Sri Lanka (Ceylon) whose large-scale producers had an advantage over the small Chinese growers in their ability to sustain a high quality product by investing in fertilizer, replacement bushes, and labor at the crucial picking time. Furthermore, the elaborate structure of the Chinese collection system, that worked so well internally, was too unwieldy to organize an adequate response to international competition. After 1887, with the decline of exported tea, raw silk became China's main export. In the mid-1890s China was the world's largest exporter of silk (although by 1904 Japan had supplanted her in that role).

Beyond the treaty ports and their immediate hinterlands the penetration of foreign imports appears to have been slow and their impact varied. Statistics are hard to come by, and it is easier to understand broad processes than to trace their timing with precision. One model for the way in which the world economy interacted with forces already at work in the Chinese countryside is provided by Philip Huang's study of an area of North China where farmers had been growing cotton for a long time. Since cotton brought a better price than grain but also, being susceptible to drought, entailed larger risks, the difference between the successful rich and those pushed into poverty by failure was increasing. This, combined with population pressure and an absence of other opportunities for employment, set in motion an invidious process of "agriculture involution" as poor peasants worked the land for marginal and diminishing returns. Meanwhile their women, supplemented family income by laboring at spinning wheel and loom, often at less than subsistence wages. Whereas spinning was practically eliminated by machine-made thread, the low prices paid to the weavers, kept the price of native cloth below that of the factory-made product, which had to be shipped into the interior. The world economy thus did not undermine the rural economic system or provide the impetus for new departures but accelerated processes already underway. "The incorporation of Chinese agriculture into the world economy telescoped and greatly accelerated change in the small peasant economy."[3] Whether or to what degree this thesis holds elsewhere and for other sectors of the economy remains to be investigated, but whatever further research may reveal, it has the great merit of focusing attention on long-term internal processes rather than attributing fundamental change exclusively to the impact from abroad of imperialism or to the spread of an international economic system.

Missionary Efforts and Christian Influence

The Western presence in nineteenth-century China was no more confined to trade and politics than it had been during the Late Ming encounter. Once again missionaries were drawn to China as a promising area for their endeavors, but now there were Protestant as well as Catholic missionaries. An early Protestant arrival was Robert Morrison of the London Missionary Society. He reached Canton in 1807, learned the language, brought out a Chinese-English dictionary and a Chinese version of the Bible (later used by the Taipings), founded the school where Yung Wing received his early education, and set up a printing press. Other missionaries, many of them Americans, brought Western medicine and other aspects of Western secular knowledge to China.

The missionaries made a notable effort in education: by 1877 there were 347 missionary schools in China with almost 6,000 pupils. Such schools helped spread knowledge about the West as well as helping to propagate the religion. A notable missionary-educator was W. A. P. Martin, who contributed to the Self-Strengthening movement and became the first president of Beijing University. Missionaries were also important as a major source of information about China for their home countries. The first foreign language newspaper published in China was a missionary publication, and missionaries also contributed to scholarship. Outstanding among the missionaries who became Sinologists was James Legge, a master translator who rendered the Chinese classics into sonorous Victorian prose. In this and other ways, missionaries with varying degrees of sophistication and self-awareness served as cultural intermediaries.

As indicated by the growth of their schools, the missionaries met with some success, but their strength was largely in the treaty ports, and the results were hardly commensurate with their efforts. By the end of the century, the number of Catholic missionaries in China had climbed to about 750, and there were approximately half a million Catholics in China, up from around 160,000 at the beginning of the century (see Figure 12-2). The Protestants had less success: in 1890 there appear to have been only slightly over 37,000 converts served by roughly 1,300 missionaries, representing 41 different religious societies. The Tianjin Massacre of 1870 had demonstrated the potential fervor of antimissionary sentiment, and nothing happened to reduce hostilities during the next quarter of a century.

The reasons for the poor showing of Christianity are many and various. They include difficulties in translation and communication analogous to those that plagued Buddhist missionaries a millennium and a half earlier. The most important concepts of Christianity such as sin or the trinity were the most difficult to translate, none more so than the most sacred idea of all, the idea of God. Agreement on how to translate "God" into Chinese was never reached; three versions, one Catholic and two Protestant, remained current. As before, differences in culture compounded the difficulties in communication.

The nineteenth-century missionary, however, also encountered problems that he did not share with his predecessors, for the Chinese associated

Figure 12-2   The French Cathedral at Canton, built on the former site of the governor's yamen.

Christianity with both the Taiping Rebellion and the unequal treaties. The former showed Christianity as subversive to the social and political order, while the latter brought the missionaries special privileges. Both were resented. Furthermore, the aura of power also drew to Christian establishments false converts; individuals attracted by the possibilities of a treaty port career, and opportunists out to obtain missionary protection for their own ends. Popular resentment of the missions was fired by scurrilous stories and bitter attacks, such as those that employed a homonym for the transliteration of "Jesus" to depict Christ as a pig (see Figure 12-3). This hostility was encouraged by the elite who saw in Christianity a superstitious religion that threatened their own status and values. It was no accident that anti-Christian riots often occurred when the examinations were being held in the provincial capitals.

Here there is an interesting contrast with the situation in Japan, where 30 percent of Christian converts during the Meiji period were from samurai backgrounds. Christianity served the spiritual needs and provided a vehicle for social protest for samurai who found themselves on the losing side of the Restoration struggle. As a result in the 1880s and 1890s a prestigious native clergy was developing in Japan, and Christianity remained more influential than the slow growth of the churches would indicate. In post-Taiping China

Figure 12-3   *The [Foreign] Devils Worshipping the Incarnation of the Pig [Jesus].*

too, Christianity continued to appeal to people dissatisfied with the status quo, and it counted among its converts some notable protesters, including Sun Yat-sen. But the elite remained hostile, and the real cutting edge of protest was to be elsewhere: too radical for the nineteenth century, Christianity turned out to be insufficiently radical for the twentieth.

In the meantime, missionaries contributed to the Western perception of China. Working in the treaty ports, dealing not with Confucian gentlemen but with men on the margin of respectable society, the missionaries frequently developed a very negative view of China and its inhabitants, an image the reverse of the idealistic picture painted earlier by the Jesuits:

> The universal practice of lying and dishonest dealings; the unblushing lewdness of old and young; harsh cruelty toward prisoners by officers, and tyranny over slaves by masters — all form a full unchecked torrent of human depravity, and prove the existence of a kind and degree of moral degeneration of which an excessive statement can scarcely be made, or an adequate conception hardly be formed.[4]

These words, dated 1848, were written by S. Wells Williams who, after his service in China, became an influential American expert on China. Similar sentiments were expressed throughout the century.

Endings and Beginnings

Perhaps the most interesting themes in the intellectual and artistic life of an era are those that reflect the end of a tradition and look toward a new future. Such a time had arrived in China. For some time sensitive men had been conscious that they were living in a late stage of a great tradition. The sense of ending was intensified by awareness of dynastic decay. For some, the sense of impending national change represented an exciting challenge. For many, however, the mood was one of uncertainty, apprehension, and regret. This mood is caught in a poem by Wang Pengyun (Wang P'eng-yün, 1848 – 1904), an official who served as a Qing censor:

Tune: "The Fish Poacher"

In Reply to a Poem from Cishan, Thanking Me for
the Gift of Song and Yuan Lyrics I Had Had Printed

Now that the lyric voice wavers in wind-blown dust
Who is to speak the sorrows of his heart?
Ten years of carving, seeking from each new block
The truest music of the string unswept,
Only to sigh now
Finding my griefs in tune
With every beat that leaves the ivory fret!
I sigh for the men of old
Pour wine in honor of the noble dead:
Does any spirit rhymester
Understand my heartbreak?

The craft of letters
Furnishes kindling, covers jars:
True bell or tinkling cymbal, who can tell?
Du Fu, who lifelong courted the perfect phrase
— Did his verse help him, though it made men marvel?
Take what you find here,
See if an odd page, a forgotten tune
Still has the power to engage your mind.
My toiling over
I'll drink myself merry, climb the Golden Terrace,
Thrash out a wild song from my lute
And let the storms rage at will.[5]

Among those who welcomed the winds from the West were a small group of remarkable men, some with experience abroad in an official or unofficial capacity. An example of the former is Guo Songdao (Kuo Sung-tao, 1818–91), China's first minister to England and the first Chinese representative to be stationed in any Western country. Another was Wang Tao (Wang T'ao, 1828–97), who spent two years in Scotland assisting James Legge in his translations and who also visited Japan. One of the founders of modern journalism in China, he favored the adoption of Western political institutions, not just their science and technology. Another remarkable man was Zheng Guangming (Cheng Kuan-ying, 1842–1921), a famous scholar-comprador, modernizer, and writer. Such men were interested in Western "substance" (not just "function"), while retaining their prime commitment to the Confucian tradition.

Still more important for the future were a number of younger men whose formative years fell into this period, although they did not become influential until the late nineties. There are three names in particular to which we will return: Yan Fu, born in 1853; Kang Yuwei (K'ang Yu-wei), 1858; and Sun Yat-sen, 1866. The discussion of their ideas must wait, however, for it was not until China was jolted by her defeat in the Sino-Japanese War that they came to the fore.

Foreign Relations

Western pressures continued to affect China's foreign relations in the 20 years prior to the Sino-Japanese War, but the nature of these pressures began to alter. The initial conflicts had been over Western efforts to open trade and diplomatic relations with China proper; in the 1870s and 1880s foreign intervention in lands constituting peripheral areas of the empire or traditionally tributary states were the major causes of friction (see map, Figure 12-4).

Even as Japan was engaged in the Taiwan expedition, the Qing government was troubled by a dangerous situation in Central Asia. In 1871 the Russians used a Muslim rebellion in Xinjiang as a pretext for occupying the Ili region,

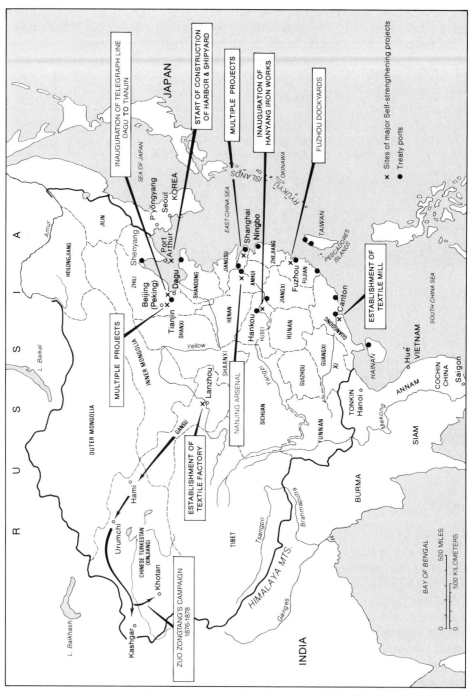

Figure 12-4   China During the Self-Strengthening Period

where a lucrative trade had developed. In Xinjiang itself, Yakub Beg (1830–77), a Muslim leader from Kokand in Central Asia, obtained Russian and British recognition for his breakaway state. In response to these alarming developments, the Qing court assigned the task of suppressing the rebellion to Zuo Zongtang, who had just finished crushing Muslim rebellions in Shaanxi and Gansu. He carried out the task with great success. By 1877, the government's control over Xinjiang was being reestablished and Yakub Beg was driven to his death. After difficult and protracted negotiations, the Russians returned nearly all of Ili (1881).

This strong showing in Central Asia, an area to which the Chinese were traditionally sensitive, bolstered morale, and Chinese successes in the diplomatic negotiations that followed encouraged those who were opposed to accommodation with the West. Indeed, the success of China's Central Asian policy encouraged them to demand an equally strong policy in dealing with the maritime powers. Pressure from this source was too strong to be ignored and constituted a major factor leading to confrontation and then to war with France in 1884–85. At issue was French expansion into Vietnam.

Vietnam and the Sino-French War of 1884–1885

North Vietnam had been annexed by the Han in 111 B.C., but after A.D. 939 native Vietnamese regimes prevailed, the major exception being the short period of Ming domination, 1406–26. The leader of the resistance against the Ming, Le Loi, established the Later Li dynasty (1428–1789), with its capital at Hanoi and its government organized along Chinese lines. As in Korea, the determination to maintain political independence from China went hand in hand with admiration for Chinese culture and institutions. It is the Chinese influence on Vietnam which sets it apart from the other, more Indian oriented states of Southeast Asia.

China also served as the model for the Nguyen dynasty (1802–1945), which from its capital at Húe in Central Vietnam ruled the country through a bureaucracy modeled as closely as possible on that of China. The Chinese model was powerful, yet differences in size and culture between China and Vietnam required adjustments and compromises. To give just one example, Chinese influence was much stronger on civil government than on the military, for military theory and practice in Vietnam (as in the rest of continental Southeast Asia) centered on the elephant.

Vietnam's location in a cultural frontier area made for a rich and complex culture but was also a source of political weakness. One result was that the social and cultural gap between village and bureaucracy was greater in Vietnam than in China. Another result was the difficulty the Vietnamese state experienced in its efforts to incorporate the south, which had been gradually taken over from the Cambodians (regarded by the Vietnamese as "barbarians") during the century from roughly 1650 to 1750. Under the Nguyen dynasty this continued to be an area of large landlords and impoverished peasants, a region where the central bureaucracy operated inadequately. The area also suffered from educational backwardness, with the result that very few southerners were able to succeed in Vietnam's Chinese-style civil service examination system.

Vietnam's long coastline and elongated shape, as well as the presence of minority peoples within its boundaries, further hampered government efforts to fashion a strong unified state capable of withstanding Western encroachments. French missionaries and military men had early shown an interest in the area and had assisted in the founding of the Nguyen dynasty itself. Nearly 400 Frenchmen served the dynasty's founder and first emperor, Gia-long (r. 1801–20). Catholicism also made headway: it has been estimated that there were more Catholics in Vietnam than in all of China. For much the same reasons as had earlier animated anti-Christian policies in China and Japan, the Vietnamese authorities turned against the foreign religion, but their suppression of Catholicism gave the French an excuse for intervention.

French interest in Vietnam increased during the reign of Louis Napoleon. In 1859 France seized Saigon. Under a treaty signed three years later, the French gained control over three southern provinces, and five years later they seized the remaining three provinces in the South. These southern provinces became the French colony called Cochin China. During 1862–63 the French also established a protectorate over Cambodia. French interests were not limited to the South but included Central and North Vietnam (Annam and Tonkin). Treaties concluded in 1862 and 1874 contained various provisions eroding Vietnamese sovereignty, and when disorders occurred in North Vietnam in 1882, France used the occasion to seize Hanoi.

Throughout this period of increasing French penetration, the Vietnamese court had continued its traditional tributary relations with Beijing. When the French took Hanoi, the Vietnamese court responded by seeking both help from the Qing and support from the Black Flags, an armed remnant of the Taipings, which had been forced out of China and was fighting the French in Vietnam.

The Qing responded by sending troops. Considerable wavering and diplomatic maneuvering followed in both Beijing and Paris, but in the end no means were found to reconcile the Chinese wish to preserve their historic tributary relations with Southeast Asia and the French determination to create an empire in this region. The resulting war was fought in Vietnam, on Taiwan and the Pescadores, and along the nearby coast of China proper, where the Fuzhou dockyards and the fleet built there were among the war's casualties.

In the peace agreement that followed, China was forced to abandon her claim to suzerainty over Vietnam. The French colony of Cochin China, and the French protectorates of Annam and Tonkin, were joined by protectorates over Cambodia and (in the 1890s) Laos, to constitute French Indo-China.

Chinese influence in Southeast Asia was further diminished in 1886 when Britain completed the conquest of Burma, and China formally recognized this situation as well. Then in 1887, China ceded Macao to Portugal, officially recognizing the de facto situation there. Thus in the last third of the nineteenth century the foreign powers tried to gain further concessions and proceeded to establish themselves in tributary areas that had been part of the traditional Chinese imperial order, although not of China proper. In the face of this challenge, the Chinese made concessions where necessary and resisted where feasible. When areas of major importance were at stake, their policy was quite forceful. The struggle over Korea is an example.

Korea and the Sino-Japanese War of 1894–1895

Like Vietnam, Korea had adopted Chinese political institutions and ideology and maintained a tributary relationship with China while guarding her political independence. Again, as in Vietnam, differences in size, social organization, and cultural tradition insured the development of a distinct Sino-Korean culture. In the nineteenth century, however, Korea was sorely troubled by internal problems and external pressures. The Yi dynasty (1392–1910), then in its fifth century, was in serious decline. Korea's peasantry suffered from "a skewered or concentrated pattern of landholding; small average per capita holdings; high rates of tenancy; a regressive tax structure; false registration of taxable land; extortion and illegal charges and gratuities at tax collection time; and usury, especially official usury in the management of the grain loan system." [6] There was a serious uprising in the North in 1811. In 1833 there were rice riots in Seoul. And in 1862 there were rebellions in the South.

During the years 1864 to 1873, there was a last attempt to save the situation by means of a traditional program of reform initiated by the regent, or Taewŏngun (Grand Prince, 1821–98), who was the father of the king. The reform program proved strong enough to provoke a reaction but was not sufficiently drastic, even in conception, to transform Korea into a strong and viable state capable of dealing with the dangers of the modern world.

That world was gradually closing in on Korea. During the first two-thirds of the century a number of incidents occurred involving Western ships and foreign demands. Korea's initial policy was to resist all attempts to "open" the country by referring those seeking to establish diplomatic relations back to Beijing. This policy was successful as long as it was directed at countries for whom Korea was of peripheral concern, but this had never been the case for Japan. Japan, therefore, was the most insistent of the powers trying to pry Korea loose from the Chinese orbit. In 1876 Japan forced Korea to sign a treaty establishing diplomatic relations and providing for the opening of three ports to trade. The treaty also stipulated that Korea was now "independent," but this did not settle matters since China still considered Korea a tributary. Insurrections in Seoul in 1882 and 1884 led to increased Chinese and Japanese involvement in Korea, including military involvement, always on opposing sides. But outright war was averted by talks between Itō Hirobumi and Li

Hongzhang, which led to a formal agreement between China and Japan to withdraw their forces and inform each other if either decided in the future that it was necessary to send in troops.

During the next years the Chinese Resident in Korea was Yuan Shikai (Yüan Shih-k'ai, 1859–1916), a protégé of Li Hongzhang, originally sent to Korea to train Korean troops. Yuan successfully executed Li's policy of vigorous assertion of Chinese control, dominating the court, effecting a partial union of Korean and Chinese commercial customs, and setting up a telegraph service and a merchant route between Korea and China.

Conflicting ambitions in Korea made war between China and Japan highly probable; the catalyst was the Tonghak Rebellion. Tonghak, literally "Eastern Learning," was a religion founded by Ch'oe Si-hyong (1824–64). In content it consisted of an amalgam of Chinese, Buddhist, and native Korean religious ideas and practices. As so often before in East Asian history, the religious organization took on a political dimension, serving as a vehicle for expressions of discontent with a regime in decay, and for agitation against government corruption and foreign encroachments. Finally outlawed, it was involved in considerable rioting in 1893, which turned to rebellion the following year when Korea was struck by famine. When the Korean government requested Chinese assistance, Li Hongzhang responded by sending 1,500 men and informing the Japanese, whose troops were already on the way. The rebellion was quickly suppressed, but it proved easier to send than to remove the troops.

When Japanese soldiers entered Seoul, broke into the palace, and kidnapped the king and queen, Li responded by sending more troops and war was inevitable. It was a war that everyone, except the Japanese, expected China to win, but all parties were stunned when Japan defeated China on sea and on land. Begun in July 1894, the war was all over by March of 1895. In retrospect the reasons for the outcome are easy to see: Japan was better equipped, better led, and more united than China, a country which was hampered by internal division, corruption and inadequate leadership in the field. Equipped with shells some of which were filled with sawdust rather than gunpowder, and commanded by an old general who lined up the fleet as though he were still organizing a cavalry charge, it is no wonder that China lost the war at sea. Furthermore, powerful governors-general considered it Li Hongzhang's war, not theirs, and were slow in participating; the southern navy remained aloof.

The Treaty of Shimonoseki (April 1895)

The war was terminated by the Treaty of Shimonoseki. China relinquished all claims to a special role in Korea and recognized that country as an independent state (although its troubles were far from over). In addition, China paid Japan an indemnity and ceded it Taiwan and the Pescadores, thus starting the formation of the Japanese empire. A further indication that the Japanese had now joined the ranks of the imperialist nations was the extension to Japan of most-favored-nation status, along with the opening of seven additional Chinese ports. Japan was also to receive the Liaodong Peninsula but, after diplomatic intervention by Russia, Germany, and France, had to settle for an additional indemnity instead. The effects of the treaty on Korea, on domestic Chinese politics, and on international relations in the area are discussed in the following chapters. Here it should be noted that the treaty marked an unprecedented shift in the East Asian balance of power, a shift from China to Japan that was to continue until Japan's defeat in the Second World War.

NOTES

1. John King Fairbank, *The Great Chinese Revolution 1800–1985* (New York: Harper & Row, 1986), p. 113.

2. Albert Feuerwerker, *China's Early Industrialization: Sheng Hsuan-huai (1844–1916) and Mandarin Enterprise* (Cambridge: Harvard Univ. Press, 1958).

3. Philp C. C. Huang, *The Peasant Economy and Social Change in North China* (Stanford: Stanford Univ. Press, 1985), p. 137.

4. Harold Isaacs, *Images of Asia: American Views of China and India* (New York: Capricorn, 1962), p. 136, quoting S. Wells Williams, *The Middle Kingdom* (New York: 1883), 1: xiv–xv.

5. Cyril Birch, ed., *Anthology of Chinese Literature* (New York: Grove Press, 1972), 2: 294.

6. James B. Palais, *Politics and Policy in Traditional Korea* (Cambridge: Harvard Univ. Press, 1975), p. 63.

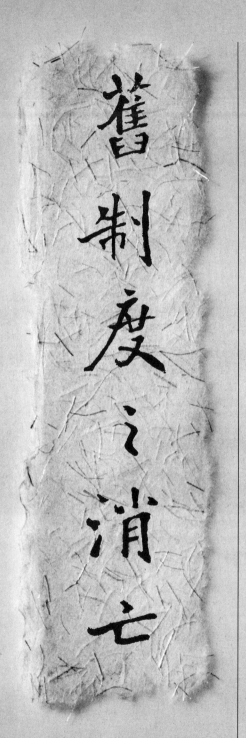

13

The End of the Old Order, 1895 – 1912

REFORMERS IN THOUGHT AND
  ACTION
THE SCRAMBLE FOR CONCESSIONS
THE BOXER RISING
WINDS OF CHANGE
REVOLUTIONARIES
ELEVENTH-HOUR REFORM
THE REVOLUTION OF 1911

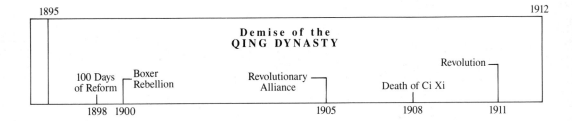

Demise of the
QING DYNASTY

Revolution

100 Days   Boxer   Revolutionary   Revolution
of Reform   Rebellion   Alliance   Death of Ci Xi

1898   1900   1905   1908   1911

C hina's defeat in the war of 1894–95 ushered in a period of accelerating change as the forces of reform, reaction, and revolution interacted and interlocked in complex patterns while the Chinese people continued to face an international environment full of menace.

The revelation of the dynasty's military weakness brought on demands for new concessions by the imperialist powers in a process that reached its greatest intensity during the first six months of 1898. Within China the parameters of political discourse were expanded and the pace of political activity quickened, reaching a climax in the "hundred days of reform," from June 11 to September 20 of that same year. The new foreign demands helped to spur the reformers in their efforts, but it was the defeat of 1895 that brought them to the fore and gave them an audience.

Reformers in Thought and Action

The new reformers who emerged in the nineties were distinguished from their modernizing predecessors both in the scope of the changes they advocated and in a willingness to reexamine basic assumptions about the very nature of the world. At the same time, however, the radicals of this generation consisted of men who still had received a thorough Confucian education and had a command of traditional learning.

A major influence on a whole generation of reformers was Yan Fu (Yen Fu), the one-time naval student at Greenwich, who voiced the bitter resentment of many:

> We thought that of all the human race none was nobler than we. And then one day from tens and thousands of miles away came island barbarians from beyond the pale, with bird-like language and beastly features, who floated in and pounded on our gates requesting entrance and, when they did not get what they asked for, they attacked our coasts and took captive our officials and even burned our palaces and alarmed our Emperor. When this happened, the only reason we did not devour their flesh and sleep on their hides was that we had not the power.[1]

297

Emboldened by the more open atmosphere, Yan publicized his ideas, first in a series of essays, and then in a number of extremely influential translations, notably Thomas Huxley's *Ethics and Evolution* (1898), Adam Smith's *Wealth of Nations* (1900), and John Stuart Mill's *On Liberty* (1903). Yan argued that Western learning was needed to release Chinese energies and rejected much of Chinese tradition. By 1904 he was denouncing even Confucius for keeping China backwards. Yan was especially attracted to Social Darwinism with its dynamic view of history as evolutionary and progressive and the hope it held out, on a supposedly modern scientific basis, for those who would struggle.

Yan Fu was no political activist, but others, notably Kang Youwei (K'ang Yu-wei, 1858–1927) and his followers Tan Sitong (T'an Ssu-t'ung, 1865–98) and Liang Qichao (Liang Ch'i-ch'ao, 1873–1929) tried to implement programs as well as exercise intellectual leadership. Working primarily through study groups and journalism, the reformers tried to spread their ideas.

Kang was an original thinker who, deeply grounded in Buddhism as well as Confucianism, elaborated a highly original theory to provide a seemingly Confucian basis for ideas that went well beyond the Confucian tradition. Drawing on the Modern Text school of classical interpretation, which, founded in the Han, enjoyed something of a revival in the late Qing, Kang argued that Confucius was not merely a transmitter of ancient teachings but a prophet who, ahead of his time, cast his message in subtle language full of hidden meanings. Confucius, according to Kang, saw history as a universal progress through three stages, each with its appropriate form of government: the Age of Disorder (rule by an absolute monarch), the Age of Approaching Peace (rule by a constitutional monarch), and the Age of Great Peace (rule by the people). Kang's Confucius was thus a seer and prophet not only for China but for the entire world. This was Kang's solution to the problem of how to be modern without rejecting everything that was native and old, when modernization implied wholesale borrowing from abroad, not only of technology but of institutions and ideas.

Another radical reinterpretation of tradition came from Tan Sitong, a brilliant man who did not confine his radical vision to a distant utopia but argued that the monarchy should be replaced by a republic, and attacked the traditional Confucian family distinctions in the name of *ren (jen)*, the central Confucian virtue frequently translated "benevolence" or "humanity." Neo-Confucian thinkers had earlier given *ren* a cosmic dimension, but Tan drew on modern scientific concepts to develop his metaphysics of *ren* in which *ren* is identified with ether (*yitai*, a transliteration of the Western word). Kang Youwei, too, equated *ren* with ether and electricity.

In their political program, Kang and his followers sought to transform the Chinese government into a modern and modernizing constitutional monarchy along the lines of Meiji Japan. Thanks to a sympathetic governor, they were able to carry out some reforms in Hunan, but their greatest opportunity came during the "Hundred Days of Reform" (actually 103 days), when a flood of edicts aimed at reforming the examination system, remodeling the bureaucracy, and promoting modernization seemed to signal the government's willingness to change course in a major way. It was an ambitious program, but the edicts were to remain more significant as expressions of intent than indicators of accomplishment, for many of them were never implemented.

The reforms were initiated by moderately experienced statesmen, but later accounts have exaggerated both the influence of Kang and his associates on this program and the degree to which it was from the beginning part of a struggle between a progressive Guangxu Emperor and a supposedly reactionary Empress Dowager (see Figure 13-1). However, rumors of Kang's supposedly extremist influence on the emperor helped to solidify the opposition and pave the way for the Empress Dowager, backed by General Ronglu (Jung-lu), to stage a coup against Emperor Guangxu, who was placed under house arrest and relegated to the role of figurehead for the remaining ten years of his life.

After the coup, Tan Sitong remained in China to suffer martyrdom, but Kang Yuwei and Liang Qichao managed to flee to Japan where they continued to write and work for renewal and reform. Kang, elaborating on his vision of utopia, dreamt of a future when the whole world would be united in love and harmony under a single popularly elected government, which would operate

Figure 13-1   The Empress Dowager seated on the Imperial Throne.

hospitals, schools, and nurseries, administering a society in which all divisive institutions would have disappeared, including even the family. Meanwhile, Liang continued to develop his ideas and to expand his horizons as well as those of his numerous readers. Like many of his contemporaries throughout the world, he championed evolution and progress, processes which he conflated and, contrary to Darwin among others, saw as products of human will. But this will had to serve the group. Like most Chinese and Japanese thinkers, Liang was not an individualist. His focus was on the group: good values were those that helped the group to progress.

The Empress Dowager's coup sent China's most advanced thinkers into exile but did not spell a wholesale reaction against reform. The Empress Dowager approved moderate reforms, including military modernization and reforms in education and the monetary and fiscal systems. That little was accomplished was due to the weakness of the central government and the enormity of the problems facing the dynasty. By no means the least of these was China's perilous international situation.

The Scramble for Concessions

China's display of weakness in the war against Japan set in motion an imperialist scramble for special rights and privileges in which Russia, France, Britain, Germany, and Japan pursued their immediate national interests and jockeyed for position in case China collapsed completely (see Figure 13-2). At the time, this seemed quite likely, and in a world in which colonies were valued as a measure of a country's greatness but little territory remained unclaimed, none of the major powers wanted to be left out.

The concessions extracted from China were economic and political. For example, the powers forced loans on the Qing, which were secured by Chinese tax revenues, such as maritime customs. Long-term leases of Chinese territory were granted to the powers, including the right to develop economic resources such as mines and railroads. Thus Germany leased territory in Shandong; Russia leased Port Arthur in the southern Liaodong Peninsula; France held leases on land around Guangzhou Bay; and Britain obtained Weihaiwei and the New Territories, adjacent to the Kowloon area of Hong Kong ceded in 1860. The powers also frequently obtained the right to police the areas they leased. Often the powers combined leaseholds, railroad rights, and commercial rights, to create a "sphere of interest," that is, an area in which they were the privileged foreign power, as, for example, Germany was in Shandong. Finally, there were "non-alienation" pacts by which China agreed not to cede a given area to any power other than the signatory: the Yangzi Valley to Britain, the provinces bordering French Indo-China to France, Fujian to Japan. In addition, Russia received special rights in Manchuria.

Britain, as the prime trading nation in China, pursued an ambiguous policy, concerned on the one hand to retain access to all of China and on the other to

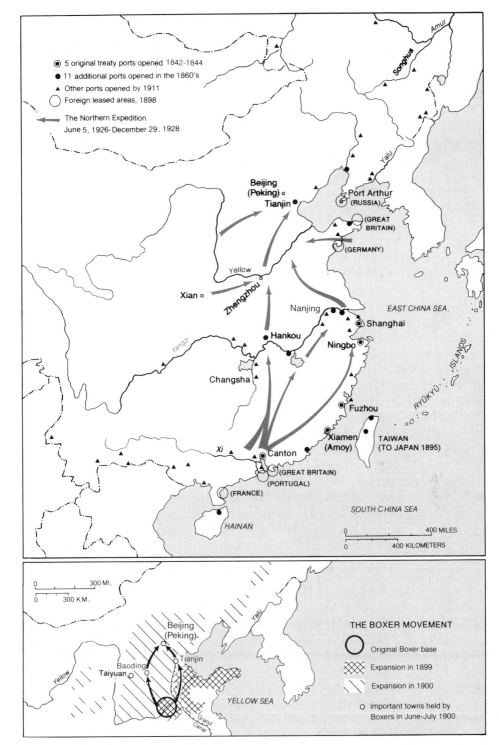

Legend:
- ◉ 5 original treaty ports opened 1842–1844
- ● 11 additional ports opened in the 1860's
- ▲ Other ports opened by 1911
- ○ Foreign leased areas, 1898
- → The Northern Expedition June 5, 1926–December 29, 1928

Beijing (Peking)
Tianjin
Port Arthur (RUSSIA)
(GREAT BRITAIN)
(GERMANY)
Yellow
Xian
Zhengzhou
Nanjing
EAST CHINA SEA
Shanghai
Hankou
Ningbo
Yangzi
Changsha
Fuzhou
RYŪKYŪ ISLANDS
Xi
Canton
Xiamen (Amoy)
TAIWAN (TO JAPAN 1895)
(GREAT BRITAIN)
(PORTUGAL)
(FRANCE)
SOUTH CHINA SEA
HAINAN

0   400 MILES
0   400 KILOMETERS

Songhua
Amur
Yalu

0   300 MI.
0   300 K.M.

THE BOXER MOVEMENT
- ◯ Original Boxer base
- ▨ Expansion in 1899
- ▨ Expansion in 1900
- ○ Important towns held by Boxers in June–July 1900

Beijing (Peking)
Baoding
Tianjin
Taiyuan
Yellow
Yalu
YELLOW SEA
Grand Canal

Figure 13-2   China, 1895–1928

obtain a share of the concessions. The United States at this time was acquiring a Pacific empire. In 1898 it annexed Hawaii and, after war with Spain, the Philippines and Guam. At the urging of Britain, the United States then adopted an "Open Door" policy enunciated in two diplomatic notes. The first of these (1899) merely demanded equality of commercial opportunity for all the powers in China, while the second (1900) also affirmed a desire to preserve the integrity of the Chinese state and Chinese territory. This was a declaration of principle, not backed by force; neither its altruism nor its effectiveness should be exaggerated.

Resentment against the encroachments of the powers was strong, not only among conservatives in office and the exiled opposition, but also among the poor and illiterate. In 1900 it flared up in violence.

The Boxer Rising

The Boxers, members of the Yihequan (*I-ho ch'üan*, Righteous and Harmonious Fists), developed in response to harsh economic conditions and resentment over the privileges enjoyed by missionaries and their converts. Passions were further fueled by alarm over the spread of railways, which cut across the land regardless of the graves of ancestors or the requirements of geomancy, railways along which stood telephone poles carrying wires from which rust-filled rainwater dripped blood red. As a counterforce the Boxers relied on rituals, spells, and amulets to endow them with supernatural powers, including invulnerability to bullets. In 1898 flood and famine in Shandong combined with the advance of the Germans in that province to create conditions that led to the first Boxer rising there in May of that year.

Originally antidynastic, the Boxers changed direction when they received the support of Qing officials prepared to use the movement against the foreign powers. Thus encouraged, the Boxers spread, venting their rage on Chinese and foreign Christians, especially Catholics. On June 13, 1900, they entered Beijing. Eight days later the court issued a declaration of war on all the treaty powers. Officially the Boxers were placed under the command of imperial princes, and there followed a dramatic two-month siege of the legation quarter in Beijing, where 451 guards defended 473 foreign civilians and some 3,000 Chinese Christians who had fled there for protection. The ordeal of the besieged was grim, but they were spared the worst, for the Boxers and the Chinese troops were undisciplined, ill-organized, and uncoordinated. The city was full of looting and violence, but the legation quarter was still intact when an international relief expedition reached Beijing on August 15 and forced the court to flee the capital.

During these dangerous and dramatic events, southern governors-general chose to ignore the court's declaration of war, claiming it was made under duress (forced by the Boxers); hence the term "Boxer Rebellion." The powers, nevertheless, demanded from the Qing court a very harsh settlement. It included a huge indemnity (450 million taels, 67.5 million pounds sterling) to be paid from customs and salt revenues. Other provisions required the punishment of pro-Boxer officials and of certain cities, where the civil service examinations were suspended. The powers received the right to station permanent legation guards in the capital and to place troops between Beijing and the sea. The Boxer rising also provided Russia with an excuse to occupy Manchuria, where some Russians remained until Russia's defeat by Japan in the war of 1904–05.

The failure of the Boxers meant a further decline in China's international position and struck a blow at the dynasty whose policies had led to ignominious flight. A convincing demonstration of the futility of the old ways, it propelled the Qing government into a serious attempt at reform.

Winds of Change

During the period 1895–1911, the modern sector of the Chinese economy continued to develop at a steady pace, but it was dominated by foreign capital. Not only were extensive railway concessions granted to the treaty powers, but Chinese railroads, like that linking Beijing and Hankou, were financed by foreign capital. Foreign capital also controlled much of China's mining and shipping, and it was a major factor in manufacturing, both for the export trade (tea, silk, soybeans, and so forth) and for the domestic market (textiles, tobacco, and so forth). Modern banking was another area of foreign domination, prompting the Qing government in 1898 to approve the creation of the Commercial Bank of China, a modern bank functioning as a "government operated merchant enterprise." Two more banks were formed in 1905 and 1907.

Except for railways and mines, foreign investments were concentrated in the treaty ports, and it was there also that Chinese factories gradually developed, taking advantage of modern services and the security to be found in foreign concession areas. Chinese enterprises were particularly important in textile manufacturing. Most remained small (by 1912 only 750 employed more than 100 workers), but they were an important part of China's economic modernization. It was also during this period that Shanghai became China's largest city, a status it retains today.

The development of a modern economic sector in Shanghai and, to a lesser extent, in other treaty ports, was accompanied by changes in social structure, but only during the last five years of the dynasty did there emerge a bourgoisie, "a group of modern or semimodern entrepreneurs, tradesmen, financiers, and industrial leaders, unified by material interests, common political aspirations, a sense of their collective destiny, a common mentality, and specific daily habits."[2] By then there was also the beginnings of an urban working class who at times expressed their resentment over terrible working conditions by going on strike. In the city, too, the old family system lost some of its economic underpinnings, and there developed an audience receptive to new values and ideas.

A strong influence on provincial affairs was exercised by a semimodern urban elite composed of merchants and bankers (more or less traditional), military and professional men (among them journalists) trained in modern methods, and absentee landowners, an elite whose interests and even values often differed from those of the landed gentry on the one hand and from the central government on the other. The very definition of elite status was changed forever when the examination system was abolished in 1905 — abolished both because the government saw the need for more modern specialists but also to secure the loyalty of graduates of new schools by reassuring them in their career expectation.

Accompanying the formation of a new elite was the emergence of a new public opinion and organized attempts to induce further changes. An early and notable example is formation of the first antifootbinding movement in 1894, which resulted in a law banning the practice in 1902, although enforcement was limited to cities. Other expressions of public opinion included a flurry of criticism at what appeared to be a maneuver to depose the emperor (1900), protests at Russia's refusal to leave Manchuria (1903), a boycott against the United States protesting exclusionary immigration laws (1905), and a boycott against Japan (1908), as well as movements to regain railway rights. The provincial urban elite's demands for modernization and building national strength were linked to their conviction that they would lead the effort.

Perhaps the most successful governor in enlisting elite cooperation during this period was Yuan Shikai, who had greatly improved his position by siding with the Empress Dowager when she decided on her coup. Yuan was able to enlist the elite of Zhili into supporting his program of police and educational reform although his economic program for the province faltered after he left. However, Yuan, like the other major reformist governor Zhang Zhidong looked to the center to take the lead.

Revolutionaries

The defeat of 1895 marked not only the emergence of radical reformism, but also led Sun Yat-sen (in Mandarin Sun Zhongshan, Sun Chung-shan, 1866 – 1925) on the path of revolution. Sun was born into a Guangdong peasant family, received a Christian education in Hawaii, and studied medicine in Hong Kong. He founded his first revolutionary organization in Hawaii in 1894, and overseas Chinese communities remained an important source of moral and financial support. Over the years he elaborated his "Three Principles of the People" — nationalism, democracy, and the people's livelihood. His political program called for the toppling of the Qing dynasty and the establishment of a republic. Sun was influenced by Henry George's "single tax'' theory, which held that unearned increases in land values (as when farm land rises in value because it is sought for commercial development) should go to the community rather than to the individual landholder. Sun, however, did not work out a full-fledged economic program. This may have been just as well, since the Three Principles were broad enough to attract the varied and loosely organized membership of Sun's Revolutionary Alliance (Tongmenhui, T'ung-men hui), formed in Tokyo in 1905 when a number of revolutionary groups merged.

The mainstream followers looked to political revolution to solve China's ills, but there were also some more radical voices, important as precursors and exemplars for future revolutionaries. One such was the pioneer feminist Qin Jin (Ch'in Chin), born in 1877 and executed as a revolutionary in 1907. The poem reproduced here was written in 1904 shortly after she had left not only the husband her family had selected for her but also a son and a daughter:

Regrets: Lines Written en Route to Japan

Sun and moon have no light left, earth is dark;
Our women's world is sunk so deep, who can help us?
Jewelry sold to pay this trip across the seas,
Cut off from family I leave my native land.
Unbinding my feet I clear out a thousand years of poison,
With heated heart arouse all women's spirits.
Alas, this delicate kerchief here
Is half stained with blood, and half with tears.[3]

Eleventh-Hour Reform

The abolition of the examination system was only the most drastic of a series of reforms in a program by which the Empress Dowager hoped to save the dynasty. The reforms were in earnest, and some, like the drive against opium, accomplished much, but frequently the measures taken to save the Qing had a way of working against the dynasty instead.

The educational reforms, which received high priority, are an example. By 1911 even remote provinces boasted new schools, teaching new subjects and ideas. Chinese students also studied abroad in record numbers, especially in Japan where by 1906 there were at least 8,000 of them, many supported by their provincial governments. There, away from their families, they enjoyed a new personal and intellectual liberty. Even those who did not manage to complete their education drank in the heady wine of new ideas. The most influential intellectual of the decade was Liang Qichao, from whose writings many learned about the major events of world history for the first time, and were introduced to Western social and political thought from Rousseau to the twentieth century. The example of Japan was itself a powerful influence, as were books translated from Japanese. More books were translated into Chinese from Japanese than from any other language, and many Japanese loan words entered the Chinese language, thus reversing the flow that had taken place over a millenium before.

In this way Chinese students learned about Western history and law, science and logic, and above all became convinced of the truths of evolutionism, with its positive evaluation of struggle, and of nationalism, with its shift of loyalty from culture to nation. The Japanese example showed that nationalism was compatible with the preservation of elements of traditional culture, but a commitment to nationalism did imply a willingness to jettison those elements of tradition that failed to contribute to national development. Toward the end of the decade students became increasingly restive and revolutionary.

Manchu political reform included restructuring the government along modern lines and the development of a constitution. After a study mission abroad (1905–06) and subsequent deliberations, the government in 1908 announced a nine-year plan of constitutional reform beginning with provincial assemblies in 1909. Although elected on a limited franchise, these assemblies, as well as the central legislative council convened in 1910, became not sources of popular support but centers of opposition.

Nothing was more urgent than the creation of a modern military force, but here too the reform program backfired. The new forces proved unreliable because they were either influenced by new, subversive ideas or were loyal to their commanders rather than the throne. The main beneficiary of military modernization turned out to be Yuan Shikai, who as governor-general of Zhihli from 1901 to 1907 built up an army with which he retained ties even after he was dismissed from the government in 1908.

The government had some foreign policy success, especially in reasserting Chinese sovereignty over Tibet, but failed to emerge as a plausible focus for nationalism. Not only was it handicapped by its non-Han ethnic origins, but during this very difficult and dangerous period of rapid change, there was a deterioration in the quality of dynastic leadership after the Empress Dowager and Emperor Guangxu both died in 1908. The new emperor was an infant, and the regent was inept.

The Revolution of 1911

In its program of modernization the dynasty was seriously handicapped by its financial weakness. This became painfully apparent in its handling of the railway issue. In order to regain foreign railway concessions, a railway recovery movement was organized by provincial gentry and merchants who created their own railway companies. The Qing government, however, wanted to centralize power, and in 1911 decided to nationalize the major railway lines. Lacking the necessary financial resources, it was able to do so only by contacting foreign loans, inevitably with strings attached. The loans and the subsequent disbanding of provincial railway companies caused a furor, nowhere more so than in Sichuan, where local gentry who had invested in the provincial railway company felt cheated by the price the government was willing to pay for their shares. Provincial interests resented the threat to provincial autonomy. Nationalists were indignant over the foreign loans that financed the transaction. This was the prelude to revolt. The insurrection which actually set off the revolution took place in Wuchang on October 10 and was conducted by men only very loosely connected with the Revolutionary Alliance, the main revolutionary organization in the land.

After the October 10 incident, province after province broke with the dynasty. It turned for help to Yuan Shikai who had last served as Grand Councillor and Foreign Minister in 1907–08 but had been dismissed after the change of throne. Yuan was the obvious man to turn to, for he enjoyed foreign support as well as the loyalty of China's best army and had prestige as a reformer. However, he was not about to sacrifice himself for a losing cause. On the other hand, he was not strong enough to impose his will on all of China. A compromise with the revolutionaries was clearly called for if China was to avoid prolonged civil war and the nightmare of direct foreign intervention. The outcome was that the Manchu child-emperor formally abdicated on February 12, 1912. Next, Sun Yat-sen stepped aside, and Yuan accepted the presidency of a republic with a two-chambered legislature. He also agreed to move the capital to Nanjing, but once in office he evaded this provision and Beijing remained the capital of the Republic. Clearly the dynastic era was over, but the immediate question was just what would replace it — or indeed, whether anything could.

NOTES

1. Quoted in James Reeve Pusey, *China and Charles Darwin* (Cambridge: Harvard Univ. Press, 1983), p. 50.
2. Marianne Bastid-Bruguiere, "Currents of Social Change," in John K. Fairbank and Kwang-Ching Liu, eds. *The Cambridge History of China*, Vol. 11 (Cambridge: Cambridge Univ. Press, 1980), pp. 558–59.
3. Quoted in Jonathan D. Spence, *The Gate of Heavenly Peace: The Chinese and Their Revolution, 1895–1980* (New York: Viking, 1981), p. 52.

PART FIVE

Post-Imperial China

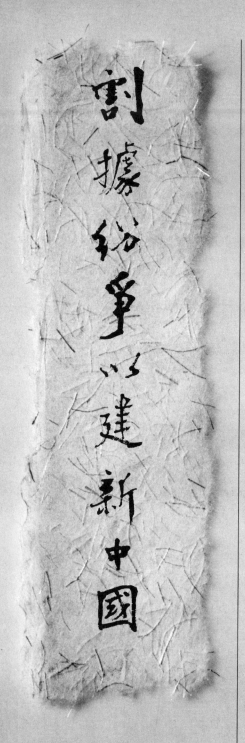

14

Fragmentation and Struggle for a New China, 1912–1927

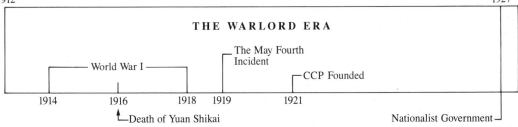

T he forces threatening to pull China apart were formidable. They included not only old tendencies toward provincialism and warlordism but also new forces making for drastic divisions within the elite while new ideologies offered inspiration as well as analysis. And as we consider these years, we need also keep in mind that the rest of the world too experienced monumental changes as World War I brought an end not only to the old international political order but to much of the mental world that had sustained it and set off a revolution in Russia that was to have profound effects everywhere.

Yuan Shikai

In the absence of well-organized political parties or deep-rooted republican sentiment among the public, there was little to restrain Yuan, who rapidly developed into a dictator. To be sure, elections were duly held in February 1913 with about 5 percent of China's population entitled to vote, but Yuan bullied the elected parliament. In March 1913 Song Jiaoren (Sung Chiao-jen, 1882–1913), architect of the constitution and leader of the largest party in parliament, the Nationalist Party (Guomindang, Kuomintang) was assassinated on Yuan's orders. That summer Yuan forced a showdown by ordering the dismissal of pro-Nationalist southern military governors. When they revolted in what is sometimes known as the Second Revolution, Yuan crushed them easily. For the next two years, the other military governors remained loyal.

Essentially Yuan sought to continue the late Qing program of centralization as the way to strengthen China internationally, but to do so he had to struggle against the forces of reformist provincialism as well as revolutionary nationalism. Often the two combined, because to finance a program regarded with suspicion by provincial interests, Yuan needed funds, and, in the absence of a radical social revolution, this meant obtaining foreign loans, which antagonized nationalists because they came with foreign strings and "advisors."

During the First World War, Japan presented China with the notorious twenty-one demands, divided into five groups: (1) recognition of Japanese

311

rights in Shandong; (2) extension of Japanese rights in Mongolia and Manchuria; (3) Sino-Japanese joint operation of China's largest iron and steel company; (4) China not to cede or lease any coastal area to any power other than Japan; and (5) provisions that would have obliged the Chinese government to employ Japanese political, financial, and military advisers, given the Japanese partial control over the police, and obliged China to purchase Japanese arms. Yuan managed to avoid the last and most onerous group of demands, which would have reduced China to a virtual Japanese satellite. However, with the other powers preoccupied in Europe, Yuan was forced to accept Japan's seizure of Germany's holdings in Shandong, grant Japan new rights in Southern Manchuria and Inner Mongolia, and acknowledge her special interest in China's largest iron and steel works, which had previously served as security for Japanese loans. The domestic result was a wave of anti-Japanese nationalist outrage, which expressed itself in protests and boycotts.

Yuan made no attempt to harness nationalist feelings to his own cause but occupied himself in preparing for restoration of dynastic rule with himself as emperor. According to an American advisor to Yuan, China was not ready for a republic. Yuan probably was not off the mark in believing that bringing back the emperorship would follow the preferences and meet the expectations of the vast majority of China's population, but he did nothing to tap or mobilize mass support or to mollify the resentment of the educated. He just went ahead. The new regime was proclaimed in December 1915 to begin on New Year's Day. Hostility to the new dynasty was so overwhelming that in March 1916 Yuan gave way and officials abandoned his imperial ambitions. But he never regained his old prestige, and died a failure in June of that year.

The Warlord Era

After the fall of Yuan Shikai, the pattern of Chinese politics became exceedingly complex. Although a national government ruled in Beijing, actual power lay in the hands of regional strongmen (warlords) who dominated the areas under their control largely through force of arms, and who struggled with each other to enlarge or protect their holdings. They constantly entered into and betrayed alliances with each other, and the foreign powers (especially Japan and the Soviet Union), fishing in these troubled waters, sought to play the warlords off against each other, and against the central government, for their own benefit.

Some of the warlords had been generals under Yuan Shikai; others had begun their careers as bandits and more or less continued to behave as such. One of the most notorious was the "Dog-Meat General," of Shandong with his entourage of White Russian guards and women. A huge brute of a man, greedy and cruel, he decorated his telegraph poles with the severed heads of secret society members. Other warlords showed a genuine interest in social welfare and education and tried to build up their areas economically, but they lacked the vision and organization to clear a way for the future. Conditions varied widely, but for many these were years of suffering and disintegration.

Internationally the 1920s were peaceful, but China's sovereignty was more impaired than ever. Its customs and salt revenues were committed to payment of foreign obligations and tariffs were kept artificially low. China's major cities were designated as treaty ports, some, most notably Shanghai, with foreign concessions under foreign jurisdiction. In these foreign enclaves foreigners lead privileged lives. They also continued to enjoy extraterritoriality wherever they went. While the foreigners' economic impact should not be exaggerated, not only commercial travelers but also missionaries used British steamers to travel inland on waterways, policed if necessary by foreign gunboats, to service churches and clinics. In short, the "foreign omnipresence"[1]—evident already in the decade before the revolution—only increased thereafter. It was both politically offensive and profoundly degrading psychologically.

Economically the modern sector expanded during the worldwide postwar boom so that 1917–23 has been called "the golden age of Chinese capitalism."[2] Yet, on the whole, economic change was incremental as the influence of the world economy on China expanded with, for example, the sale of kerosene spreading into interior villages. Over all, these economic developments were insufficient to destabilizing the economy to bring on either a fundamental breakdown or set off a breakthrough to growth. However, economic developments can never be separated from other aspects of human activity, and we may speculate that with the state too weak to exert pressure, the examination system no longer in place to reward Confucian learning and the old paternalistic ideology itself tarnished, there was increasingly little to prevent former gentry families from turning into landlords pure and simple. If so, this suggests fragmentation of the social fabric analogous to the political fragmentation produced by the warlords. Meanwhile the shattering of the old world was most visible in the intellectual arena.

Intellectual Ferment

It did not take the fall of the Qing to produce iconoclasm and protest. Revolutionary ideas had been current among Chinese students in Tokyo and were welcomed by magazines and schools in China as well. Pedants were mocked and corruption was castigated. As already noted, there were the beginnings of feminism while anarchism attracted those who thought political revolution was not enough. The abolition of the examinations by removing the institutional prop for Confucianism opened the way for new ideas, without, however, destroying the respect accorded scholars and intellectuals, their activist commitment to society, or their sense of their own importance. What the collapse of the dynasty did do however was to intensify these tendencies and produce a veritable explosion.

A major landmark was the founding in 1915 of *New Youth*, the journal that came to stand at the core of the new intellectual tide. In the first issue, its founder Chen Duxiu (Ch'en Tu-hsiu, 1879–1942), just returned from Japan, issued an eloquent call for the rejuvenation of China accompanied by an equally strong denunciation of the old tradition. A prime target for the new intellectuals was Confucianism, still advocated by, among others, Kang You-wei, who tried to cast it in a new role as an official religion for the Chinese state. It was Kang's great misfortune that in the late Qing he could not construct a Confucian justification for modernization that was persuasive to scholars grounded in the classics, and that afterward he was equally unsuccessful in devising a modern justification for making Confucianism acceptable to those whose primary loyalty was to the nation. Kang was not the only intellectual whom the world passed by as ideas once considered radical appeared conservative in a changed world. As for Confucianism, it was not destroyed, but it was very much put on the defensive.

New Youth not only opposed the traditional teachings, it also opposed the language in which they were written. The journal opened its pages to Hu Shi (Hu Shih, 1891–1962), a former student of the American philosopher John Dewey, and China's leading champion of the vernacular language *(baihua, pai-hua)*. Hu Shi argued that people should write the spoken language not the language of the classics, and that the vernacular should be taught in the schools. He praised the literary merits of the old novels written in the vernacular, which had long been widely read but had not been considered respectable. The campaign for the vernacular was a success. The transition did not come all at once: classical expressions had a way of creeping into the vernacular, and newly borrowed terms stood in the way of easy comprehension. Nevertheless, the new language was both more accessible and more modern than the old. Introduced into the elementary schools in 1920, it was universally used in the schools by the end of the decade.

New Youth was also the first magazine to publish Lu Xun (Lu Hsün), pen name of Zhou Shuren (Chou Shu-jen, 1881–1936) who became China's most acclaimed writer of the twentieth century. Lu Xun had gone to Japan to study medicine but decided to devote himself to combating not physical ailments but China's spiritual ills. His bitter satire cut like a sharp scalpel, but a scalpel wielded by a humanist who hoped to cure, not kill. His protagonist in "A Madman's Diary" *(New Youth*, 1918) discovers the reality underneath the gloss of "virtue and morality" in the old histories: a history of man eating man. He ends with the plea, "Perhaps there are still children who have not eaten men? Save the children. . . ."[3]

Many of the leaders of the new thought were on the faculty of Beijing University, now directed by a tolerant European-educated intellectual who brought in Chen Duxiu as dean. Their ideas found a ready following among the students at this and other Chinese universities. On May 4, 1919, some 3,000 of these students staged a dramatic demonstration to protest further interference in Chinese affairs by the imperialist powers. China had entered the World War on the allied side, and sent labor battalions to France, in order to gain a voice in the peace settlement. But when the powers met at Versailles, they ignored China, and assigned Germany's former possessions in Shandong to Japan. The students were outraged. The demonstration became violent.

There were arrests. These were followed by more protest: a wave of strikes and a show of merchant and labor support for the students. This was particularly significant because the growth of the modern-minded merchant and labor classes in China's large cities had been stimulated by the wartime withdrawal of European firms from East Asia.

In the end the government had to retreat. Those who had been arrested were released, and those who had ordered the arrests were forced to resign. China never signed the ill-fated Treaty of Versailles.

The May Fourth incident came to symbolize the currents of intellectual and cultural change first articulated in *New Youth* and gave rise to the term "May Fourth movement," usually used to designate the whole period from 1915 to the early 1920s. The incident gave intellectuals a heightened sense of urgency and turned what had been a trickle of protest into a tide. A flood of publications followed, attacking just about every aspect of Chinese traditional culture in a total rejection of the past, including such basic institutions as the family, and introducing a host of new and radical ideas. There was much heady and excited talk but also action as young people spurned the conventions of arranged marriage. There was also increased social action, particularly in the area of organizing labor unions.

The May Fourth movement had long-term revolutionary consequences both in what it destroyed and in what it introduced. In the short term, however, although the current of nationalism ran deep and strong, there were intense disagreements concerning the future direction of Chinese culture, and in the absence of an official orthodoxy, a tremendous variety of ideas, theories, and styles swelled the eddies of Chinese intellectual and cultural life.

Intellectual Alternatives

The spectacle of Europe's self-destruction in World War I as well as the failure of liberal principles at Versailles prompted some to be as critical of the Western tradition as of their own and others to reaffirm the value of things Chinese. Among those who turned back to the Chinese tradition was Liang Qichao, who now hoped to combine the best of both worlds and achieve a synthesis in which the Chinese elements would predominate (just as Song Neo-Confucianism had synthesized Buddhism into an essentially Confucian framework), but in the twentieth century this turned out to be an extraordinarily difficult task.

An important debate began in 1923 between the proponents of science and metaphysics, a debate which also involved differences over the interpretation and evaluation of Chinese and Western cultures. Among the advocates of the former were the proponents of scientism, that is, the belief that science holds the answers for all intellectual problems (including problems of value) and that the scientific method is the only method for arriving at truth. These tenets were challenged by those who argued that science is applicable only to a limited field of study, such as the study of nature, and that moral values have to be based on deeper metaphysical truths that by their very nature are beyond the reach of scientific methodology. Since similar problems agitated the West as this time, Chinese thinkers drew not only on the ideas of such classic European philosophers as Immanuel Kant but also on the thought of contemporaries as varied as John Dewey and Henri Bergson, the French exponent of vitalism. Those who identified with the Chinese tradition further drew on the insights of Neo-Confucianism and Buddhism, particularly the former.

One of the most noteworthy defenders of tradition was Liang Shuming (Liang Shou-ming, 1893 – 1988) who put his Confucian principles into action by working on rural reconstruction. Another was Zhang Junmai (1887 – 1969), later the leader of a small political party opposed to both the Communists and the Nationalists. Among influential philosophers were Feng Yulan (Fung Yu-lan, 1895 –), a proponent of Zhu Xi's (Chu Hsi's) Neo-Confucianism interpreted in a Platonic fashion, and Xiong Shili (Hsiung Shih-li, 1885 – 1969) whose intuitionist philosophy drew on the thought of Wang Yangming.

Among the champions of science and Western values were the scientist Ding Wenjiang (Ting Wen-chiang, T. V. Ding, 1887 – 1937) and Hu Shi the father of the vernacular language movement. Hu Shi was a leading liberal who advocated a gradualist, piecemeal problem-solving approach to China's ills in the face of attacks not only from the traditionalists on the right but also from the left. His message increasingly fell on deaf ears, for his approach required time, and time was precisely what China lacked. More often than not, this included time to digest the heady dose of new intellectual imports. Similarly, liberal individualism was another luxury which many felt a nation and a civilization in crisis could ill afford as Marxism became increasingly attractive to those hungry for change.

Cultural Alternatives

In China, as elsewhere, art usually reflects the times, yet the most beloved twentieth-century painter was singularly unaffected by either the impact of the West or the excitement of the May Fourth movement. This was Qi Baishi (Ch'i Pai-shih, 1863 – 1957), already in his fifties at the time of the May Fourth incident. Qi began as a humble carpenter and did not turn to painting until his mid-twenties, but his industry and longevity more than made up for his late start. It is estimated that he produced more than 10,000 paintings. Qi was a great admirer of the seventeenth-century individualist Zhu Da (Chu Ta) but essentially followed his own inner vision. He was not given to theorizing but did express his attitude toward representation: "The excellence of a painting lies in its being like, yet unlike. Too much likeness flatters the vulgar taste; too much unlikeness deceives the world." [4] Although his work includes landscapes and portraits, he is at his best in depicting the humble forms of life, including rodents and insects, with a loving and gentle humor reminiscent of the haiku of Kobayashi Issa (see Figure 14-1). His pictures are statements of his

Figure 14-1   Qi Baishi,
The Night Marauders.
Hanging scroll, Chinese ink
on paper.

own benevolent vision. They show, to quote a Chinese critic, "a loving sympathy for the little insects and crabs and flowers he draws," and have "an enlivening gaiety of manner and spirit," so that, "his pictures are really all pictures of his own gentle humanism."[5]

There were other painters and calligraphers in the twenties and thirties who remained uninfluenced by the West, but many felt that the new age required a new style. Among those who tried to combine elements of the Chinese and Western traditions were the followers of a school of painters established in Canton by Gao Lun (Kao Lun also, known as Gao Jianfu, Kao Chien-fu, 1879–

1951). Gao sought to combine Western shading and perspective with Chinese brushwork. He was also influenced by Japanese decorativeness. He further sought to bring Chinese painting up to date by including in his works new subject matter, such as the airplanes in Figure 14-2.

In Shanghai, meanwhile, a small group of artists tried to transplant French-style bohemianism into that international city. Xu Beihong (Hsü Pei-hung, Péon Ju, 1895–1953), for example, affected the long hair and general appearance popular in the artists' quarter of Paris when he returned from that city in 1927. Xu also brought back a thorough mastery of the French academic style. The subject of the painting shown in Figure 14-3 comes from the Warring States period, but in style it is a typical product of a European art school of the time, although it is executed with great technical skill. Somewhat more contemporary in his Western tastes was Liu Haisu (b. 1895), founder of the Shanghai Art School (1920), where he introduced the use of a nude model for the first time in China. This was also one of the first schools to offer a full course of instruction in Western music. Liu drew his inspiration from French postimpressionists like Matisse and Cézanne. Later, however, Liu returned to

Figure 14-2 Gao Lun, *Landscape with Airplanes.* Hanging scroll. Art Gallery, Chinese University of Hong Kong.

Figure 14-3   Xu Beihong, *Tianheng Wupai Shi.* Oil.

painting in a traditional manner, and Xu too abandoned his Western dress for a Chinese gown. Today Xu is perhaps most appreciated for his later paintings of horses, which are modern, yet essentially Chinese.

Modern Chinese literature had its origins in the social and sentimental novels of the late Qing. Next came the very popular but superficial best-seller "Butterfly" literature, named after poems inserted into a novel, comparing lovers to pairs of butterflies. Between 1910 and 1930, around 2,215 novels were produced in this genre, offering a literate but unlearned public amusement and escape from the trials and tribulations of the real world. Also going back to the late Qing there was a steady and swelling stream of translations. The most famous and prolific early translator was Lin Shu (1852–1924) who rendered into classical Chinese the novels of Charles Dickens, Walter Scott, and others in an opus that grew to some 180 works. By the end of the twenties all the major European literary traditions as well as that of Japan were accessible in translation.

As suggested in our discussion of Hu Shi and Lu Xun, the May Fourth movement had a strong effect on literature. The intellectual revolution was accompanied by one in literature. This brought with it experiments in form such as those of Xu Zhimo (Hsü Chih-mo, 1896–1931) who modeled his poetry on English verse complete with rhyme. More widespread was a tendency toward romantic emotionalism, an outpouring of feelings released by the removal of Confucian restraints and encouraged by the example of European romanticism.

One strain, as analyzed by Lee, was the passive-sentimental, presided over by the hero of Goethe's *The Sorrows of Young Werther* read in China (as in Japan) as "a sentimental sob story." The subjectivism of these writers was not unlike that of the writers of "I" novels in Japan. Another strain was dynamic and heroic. Its ideal was Prometheus, who braved Zeus's wrath and stole fire for mankind. Holding a promise of release from alienation, it was compatible with a revolutionary political stance. For Guo Moro (Kuo Mo-jo, 1892–1978), once an admirer of Goethe, Lenin became beyond all else a Promethean hero. Perhaps the strongest expression of Promethean martyrdom came from Lu Xun, "I have stolen fire from other countries, intending to cook my own flesh. I think that if the taste is good, the other chewers on their part may get something out of it, and I shall not sacrifice my body in vain."[6]

Controversies and rivalries stimulated the formation of literary and intellectual societies as like-minded men joined together to publish journals for their causes and denounce those of the opposition. Revolutionaries were not alone in arguing that literature should have a social purpose, but as the years passed without any improvement in Chinese conditions, the attractions of revolutionary creeds increased. Writers of revolutionary persuasion such as Mao Dun (Mao Tun, Shen Yanbing, Shen Yen-ping, 1896–1981) employed their talents in depicting and analyzing the defects in the old society and portraying the idealism of those out to change things. Such themes appeared not only in the work of Communist writers like Mao Dun but are found also in the work of the anarchist Ba Jin (Pa Chin, Li Feigang, Li Fei-kang, 1905–), best known for his depiction of the disintegration of a large, eminent family in the novel appropriately entitled *Family* (1931), a part of his *Turbulent Stream* trilogy (1931–40). Such works provide important material for the student of social as well as literary history.

Marxism in China: The Early Years

Marxism was not unknown in China, but it held little appeal prior to the Russian Revolution. The most radical Chinese, like their Japanese counterparts, were most impressed by the teachings of anarchism, which opposed the state as an authoritarian institution and sought to rely on man's natural social tendencies to create a just society. Those few who were drawn to socialism were attracted more by its egalitarianism than by concepts of class warfare. The writings of Marx and Engels offered the vision of a perfect society, but their thesis that socialism could only be achieved after capitalism had run its course suggested that Marxism was inappropriate for a society only just entering "the capitalist stage of development."

The success of the Russian Revolution (1917) altered the picture considerably. Faced with a similar problem in applying Marxism to Russia, Lenin amended Marxist theory to fit the needs of his own country, and thereby also made it more relevant to the Chinese. His theory that imperialism was the last stage of capitalism gave new historical importance to countries such as China, which were the objects of imperialist expansion. It also suggested that the imperialist nations were themselves on the verge of the transition to socialist states. Most significant for the Chinese situation, perhaps, was Lenin's concept of the Communist party as the vanguard of revolution, which showed a way in which party intellectuals could help make history even in a precapitalist state, and thus justified their efforts.

Furthermore, Marxism was modern and claimed "scientific" validity for its doctrines. It shared the prestige accorded by Chinese intellectuals to what was Western and "advanced," even as it opposed the dominant forms of social, economic, and political organization in the West. A Western heresy that could be used against the West, it promised to undo China's humiliation and to place China once again in the forefront of world history. Most important of all, it worked. The Russian Revolution demonstrated its effectiveness. To many, and not only in China, it seemed the wave of the future.

The appeal of Marxism in China was varied. Li Dazhao (Li Ta-chao, 1888–1927), professor and librarian at Beijing University and an ardent revolutionary, was attracted to it initially as a vehicle for national revolution. Chen Duxiu, dean and editor of *New Youth*, for a time championed science and democracy but turned to Marxism as a more effective means of achieving modernization. Others were drawn to it for a mixture of reasons, high among them the promise it held for solving China's ills. Whatever their reasons, a core of Marxist intellectuals was available as potential leaders by the time the Comintern* agent Grigorii Voitinsky arrived in China, in the spring of 1920, to prepare for the organization of the Chinese Communist party (CCP). Organization of the CCP took place in the following year.

At its first gathering in July 1921, the CCP elected Chen Duxiu its Secretary General. Despite very considerable misgivings, the leadership of the fledgling party submitted to a Comintern policy of maximum cooperation with the Guomindang, with which a formal agreement was reached in 1923. Under this arrangement, at the insistence of Sun Yat-sen, the two parties were not allied as equals with the CCP as a "block without," but CCP members were admitted into the Guomindang as individuals, forming a "block within," and subjecting themselves to Guomindang party discipline. The CCP leadership was suspicious of the Guomindang and found it difficult to accept the Comintern's theoretical analysis of the Guomindang as a multiclass party. But it submitted to Comintern discipline and the logic of the situation in China, where the few hundred Communists were outnumbered by the thousands of Guomindang members and had little contact with the masses they sought to lead. This initial period of cooperation lasted until 1927. Although the CCP greatly expanded during these years, the Guomindang remained definitely the senior partner.

---

* The Third International (*Communist International*) founded in Moscow in 1919 to coordinate Communist movements around the world.

The Guomindang and Sun Yat-sen (1913–1923)

After the failure of the "second revolution" of 1913, Sun Yat-sen was once again forced into exile in Japan, where he tried to win Japanese support for his revolution. After the death of Yuan Shikai, he was able to return to China and establish a revolutionary base in Canton, where he retained a precarious foothold dependent on the good will of the local warlord.

Denied foreign backing despite his efforts to obtain support in Japan and elsewhere, Sun was also handicapped by the weakness of the Guomindang party organization, which was held together only loosely, and largely through loyalty to Sun himself. Meanwhile, the success of the Russian Revolution provided a striking contrast to the failure of the revolution Sun tried to lead in China. Further, Sun was favorably disposed to the U.S.S.R. by the Soviet Union's initial renunciation of Czarist rights in China. This corresponded to a new anti-imperialist emphasis in his own thought and rhetoric. The end of Manchu rule had not led to marked improvement in China's lot vis-à-vis the foreign powers, and a stronger anti-imperialist line seemed called for.

Sun was therefore ready to work with the Communists, and in 1923 he concluded an agreement with the Comintern agent Adolf Joffe, who concurred with Sun's view that China was not ready for socialism and that the immediate task ahead was the achievement of national unity and independence. Through this pact with Joffe, Sun received valuable assistance and aid. Under the guidance of the Comintern agent Mikhail Borodin (Grusenberg), the Guomindang was reorganized into a more structured and disciplined organization than ever before, while General Galen (Blücher) performed the same service for the Guomindang army. Sun Yat-sen made some minor ideological compromises but did not basically depart from his previous views. Of his Three Principles of the People, that of nationalism was now redirected so as to be anti-imperialist rather than anti-Manchu. The principle of the people's livelihood now gave greater emphasis to farmers.

Guomindang and CCP Cooperation (1923–1927)

For both sides, the agreement of 1923 was a marriage of convenience, and at first it worked to the advantage of both parties. The Guomindang gained guidance and support while CCP members rose to important positions in the Guomindang organization, and the party reached out to organize urban workers and made a beginning in rural organization. A good example of a CCP leader occupying an important Guomindang office is provided by Zhou Enlai (Chou En-lai, 1898–1976), who became head of the political department of the Whampoa Military Academy, headed by Chiang Kai-shek (in Mandarin Jiang Jieshi, Chiang Chieh-shih, 1887–1975). At Whampoa the cream of the Guomindang officer corps was trained and prepared to lead an army to reunify China and establish a national regime.

In accord with Marxist principles, the CCP devoted its main efforts to organizing the urban labor movement, which had already won its first victory in the Hong Kong Seamen's Strike of 1922. Shanghai and Canton were particularly fertile grounds for the labor organizer, since in these cities the textile and other light industries continued their pre–First World War growth, assisted in part by the wartime lull in foreign competition. Of some 2.7 million cotton spindles in China around 1920, 1.3 million were in Chinese controlled factories, and 500,000 were owned by Japanese. In Chinese and foreign plants alike, working conditions remained very harsh.

Under these circumstances, the CCP's work met with substantial success. It gained greatly by its leadership during and following the incident of May 30, 1925, when Chinese demonstrators were fired on by the police of the International Settlement in Shanghai, killing 10 and wounding more than 50. A general strike and boycott followed; in Hong Kong and Canton the labor movement held out for 16 months. The strike did not achieve its goals, but CCP party membership increased from around 1,000 in early 1925 to an estimated 20,000 by the summer of 1926.

Sun Yat-sen did not live to witness the May 30 incident, for he died of liver cancer in March 1925. In death he was glorified even more than he had been while alive, but his image as the father of the revolution did not suffice, in the absence of a clearly designated heir apparent, to keep the only-recently reorganized Guomindang united. Furthermore, his ideological legacy was open to a variety of interpretations. His last major statement of the Three Principles of the People, issued in 1924, stressed the first principle, nationalism, which included opposition to foreign imperialism and also provided for self-determination for China's minorities.

The second principle, democracy, contained proposals for popular elections, initiative, recall, and referendum, but full democracy was to come about only after a preparatory period of political tutelage. In terms of political structure, Sun envisioned a republic with five branches of government: the standard Western triad (legislative, executive, judicial), plus two contributions from traditional Chinese government: an examination branch to test applicants for government posts, and a censorial branch to monitor the performance of government officials and to control corruption.

Finally, the principle of the people's livelihood aimed at both economic egalitarianism and economic development. It incorporated a Henry Georgian plan to tax the unearned increment on land values in order to equalize land holdings. An additional refinement was a land tax based on each landholder's assessment of the value of his land. To prevent underassessment, the state was to have the right to purchase the land at the declared value. Sun also had a grandiose vision of Chinese industrialization, but this was unrealistic since it called for enormous investments from a Europe which could ill afford them. More realistic was a proposal for state ownership of major industries. He remained critical of Marxist ideas of class struggle, preferring an emphasis on the unification of the Chinese people.

Prominent among the leaders competing for Guomindang leadership after Sun Yat-sen's death was Wang Jingwei (Wang Ching-wei, 1883–1944), who had been associated with Sun in Japan and gained a reputation for revolutionary heroism when he attempted to assassinate the Manchu Prince Regent in 1910. Wang, however, could not dominate the party and had to work with various factions and other leaders. In 1926 it became apparent that the most formidable challenger for the leadership was Chiang Kai-shek. After the pact with Joffe in 1923, Sun had sent Chiang to Moscow to study the Soviet military. On his return to China, Chiang was appointed to head the newly formed Whampoa Military Academy, where he was highly successful, esteemed alike by the Soviet advisors and by the officer candidates, whom he exhorted to do their utmost for the Guomindang and the Three Principles of the People.

While Wang Jingwei loosely presided over the Guomindang, the CCP steadily gained influence in the party, much to the alarm of the Guomindang right and of Chiang Kai-shek. In March, 1926, Chiang decided to act: he declared martial law, arrested Soviet advisors, and took steps to restrain the CCP influence in the Guomindang, while managing to retain the cooperation of both the CCP and of its Soviet supporters, since he required their assistance for the military unification of the country. This he began in the summer of 1926, when he embarked on the Northern Expedition (see Figure 14-4), setting out with his army from Canton. Although there was some heavy fighting against warlord armies, the force made rapid headway on its march to the Yangzi, and some warlords decided to bring their forces over to the Nationalist side. In the fall of 1926, the Nationalist victories enabled them to shift the capital from Canton to more centrally located Wuhan.* There Wang Jingwei headed a civilian Guomindang government but lacked the power to control Chiang and his army.

The Break

On its march north to the Yangzi, the Guomindang army was assisted by popular support for the revolutionary cause, and nowhere was this support more enthusiastic than among the Communist-led workers of Shanghai, where the General Labor Union seized control of the city even before the arrival of the Nationalist troops. Elsewhere too there was an increase in labor activity. This alarmed Chinese bankers and industrialists who, ready to support a national but not a social revolution, financed the increasingly anti-Communist Chiang Kai-shek. In April, 1927, Chiang finally broke with the CCP completely by initiating a bloody campaign of suppression in Shanghai, which then spread to other cities. Union and party headquarters were raided; those who resisted were killed; suspected Communists were shot on sight.

* Wuhan refers to the three cities (Wuzhang, Hanyang, and Hankou) where the Han River flows into the Yangzi.

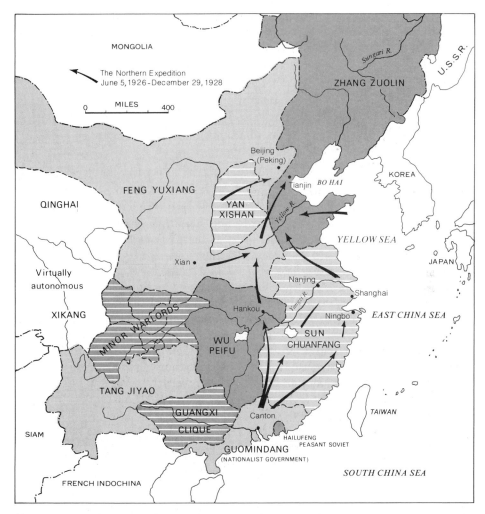

Figure 14-4   China and the Northern Expedition   1926–1928

CCP cells were destroyed and unions disbanded in a devastating sweep that left the urban CCP shattered.

The CCP's work in organizing city factory workers was entirely consistent with Marxist theory, but the majority of the Chinese people continued to be peasants. Marx, as a student of the French Revolution, despised the peasantry as "the class which represents barbarism within civilization."[7] But Lenin, operating in a primarily agrarian land, assigned the peasantry a supporting role in the Russian Revolution. The CCP, although it concentrated on the cities, had not neglected the peasants. In 1921, China's first modern peasant movement was organized by Peng Bai (P'eng Pai, 1896–1929), and by 1927 the CCP was at work in a number of provinces, most notably Hunan, where the young Mao Zedong (Mao Tse-tung, 1893–1976) wrote a famous report urging the party to concentrate on rural revolution and predicting, "In a very short time . . . several hundred million peasants will rise like a mighty storm, like a hurricane, a force so swift and violent that no power, however great, will be able to hold it back."[8] In another famous passage in the same report, he defended the need for peasant violence:

> A revolution is not a dinner party, or writing an essay, or painting a picture, or doing embroidery; it cannot be so refined, so leisurely and gentle, so temperate, kind, courteous, restrained, and magnanimous. A revolution is an insurrection, an act of violence by which one class overthrows another.[9]

In Hunan, as in other parts of China's rice producing region, tenancy rates were high, and the poorer peasants were sorely burdened by heavy rental payments and crushing debts. Tenants had few rights, and they faced the recurring specter of losing their leases. It was, as Mao saw, a volatile situation, fraught with revolutionary potential. But the Chinese party and its Soviet advisers remained urban minded.

After Chiang's April coup, the CCP broke with him but continued to work with the government at Wuhan, which also broke with Chiang. But here again the needs of the social revolution clashed with those of the national revolution, since the Wuhan regime depended for military support on armies officered largely by men of the landlord class, which was the prime object of peasant wrath. In this situation Comintern directives were wavering and contradictory, reflecting not Chinese realities but rather the exigencies of Stalin's intraparty maneuvers back in Moscow. The end result was that in June the CCP was expelled from Wuhan. Borodin and other Soviet advisers had to return to the U.S.S.R. For the CCP there began a difficult period of regrouping and reorganization.

Establishment of the Nationalist Government

After Chiang Kai-shek's coup in Shanghai, he established a government in Nanjing, which remained the capital after the completion of the Northern Expedition. The expedition was resumed in 1928, by which time the Wuhan leaders had bowed to the inevitable and made their peace with Chiang, as had a number of warlords whose forces now assisted the Nationalist army in its drive north and actually outnumbered the Guomindang's own troops. In June 1928, after a scant two months of fighting, Beijing fell. China again had a national government, but the often nominal incorporation of warlord armies into the government forces meant that national unification was far from complete. Warlordism remained an essential feature of Chinese politics until the very end of the republican period in 1949.

During 1927 anti-imperialist mobs attacked British concessions in two cities, and violence in Nanjing in March left six foreigners dead, a number wounded, and foreign businesses and homes raided. Such incidents were officially attributed to Chiang Kai-shek's leftist rivals, and the foreign powers concluded that he was the most acceptable leader for China, that is, that his government would negotiate rather than expropriate their holdings. Thus Chiang's victory reassured the powers; except for the Japanese, who had plans of their own for Manchuria and Inner Mongolia. Japan had restored its holdings in Shandong to Chinese sovereignty after the American-sponsored Washington Conference of 1921–22 attended by nine powers with an interest in East Asia (Britain, the United States, France, Italy, Japan, China, Belgium, the Netherlands, and Portugal) to settle issues left over from the First World War. But now Japan sent troops to Shandong claiming that they were needed to protect Japanese lives and property, and there was fighting with Chinese soldiers in 1928. Still more ominous was the assassination that same year of the warlord of Manchuria, Zhang Zuolin (Chang Tso-lin), by a group of Japanese army officers who hoped this would pave the way for seizure of Manchuria. Acting on their own, without the knowledge or approval of their government, the Japanese officers did not get their way in 1928, but their act did serve as a prelude to the Japanese militarism and expansionism that threatened China during the thirties, even as the Nanjing government tried to cope with warlords and revolutionaries at home, in its attempt to achieve a stable government.

NOTES

1. Term coined by Mary Wright, cf. her *China in Revolution: The First Phase, 1900–1913* (New Haven: Yale Univ. Press, 1968), pp. 54–58.

2. Marie-Claire Bergère, in John K. Fairbank, ed. *The Cambridge History of China*, Vol. 12, (Cambridge: Cambridge Univ. Press, 1983), pp. 745–51.

3. Lu Hsün, "A Madman's Diary," in *Selected Works of Lu Hsün* (Peking: Foreign Language Press, 1956), pp. 8–21; reprinted in Ranbir Vohra, *The Chinese Revolution: 1900–1950* (Boston: Houghton Mifflin, 1974), pp. 62–71; quote p. 71.

4. See the biographical entry for Ch'i Pai-shih in Howard L. Boorman, ed., *Biographical Dictionary of Republican China* (New York: Columbia Univ. Press, 1967–71) 1:302–04. Qi's statement is quoted on p. 302.

5. Michael Sullivan, *Chinese Art in the Twentieth Century* (Berkeley: Univ. of California Press, 1959), p. 42.

6. Quoted in Leo Ou-fan Lee, *The Romantic Generation of Modern Chinese Writers* (Cambridge: Harvard Univ. Press, 1973), 291.

7. Karl Marx, quoted in Lucien Bianco, *Origins of the Chinese Revolution: 1915–1949*, trans. Murial Bell (Stanford: Stanford Univ. Press, 1971), p. 74.

8. Mao Tse-tung, "Report on an Investigation of the Peasant Movement in Hunan," in *Selected Works of Mao Tse-tung* (Peking: Foreign Languages Press, 1967), Vol. 1; reprinted in Ranbir Vohra, *The Chinese Revolution: 1900–1950* (Boston: Houghton Mifflin, 1974) p. 115.

9. *Ibid.*, p. 117.

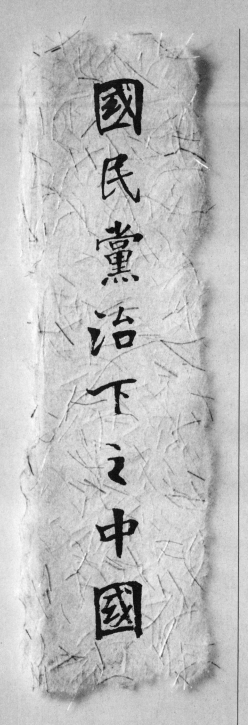

國民黨治下之中國

15
China under the Nationalists, 1927 – 1949

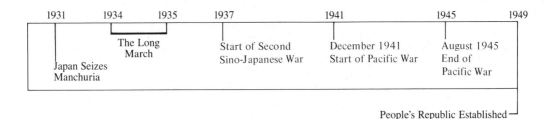

1931	1934	1935	1937	1941	1945	1949

The Long
March

Start of Second
Sino-Japanese War

December 1941
Start of Pacific War

August 1945
End of
Pacific War

Japan Seizes
Manchuria

People's Republic Established

F or much of the world the 1930s were bleak and somber years, and they were followed by global warfare. In considering China during this period, we need to bear in mind not only that external military and economic forces constrained China's freedom to act, but that in the wake of the Great Depression, people in many lands, desperate for vigorous action, accepted dictatorship of one kind or another as the most effective way of pulling a nation together. It was not in Italy and Germany alone that fascism was viewed as the wave of the future. In Japan, militarists seized power from the political parties and in China, too, the military gained in power and prestige.

The Nanjing Decade: An Uneasy Peace

From 1927 to 1937, the Nationalist government in Nanjing remained at peace with Japan, but from the start these were hardly peaceful years. Even after the completion of the Northern Expedition in 1928, the government actually controlled only the lower Yangzi Valley. Elsewhere it was dependent on the unreliable allegiance of local powerholders. In 1930 the government secured its authority in the North after waging a costly campaign with heavy casualties on both sides against the combined armies of two warlords. Nanjing was strengthened by this victory but still lacked the power to subdue the remaining warlords once and for all. There was therefore a strong tendency to give highest priority to building military strength even before Japan's seizure of Manchuria and the looming threat of further Japanese aggression made such a policy imperative.

The attack on Manchuria took place in the fall of 1931 while China was hampered by floods in the Yangzi Valley and the Western powers were neutralized by depression. It was masterminded by a small group of officers of the Japanese Army on the Liaodong Peninsula. Without government authorization, these officers, none with a rank higher than colonel, fabricated an excuse for hostilities: a supposed Chinese attempt to sabotage the South Manchurian Railway Company. And they saw to it that the fighting continued until the army controlled the entire area. Once this was accomplished, the army estab-

329

lished the puppet state of Manchukuo, which early in 1932 declared its independence from China with its titular ruler, Puyi, who as an infant had been the last emperor of China.

Meanwhile the fighting had spread to China proper; for six strenuous weeks, Japanese and Chinese fought around Shanghai until a truce was finally arranged. Japanese efforts to make a general settlement with China and obtain recognition of Manchukuo were rebuffed and condemned by the League of Nations from which Japan withdrew in March 1933. In Japan, the Manchurian incident tolled the death knell for civilian rule, while for China a militarized Japan posed a constant threat.

A truce was concluded in May 1933 after the Japanese had crossed the Great Wall that spring. The temporary accord left Japanese troops in control of the area north of the Great Wall and provided for a demilitarized zone whose boundaries were marked by the railway line running between Beijing, Tianjing, and Tanggu, but it did not prevent the Japanese from setting up a puppet regime in that area nor from exerting continuous pressure on North China. In December 1935, Japanese army officers failed in their plans to engineer a North Chinese puppet regime, but that there was no common ground for real peace became crystal clear when full-scale war broke out in the summer of 1937. In Manchuria, and now also in Korea, the Japanese concentrated on the development of heavy industry, building up an industrial base on the continent under army control.

At home, the government at Nanjing had to deal with warlords and Communists. The government's policy toward the warlords was to temporize, try to prevent the formation of antigovernment warlord coalitions, and to settle for expressions of allegiance until such time as it could establish central control. Its power and prestige were increased when it defeated a rebellion in Fujian in 1933–34, and especially after it obtained control over Guangdong and the submission of Guangxi in 1936. Its campaigns against the Communists also provided occasions for the dispatch of central government troops into warlord provinces, especially after the Communists began their Long March in 1934, and similarly the Japanese threat proved useful in eventually bringing certain warlords into line. Thus the trend was in favor of Nanjing, but the actual balance between central and local power varied widely in different parts of China. The tenacity of the warlord phenomenon in certain regions is illustrated by Sichuan, in parts of which warlords remained powerful even after the Nationalists moved their wartime capital to that province. Similarly, Xinjiang, in the far west, remained virtually autonomous.

The Nanjing Decade: Domestic Policies

The regime's military emphasis was reflected in government expenditures with 60 to 80 percent of the annual outlay going to military expenses and debt service. Military considerations were paramount also in such projects as road and railway construction. Taking the place of the ousted Russian military advisors were a series of German military men, who tried to introduce German military doctrines (including concepts of military organization not necessarily suitable to the Chinese situation) and also helped to arrange for the import of German arms and munitions. In 1935, at the height of their influence, there were 70 German advisors in China. After the anti-Comintern pact between Germany and Japan, their number decreased until the last men were recalled in 1938. Noteworthy within the army were the graduates of the Whampoa Military Academy, particularly those who completed the course during Chiang Kai-shek's tenure as director, for they enjoyed an especially close relationship with their supreme commander.

It was also Whampoa graduates who during 1931 formed the Blue Shirts, a secret police group pledged to complete obedience to Chiang Kai-shek. They and the so-called CC clique (led by two Chen brothers trusted by Chiang) were influenced in ideology and organization by European fascism. The Blue Shirts were greatly feared because of their spying and terrorist activities, including assassinations. The CC clique, too, had considerable power but it failed in its prime aim, which was to revitalize the Guomindang. After the split with the Communists, the Guomindang purged many of its own most dedicated revolutionaries. One result was that young activists, often from the same modern schools that had earlier supplied recruits for the Guomindang, were drawn to the Communist Party. Another was to create within the ruling party an atmosphere attractive to careerists who, concentrating on their own personal advancement, were disinclined to rock the boat. Meanwhile Chiang saw to it that the party remained just one of several centers of power.

The deterioration of the party was a particularly serious matter because the Nanjing government suffered from factional politics and favoritism as well as from bureaucratic overorganization, which spawned departments with overlapping functions and countless committees grinding out lengthy reports and recommendations, detailing programs that consumed vast quantities of paper but were rarely implemented. Coordination was poor. It sometimes happened, for example, that government censors suppressed news items deliberately issued by the government itself. The conduct of official business lumbered along unless quickened by the personal intervention of Chiang Kai-shek, whose power was steadily on the increase. It was power based on the loyalty of the military and the Blue Shirts, core partisans such as the CC clique, the financial backing of bankers and businessmen (including the relatives of Chiang's wife), and on a semblance of balance of various political cliques and factions manipulated by Chiang himself. It was a power that made Chiang indispensable to government, but he lacked the charisma to inspire his officials, who feared rather than loved him. Nor did he have the gift of eloquence with which to rouse the people had he so desired. Negative sanctions, such as the executions sporadically ordered by Chiang when an exceptionally flagrant case of corruption was brought to his attention, were not enough; the regime lacked drive and direction.

One problem was that the regime was ideologically weak. Sun Yat-sen became the object of an official cult, but his ideas were not further refined or developed. Instead emphasis was shifted toward a revival of Confucianism. In contrast to Sun's admiration for the Taipings, Chiang sought to emulate Zeng Guofan (Tseng Kuo-fan), who in his day had successfully stemmed a revolution by revitalizing Confucian values. Chiang's regard for Confucius and Zeng was already apparent during his days at Whampoa but became even more obvious in 1934 when he launched an extensive program to foster traditional values known as the New Life movement. This movement exhorted the populace to observe four vaguely defined Confucian virtues and spelled out the criteria for proper behavior in detailed instructions. The people were to sit and stand straight, eat quietly, refrain from indiscriminate spitting, and so forth, in the hope that they would thus acquire discipline. It did not work. Officials and commoners continued to act much as before. The government never did devise an ideology able to arouse the enthusiasm of its own personnel, command the respect of the people, or convince intellectuals. Censorship clearly was not the answer, although even foreign correspondents were subjected to it, some complaining that it was worse in China than in Japan.

Ineffectiveness also characterized local government under the Nationalists. It did restructure county government and established four bureaus charged with education, construction, public security, and finance, and it even attempted to reach down below that level by assigning officials to the wards into which they divided the counties, but it failed to wrest control over taxes and local security from the entrenched local elite who in practice continued to exercise actual power. Thus, like its predecessors, the Nanjing regime failed to mobilize the financial or human resources of the village. With income from land taxes remaining in the provinces, the government was financed primarily from the modern sector.

Despite early links with the business community, the Guomindang tended to regard business as a source to be exploited for revenue rather than as an asset to be fostered as a component of national strength. Thanks to the Nationalists, during 1928 and 1929 China at long last regained the tariff autonomy lost in the Opium War, but it was not of much help to China's industries since exports were subjected to the same tariffs as imports, and imports of raw materials were taxed as heavily as those of finished goods. In 1933, heavily in debt to the banks, the government took control of the banking system in a move that benefitted the treasury but not the private sector. Overall, the modern sector did grow during the first ten years of Nationalist rule but only at roughly the same pace as during the years between the fall of the Qing and the establishment of the regime in Nanjing.

During the early thirties the traditional agrarian sector of the economy, which accounted for most of China's production and employed the vast majority of its people, was sorely hurt by the fall of prices produced by the depression. The agrarian sector was further afflicted by severe weather conditions, including the Yangzi flood of 1931, and by the exactions of the tax collector who piled surtax on surtax (later changed to special assessments), with the result that the taxes on agriculture continued to increase despite the decline in farm prices. Taxation, like the climate, varied widely, making generalization very risky. Even in the same province, the tax burden paid by one district was often much more than that paid by another, and this was true even in provinces like Jiangsu and Zhejiang that were firmly controlled by the government.

It is difficult to generalize about the conditions of the peasantry, but it is clear that some, such as the peasants of Wuxi County in Jiangsu, who had come to depend on sericulture, were badly hurt by the depression and that agricultural involution occurred in the South as well as in the North. Statistics for parts of North China indicating that by 1934–35 nearly half of the peasant households were farming less than 10 *mu* (1 *mu* = .167 acres), when 15 were needed for subsistence, reflect a deepening agrarian crisis. Elsewhere too, since the government did nothing to change the status quo in the village and on the land, the poorest and the weakest suffered most. Like so much legislation promulgated during those years, the law passed in 1930 limiting rents to 37½ percent of the harvest was not enforced. Payments of 50 percent were common and 60 percent was not unusual. Programs for developing cooperatives and fostering rural reconstruction were organized, but their benefits rarely filtered down to the rural poor. In 1937 there was a price recovery, and harvests were good, but by that time millions had suffered bitter poverty and despair.

Chiang Kai-shek and his supporters wanted to unify the country and to stabilize society. They wished to consolidate the revolution that had brought them into power, not to expand it. Therefore they put a premium on suppressing those forces that would lead to further and continued revolution. The regime was intent on destroying communism and the Communists, who maintained that the revolution was unfinished and proclaimed their readiness to lead it to completion. To Chiang Kai-shek nothing was more urgent than the elimination, once and for all, of his old enemies, the Chinese Communist Party. For the CCP too these were crucial years.

The Chinese Communists (1927–1934)

The Shanghai massacre and the subsequent suppression of the CCP and its associated labor movement had effectively eliminated the party as an urban force and thereby altered its geographical distribution and profoundly affected its strategy and leadership. For some years it remained unclear just what direction the movement would take. Neither the Comintern nor its Chinese followers was willing simply to write off the cities. After urban insurrection failed, as in the Canton Commune established for four days in December 1927 and greeted by the populace with profound apathy, an attempt was made to capture cities by armed force, as in the case of Changsha in Hunan in 1930. But this also failed. Although no one was ready to say so, at least in public, Moscow clearly did not have the formula for success. Meanwhile in China various groups and factions contended for power and the adoption of their policies.

One of these groups was the CCP military force, which underwent a crucial reorganization in the mountains on the Hunan-Jiangxi border, where, in the spring of 1928, Zhu De (Chu Teh, 1886–1976) joined Mao Zedong, who had arrived the previous fall. In command of some 2,000 troops, the two leaders laid the groundwork for the Red Army, with Zhu De taking military command and Mao in charge of political organization and indoctrination. As Mao was to say in 1938: "Political power grows out of the barrel of a gun. Our principle is that the Party commands the gun; the gun shall never be allowed to command the Party."[1] Through indoctrination, the recruitment of soldiers into the party, and the formation of soldiers' committees, Mao secured the control of the party over the army, while on the military side Zhu and Mao emphasized guerrilla warfare, which put a premium on mobility and surprise, rapid retreats to avoid battle with superior enemy forces, lightning strikes to pick off small contingents of the enemy, and constant harassment to keep the enemy off balance. Essential to this type of warfare is popular support to provide intelligence, supplies, and recruits, as well as cover for guerrillas under enemy pursuit. Peasant participation and support were secured by redistributing land and furthering the revolution in the countryside.

This strategy focused on the development and expansion of rural CCP controlled bases, and in the early thirties there were a number of such areas. The largest were in Jiangxi, where in December 1931 the founding of the Chinese Soviet Republic was proclaimed. The basic agrarian policy was "land to the tiller," involving the confiscation of large holdings and their reassignment to the poor, with "middle peasants" left largely unaffected, but there was a good deal of disagreement over definitions as well as wide variations in the degree of local implementation of the program. During the Jiangxi period, Mao and Zhu were influential leaders, but they had by no means won complete acceptance of either their programs or their leadership, even after party headquarters were moved to Jiangxi from Shanghai, a shift which signified recognition of the new power center in the CCP and a defeat for those oriented toward the Comintern in Moscow. Factionalism continued to undermine party unity, but the most severe challenge was external.

Chiang Kai-shek's first three "annihilation campaigns" came in 1930–31 and helped strengthen rather than weaken the CCP as the Red Army employed its tactics to good effect and captured weapons, men, and land. The fourth campaign, 1932–33, again ended in defeat for the Nationalists. In the fifth campaign, begun late in 1933, Chiang, on German advice, changed his strategy. Deploying some 750,000 men supported by 150 airplanes, he surrounded the Jiangxi Soviet and gradually tightened the circle of his blockade. When in the fall of 1934 their situation became untenable, the Communist forces abandoned their Jiangxi base, broke through a point in the Guomindang blockade manned by former warlord armies, and began their Long March (see Figure 15-1).

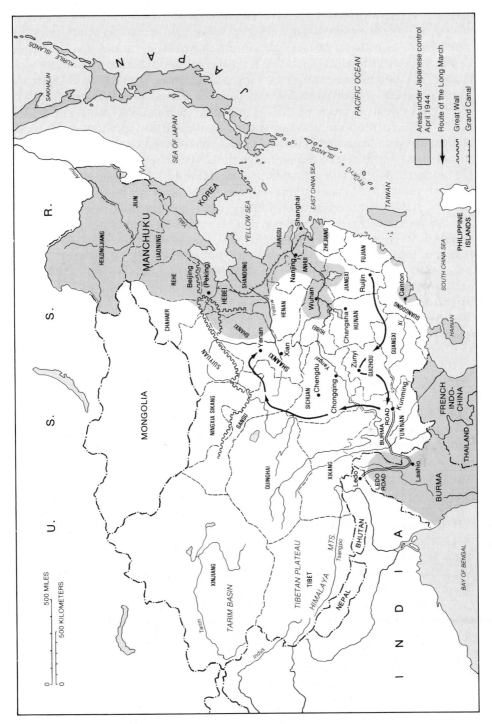

Figure 15-1 China, 1930—Spring 1944
(For Japan's maximum occupation of China, see Figure 15-3.)

The Long March

When the Communists left Jiangxi, their first priority was survival, and their destination was not clear. That was settled at an important conference held at Zunyi in Gueizhou in January 1935, when it was decided to proceed to Shaanxi, where a small soviet was already in existence. In Shaanxi the CCP would be out of easy reach of the Guomindang armies. They would be able to act on their earlier declaration of war against Japan and might even hope for some assistance from the U.S.S.R. At the Zunyi conference Mao gained a new prominence, although he did not actually control the party until the forties.

The march itself, was a heroic accomplishment, a vindication of Mao's belief in the power of the human will and determination. In just over a year, the marchers covered some 6,000 miles, traversing snow-covered mountain passes where they froze in their thin clothes and crossing treacherous bogs and marshes. To the hardships provided by nature was added the hostility of man, for there was rarely a day without some fighting. At one point they had no alternative but to cross a mountain torrent spanned by a thirteen-chain suspension bridge from which the enemy, armed and waiting on the other side, had removed the planks.

A terrible ordeal was the six- or seven-day crossing of grasslands in the Chinese-Tibetan border region. Here heavy rainfall and poor drainage had created a waterlogged plain in which green grass grew on multiple layers of rotting grass beneath. First a vanguard was sent to chart the way, and in the central grasslands they could find no place dry enough to sleep so the men had to remain standing all night long, leaning against each other. The rest of the army followed through the slippery, treacherous terrain, trudging on despite hunger and fatigue, trying to ward off rain and hail and survive the unbearable cold of the nights. Since the men carried only a very small amount of grain, they subsisted mostly on wild grasses and vegetables eaten raw because there was no firewood for cooking. Sometimes the vegetables turned out to be poisonous, and the stagnant water reportedly smelled of horse's urine.

The marchers succeeded in overcoming this and other obstacles but at great cost. Of about 100,000 who set out from Jiangxi, less than 10 percent completed the march. Some were left behind to work in various areas, but many more perished. The loss was only partially offset by new recruits who joined along the way. After completion of the march, including the men already in Shaanxi, the Communists were about 20,000 strong.

The survivors of the march emerged toughened and filled with a sense of solidarity forged by shared hardships and common suffering. There was also a heightened self-confidence, a conviction that the movement would surmount all obstacles. Something of this spirit is conveyed in a poem Mao wrote shortly before reaching Shaanxi:

> Lofty the sky
>   and pale the clouds—
> We watch the wild geese
>   fly south till they vanish.

We count the thousand
  leagues already travelled.
If we do not reach
  the Great Wall we are not true men.

High on the crest
  of Liupan Mountain
Our banners billow
  in the west wind.
Today we hold
  a long rope in our hands.
When shall we put bonds
  upon the grey dragon?[2]

The saga of the Long March continued to be celebrated in poetry and prose. It remains today a source of heroic inspiration.

United Front and War

With the Communists in Shaanxi, Chiang remained as determined as ever to crush them, but their call for a united front against Japan had special appeal for the troops of Marshal Zhang Xueliang, son of Zhang Zuolin, the former warlord of Manchuria. Although assigned to the task, Zhang's forces were less than enthusiastic in fighting the CCP. To breathe some life into the anti-Communist campaign, Chiang Kai-shek flew to Xian in December. But he had misjudged the situation. Instead of pledging themselves to renewed anti-Communist efforts, Marshal Zhang and some of his men seized Chiang Kai-shek and held him prisoner for two weeks while his fate was being negotiated. Exactly what transpired is not clear, but, after Communist intercession, Chiang was finally released, having agreed to terminate his campaign against the Communists and lead a united front against Japan. He was at the time China's most distinguished military man, the leader of the government recognized as legitimate at home and abroad, the heir to the mantle of Sun Yat-sen. Even his enemies saw him as the only man possessing the political, military, and ideological authority to lead China in an effort to stop the Japanese.

The Xian incident led to the formation of a united front in 1937. Following the Guomindang's 1936 success against Guangdong and Guangxi, formation of the united front was viewed with dismay by Japanese army officers intent on dominating China. As it was, even though after 1933 Japanese pressure had been primarily economic and political, there was always the danger that an unplanned military incident might escalate into a major war. This is, in effect, what happened after a clash between Chinese and Japanese soldiers in July on the Marco Polo Bridge outside Beijing, when the Chinese drew the line and refused further concessions. The ensuing hostilities signified the beginnings of a war that in 1941 became part of an even more extensive and destructive war (the Second World War), although this is not what the Japanese intended in 1937.

The fighting went badly for the Chinese. By the end of July the Japanese were in possession of Beijing and Tianjin, and in August Japanese forces attacked Shanghai, where Chiang used some of his best German-trained troops in three months of bloody fighting, with heavy casualties. After Shanghai came Nanjing, which fell in December, followed by the notorious "Rape of Nanjing." Japanese soldiers went on a rampage, terrorized the inhabitants, killing and raping, burning and looting. When, after seven weeks, it was all over, at least 42,000 people were dead. The Japanese acquired a reputation for terrible cruelty, which stiffened the Chinese determination to resist.

As the war escalated so did the Japanese government's aims and rhetoric. What had begun as a search for a pro-Japanese North China turned into a holy crusade against the West and Communism. Unable to obtain Chinese recognition of Manchukuo, in 1938 the government of prime minister Prince Konoe Fumimaro (1891–1945) declared Chiang's regime illegitimate and vowed to destroy it. Japanese troops continued their advance, taking Canton in October, Wuhan in December. Chiang still showed no inclination to submit. In November Konoe proclaimed Japan's determination to establish a "New Order in East Asia" to include Japan, Manchukuo, and China in a political, economic, and cultural union, a bastion against (Western) imperialism and against Soviet Communism. Those who did not see the light were to be brought to their senses by force. In the summer of 1937 Japanese plans had called for a three-month campaign by three divisions at a cost of 100 million yen to destroy the main Chinese force and take possession of key areas while waiting for Chiang to ask for peace, but by the following spring they were preparing orders for 20 divisions, had appropriated over 2.5 billion yen with promise of more to come and no end in sight.

The Nationalist government followed a strategy of "trading space for time" moved its capital to Chongjing in Sichuan. Many refuges from Japaneses-occupied China followed the government to the southwest (see Figure 15-2). Not only universities but hundreds of factories were transported piecemeal to the wartime capital to help produce for the war effort. In Chongjing, Chiang held on gamely, on the defensive. Before the Japanese attack on Pearl Harbor, the Chinese did obtain some financial assistance from outside, and beginning in August 1941, they were also aided by the Flying Tigers, volunteer American pilots later incorporated into the Fourteenth U.S. Air Force, commanded by General Claire L. Chennault. However, the West's support remained primarily moral, and the U.S.S.R. alone sent some official assistance. Although Chongjing suffered repeated bombings during 1939–41, at the battlefront these two years were marked by skirmishes rather than massive campaigns, as both sides worked to consolidate their positions. In 1940 the Japanese established a puppet regime in Nanjing headed by Wang Jingwei (Wang Ching-wei), the erstwhile follower of Sun Yat-sen and leader of the left wing of the Guomindang.

Figure 15-2   *Refugees Crowding onto Trains Bound for Guilin*, woodcut by Cai Dizhi.

Expansion of the War into a Pacific War

A major Japanese foreign policy concern during the thirties was Japanese relations with the U.S.S.R. During 1938–39 there were several military clashes in the border area along Russia's frontier with Korea and Manchukuo. In these operations, quite large in scale and involving the deployment of armor, Japan was not successful. Furthermore, the Japanese were caught off guard diplomatically when Germany, without any warning, came to terms with the Soviet Union in August 1939. Japan was therefore neutral when the Second World War began in Europe shortly afterward. However, the dramatic success of the German blitzkrieg strengthened the hands of those in Tokyo who favored a pro-German policy, and in September 1940, Konoe signed the Tripartite Pact forming an alliance with Germany and Italy.

The Germans again surprised the Japanese in June 1941 when Hitler invaded Russia. While some army men maintained that Japan should join the attack on the U.S.S.R., the navy wanted to advance into the oil and mineral rich south. Officially, Japan's mission was now expanded into the creation of a "Greater East Asian Co-Prosperity Sphere," but the underlying perception was that without the resources of Southeast Asia Japan would never attain economic security.

Konoe hoped that, armed with the Tripartite Pact, he would be able to reach his aims without going to war with the United States, but the American government was becoming increasingly alarmed over Japanese expansion. When in the summer of 1941 Japan moved troops into southern Indo-China, the United States, Britain, and Holland (then in control of the East Indies, modern Indonesia) retaliated by applying the economic sanctions they had withheld in 1931. An embargo on scrap iron was serious, but the crucial product cut off from Japan was oil.

America and Japan were on a collision course. To quote Michael Barnhart, "The Japanese Empire was determined to retain the rights and privileges it considered necessary for its economic and political security. The United States thought these rights and privileges contrary to its own deeply held principles and to the survival of what were now in effect its allies in the struggle against global aggression."[3] The United States was determined that Japan should withdraw from China as well as Indo-China. For Japan this would have meant a reversal of the policy pursued in China since 1931 and the relinquishment of the vision of Japanese primacy in East Asia. Dependent on oil and rubber from Southeast Asia, the Japanese were in no position to carry on protracted negotiations. Their choice was to fight or retreat. It is a bitter irony that Japan now prepared to go to war to attain the self-sufficiency that its proponents of total war had once considered a precondition for war.

When it became clear to Konoe that the situation had reached an impasse, he resigned, to be followed by General Tōjō Hideki (1884 – 1948), prime minister from October 1941 to July 1944. When last minute negotiations proved fruit-less, the Japanese decided on war as the least unpalatable alternative. It began on December 7, 1941, with a surprise attack on Pearl Harbor, in Hawaii, which destroyed 7 American battleships and 120 aircraft, and left 2,400 dead.

China during the War

The conviction that eventually the United States would enter the war against Japan sustained Chiang Kai-shek during the long years when China faced Japan virtually alone. When as a result of Pearl Harbor this did happen, it buoyed the spirit of the Chinese, now allied to the one country powerful enough to crush Japan. More material forms of support were also soon forth-coming, although there was never enough because in 1942 Japan cut off the government's last land route to its allies by seizing Burma and closing the Burma Road. Thereafter, supplies had to be flown in from India to Yunnan over the Himalaya Mountains (the "hump"). In addition, China ranked low in the American war effort. The Allies decided first to concentrate on the defeat of Germany, and the island-hopping strategy adopted against Japan largely bypassed China, although the Allies appreciated the fact that China tied down

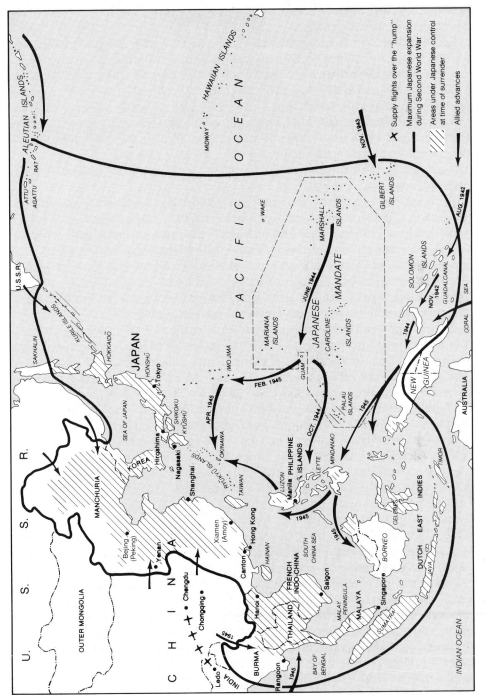

Figure 15-3   The Pacific War

vast numbers of Japanese troops that otherwise might have been used elsewhere (see Figure 15-3).

The top American military man in China was General Joseph Stilwell, who in 1942 became Chiang's chief-of-staff as well as commander of American forces in the China-Burma-India theater. Stilwell was a fine soldier but no diplomat. He had high regard for the ordinary Chinese fighting man but scarcely concealed his irritation and impatience with the inefficiencies and corruption he encountered in Chongjing, and his disgust at Chiang's policy of preparing for a postwar showdown with the CCP rather than joining in a single-minded effort against the Japanese enemy. The relationship between the two men deteriorated until Chiang requested and received Stilwell's recall in 1944.

Stilwell was replaced by General Albert Wedemeyer, who was more friendly to Chiang, but also was critical of conditions in the Chinese army, which were, by all accounts, horrendous. Induction was tantamount to a death sentence. Those who could possibly afford to do so bribed the conscription officer. The remainder were marched off, bound together with ropes, to join their units, often many miles and days away. Underfed and exhausted, many recruits never completed the trip. Those who did found that food was equally scarce at the front and medical services almost completely lacking.

Misery and corruption were not unique to the military. Even in times of famine (as in Henan during 1942–43) peasants were sorely oppressed by the demands of the landlord and the tax collector, while the urban middle class suffered from mounting inflation. This had already reached an annual rate of 40 to 50 percent between 1937 and 1939, climbed to 160 percent for 1939–42, and mounted to an average of 300 percent for 1942–45. By 1943 the real value in terms of purchasing power of the salaries paid to bureaucrats was only one-tenth what they had received in 1937, while teachers were down to 5 percent of their former earnings. The result was widespread demoralization of the Chinese military and civilian populations under Nationalist control. The secret police were unable to root out corruption. Government exhortations and the publication of Chiang Kai-shek's book *China's Destiny* (1943) did not suffice to reinvigorate ideological commitment to the government and the Guomindang.

A major reason for the wartime deterioration of the Guomindang was that Japan's seizure of the eastern seaboard and China's major cities had deprived the Nationalists of their usual sources of support, the great business centers of east China. In Sichuan they became critically dependent on the local landlords, precisely the elements in society that were most resistant to change and reform. Moreover, Chiang was unwilling to commit his troops to battle with the Japanese more than was absolutely necessary, or to do anything that might strengthen the armies of the CCP, because he was convinced that after the war with Japan there would be an all-out confrontation with the Communists that would determine China's future. As a consequence, he missed whatever opportunity existed for building a modern Chinese force with American assistance, and for translating anti-Japanese nationalism into support for his own regime.

The shortcomings of the Chongjing government were highlighted by the accomplishments of the Communists, headquartered in Yenan (see Figure 15-4). During the war years, from 1937 to 1945, the party expanded its membership from roughly 40,000 to over 1 million, and its troop strength increased tenfold to an estimated 900,000, not counting guerrillas and militiamen. Furthermore, the Communists enjoyed widespread peasant support in North China, where they established themselves as the effective government in the countryside behind the Japanese lines. The Japanese, concentrated in the cities and guarding their lines of supply, did not have the manpower to patrol the rural areas constantly and effectively.

In the areas nominally under Japanese control, the Communists skillfully pursued flexible policies to fuse national resistance and social revolution. The key to their ultimate success was mass mobilization of the peasantry, but the mix of policies and the pace of change varied according to local conditions. Carefully avoiding premature class warfare, they frequently began by organiz-

Figure 15-4   Yenan in 1960. After the Long March and during the war, the CCP leaders lived and worked in the Yenan caves.

ing the peasants to wage guerrilla war, enlisting support from the village elites for the war effort, and manipulating them into going along with rent and interest reduction. While building up their military power, they enlisted elite support even as they undermined elite power.

Crucial was the creation of new mass organizations led by poor peasant activists, who, freed from the exactions of landlords and given a voice in government, became enthusiastic supporters of the Communist Party and government. Similarly, new energies were released by organizing women and young people in an attack on traditional family authority. Actual or potential rivals such as secret societies or bandits were attacked and eliminated. The twin lessons of nationalism and revolution were further brought home to the people through indoctrination programs and a campaign to combat illiteracy, conveying new ideas to the peasantry even as they gained access to the written word, shattering the old monopoly on learning.

The peasant associations along with local Party branches took the lead in effecting changes in taxation and reducing rent and interest payments thus destroying the economic foundations of the old system. The end result was the transformation of the elite power structure into one based on the poor peasantry and led by the Party.

The Japanese for their part patronized puppet armies and even tolerated trade with the Guomindang-controlled areas of China, but the Wang Jingwei regime was too obviously controlled by the Japanese ever to gain credibility let alone enthusiastic support. At best, life in occupied China went on as usual, but Japanese arrogance alienated many Chinese while humane behavior on the part of some individuals was overshadowed by acts of cruelty that evoked Chinese hatred and resistance. An example is the notorious "kill all, burn all, destroy all" campaign carried out in 1941 and 1942 in parts of North China in retaliation for a CCP offensive. Implemented literally, the Japanese did hurt the CCP badly, but they also helped turn apolitical peasants into determined fighters.

The policies and record of the CCP also helped to attract urban intellectuals to the party. To insure discipline and preserve the cohesion of the movement swollen by new adherents, the party under Mao (now firmly established as leader) organized a rectification campaign to assure "correct" understanding of party ideology and to bring art and literature into line. Art for its own sake or for the purpose of self-expression was condemned, and those guilty of being insufficiently mass oriented were induced to confess their faults. Many were sent down to work in villages, factories, or battle zones to "learn from the masses."

From the war, the CCP emerged stronger than it had ever been before, although the outcome of the civil war that followed was by no means obvious to observers at the time. It is one of the ironies of the war that the Japanese, who proclaimed that they were combating communism in China, instead contributed to its ultimate victory.

The End of the Second World War

Japan's surrender on August 15, 1945, brought an end to half a century during which Japan was the dominant military and political power in East Asia. Japan's defeat also initiated a new phase in the history of South and Southeast Asia, as former colonies resisted the return of Western colonial masters. On the broader international scene, the war left the United States and the Soviet Union as the two giant powers who maintained a presence in East Asia and had the capacity to influence events in that part of the world. And the bombing of Hiroshima and Nagasaki had demonstrated just how dangerous a place that world could be.

An immediate result of the war was that Japan had to relinquish not only Manchuria and other areas seized since 1931 but all lands acquired since 1895, most notably Taiwan and Korea. China had preserved its national independence, but the end of the war did not lead to demobilization and peace. The country that had been at war for four years before Pearl Harbor did not attain peace until four years after Japan's surrender.

When Japan surrendered, its generals in China were ordered to submit only to Nationalist forces. To enable the Guomindang armies to accept the Japanese surrender, the United States undertook to transport them by water and by air to those parts of the country then occupied by Japan. However, they were not allowed into Manchuria until January 1946. Manchuria had been occupied by the U.S.S.R. during the last days of the war, and the Russians did not completely withdraw their troops until May 1946, by which time they had allowed the CCP to gain substantial control of the countryside there. Chiang Kai-shek, determined to retain the area where the Japanese had begun their aggression, disregarded American warnings against overextending his forces and stationed almost half a million of his best troops in Manchuria.

During the year or so immediately after the war, the Nationalists appeared to have formidable resources, at least on paper. Recognized as the legitimate government of China by all the Allies, including the Soviet Union, they had three or four times as many men under arms as their Communist rivals and enjoyed a similar superiority in armament. They were, therefore, in no mood to make concessions to the CCP. The Communists, on the other hand, had come through the war battle hardened, with well-established bases of support in the countryside, and high morale. Their leaders, too, were convinced that victory would in the end be theirs in the coming struggle. It was against this background that the United States sought to mediate between the Guomindang and CCP. In December 1945, President Truman sent General George C. Marshall to China to help the parties compose their differences. Given their history of conflict, divergence of views, and confidence in their respective causes, there was little chance that American mediation could bring about a genuine meeting of minds between the bitter Chinese antagonists. The American initiative was probably doomed from the start. Marshall's efforts were also hampered by general American support of the Nanjing government, even though President Truman stipulated that large-scale aid to China was contingent on a settlement. As during Mao's visit to Chongqing in August – October 1945 (see Figure 15-5), there was a show of cordiality, but the Marshall mission produced only a brief breathing spell before fighting broke out in earnest in mid-1946.

Civil War and Communist Triumph, 1946 – 1949

Initially, until July 1947, the Guomindang armies enjoyed success, even capturing the wartime CCP capital at Yenan. However, these were hollow victories. Like the Japanese before them, in North China and Manchuria the Guomindang controlled only the cities in the midst of a hostile countryside. Moreover, the military efficacy of the armies was undermined by the rivalries between their commanders; by Chiang Kai-shek's penchant for personal decision making even when he was far removed from the scene; and by his abiding concern to prevent any possible rival from amassing too much power. Also much in evidence were the harshness and corruption that had sapped the soldiers' morale during the war against Japan and were even more demoralizing now that they were supposed to fight fellow Chinese.

In other respects too, far from stimulating reform, the defeat of Japan re-

Figure 15-5   Chiang Kai-shek and Mao Zedong exchanging toasts, Chongqing, August – October 1945.

sulted merely in the transfer to the rest of China of the ills that had been incubating in wartime Chongqing. A nation badly in need of political, economic, and social reconstruction was subjected to a heavy dose of autocracy and to a galloping inflation. There was talk of reform, but the assassination, in the summer of 1946, of the poet and professor Wen Yiduo (Wen I-to, 1899–1946) disheartened intellectuals who shared his liberal ideas and hoped for greater freedom to criticize the government. But intellectuals and students were not the only ones disenchanted with the regime, for many suffered from the arrogance of the Nationalist soldiers and the rapacity of those with political connections.

The situation was particularly bad on Taiwan, where carpetbaggers from the mainland enriched themselves at the expense of alleged Taiwanese "collaborators"—a convenient charge against any noncooperative Taiwanese who had done at all well during the preceding half century of Japanese rule. When the Taiwanese rioted in protest in 1947, the Nationalist government responded with brutal and bloody repression. The exact number of casualties is not known — Taiwanese leaders in exile claim that over 10,000 were killed.

The government, inefficient as well as autocratic, proved unable to halt rapidly accelerating inflation that threatened all those whose incomes did not keep up with rising costs. Toward the end, people in the cities had to carry enormous bundles of paper money on their daily rounds of shopping for the necessities of life.

In the CCP areas, in contrast, a disciplined and well-organized political and military leadership offered models of earnest dedication to their cause based on the conviction that this cause was just and would ultimately triumph. Unlike the Guomindang, which promised reform only after fighting was finished, the CCP implemented one change after another. A crucial and impressive demonstration of their expertise in mass mobilization took place in Manchuria where they made the most of the window of opportunity granted them by the Soviet Union before it withdrew. Here, once their military presence was established, they were able in a mere 18 months to transform indifferent, suspicious peasants into ardent participants in and supporters of the party and of the military campaigns directed by the brilliant general Lin Biao (Lin Piao, 1907–71). Cooperation was secured by a mixture of hope and fear that varied with groups and individuals while party cadres led a series of carefully orchestrated campaigns attacking and systematically displacing the old elite that no longer could summon external support from a provincial or regional elite undermined and compromised during the preceding 14 years of Japanese rule. The campaigns culminated in land redistribution (see Figure 15-6), which revolutionized the local power structure.

The contrast between CCP dynamism and Guomindang decay helps explain not only the ultimate outcome but also the unexpected rapidity of the course of events. The military turning point came in July 1947 when Communist armies attacked along several fronts in North China. In Manchuria, Lin Biao commanded a campaign that put the Guomindang forces on the defensive and

Figure 15-6   *Seizing the landlord and transporting his movable property (Dongbei zhibao)*, October 9, 1947.

ended, in October 1948, by completely routing them. During that same month and into November, the last great battle of the war was fought at the strategic city of Xuzhou on the Huai River where the Beijing-Nanjing Railway line joined the Longhai line, which runs from Shaanxi to the sea. Around half a million men on each side were involved in this battle, generally known as the battle of Huai-Hai after the Huai River and the Longhai Railway. When it was all over, the Nationalists, under Chiang Kai-shek's personal command, had lost 200,000 men and no longer had any way to supply their forces to the north. In January 1949 Nationalist generals surrendered Beijing and Tianjin. Throughout the campaigns the Communist army gained not only military advantages from its victories, but also captured valuable military equipment and supplies and increased its manpower as Nationalist soldiers defected or surrendered and were incorporated into the People's Liberation Army.

During 1949 the Communists continued their advance. They crossed the Yangzi in April, took Nanjing the same month, and were in control of Shanghai by the end of May. On October 1 Mao Zedong, in a great ceremony in Beijing, formally proclaimed the establishment of the People's Republic of China (see Figure 15-7.) There was still some fighting in the south, but clearly the CCP had won control of the Chinese mainland. Meanwhile, Chiang Kai-shek and other Nationalists took refuge on Taiwan and vowed continued resistance.

The triumph of the Communists in 1949 began a new chapter in China's long history. It was the result of a long revolutionary process that had begun well before the founding of the CCP, but in terms of the party's own programs and goals the revolution had only just begun.

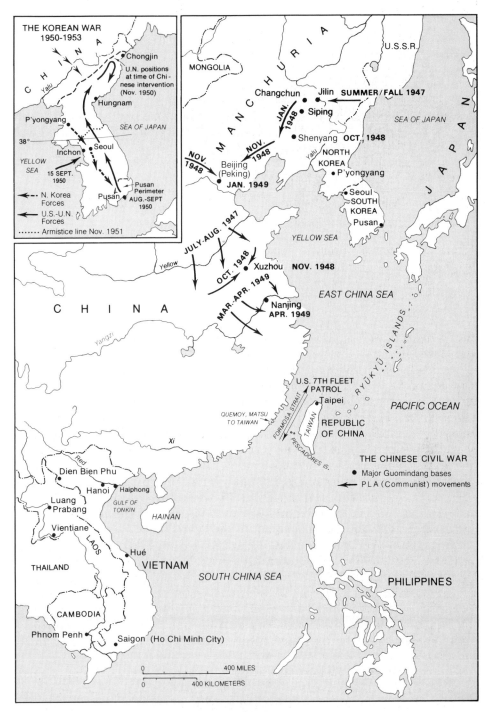

Figure 15-7   **East Asia after the Second World War**

NOTES

1. Stuart R. Schram, *The Political Thought of Mao Tse-tung* (New York: Frederick A. Praeger, 1963), p. 209.
2. Jerome Ch'en, *Mao and the Chinese Revolution* (New York: Oxford Univ. Press, 1965), p. 337.
3. Michael A. Barnhart, *Japan Prepares for Total War: The Search for Economic Security, 1919–1941* (Ithaca: Cornell Univ. Press, 1987), p. 234.

16
The
New China

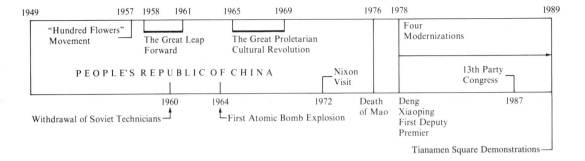

W hen Mao Zedong proclaimed the People's Republic on October 1, 1949, it marked a watershed in the history of modern China. After a century of suffering because of internal disintegration and foreign aggression, China made a new beginning under leaders deeply committed to the revolutionary transformation of the nation. Mao and his associates were determined to create an egalitarian society and make China strong and prosperous. While the road to these goals was to prove neither smooth nor easy, clearly China was moving in a new direction.

In taking control of the entire country and then restructuring Chinese society, the new leaders faced problems as immense as China itself. They were dedicated Marxists and in their march to power had brilliantly adapted the foreign ideology to Chinese conditions. The challenge that now awaited them of transforming China in the spirit of that ideology proved a formidable one, and, in terms of the broad sweep of Chinese history, it may be too early to assess their achievement.

PART I. CONSOLIDATION AND CONSTRUCTION SOVIET STYLE (1949–1958)

The first nine years of the People's Republic began with an initial period (1949–52), during which the regime consolidated its rule and forged the basic framework of a new sociopolitical order. This was followed by a period of Socialist Construction (1953–58), initiated by the publication of the first Soviet-style five-year plan—begun in 1953, although not published until 1955.

Government and Politics

Politically, the years after 1949 saw the establishment of the basic machinery for governing China. A characteristic feature of the Chinese system (as it was, also, in the Soviet Union) was the creation of parallel government and party structures, and the practice of appointing high party officials to top government posts. Thus Mao was head of the party (that is, Chairman of the CCP

352

Central Committee) and, until 1959, also officially head of state. Party control was also exercised in other sectors by the same means. High party members held positions of leadership in various quasi-official organizations such as trade unions, and, as during the pre-1949 years, party members served as political commissars in the army, which was responsible to the Military Affairs Commission headed by Mao.

Administratively China was divided into provinces, and these remained the primary political subdivisions after an additional governmental level between the provinces and the central government was tried but discarded. The three most highly populated metropolitan areas, Shanghai, Beijing, and Tianjin, were placed under the central government, and "autonomous regions" were created in areas inhabited by a significant number of minority people. One such "autonomous regions" was Inner Mongolia. (The new government recognized the independence of Outer Mongolia where the Mongolian People's Republic had been established in 1924, under Soviet sponsorship.) The other autonomous regions were Guangxi, Ningxia (southeast of Inner Mongolia), and the vast western regions of Xinjiang and Tibet. The latter was incorporated into the People's Republic after Chinese troops entered that mountainous land in October 1950, but Tibet did not receive autonomous region status until 1965. (See map, pp. xxiv – xxv.) Aside from their strategic importance, the Inner Asian territories were significant because the Chinese government now had to deal with the interests and sensitivities of ethnic minorities.

An important factor in establishing and operating the new system was the cohesiveness of the Party leadership. The only political conflict to erupt openly was an attack on Gao Gang (Kao Kang), the CCP leader in Manchuria who was accused of separatist ambitions. Also a factor were Gao's ties with the Soviet Union and the issue of Soviet influence in Manchuria. Gao's suicide was reported in 1955. Another prominent leader purged at the same time was Rao Shushi (Jao Shu-shih), who was based in Shanghai. Rao, like Gao, was charged with operating "an independent kingdom." These two leaders, in charge of China's two prime industrial centers, were also accused of forming a political alliance.

To achieve its goals, the leadership launched massive national campaigns. Thus, during 1951 – 52 there was a "three anti" campaign against waste, corruption, and bureaucratism aimed at disciplining the greatly enlarged CCP membership, and a "five anti" campaign against bribery, tax evasion, fraud, the stealing of state property, and the theft of economic secrets. During this campaign many wealthy men had to pay heavy fines. In accordance with Mao's "On the New Democracy" (1940), members of the national bourgeoisie were initially tolerated, and only capitalists with Guomindang or foreign ties were considered enemies of the revolution. Gradually, however, private companies were turned over to the state, although their former owners often remained as managers. The owners continue to receive some dividends to this day, although payments were interrupted during the Cultural Revolution.

Not all drives were directed against human evildoers; there was also a concerted Attack on the Four Pests: a war against rats, sparrows, flies, and mosquitoes. Partly by campaigns such as this, the People's Republic achieved enormous improvements in public health. Furthermore, by involving all the people in these campaigns, the leadership not only made use of China's greatest asset (manpower) but also gave the people a sense of participation and pride in the resulting accomplishments.

Foreign Relations and the Korean War

The Communist victory was hailed with enthusiasm in Moscow and bitterly deplored in Washington. Partly for ideological reasons and partly in response to continued even if unenthusiastic American support for the Nanjing government, the CCP aligned itself with the U.S.S.R. in a policy of "leaning to one side." Mao's visit to Moscow, his first trip abroad, resulted in the February 1950 treaty with the U.S.S.R. Relations between the two allies were not easy, however, for Stalin drove a hard bargain and was slow to relinquish special interests in Manchuria and Xinjiang. Still, the relationship with the Soviet Union was very important to the Chinese, because the U.S.S.R. provided a working model for economic and political development as well as moral, political, and economic support. The Soviet alliance was the mainstay of Chinese foreign policy.

On the American side, although some observers had taken the measure of Chiang Kai-shek, large sectors of the American public continued to view him as China's savior, a view fostered by wartime propaganda and the efforts of ex-missionaries, politicians, and other supporters. Many, in and out of government, failed to appreciate that the CCP were nationalists as well as Communists. All this stood in the way of easing tensions between Washington and Beijing, but it is clear that "both Chinese and American leaders were interested in and groping uneasily toward accommodation."[1] However, time ran out with the beginning of war in Korea in June 1950.

During the Second World War, the United States and the Soviet Union had agreed on the 38th parallel as a dividing line: north of this line Japanese forces would surrender to Soviet troops; south of the line they would submit to troops of the United States. What was not clear at the time was that this was to become a semi-permanent dividing line between a Soviet-backed Communist state in the north and an American-supported state in the south. Both states harbored the ambition to rule over the entire country. These ambitions erupted into war in June 1950, when North Korea attacked the south.

The period of intense fighting can be divided into three main phases, each with its own subdivisions. First, from June to September 1950, the North Koreans were on the offensive, pushing the South Korean and American forces back until they established a defense perimeter around Pusan from which they could not be dislodged. The second phase began with MacArthur's amphibious landing at Inchon in September, which led to the recapture of Seoul and then to an offensive intended to unify Korea by force. Then, in November, the Chinese, alarmed by the American advance to the Yalu River, and having had their warnings ignored, sent massive "volunteer" armies into Korea. These succeeded in regaining the north but were unable to win control over the south. This became clear in late May 1951, and in July of that year truce talks began but not until July 1953 did they lead to an armistice, which, although marred by incidents, still remains in effect today.

The Korean War did not alter the international configuration of power in East Asia, but it did considerably embitter Sino-American relations. Both sides were now more convinced than ever of the enmity of the other. In the United States, proponents of a moderate China policy were removed from influence and subjected to slander. The American commitment to the Nationalist regime was confirmed. Taiwan was given economic and military assistance, and in 1954 the United States signed a mutual defense treaty with the government of Chiang Kai-shek. Meanwhile, American troops remained in Korea and on their bases in Japan and Okinawa. The Chinese, alarmed by these developments, were confirmed of the wisdom of allying themselves with the U.S.S.R. While the Chinese viewed America as an imperialist aggressor, throughout the 1950s many people in the United States, even those in high places, considered the People's Republic to be little more than a Soviet satellite.

If the Korean War merely solidified alliances already in the making and froze the participants into their Cold War postures, it did enhance China's international status by demonstrating the ability of her peasant army, a bare year after the triumph of the revolution, to resist the formidable armed might of the United States. Within China, the Korean War helped the government to mobilize the people under the banner of national resistance and created its share of national heroes. Above all, it meant that the revolution had now been tested in foreign as well as domestic war.

Abroad, Beijing's representatives played an important role in the Geneva Conference on Indo-China (1954) and at the conference of Asian-African states held at Bandung (Indonesia) in 1955. However, the People's Republic was not accorded membership in the United Nations, and the United States prevailed on many of its allies to withhold recognition. The buildup of Nationalist strength on Taiwan also rankled Beijing. However with the U.S. Seventh Fleet patrolling the Taiwan Strait, actual fighting was limited to sporadic shelling of two Nationalist-held islands off the coast of Fujian Province.

Economic Policies

Economic matters were of central concern to the new government right from the start. It had inherited a land ravaged by war and floods, with both agricultural and industrial output badly down from prewar levels and the monetary system wrecked by inflation. Furthermore, the underlying economy had serious structural weaknesses. In the agrarian sector, the prevalence of small, uneconomic, scattered landholdings and uneven land ownership helped to perpetuate traditional farming techniques and discouraged capital formation and investment in agriculture. China's industrial sector, on the other hand, consisted primarily of light industry concentrated around Shanghai and heavy industry in Manchuria. It had been developed to meet the requirements of foreign capital rather than the needs of China and its people.

Any government would have had to restore and strengthen the economy to increase production, but as Marxists, China's new leaders were also committed to the transfer of the means of production from private to public ownership and the creation of an egalitarian system of distribution. Their aim was to create a socialist state with a strong proletarian (working-class) base. The necessary precondition for this was vigorous industrialization, and since this was also required for the attainment of national strength, economic ideology and patriotism pointed to the same end.

By 1952, despite the strains of the Korean War, the economy had been restored to prewar levels. Factories had been put back into operation, railway lines had been repaired, and inflation had been brought under control. In the cities the private sector was temporarily retained and even encouraged, but control over materials and marketing, as well as wages, prices, and working conditions, was in the hands of the state. Meanwhile, in the countryside, land redistribution was carried out not by government decree but by mobilizing the suppressed fury of the rural poor. Landlords were denounced and humiliated in public trials and at mass "speak bitterness" meetings. The more fortunate ones were allowed to retain enough land to support themselves, but many lost their lives. The campaign became associated with a general suppression of potential counterrevolutionaries during the Korean War. The end result was not only a more equitable distribution of land but a change of village leadership, which was now in the hands of activists drawn from the poor peasantry.

The achievements of the first three years of the People's Republic were viewed as merely a necessary stage for further socialization and economic development. China was now ready to embark on planned economic growth. A planning organization was established, as was a statistical bureau, and in 1953 China took its first modern census, which registered a total population of 582,600,000 on the mainland. Although demographers have questioned its accuracy, this figure is accepted as a general indication of the size of China's population at the time.

China's First Five-Year Plan followed the model of the Soviet Union's economic development in stressing heavy industry, with some 85 percent of total investments going into this sector. The role of the Soviet Union was important also in other ways. Russia supplied technical assistance (plans, blueprints, and so forth), helped train Chinese technicians (28,000 Chinese technicians and skilled workers went to the U.S.S.R. for training during the fifties), and sent about 11,000 of its own experts to work in China. Development was also accelerated by importing entire plants from the Soviet Union. Most of what was left of the private sector was eliminated. Control over the plants was given to professional managers and technocrats, whose prime responsibility was to carry out government economic directives. To enable them to do this, they were placed firmly in charge of their factories.

Since loans advanced by the Soviet Union amounted to only 3 percent of China's total state investments, the financing of this industrialization effort was predominantly Chinese. These funds came out of the government's budget. The government, in turn, derived much of its revenue from taxes and from the income of state enterprises. Ultimately, a considerable portion of investment capital came from agriculture, which remained the heart of the Chinese economy.

To increase output and channel agricultural surplus more effectively into capital formation, the government in 1953 began a program of more radical transformation of the pattern of land management. To replace the existing system of small fields, individually owned and worked, the government planned to collectivize agriculture by pooling land, labor, and other resources. The change was not to be accomplished all at once. At first, "mutual-aid" teams, which shared labor, tools, and work animals, were organized. The next stage was to create village producers' cooperatives in which land also was pooled. Initially, agricultural collectivization was planned as a gradual program, because the Chinese leadership wanted to avoid the terrible bloodshed and suffering that had accompanied Stalin's rapid collectivization in the Soviet Union. Mao, however, in an important speech he delivered in July 1955, drew on the experience of the Chinese Revolution rather than the Russian Revolution and reaffirmed his faith in the revolutionary spirit of the Chinese peasantry. Just as the peasantry had been in the vanguard of the revolution that gave birth to the People's Republic, it would now lead the nation to socialism. In Mao's view it was the party, not the people, that was dragging its feet. The immediate effect of Mao's speech was an acceleration in the agricultural collectivization program, so much so that is was largely accomplished within a single year (1955 – 56); and the timetable for full collectivization was set ahead. A long-range effect of the speech was the emergence of a Maoist strategy of economic development distinct from that of the Soviet Union. In 1957 the process of collectivization was completed.

When the First Five-Year Plan came to an end, the Chinese viewed the results with considerable satisfaction. The government was now firmly in control of the industrial sector, and agriculture had been reorganized. In such key areas as iron, coal, and steel, the production targets set by the plan had been exceeded. Industrial production doubled between 1953 and 1957, and, altogether, remarkable progress had been made on the road to industrialization. There were problems, to be sure. One was the widening gap between the city and the country, a problem that has plagued all industrializing countries but was of special concern in China, where the peasantry remained the majority and where the party leaders identified with them. Another problem was the reappearance of bureaucracy. As Maurice Meisner put it, "Once leaders of the masses in a revolutionary situation, party cadres were becoming state administrators governing the masses."[2]

Thought Reform and Intellectuals

The leaders of the People's Republic were convinced not only of the scientific correctness of their doctrine but also of its moral rightness, and they believed that virtually everyone could be brought to share their vision and act accordingly. They were optimistic not only about the course of history but also about the nature of human beings, and they retained a traditional Chinese faith in the moral perfectibility of man as they set about creating an ideal socialist man to replace the traditional models. It was their belief that given the proper environment and correct guidance, people would become selflessly devoted to revolution and community.

Naturally the most promising were the young, uncontaminated by the old society, and the government saw to it that they were educated in the new values. Special attention was paid to the political awareness of Communist party members and cadres, who were relied on to set examples of personal conduct and lead the people. To further the thought reform and moral transformation of even the most unpromising individuals, the authorities devised techniques of group discussion, self-criticism, and public confession. By using the individual's own feeling of moral inadequacy and guilt, and by applying external pressures, the authorities induced people to renounce old values and prepared them for conversion to the new faith. Perhaps the most famous example of such a change of heart, accomplished in the controlled environment of a correctional institute, is provided by Puyi. As an infant he had been the last occupant of the Qing throne, and more recently he had served the Japanese as puppet ruler of Manchukuo. After undergoing thought reform, he reemerged as a citizen in good standing.

Not only prominent personages but also ordinary people now spent a good deal of time in small discussion groups, analyzing their lives as well as problems or incidents at their places of work. In this way the new ideology was transmitted to the people, and they were taught to use it in analyzing everyday problems. At the same time, social pressures were applied to everyone to conform to generally accepted standards of behavior.

The thought reform of intellectuals presented special problems. Highly trained and educated people were a rare and precious resource for a nation bent on industrialization and modernization. Yet few came from peasant or worker backgrounds. More serious than the question of class background was the persistence of traditional elitist attitudes among intellectuals, as well as their critical habits of mind. They tended to resent taking directions from party cadres less well educated than themselves. Their special knowledge and skills were needed, but could they be trusted? The integration of intellectuals into the new society remained a difficult problem.

The extent of dissatisfaction among intellectuals was revealed when Mao invited writers and thinkers to "let a hundred flowers bloom; let a hundred schools contend." When this invitation was first issued in May 1956, there was little response from intellectuals wary of exposing themselves to attack. Then, in February 1957, Mao said in a speech, "On the Correct Handling of Contradictions Among the People," that nonantagonistic contradictions should be resolved by persuasion rather than force. After some further reassurance, the floodgates of criticism were opened.

Criticism was directed not only against the behavior of individual party functionaries and at specific party policies but also at the CCP itself for seeking "to bring about the monolithic structure of a one-family empire."[3] Intellectuals and writers asked for independence from the party's ideological control. Academic problems should be left for professors to solve: "Perhaps Mao has not had time to solve these problems for us," one history professor suggested.[4]

Mao had intended the campaign to rectify the party, but the criticism was more than he had bargained for. Weeds grew where he had invited flowers. Soon criticism exceeded acceptable limits. In the resultant suppression, some prominent intellectual and literary figures disappeared from the public scene. The intellectuals sent to do physical labor in the countryside were soon joined by thousands of conservative or bureaucratic party members, targets of an anti-Rightist campaign that began in June 1957 and in December quickened into a massive purge of party members and cadres.

An underlying issue was how to balance the requirement for ideological purity and moral dedication to the revolution with the professional competence required to operate a modern state and build an industrial system. Without the former, a new elite of experts, technocrats, and managers would pursue its own aims, and the revolution would be jeopardized. Mao believed that progress toward Communist egalitarianism and the building of national strength went hand in hand, but for the rest of his life put his faith in Redness, often at the expense of expertise.

PART II. THE REVOLUTION CONTINUED (1958–1976)

By the end of the first five year plan there were increasing indications that following the Soviet model was not producing the desired economic or social results, but there was no agreement on what should be done. While the party establishment saw a need for only relatively minor adjustments, Mao advocated a far more radical line. In the subsequent complicated, often turbulent years, he did not always dominate events, but he did prevent the revolution from settling down into comfortable routines and remained a potent force to be reckoned with until his death in 1976.

The Great Leap Forward

The Great Leap Forward was initiated in January 1958 but lost momentum the following year; after fall 1959 it was continued but without vigor, until it was terminated in January 1961. On Mao's initiative the gradualism of Soviet-style central planning was now abandoned in favor of reliance on the energies of the masses imbued with revolutionary consciousness. A voluntarist as well as a populist, Mao believed that ideology was a force that could motivate people to heroic accomplishments. History was not confined to a series of well-defined objective stages of economic and sociopolitical development but instead was a constant process of "permanent revolution," with the subjective will transforming the objective world. The revolution had made extensive use of massive manpower in labor-intensive projects all along, projects such as the building of waterways, roads, and other giant construction works. Now all of China's human resources were to be focused in a giant leap. By emphasizing Redness and revolutionary fervor, Mao hoped to accelerate China's economic development and progress toward socialism. The spirit of the people was to be the driving force for China's continued economic growth and social transformation.

As the prime vehicle for this effort, rural communes were formed by combining the already existing cooperatives. By the end of 1958 there were 26,000 rural communes in which 98 percent of China's rural population lived. Each averaged about 25,000 people. The communes themselves were divided into production brigades, each corresponding roughly to the traditional village, and these were in turn divided into production teams. The communes were intended to function as China's basic political as well as economic and social units, integrating all aspects of the lives of their members. As economic units the communes supervised agricultural production and distribution, provided banking services, and also established small factories and machine shops operated on the commune or production brigade level, depending on the size and degree of specialization of the plant. The communes were further responsible for police functions, and they operated schools and hospitals, provided day-care facilities and mess halls, took care of the aged, and staged plays and other entertainments. They represented an ambitious attempt to create new, large-scale communities. But they turned out to be too large. Their size was therefore reduced, so that by the end of the Great Leap Forward the original number of communes had almost tripled to 74,000, with a corresponding decrease in the size of their memberships. Later the communes lost many of their functions to the smaller production brigades.

There was also a movement to establish communes in the cities by combining or transforming earlier street associations, but this movement was briefer and accomplished less than its rural counterpart, perhaps because of the greater complexities of cities or because it ran into opposition. The street associations, which included the inhabitants of one street (or of several small streets, or of a portion of a large street), had originally been organized for security and welfare purposes. They were now given additional responsibilities for economic enterprises as well as for educational and medical facilities. In general, the formation of urban communes involved the transfer of authority over factories from central and provincial ministries to the local party committee that controlled the communes. Some of the communes consisted of workers in one large factory, others included the residents of one part of a city, still others, located on the outskirts of cities, included some farmland along with an urban sector. Whatever the form of urban organization, an effort was made to release women for work by establishing mess halls, nurseries, homes for the aged, and service facilities such as laundries.

To enlist the enthusiasm of the people and encourage local initiative, local authorities were granted substantial leeway in deciding how to implement government directives. The central government still set general economic policy and retained control over the largest heavy industrial plants, but 80 percent of all enterprises were decentralized. No longer was there to be reliance on experts in far-off Beijing making all the decisions and operating with a centralized bureaucracy such as that of the U.S.S.R. This new policy was consistent with Mao's belief in mass participation and in the power of the human will.

High social as well as economic expectations were raised by the creation of the communes. According to Communist theory, the achievement of a truly communist society entails a change from paying people according to their productivity to paying "each according to his needs." In line with this, experiments were conducted in paying people approximately 70 percent of their wages in kind (produce to satisfy their needs) and the rest in cash according to their productivity. Meanwhile, impressive production targets were announced, including the goal of catching up with British industrial production in 15 years. To the Chinese leaders, the social and economic goals seemed entirely compatible.

Through the catharsis of intense participation, the Great Leap Forward furthered the emotional involvement of many people in the creation of a new order. They were made to feel that the making of a strong China was not something to be left to the experts and technocrats; it was to be done by, as well as for, the people. People and government were to join in one vast common effort.

If the Great Leap Forward achieved some of its political and psychological goals, it also turned into an economic disaster. This did not become apparent for some time; the initial statistics of production were impressive, but they turned out to have been grossly inflated. One unanticipated consequence of the Great Leap Forward was a breakdown in China's statistical services, and serious mistakes were made because the government accepted the exaggerated figures forwarded by overenthusiastic local authorities. Some projects originally pursued with enthusiasm later had to be abandoned as unworkable. Perhaps the best known was the campaign to build backyard furnaces for making iron and steel. The plan was vigorously implemented. All over China small furnaces were set up, but they proved incapable of turning out iron of acceptable quality let alone steel.

The most serious failure of the Great Leap Forward was in agriculture. Here too the government worked with misleading statistics, as local units vied with each other in reporting productivity gains. The harvest of 1958 was seriously exaggerated, leaving China poorly prepared for 1959 when bad weather harmed the crops and for the harvest of 1960, which was still worse. According to later Chinese figures over 16 million people died of famine, while Western estimates were over 25 million dead. It was a disaster. In John K. Fairbank's words, "the Chinese path to socialism had led over a cliff."[5]

The Sino-Soviet Split

From the founding of the People's Republic on, there were areas of tension and potential conflict between China and the Soviet Union. As we have seen, the CCP was not successful in achieving power until it went its own way, forging its own policies in accord with Chinese realities rather than with Moscow's theories. Furthermore, the Chinese leadership was as determinedly nationalistic as the Russians, who, ever since Stalin first came to power, had operated on the principle that what was good for the Soviet Union was also good for the cause of world communism. This was an equation with some plausibility as long as there was only one great Communist power in the world, but it was a thesis that the Chinese, sooner or later, were bound to challenge.

Initially, the forces holding the alliance together were stronger than those pulling it apart. These included not only the ties of a common ideological heritage but also a set of common Cold War enemies. However, around the mid-1950s the first cracks in the alliance began to appear.

One cause of friction and potential antagonism was territorial. The Chinese did reluctantly accept the independence of Outer Mongolia, whose historical status resembled that of Tibet, but they were very unhappy about their northern and western boundaries with the Soviet Union. These borders had been drawn in the nineteenth century and thus formed part of the history of imperialism that China's new government was pledged to undo. As early as 1954 Chinese publications indicated the country's refusal to accept vast regions of Central and Northeast Asia as permanently belonging to the U.S.S.R.

Another source of trouble was the Chinese desire for recognition as leaders within the Communist world. After the death of Stalin in 1953, they expected that Mao would be honored as the leading living contributor to Marxist ideology. Instead, Khrushchev went his own way, first shocking the Marxist world by denouncing Stalin, in a famous speech in 1956, and then by developing his theories of peaceful coexistence. Neither the rejection of Stalinism nor the U.S.S.R.'s new international stance accorded with Chinese needs, nor had the Chinese leaders been consulted before these major shifts in Soviet policy were announced. On the other hand, the Russian leaders could hardly be expected to welcome Chinese claims, made during the Great Leap Forward, that their communes represented a higher stage on the road to the ideal society than anything achieved in the Soviet Union after 40 years of Communist rule.

Despite efforts toward reconciliation such as Chinese support for the Soviet suppression of the Hungarian uprising in 1956 and Mao's visit to Moscow in 1957 and Khrushchev's to Beijing in 1958 and 1959, the strains in the alliance continued to mount. One reason for this was the U.S.S.R.'s unwillingness to exploit its temporary supremacy in rocketry to support a possible Chinese attack on Taiwan, an attack that would have had no hopes for success unless the United States were neutralized by Soviet threats. Khrushchev's relatively unbelligerent stance toward the United States seemed to the Chinese like a cowardly betrayal, while Mao's belittling of the dangers of nuclear warfare made him appear to the Russians as a dangerous adventurer gambling with the lives of millions. Consequently, the Russians were hesitant about sharing nuclear secrets with the Chinese.

The split became permanent in the summer of 1960 when the Soviets withdrew their technicians from China. The Russians even took their blueprints with them. After that, despite limited cooperation during the Vietnam War, relations remained bitter as China and the U.S.S.R. denounced the other's policies and challenged the Marxist legitimacy of the other's revolution. While the Chinese charged that the Soviets had deviated from the true revolutionary path, Russian and East European ideologists depicted Chinese aberrations as arising from their lack of a firm proletarian base as well as an inadequate understanding of Marxism.

One aspect of this situation was the Soviet Union's support of India in its disputes with China. Relations between China and India became tense in 1959, after the Chinese suppressed a revolt in Tibet and India welcomed Tibetan refugees, including the Dalai Lama, the spiritual and sometime secular leader of Tibet. Furthermore, China and India, the world's two most populous nations, were natural rivals for Asian leadership. The resulting tensions would not have led to outright hostility, however, had it not been for Indian intransigence over border disputes. The result was a short border war in 1962 in which Chinese quickly humiliated the Indian troops. The Soviet Union continued its policy of friendship for India, and China cultivated good relations with India's arch rival, Pakistan. Meanwhile, within the Communist world, China defended and allied itself with the bitterly anti-Soviet regime of Albania.

Militarily the Soviet Union remained much the stronger of the two powers, but the People's Republic was also developing its armed strength. A milestone was reached in 1964 when it exploded its first atomic bomb. Numerous clashes along the border between the U.S.S.R. and China endangered the peace between them, and both sides feared that the situation might evolve into a fullfledged war. Beijing invested in an extensive system of underground shelters for use in case of an attack by air. The hostility of the Soviet Union continued to be a basic reality in China's international situation. It was one of the principal factors that led to a gradual rapprochement between China and the United States during the 1970s.

Domestic Developments (1961–1965)

The failure of the Great Leap Forward led to retrenchment in domestic policies, a willingness to accept, for the moment, more modest interim social and economic goals. It also led to a decline in Mao's personal authority, not only because of the economic depression that had followed the Great Leap, but also because political and economic processes were becoming institutionalized and bureaucratized. The new system was settling down.

Mao was still chairman of the party, but in December 1958 he had resigned as head of the government. That post was filled by Liu Shaoqi (Liu Shao-ch'i, 1898–1969), a hard-working organization man long associated with Mao. Liu had a number of supporters in high party and government positions, but the supervision of the state's administrative machinery, including the various ministries, remained under the direction of the head of the State Administrative Council, who had the title of Premier. This position had been filled since 1949 by another trusted party veteran, Zhou Enlai (Chou En-lai). Zhou also served as Foreign Minister until 1959, and continued even after he left that post to serve as China's main spokesman in foreign affairs. By all accounts, Zhou was one of the most capable and versatile of all the CCP leaders, a superb political and military strategist, a truly gifted administrator and negotiator.

Another important government position was that of Minister of Defense. In 1959 a veteran general was ousted from this post for going too far in criticizing Mao and the Great Leap Forward, for pro-Soviet tendencies, and for overemphasizing professionalism, allegedly at the cost of failing to imbue the troops with sufficient ideological spirit. His successor as Minister of Defense was another distinguished general, Lin Biao (Lin Piao).

Under the direction of Liu Shaoqi, the government relaxed the tempo of social change. There was now greater appreciation of expertise and less reliance on the revolutionary enthusiasm of the masses. There was an increased use of economic rather than ideological incentives: in the communes the more productive workers could earn extra work points, and in the factories there were wage increases, bonuses, and promotions to be earned — measures later castigated as "economism." Peasants were also allowed now to have small private plots and to sell on the free market whatever they could grow on them, while still under the obligation to produce a fixed amount of grain for the state.

After the great exertions and the disappointments of the Great Leap Forward, there was a natural slackening not only of the pace of change but also of revolutionary fervor. This alarmed Mao, who sought to combat this trend by initiating a socialist education movement in 1962 without, however, much effect. Furthermore, there now appeared in print thinly veiled attacks on Mao himself. Among them was the historical play, "Hai Rui (Hai Jui) Dismissed from Office," written by the Deputy Mayor of Beijing. In this play the sixteenth-century Ming official (see Chapter 8) was portrayed sympathetically as an honest minister who stood up for the peasants and was dismissed by a foolish and autocratic emperor. What was implied was a critique of Mao's own dismissal, in 1959, of the then Minister of Defense. In November 1965 an article was published in the Shanghai press denouncing this play. Thus began the Cultural Revolution.

The Great Proletarian Cultural Revolution (1965–1969)

The Cultural Revolution was profoundly ideological and strongly political. It was cultural in the broadest meaning of that term, since it sought to remold the entire society and to change the consciousness of the Chinese people. Utopian in its aims, it was disastrous in its results.

Its moving force was Mao himself, determined not to allow the revolution that had been his life's work to drift into Soviet-style revisionism, resolved to combat the reemergence of old patterns of bureaucratic arrogance and careerism, convinced that drastic measures were necessary to prevent the entrenchment of new vested interests in state and party. Now an old man, Mao was unwilling to rest on his laurels as the father of the revolution. He actively involved himself in the Cultural Revolution and dramatically displayed his physical vigor by publicly swimming some ten miles across the Yangzi River five months before he turned 74 in 1966.

The obstacles to the Cultural Revolution were formidable because it affected the interests of a majority of party functionaries both at the center and in the provinces. But among Mao's assets were not only his unequaled prestige but also the support of the People's Liberation Army, which under Lin Biao, emphasized guerrilla-style revolutionary spirit and fostered solidarity among officers and men by deemphasizing rank. In the summer of 1965, insignia of rank were abolished. Nor were there any other differences in uniform to differentiate officers and men. Mao and other leaders hoped similarly to reduce or, if possible, to eliminate the distinctions and privileges of rank in society at large.

To accomplish this required the destruction of the Establishment. A popular image of the Cultural Revolution was that of Monkey from *Journey to the West* (see Chapter 8):

> The Golden Monkey wrathfully swung his massive cudgel,
> And the jade-like firmament was cleared of dust.[6]

The author of the article in which these lines appeared in May 1966 went on to explain that the cudgel was Mao's thought. To carry on the battle, the country was inundated with copied of *Quotations from Chairman Mao*, the omnipresent Little Red Book cited on all occasions as the ultimate source of authority. Similarly, Mao himself was glorified as never before.

By all accounts the most enthusiastic wielders of the cudgel were the Red Guards, young people mostly born since the founding of the People's Republic. Mao hoped that their youthful spirit would revitalize the revolution and keep it from sinking into comfortable revisionism. In Mao's view it was not enough for these young people merely to read theoretical and historical works and to sing revolutionary songs. They must actually live and make revolution, so that they would be molded by direct personal revolutionary experience, much as Mao and his generation had been. These young people formed the vanguard of the Cultural Revolution and were also responsible for most of its excesses as they organized public humiliations of prominent people, administered beatings and took captives, ransacked houses and destroyed books, art, and anything old or foreign. Among the most enthusiastic participants were urban youths of questionable class background proving to others and themselves their revolutionary purity.

Opposition to the Red Guard and the Cultural Revolution was considerable. In many places the local authorities were able to draw on popular support. There was rioting, and pitched battles were fought between rival groups, each claiming to represent the thought of Mao. Much of the information on these struggles comes from the posters written in large characters that were the prime means of public communication during the Cultural Revolution. Mao himself, in August 1966, wrote such a poster, "Let Us Bombard the Headquarters."

Many party headquarters were indeed attacked, and the party was crippled. Leaders of the government from Liu Shaoqi down were made to confess their sins in public and then disappeared from public view. Universities were closed, scientific and scholarly journals ceased publication (although nuclear development went on apace), intellectual and cultural life were disrupted, and there was turmoil in the cities. However, Zhou Enlai managed to keep the basic machinery of government working and was able to protect some from attack. Meanwhile, Mao's wife, Jiang Qing (Chiang Ch'ing, ca. 1915–), and Mao's secretary, Chen Boda (Ch'en Po-ta, 1904–), emerged as leaders of the Cultural Revolution group.

The Cultural Revolution reached its most radical phase in 1967. At the beginning of that year a dramatic series of events in Shanghai, China's largest city, led to the triumph of a workers' movement that was able to overthrow the local party apparatus by overcoming factional divisions. In February the workers formed a People's Commune, which lasted only 19 days, since it did not receive the endorsement of Mao Zedong, who thought it too radical. He preferred the formation of "revolutionary committees" in which the army played a leading role. With the CCP out of commission and the country badly divided, the army grew in importance as the single organized and disciplined institution capable of forceful action on a national scale. However, the revolution developed a new "ultraleft" intensity before the army was called in to calm things down. In the summer of 1967, hundreds of thousands demonstrated in Beijing against Liu Shaoqi and Zhou Enlai. Radicals even occupied the foreign ministry for two weeks. Outside of the capital the most dramatic events took place in July, when the army intervened to suppress local antigovernment insurgents. In September, fearing that China was on the brink of anarchy, Mao ordered the army to restore order.

Military men were prominent on the various revolutionary committees set up to administer provinces, factories, and communes as the Cultural Revolution continued, increasingly under army auspices. The revolution came to an end in 1969. In April of that year, a party congress officially confirmed the new prominence of the army by adopting a new constitution designating Lin Biao as Mao's successor. An important official criterion for party membership was class background. "Bad elements," such as the descendants of landlords, rich peasants, capitalists, and "rightists" continued to face obstacles in career advancement.

Earlier, party cadres and intellectuals were frequently "sent down" to work the land among the peasants, and now thousands of Red Guards were similarly removed from the cities for a stint of labor in the fields. This was not only a practical measure for restoring order but also had a theoretical basis in the "mass line," which embodied Mao's conviction that the people were the source of valuable ideas and that the function of leaders was to obtain these ideas from the masses, to concentrate and systematize them, and then take them back to the masses. The function of party members and other leaders was humbly to learn from the masses and also to teach them. Whatever the shortcomings of this process, it was a way to get leaders to identify with the common people.

Economically the Cultural Revolution saw the resumption of Great Leap Forward programs that had been dismantled during the early 1960s. Again ideology was emphasized over expertise and personal economic incentives. Again the focus was on the rural sector, which benefitted from programs that extended medical care and education. Plants were built in rural areas to manufacture and repair farm machinery, produce fertilizer, or process local products, thereby diminishing the distinction between city and country. After the cultural revolution, experiments in calculating work points for farm work on the basis of political criteria rather than in terms of an individual's productivity were abandoned. Similarly, in urban factories there were provisions for greater worker participation in factory management and programs to lessen the distinction between workers and managers and between mental and manual labor.

The Winding Down (1969–1976)

Although the Cultural Revolution was officially ended in 1969, Jiang Qing and her associates retained control over the media and cultural affairs. During the next seven years radical Maoists remained influential in national politics and had some victories. Nevertheless, there was a gradual turn to moderation. The party was rebuilt and moderate leaders reappeared. Mao himself wanted to curb the power of the military and turned against Lin Biao, whose downfall came in the autumn of 1971. Allegedly Lin tried to save himself by staging a coup and when that failed attempted to flee in an airplane that crashed in Mongolia.

The fate of Liu Shaoqi and Lin Biao demonstrated the hazardous position of those who rose to high leadership and were marked for the succession, but Zhou Enlai, as usual, was on the winning side. Zhou continued as Premier, and with Mao aging, he played a more important role now than ever. There was a decrease in army influence and more moderate economic policies were adopted. There was a general relaxation of emphasis on revolutionary fervor. For example, when universities were first reopened in 1970, after a four-year hiatus, admission was based on a candidate's recommendations from comrades in the candidate's work unit and the approval of the appropriate revolutionary committee. In 1972, however, academic criteria for admission were reintroduced. That year, the first scientific periodicals also reappeared, but the new emphasis was on applied rather than theoretical science. Public exaltation of Mao was toned down. There were even attacks on the Little Red Book; CCP members were now urged to pursue a thorough study of Marxist writings.

Even after his death, Lin Biao was further denounced during 1973–74 in a campaign linking him with Confucius. Both men were portrayed as "political swindlers" and sinister reactionaries. Thus Confucius was depicted as representing a declining slaveowner class, while Lin Biao was charged with wanting to restore capitalism, each man exerting himself to reinstate an outdated system.

The campaign against Confucius and Lin Biao was a sign of the continuing influence of the Cultural Revolution leaders' attack on the past, but the ancient philosopher and modern general made a strange pair, and there is some evidence suggesting that Confucius was really a surrogate for Zhou Enlai.

During and after the Cultural Revolution, Chinese relations with the Soviet Union remained tense even though both powers supported North Vietnam in its war against the Saigon regime and the United States. Concern over Soviet intentions was heightened to alarm when the U.S.S.R. invaded Czechoslovakia in 1968 and Communist Party Secretary Leonid Brezhnev announced that the U.S.S.R. had the right to intervene in socialist countries, which he accorded only "limited sovereignty." Fears of a Soviet nuclear strike, actual troop deployments along the lengthy Sino-Soviet frontier, and armed clashes in Manchuria induced China to seek broader diplomatic contacts with the United States. Although Chinese personnel did assist the North Vietnamese, there was no repetition of Korea. Chinese terrain was not threatened and no massive intervention by Chinese troops took place. Furthermore, a channel of communication was maintained through periodic meetings of the ambassadors of the two countries, held first in Geneva and later in Warsaw. The fall of Lin Biao and the emergence of Zhou Enlai also increased the prospect for improved Sino-American relations.

A contributing factor on the American side was the intention of President Nixon, elected in 1968, to withdraw the United States from the war in Vietnam. As long as China and the United States were committed to the opposing sides of a war that was raging at full force and ever threatening to escalate still further, substantial improvement in Sino-American relations remained highly unlikely. Nevertheless, a high-level Sino-American dialogue did not have to wait for the actual end of the war — a shift in direction toward peace was enough. By 1971 both sides were ready to talk. A new approach to China was deemed a logical corollary of the Kissinger-Nixon concept of international balance-of-power politics. The Chinese were receptive. The Sino-American rapprochement began informally with a Chinese invitation of an American Ping-pong team whose members were personally greeted by Zhou Enlai. Then came President Nixon's visit to Beijing in February 1972 and the Shanghai Communique, which provided for partial normalization and paved the way for the resumption of full formal diplomatic relations in 1979. In 1971, even before the Nixon visit, the United Nations had voted to admit the People's Republic in place of the Nationalists, and the new American stance now removed the last obstacle to recognition by most countries.

It remained for a new leadership to work out the implications of the change in China's international posture. When Zhou died in January 1976, his enemies banned public mourning but were unable to prevent a massive gathering at the Martyrs' Memorial in Beijing's great Tiananmen Square on China's Day of Mourning in April. This expression of reverence for the late premier was tantamount to a rejection of Cultural Revolution. Mao, aged and ailing, still had sufficient authority to designate Hua Guofeng (Hua Kuo-feng, 1920–) as Zhou's successor.

Hua was soon called upon to demonstrate his administrative talents, for in July China's worst earthquake in four centuries devastated Tangshan, an industrial and mining city a hundred miles from Beijing. In old China, statesmen would have interpreted this as a signal of further shocks to come, and they would have been vindicated for on September 9 Mao died. Architect of the triumph of the CCP, he had been responsible for most of the features that made the Chinese revolution unique. His passing marked the end of an era.

PART III. CHINA AFTER MAO (1977–)

During the years following the passing of Mao and Zhou, China undertook another profound change of course. Many of the policies of the previous quarter of a century were reversed, and new measures adopted that bore scant resemblance to either those of Mao or of his more conventional opponents.

The future, as ever, remained uncertain, but what seemed clear was that the Revolution had been more successful in destroying the old political and economic power structure than in initiating progress towards a bright new day. It was time to try something new.

The Four Modernizations

Mao's true successor was not Hua Guofeng but Deng Xiaoping (Teng Hsiao-p'ing, 1904 –), a party veteran who had once been castigated as second only to Liu Shaoqi in "taking the capitalist road" and more recently had enjoyed the backing of Zhou Enlai. In July 1977, Deng became First Deputy Premier and from 1978 on was clearly China's most powerful political figure. Blamed for all the ills of recent years were the "Gang of Four," led by Jiang Qing, Mao's widow. By November 1980 the new leadership under Deng felt sufficiently secure to put the "Gang of Four" on trial. In January 1981 Jiang Qing and another leader were given suspended death sentences later commuted to life imprisonment. Hua Guofeng was soon shunted into political obscurity.

Deng's program was epitomized by the slogan "The Four Modernizations," first introduced by Zhou Enlai in 1975. Directed at farming, industry, science, and defense, the aim was to turn China into a modern industrial state by the end of the century. The years since 1952 had seen considerable economic progress, but China remained an underdeveloped country. Furthermore, the Cultural Revolution had taken a heavy toll in lost educational and technological progress. Now under Deng, merit, not revolutionary virtue, was rewarded. Professionalism and individual initiative were encouraged, and market forces allowed greater play.

There were dramatic changes in the countryside as agriculture was decollectivized. In 1982 communes lost their social and political authority while their economic power was also curtailed. Under the "responsibility system," peasants were assigned land on contracts to produce a certain amount of grain and increasingly won both the right to decide on just how to do this and to dispose of any surplus produce on the open market. As under the old "equal-field system," the amount of land to be assigned was to depend on the number of people in each family. Gradually, restrictions on commercial activities were eased, and enterprising peasants did notably well.

Similar changes took place in light industry and commerce but at a slower pace. Official enterprises were expected to justify their existence by making a profit, government regulation was decreased, and individuals were allowed to open restaurants and workshops. Under a new "open door" policy welcoming foreign companies, special economic zones were established, where foreign investment was encouraged. At the same time, the skyline of Beijing and Shanghai was transformed by the rise of international luxury hotels where the affluent traveler could savor China in luxury and at an antiseptic distance.

The attainment of utopian egalitarianism was now postponed, and China was deemed to be only in the "initial stage of socialism" as Premier Zhao Ziyang (Chao Tzu-yang, 1919 –) put it at the Eleventh Party Congress in 1987. For the sake of building national wealth and strength, China's new pragmatic leaders were willing to try policies that would have been anathema to their more dogmatic predecessors. For example, in 1987 the mayor of Shenyang was quoted as saying, "When used to promote the development of China's socialist economy, bankruptcy, leasing, shareholding and these sorts of things are no longer capitalist."[7] Socialist aims were not renounced, but their attainment was placed in the far distant future.

Whatever vision China's leaders had of the timetable of history, it had been clear for some time that China's future would be dim indeed if something were not done to effect population control. Since the early 1970s, China had a vigorous birth-control program. Even so, since China's population was young and more people were born than died, the population continued to increase. It topped 1 billion in 1982 and will continue to grow until the early years of the next century even if each couple has only one child as the new leadership wants. Severe pressures, not always stopping short of coercion, insured virtually full compliance in China's cities, but this was not the case in the countryside where children, with good reason, continued to be regarded as an asset to a family.

Population pressures not only pose a restraint on increase in the standard of living but also threaten China's ability to respond adequately to ecological problems such as the land erosion that has caused the Yangzi River to become another Yellow River. In the mid-1980s topsoil loss of more than 5 billion tons annually deprived China of more soil nutrition than that produced by its entire synthetic fertilizer industry. Major programs of reforestation are one positive response, but it will take very strong and farsighted leadership to avert further deterioration and bring about gradual improvement.

The new policies made people more prosperous but were not beyond criticism. There was a notable increase in corruption and a general slackening of revolutionary morale, even disillusionment. People focused on improving their standard of living, and family and personal concerns often crowded out broader considerations of the public good. The demise of Maoism left a moral vacuum.

From the beginning of the Four Modernizations some people, many of them influential but elderly men, objected to the departures from orthodox socialism, but there were also voices at the opposite end of the political spectrum, calling for more rapid liberalization. During 1978 – 79 a movement to add democracy as the "fifth modernization" had found expression on "Democracy Wall" in Beijing. This was a place where, for a time, people could freely post their views. The wall was abolished and the movement's leader arrested, but critics continued to find a ready hearing among students and intellectuals. Under Deng's guidance, the regime, on its part, was concerned not to let criticism get out of hand, but for some ten years refrained from strong-armed measures that could alienate the intellectuals whose cooperation was needed for modernization. Thus campaigns against "cultural pollution" (1983) and "bourgeois liberalism" (1987) were relatively mild, and the government's response to the student demonstrations of December 1986 was to send over a million students to spend the following summer recess in the countryside.

For some ten years Deng successfully orchestrated the pace of change, and in 1987 he had the satisfaction of seeing the Thirteenth Party Congress affirm the general directions of his policies, including the primacy of economic development. This session also marked the retirement of a substantial number of the old guard, who were generally replaced by men more inclined to follow Deng in "seeking truth from facts." Deng himself felt sufficiently confident to resign as Deputy Premier although, significantly, he retained his chairmanship of the Military Commission for two more years.

However, the strains of the unprecedented move away from a command economy in the direction of a market economy were becoming more acute. As was only to be expected, the increase in agricultural productivity after the initial jump following decollectivization could not be sustained indefinitely. More threatening was the danger of accelerating inflation after the relaxation of price controls. In 1988, the government was faced with an inflation rate of over 30 percent in many urban areas, and an estimated 35 percent of all urban households suffered a decline in their standard of living. It responded by slowing down the economic reform program to regain control of the economy.

It remains to be seen whether the attempt to confine the new economic energies within acceptable channels will ultimately succeed, but a similar attempt to channel intellectual life suffered a major setback in the spring of 1989, when the government was caught off guard by the intensity of massive student demonstrations in favor of democratic reforms. Symbolic of the students' aspirations was the large statue of the Goddess of Democracy (see Figure 16–1) they erected in Beijing's Tiananmen Square. At first the government hesitated, but the upshot was that on June 4, 1989, Deng resorted to bloody military suppression of the students in Beijing. This was followed by the arrest, and in some cases execution, of student leaders in the capital and elsewhere.

Beijing's policy in the immediate aftermath of the suppression has been to increase indoctrination and thought control but otherwise maintain that essentially nothing has changed. That, however, is hardly convincing to those within China and beyond who witnessed the suppression on television. The regime emerged with its moral authority shattered and its international standing impaired. Whether it will be able, with the passage of time, to repair the damage, reassure educated people within China (and Hong Kong), and regain the confidence of foreign investors, only time would tell. Similarly, the political future is murkier than ever. As in the aftermath of the Cultural Revolution, the military once again has come to the fore. Deng's authority was reconfirmed, but the events of the spring of 1989 cost Zhao Ziyang his career. Zhao was succeeded by Jiang Zemin (1926–) who in November 1989 also replaced Deng as chairman of the Military Commission. Jiang is generally

Figure 16-1
Goddess of Democracy, Tienanmen
Square, Beijing, May 30, 1989.

considered a technocrat, but the question of who will ultimately succeed the 85-year-old supreme leader remains open.

Undoubtedly China will continue to devise its own synthesis between native and foreign, modern and old, as it copes with problems that are all magnified by sheer number and size. For example, there is no reason to doubt the continued importance of the Communist Party even as its role is being redefined, but the governance of a party composed of 46 million members is comparable in scale to governing a country rather than to running an ordinary political party elsewhere in the world.

Foreign relations during the late 1970s and 1980s remained within the pattern set earlier. Sino-Soviet relations remained correct. In 1988 the Soviet Union began to withdraw from Afghanistan thereby removing one source of friction. Sino-Vietnamese relations remained tense. There were border clashes in 1985. China continued to support the Khmer Rouge in guerrilla warfare against a government installed in Cambodia by the Vietnamese in 1978.

A notable diplomatic success was the agreement in 1984 with Great Britain to return Hong Kong to Chinese sovereignty in 1997. China in turn guaranteed that for the next 50 years Hong Kong would retain its own economic institutions. The People's Republic thus acknowledged the economic importance of Hong Kong, which by the mid-eighties had developed into a major world financial and trade center and also had a thriving manufacturing sector. After the events of June 1989, the People's Republic reaffirmed its guarantees in an attempt to reassure anxious people in Hong Kong. Beijing also hoped that the "One Country Two Systems" formula might eventually lead to a similar settlement with Taiwan.

PART IV. TAIWAN

Chinese in culture and population, Taiwan's recent history has diverged from that of the rest of China ever since it was ceded to Japan in 1895. Subsequently it was joined to the mainland only from 1945 to 1949. Since 1949 it has experienced sustained economic growth, major social change, and gradual political change as well.

Economic Growth and Modernization

As noted in Chapter 15, the first two years of Guomindang rule were so oppressive as to provoke the riots of 1947, which the government suppressed ferociously. As a result of Guomindang actions much of the Taiwanese elite was decimated. Ironically, this removed not only resistance to the political dominance of the Guomindang but also a potential source of opposition to land redistribution and other economic reforms undertaken during the fifties with American backing and advice.

During the Japanese years, Taiwan acquired much of the necessary infrastructure for industrialization, and many of the approximately 2 million civilian refugees who came to Taiwan with the Nationalists also brought training and skills that contributed to the development of light industry and commerce. Capital came in part from the great sums of money the Nationalists brought over with them. Until terminated in 1966, American economic aid also helped, and once the Japanese economy had recovered, Japanese companies too invested heavily in Taiwan. The government generally supervised and advanced development, as in 1965 when it created special Export Processing Zones where companies enjoyed tax incentives and were free of import taxes as long as they exported whatever they made or assembled.

Progress was sufficient for the economy to come through both the oil crisis and the diplomatic defeats of the seventies in good shape. As in Japan, there was a turn to more advanced technology such as computers. In 1980 the state estabished a science-oriented industrial park.

By that time Taiwan had attained a level of per capita income second in Asia only to Japan. In many ways, it became a modern country. By 1979 over half the people owned a color televison set and 90 percent had refrigerators, and during the eighties air-conditioners became common and cars largely captured the road dominated previously by motorbikes.

The government as well as many intellectuals saw its mission as that of preserving old Chinese traditions. Taiwan became the home for institutes of higher learning. A museum was built to house the priceless Palace Collection of Art, which the Nationalists brought with them from the mainland. Ideologically the regime remained committed to the reunification of China and to Sun Yat-sen's Three Principles of the People.

Originally the mainlanders, though outnumbered, were slow to share power with the Taiwanese, that is, people of Chinese stock who had settled earlier on the island. Though the native Taiwanese did win elections to local governments, real control remained in the hands of the central government, which claimed to speak for all of China. Prosperity and repression kept dissent to a minimum. When Chiang Kai-shek died in 1975, there was an easy and smooth passing of power to his son Chiang Ching-kuo (in pinyin Jiang Jingguo, 1910–88).

In the eighties, as the events of more than 30 years earlier receded into the past while economic growth continued to transfigure the land, differences in economic stratification were becoming more important than those between mainlanders and Taiwanese. This may have been one of the factors prompting the government to meet popular pressures for more democracy. In any case, in 1987 martial law was revoked, press restrictions were eased, and inhabitants of Taiwan were, for the first time in 38 years, allowed to visit relatives on the mainland. The government was confident that they would return appreciating the higher standard of living they enjoyed on Taiwan.

When Chiang Ching-kuo died in January 1988, he was succeeded by Lee Teng-hui (in pinyin Li Denghui, 1923–), a Taiwanese with a Ph.D. in agricultural economics from Cornell, who made good on his pledge for further democratic reforms by conducting a free election in December 1989. Since the island continued to enjoy a favorable balance of trade and general prosperity, there seemed little inducement to respond to Beijing's invitation to begin a dialogue leading toward reunification. Economic relations were relatively unaffected by Beijing's supression of the students in June 1989, but this did cost the People's Republic a loss of good will and esteem.

PART V. ARTISTIC AND INTELLECTUAL LIFE

The turbulence of the years since the great war was mirrored in literature and the arts, and the changes that took place, in content and style, were as revolutionary as those affecting other aspects of life.

Serving the People

After the establishment of the People's Republic and in line with policies enunciated by Mao in Yenan, art was to speak to a mass audience and serve the revolution. What was valued was not technique, or subtlety of expression, but revolutionary content and easy communication with the people. In keeping with this approach, major efforts were made both to broaden popular participation in the arts and to put artists in closer touch with the masses, so that they might draw inspiration from them.

As far as possible, literature and the visual arts were to be not only for the people but also by the people. Thus, during the Great Leap Forward, teams were sent out to collect the people's literature and to encourage peasants and workers to compose poetry and otherwise participate in the creation of art. As a result, in Shanghai alone some 200,000 people participated in producing 5 million poems. Many thousands undoubtedly were exhilarated at achieving recognition in a field previously reserved for an exclusive elite.

During the sixties and seventies, workers and peasants continued to be encouraged to participate in the creation of art. There were efforts at collective writing and painting. Another arrangement was for part-time writers to get a day off from their factory jobs in order to work on their literary projects. Professional writers were periodically "sent down" to factory or commune, so that they would not lose touch with the people. They also, as a matter of routine, invited popular criticism of their work and responded to suggestions for changes. For example, before The Broad Road to Golden Light (1972) was issued, 200 copies were sent to communes and factories for criticism. This novel by Hao Ran (Liang Jinguang, 1932 –) went on to sell 4 million copies.

As earlier in the Soviet Union, the challenges and triumphs of a socialist society became the main topics of art and literature. The theme of Broad Road, for example, is the change from individual farming to the creation of mutual-aid teams. The same themes occur over and over: the ideals and struggles of the revolution, the wisdom of Mao, the heroism of soldiers, the triumph of socialist virtue over selfishness, and the glories of work. Although the style is usually designated "socialist realism," it is romantic rather than realistic, intended to inspire, not to mirror life, which in practice inevitably falls short of the ideal.

A central reality in Chinese life is the importance of work. This is hardly surprising in a socialist state striving to feed its people, assure its national security, and otherwise catch up with the advanced industrial nations of the world. Everyone is exhorted to work hard and to contribute to the building of a new society; indeed, there is an almost puritan ethos of devotion to work. The arts both encourage and reflect this tendency. Thus Yuan Kejia (Yüan K'o-chia, 1921 –), once an admirer of T. S. Eliot, wrote in 1958:

> Labor is joy; how joyful is it?
> Bathed in sweat and two hands full of mud,
> Like sweet rain my sweat waters the land
> And the land issues scent, better than milk.
>
> Labor is joy; how joyful is it?
> Home from a night attack, hoe in hand,
> The hoe's handle is still warm,
> But in bed, the warrior is already snoring.[8]

Content was emphasized over form in the arts, and since that content was determined by the political authorities, the line between art and propaganda was often thin. To Western eyes, much that is now produced lacks appeal. Thus, none of the numerous paintings glorifying Mao Zedong matches in human appeal the sympathetic photograph shown in Figure 16-2.

Perhaps the most refreshing and enjoyable paintings came from the brushes of peasants and showed scenes of people at work. Figure 16-3 shows a work of peasant art exhibited in Beijing in 1973. It is filled with people at work. Most of the work is done by human muscle; children too are mobilized to help out, as in old China, although now they march in formation behind a red banner identifying them as little red soldiers. But there are other sources of power too, including a power station testifying to the electrification of irrigation, which is now general in China and has greatly helped agriculture. In accordance with the time, the painting also has an immediate political messsage: in front of the wall-poster stand, in the lower right, is a man making posters, "Criticize Lin, Criticize Confucius," and the theme is repeated in the painting's title. Like many peasant paintings, this one is done in bright and cheerful colors. Its tone is optimistic. As urban counterparts there were paintings showing people working in factories. Many show women at work, for China was determined

Figure 16-2   Mao Zedong.

Figure 16-3   Hang Gaoshe
*Criticizing Lin Biao and
Confucius Promotes Production.*
Peasant Painting from Huxian.
Exhibited in Beijing in 1973.

that women were to become fully equal with men. In *Youth Red as Fire* (see Figure 16-4) a young woman sits at the controls of a huge steel furnace, and the red of the title is echoed by the red glow of the furnace pouring out liquid white steel. Such examples of "socialist realism," represent a break with the artistic past. However, tradition was not rejected in its entirety, for there were artists who used old techniques to render modern subjects. In Figure 16-5, the Beijing Express emerges from "Victory Tunnel," which is given depth by the use of Western perspective; but even the train on the bridge high above does not destroy the traditional flavor of the mountain setting and the overall composition.

Writers and artists were prominent among the victims of the Cultural Revolution, and a narrow orthodoxy was also enforced in the other arts. Jiang Qing, herself once an actress, championed revolutionary operas celebrating contemporary themes. In place of traditional Chinese Opera audiences were now treated to dances on the theme "We Are So Happy Because We Are Delivering Grain to the State." After describing a dance featuring a father-daughter duet expressing their joy at the completion of an electric power plant, Clive Barnes, formerly the dance critic for the *New York Times*, suggested that if this seems bizarre to us, the Chinese might be just as startled by the story of a prince falling in love with a swan (Swan Lake).[9]

While mainland artists were caught in the political storms, Chinese artists elsewhere were freer to explore new ways to draw on their tradition in order to create forms of expression suitable for the twentieth century. One of the most gifted of these was Liu Guosong (Liu Kuo-sung, 1932–) who was born in Shandong, educated in Taiwan, and eventually settled in Hong Kong. As Liu explained, "We are no longer ancient Chinese nor modern Westerners. We do not live in the Song or Yuan society, nor in the modern European or American environment. If it is false for us to copy old Chinese paintings, isn't it the same to copy modern Western Painting?"[10] Liu is deeply conversant with both

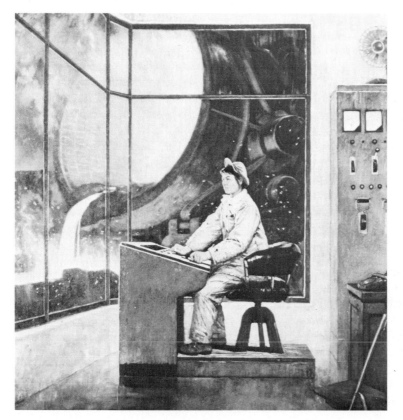

Figure 16-4
Liu Qing,
Youth Red as Fire.
Oil. Exhibited at the
National Exhibition
Commemorating
the 25th Anniversary
of the Founding of
the People's Republic
of China.

Figure 16-5   Ma Lizhou and Yao
Lifang, *The Iron Dragon Bores
Through Ten Thousand Layers
of Mountains.* 1974.

traditions. His *Metaphysics of Rocks* (see Figure 16-6) includes calligraphic
brushwork and collage. The latter is described by Chu-tsing Li as follows:

> In the lower middle part are two pieces of collage, one large and the other small,
> both suggesting rock shapes. The paper is in color, but combined with some tex-
> tures printed with wrinkled paper. Thus there seem to be several kinds of rocks,
> done with different techniques and brushwork. Yet none of them are realistic
> enough to resemble real rocks. But each gives us an idea of some quality of rocks,
> such as jutting up, having interesting textures, or showing watery surfaces.[11]

New Beginnings

After 1976 mainland intellectuals enjoyed an atmosphere of greater freedom.
People long silenced in prison or obscurity were seen and heard once more.

Figure 16-6
Liu Kuo-sung,
The Metaphysics of Rocks.
Ink and acrylic with
collage on paper, 1968,
68.6 cm × 67.3 cm.

Initially there was an outpouring of sorrow and bitterness in "the literature of the wounded," which revealed how much suffering the Cultural Revolution had brought about. Subsequently writers turned more to psychological themes or to the interplay of human feelings and also engaged in stylistic experiments such as the flow of consciousness technique used by Wang Meng (1934–).

In intellectual and artistic life, there was a new opening to the West facilitated by intellectual exchanges, new translations, exhibitions, and concerts. During the eighties historians read Max Weber as well as Marx, English professors delved into the latest Western literary theories, and the autobiography of Lee Iacocca, chairman of Chrysler, was on sale on the sidewalks of Beijing. Chinese scholars in all fields of specialization rejoined the international intellectual community and undertook a reexamination of their own past. Foreign scholars too were welcomed, as at conferences on Confucius and Zhu Xi (1987) held in both cases in the philosopher's home province. Temples and monuments were restored as were mosques and churches.

Jiang Qing's revolutionary operas disappeared from the stage, and Arthur Miller was invited to help prepare a Chinese performance of *Death of a Salesman* (1985). Now too the Chinese public had its first look at modern artists ranging from Picasso to Jackson Pollock. Among those now exhibited were overseas Chinese artists including Liu Guosong.

Mainland painting became more diverse than ever. While traditionalists added new variations to old genres, and a number of painters expressed their own distinct visions, artists were free to experiment as long as they kept within certain limits of decorum and refrained from hostile political statements. Stage and film too showed new life, and big city audiences now could again enjoy not only Beethoven but even jazz (Figure 16-7). Like proper jazz musicians the world over, Zhang Peili's young men play without a score: what tunes they will improvise we do not know, nor can we tell whether they will be heard in the vast countryside or drowned out by the clamor of those marching to other drummers. We do not even know whether they will be allowed to play at all. China moves at various rhythms and speeds, but these musicians are preparing to play to a new beat.

Figure 16-7 *Jazz* by Zhang Peili. 72 × 56 inches. Oil on canvas. 1985.

NOTES

1. Warren I. Cohen, ed., *New Frontiers in American-East Asian Relations* (New York: Columbia Univ. Press, 1983), p. 144.

2. Maurice Meisner, *Mao's China: A History of the People's Republic* (New York: The Free Press, 1977), p. 129.

3. Chu Anping (Ch'u An-p'ing), quoted in Merle Goldman, *Literary Dissent in Communist China* (Cambridge: Harvard Univ. Press, 1967), p. 192.

4. Yang Xiangkuei (Yang Hsiang-k'uei), quoted in Goldman, p. 193.

5. John K. Fairbank, *The Great Chinese Revolution 1800–1985* (New York: Harper & Row, 1986), p. 305.

6. Quoted in *The Great Cultural Revolution in China*, compiled and edited by the Asia Research Center (Rutland, Vt. and Tokyo: Charles E. Tuttle, 1968), p. 114.

7. Christopher R. Wren, "Comparing Two Communist Paths to 'Reform,'" *The New York Times*, Sept. 6, 1987, Section 4, p. 2.

8. Hsu Kai-yu, *The Chinese Literary Scene — A Writer's Visit to the People's Republic* (New York: Vintage Books, Random House, 1975), p. 227.

9. Clive Barnes, "Shanghai Ballet and Us — Two Different Worlds," *New York Times*, June 12, 1966, sec. D, pp. 5, 6, 24.

10. Quoted in Chu-tsing Li, *Liu Kuo-sung — The Growth of a Modern Chinese Artist* (Taipei: The National Gallery of Art and Museum of History, 1969), p. 32.

11. *Ibid.*, p. 53.

Suggestions for Further Reading

*T*he literature in English on the history and civilizations of China is so extensive that careful selection is imperative for student and researcher alike. The effort here has been to suggest books that are broad enough to serve as introductions to their topics, that incorporate sound and recent scholarship, that make for good reading, and that in their totality reflect a variety of approaches. This listing gives special attention to sources of well-researched bibliography. When such sources are up-to-date and readily available, additional readings are generally not given. Please also note that the length of individual subsections depends in part on the availability of a good recent source for further readings — not on the intrinsic importance of a topic nor on the current state of research. Therefore, there may be fewer items given for a well-researched topic on which there is a recent bibliographical essay or other source of readings than for a topic on which less work has been done but for which there exists no good bibliography. Textbooks and collections of classroom readings are not included. Years given are dates of first publication.

GENERAL WORKS

1. Reference

The Bibliography of Asian Studies published annually by the Association for Asian Studies, Inc., is a basic resource. Tsuen-Hsuin Tsien, *China: An Annotated Bibliography of Bibliographies* (1978) is an impressive research aid which provides an overview of scholarship on China in all languages.

2. General Overviews and Interpretations

A book stimulating to neophyte and expert alike is *Cultural Atlas of China* (1983) by Caroline Blunden and Mark Elvin. For anthropological perspectives on Chinese society see Maurice Freedman, ed., *Family and Kinship in Chinese Society* (1974); Arthur Wolf, ed., *Religion and Ritual in Chinese Society* (1974); and Patricia B. Ebrey and James L. Watson, *Kinship Organization in Late Imperial China, 1000–1940* (1986). K. C. Chang, ed., *Food in Chinese Culture: Anthropological and Historical Perspectives* (1977), is an important book on an important (and delicious) subject. Language provides a key to any civilization: John de Francis, *The Chinese Language: Fact and Fantasy* (1984), and S. Robert Ramsey, *The Languages of China* (1987), are recommended.

3. Surveys and Broad Histories

Jacques Gernet, *A History of Chinese Civilization* (Eng. trans. 1982), is the most extensive single-volume history in English. A truly comprehensive project, *The Cambridge History of China* began publication in 1978; individual volumes are noted where appropriate. Also recommended are Charles O. Hucker, *China's Imperial Past: An Introduction to Chinese History and Culture* (1975), and Immanuel C. Y. Hsü, *The Rise of Modern China*, 3rd. ed. (1983). In *The Pattern of the Chinese Past* (1973), Mark Elvin develops the stimulating and influential thesis that late imperial China found itself in a high-level equilibrium trap. Kang Chao, *Man and Land in Chinese History* (1986), is an ambitious interpretation of China's premodern economic history.

4. The Arts and Literature

Sherman E. Lee, *A History of Far Eastern Art*, rev. ed. (1973), includes a consideration of Indian art that is helpful for understanding the Buddhist art of East Asia. It is a well-written perceptive but also a demanding book. Michael Sullivan, *The Arts of China*, 3rd. ed. (1984) is highly recommended. *Theories of the Arts in China* (1983), ed. Susan Bush and Christian Murck, is a stimulating collection of essays on a variety of important topics. Also see Christian Murck, ed., *Artists and Tradition: Uses of the Past in Chinese Culture* (1976). On Chinese painting see the "state of the field" article by Jerome Silberberg "Chinese Painting Studies in the West," *The Journal of Asian Studies* 46, no. 4 (Nov. 1987): 849–97.

The best brief general survey of Chinese literature remains Liu Wu-chi, *An Introduction to Chinese Literature* (1966). A concise introduction is provided by J. Y. Liu, *Essentials of Chinese Literary Art* (1979). Liu also surveyed the field in "The Study of Chinese Literature in the West: Recent Developments, Current Trends, Future Prospects," *The Journal of Asian Studies* 35, no. 1 (Nov. 1975): 21–30. Cyril Birch, ed., *Anthology of Chinese Literature*, 2 vols. (1965, 1972), is also recommended. *The Indiana Companion To Traditional Chinese Literature* (1985), William H. Nienhauser, Jr., et al. eds., is useful but uneven (see review in *Journal of the American Oriental Society* 107 [1987]: 293–304). For a sensitive reading of Chinese poetry see Stephen Owen, *Traditional Chinese Poetry and Poetics: Omens of the World* (1985). Tao-Ching Hsu, *The Chinese Concept of Theater* (1985), is multifaceted and highly informative.

5. Thought and Religion

East Asian Civilizations: A Dialogue in Five Stages (1988), by Wm. Theodore de Bary, is a masterful summation that concludes by pointing to the need for both East Asia and the West to catch up with each other. A basic resource for the student of Chinese philosophy is Wing-tsit Chan, *A Source Book in Chinese Philosophy* (1963), which covers all periods. Also see Charles W. Fu and Wing-tsit Chan, eds., *Guide to Chinese Philosophy* (1978). On the natural sciences see "Science and Medicine in Imperial China — The State of the Field," by Nathan Sivin in *The Journal of Asian Studies* 47, no. 1 (Feb. 1988): 41–90.

Introductory surveys of Chinese religion are provided by Daniel L. Overmyer, *Religions of China* (1986) and Christian Jochim, *Chinese Religions* (1986). The best bibliographic reference is Laurence G. Thompson, *Chinese Religion in Western Languages: A Comprehensive and Classified Bibliography of Publications in English French, and German Through 1980* (1985). There are also good discussions on many Chinese topics in Mircea Eliade, ed., *The Encyclopedia of Religion* 16 vols. (1987).

PART I THE CLASSICAL CIVILIZATION OF CHINA (Through the Han)

Archaeology not only illuminates the beginnings of Chinese civilization but also provides valuable information concerning its development. The leading American authority is Kwang-chih Chang, who has periodically revised his *The Archeology of Ancient China*, 4th ed. (1986), to reflect recent developments. Both it and David N. Keightley, ed., *The Origins of Chinese Civilization* (1983), are rather technical in places but indispensable.

The historical changes that took place during the Eastern Zhou are analyzed in Cho-yun Hsu, *Ancient China in Transition: An Analysis of Social Mobility, 722–222 B.C.* (1965). Burton Watson, *Early Chinese Literature* (1962), is a masterly account that takes its subject through the Han. Also recommended is Watson's *The Tso Chuan: Selections from China's Oldest Narrative History* (1989), and two fine translations of early Chinese poetry: Arthur Waley, *The Book of Songs* (1937), and David Hawks, *Ch'u Tz'u: The Songs of the South* (1959). Still useful is the monumental work by James Legge, *The Chinese Classics*, 5 vols. (1893–95; reissued 1960).

A. C. Graham, *Disputers of the Tao: Philosophical Argument in Ancient China* (1989), is a masterful history of classical Chinese philosophy. Other studies that have appeared since the publication of Fu and Chan's *Guide* include Chad Hansen, *Language and Logic in Ancient China* (1983); Benjamin Schwartz, *The World of Thought in Ancient China* (1985); A. C. Graham, *Chuang Tzu: The Inner Chapters* (1981); Hsiao Kung-chuan, *A History of Chinese Political Thought*, Vol. 1, *From the Beginnings to the Sixth Century* (1979), trans. F. W. Mote; David L. Hall and Roger T. Ames, *Thinking Through Confucius* (1987) and John Knoblock, *Xunzi: A Translation and Study of the Complete Works*, Vol. 1 (1988).

The obvious starting point for additional reading on the first empire is Denis Twitchett and Michael Loewe, eds., *The Cambridge History of China*, Vol. 1: *The Ch'in and Han Empires, 221 B.C.–A.D. 220* (1986). For the period's (and China's) own greatest historian there is Burton Watson's *Ssu-ma Ch'ien: Grand Historian of China* (1958), and Watson's translation, *Records of the Historian: Chapters from the Shih Chi of Ssu-ma Ch'ien*, 2 vols. (1961). For life and poetry, also see Anne Birrell, *Popular Songs and Ballads of Han China* (1988).

PART II CHINA IN A BUDDHIST AGE

Buddhism in China

The literature on Buddhism in English is rich and varied. A straightforward introduction, written in sample language and presuming no background is Kenneth Chen, *Buddhism: The Light of Asia* (1968). A useful collection of Buddhist writings is Wm. Theodore de Bary, ed., *The Buddhist Tradition in India, China, and Japan* (1972).

The relationship between Chan (Zen) and the arts remains as difficult to define as the religion itself, but the arts, especially painting, testify to the power of Zen even as they offer an approach to understanding. Enthusiastically recommended is Jan Fontain and Money L. Hickman, *Zen Painting and Calligraphy* (1970), a catalog of an exhibition of both Chinese and Japanese works. Another fine catalog broad in subject matter is Pratapaditya Pal, *Light of Asia: Buddha Sakyamuni in Asian Art* (1984). A major study is J. Leroy Davidson, *The Lotus Sutra in Chinese Art* (1954).

For a brief account of Buddhism in China viewed as a rich and complex historical process of interaction between China and the Indian religion, see Arthur F. Wright, *Buddhism in Chinese History* (1959). Of all the sects of East Asian Buddhism, Chan has attracted the most attention in the West. The most scholarly translation of a key text is Philip P. Yampolsky, *The Platform Sutra of the Sixth Patriarch: The Text of the Tun-huang Manuscript* (1967). The standard history is still Heinrich Dumoulin, *A History of Zen Buddhism* (1963). For additional references see the bibliographies in the works on religion listed in Section 5 under "General Works."

Secular Developments

The interaction between Chinese and non-Chinese peoples is a major theme in the history of China during the period of disunion between Han and Sui. A pathbreaking work on this subject is Owen Lattimore, *Inner Asian Frontiers of China* (1940). Michael C. Rogers, *The Chronicle of Fu Chien: A Case of Exemplary History* (1968), is an important contribution to the historiography as well as the history of the period. For social history see Patricia B. Ebrey, *The Aristocratic Families of Early Imperial China: A Case Study of the Po-ling Ts'ui Family* (1978). Also recommended is Yen Chih-t'ui, *Family Instructions for the Yen Clan: Yen-shih Chia-hsün* (1966), trans. Teng Ssu-yu.

Studies in Chinese secular culture during the period of division include Robert Van Gulik, *Hsi K'ang and His Poetic Essay on the Lute* (1940). Richard B. Mather has translated the *Shishuo Xinyu (Shih-shuo hsin-yü)* under the title *A New Account of Tales of the World* (1976). This very learned and meticulous translation makes available in English a major source for the study of the period's sophisticates. Two out of a projected 8 volumes have been published to date of David Knechtges' monumental translation of China's oldest surviving literary anthology, *Wen Xuan or Selections of Refined Literature* by Xiao Tong (Hsiao T'ung) (1982, 1987).

Sui and Tang

The Cambridge History of China, Vol. 3, *Sui and T'ang, 580–906*, Part 1, (1979), ed. Denis Twitchett, is a major resource. Major recent publications include Arthur F. Wright, *The Sui Dynasty* (1978), and Howard J. Wechsler, *Offerings of Jade and Silk: Ritual and Symbol in the Legitimation of the T'ang Dynasty* (1985). Stanley Weinstein, *Buddhism under the T'ang* (1987), is a chronological account concentrating on the interaction of state and religion, while Charles Hartman, *Han Yü and the T'ang Search for Unity* (1986), deals with political as well as literary and intellectual history. David McMullen, *State and Scholars in T'ang China* (1988) is a major work of scholarship.

Tang poetry is well represented in anthologies as well as in studies of individual poets. Selecting from a number of titles is in part a matter of taste, but it is generally recognized that one of the best books by a master translator is Arthur Waley, *The Life and Times of Po Chü-i* (1949). Although not as fully biographical as Waley's book, the following studies also provide windows on Tang life: Arthur Cooper, *Li Po and Tu Fu* (1973); A. R. Davis, *Tu Fu* (1971); and three books by Stephen Owen: *The Poetry of Meng Chiao and Han Yü* (1975), *The Poetry of the Early T'ang* (1977), and *The Great Age of Chinese Poetry: The High T'ang* (1981). For late Tang poetry see A. C. Graham, *Poems of the late T'ang* (1965), and James J. Y. Liu, *The Poetry of Li Shang-yin* (1969). A leading student of T'ang culture is Edward H. Schafer. Two of his finest books are *The Golden Peaches of Samarkand: A Study of T'ang Exotics* (1963) and *The Vermillion Bird: T'ang Images of the South* (1967). For a fascinating view of T'ang China as seen through the eyes of a visiting Japanese monk, see Edwin O. Reischauer, *Ennin's Travels in T'ang China* (1955).

PART III LATE IMPERIAL CHINA

Song China

James T. C. Liu and Peter J. Golas, *Change in Sung China: Innovation or Renovation* (1969), is still useful, and Liu's *Reform in Sung China: Wang An-shih (1021–1086) and His New Policies* (1959), remains the standard treatment of China's foremost reformer. Robert P. Hymes, *Statesmen and Gentlemen: The Elite of Fu-Chou, Chiang-Hsi in Northern and Southern Sung* (1986), is essential reading for social history as is John W. Chaffee, *The Thorny Gates of Learning in Sung China: A Social History of Examinations* (1985). Recommended as another major study is Thomas H. C. Lee, *Government Education and Examinations in Sung China* (1985). Village structure is analyzed in Brian E. McKnight, *Village and Bureaucracy in Southern Sung China* (1971). For insight and information on Southern Sung politics, see Richard L. Davis, *Court and Family in Sung China, 960–1279: Bureaucratic Success and Kinship Fortunes for the Shih of Min-chou* (1986) as well as James T. C. Liu, *China Turning Inward: Intellectual and Political Changes in the Early Twelfth Century* (1988).

A stimulating discussion of the Sung economy in the light of world history is provided in the first chapter of William H. McNeill, *The Pursuit of Power: Technology, Armed Force, and Society since A.D. 1000* (1982). Peter J. Golas, "Rural China in the Song," *The Journal of Asian Studies* 39, No. 2 (Feb. 1980): 291–325, is a survey of "the state of the field" (in more than one sense.) For other aspects of the economy see Shiba

Yoshinobu, *Commerce and Society in Sung China* (1970), trans. Mark Elvin, and several important articles by Robert Hartwell including "A Cycle of Economic Change in Imperial China: Coal and Iron in Northeast China, 750–1350," *Journal of the Economic History of the Orient* 10 (July 1967): 102–59, and "Financial Expertise, Examinations, and the Formulation of Economic Policy in Northern Sung China," *Journal of Asia Studies* 30 (Feb. 1971): 281–314. *Family and Property in Sung China: Yüan Ts'ai's Precepts for Social Life* (1984), trans. Patricia B. Ebrey is a fascinating and important contribution to social history. Richard von Glahn, *The Country of Streams and Grottoes: Expansion, Settlement, and the Civilizing of the Sichuan Frontier in Song Times* (1987), deals with a major theme in a sophisticated manner. A book filled with interesting detail is Jacques Gernet, *Daily Life in China on the Eve of the Mongol Invasion, 1250–1276* (1962), trans. H. M. Wright.

Ronald C. Egan, *The Literary Works of Ou-yang Hsiu (1007–72)* (1984), examines a key literary and intellectual figure. For the study of Song poetry, James J. Y. Liu, *Major Lyricists of the Northern Sung* (1974) has the great merit of including for each poem the Chinese text, a word for word rendition, and a polished translation. A thoughtful and highly commendable book is Jonathan Chaves, *Mei Yao-ch'en and the Development of Early Sung Poetry* (1976). Chaves is also the author of the excellent and delightful, *Heaven My Blanket, Earth My Pillow—Poems from the Sung Dynasty by Yang Wan-li* (1975). Two of the dynasty's most beloved poets have been sensitively translated by Burton Watson: *Su Tung-p'o—Selections from a Sung Dynasty Poet* (1965), and *The Old Man Who Does As He Pleases—Poems and Prose by Lu Yu* (1973). There are a number of other worthy books on Song poetry that cannot be listed here, but we should mention a study of China's foremost woman poet: *Li Ch'ing-chao* by P'in-ch'ing Hu (1966). For readers interested in the history of music, there is Rulan Chao Pian, *Song Dynasty Musical Sources and Their Interpretation* (1967). Also recommended is Lothar Ledderose, *Mi Fu and the Classical Tradition of Chinese Calligraphy* (1979).

A prime source for the study of Neo-Confucian thought is Wing-tsit Chan, trans., *Reflections on Things at Hand: The Neo-Confucian Anthology Compiled by Chu Hsi and Lü Tsu-ch'ien* (1967). Among the many other outstanding contributions by Wing-tsit Chan to the study of Neo-Confucianism are his translation of *Neo-Confucian Terms Explained (The Pei-hsi tzu-i) by Ch'en Ch'un, 1159–1223* (1986), and his editing of *Chu Hsi and Neo-Confucianism* (1986), a wide-ranging volume of essays by East Asian as well as Western scholars. Also see his, "This Study of Chu Hsi in the West," *The Journal of Asian Studies* 35 (Aug. 1976): 555–77. A fine study of one of the alternatives to Zhu Xi is Hoyt C. Tillman, *Utilitarian Confucianism: Ch'en Liang's Challenge to Chu Hsi* (1982). For a study of one of the dynasty's most fascinating thinkers, see Anne D. Birdwhistell, *Transition to Neo-Confucianism: Shao Yung on Knowledge and Symbol of Reality.* (1989)

The Yuan

For a general history of the Mongols, see Berthold Spuler, *The Mongols in History* (1971). Morris Rossabi, *Khubilai Khan: His Life and Times* (1987), is a scholarly biography of the Mongol emperor most important for China. John W. Dardess, *Conquerors and Confucians: Aspects of Political Change in Late Yüan China* (1973), is an important study of Yuan political history while John D. Langlois, Jr., ed., *China under Mongol Rule* (1981), is a far-ranging collection of essays. For those who would like to explore Yuan culture, there are two books that are authoritative and sensitive: Chung-wen Shih, *The Golden Age of Chinese Drama* (1976), and James Cahill, *Hills Beyond a River: Chinese Painting of the Yüan Dynasty 1279–1368* (1976). Hok-lam Chan and Wm. Theodore de Bary, eds., *Yüan Thought* (1982), is the best book on its subject.

The study of Marco Polo is a field all to itself. His account of his travels, a subject of enduring fascination, may be read in *The Travels of Marco Polo* (1958), trans. R. E. Latham. Also very highly recommended is Leonardo Olschki, *Marco Polo's Asia: An Introduction to His "Description of the World" Called "il Milione"* (1960). For other travel accounts see Christopher Dawson ed., *Mission to Asia: Narratives and Letters of the Fransiscan Missionaries in Mongolia and China in the Thirteenth and Fourteenth Centuries* (1955). Also see Jeannette Mirsky, ed., *The Great Chinese Travelers* (1964), which includes three accounts falling into this period.

Ming

The Cambridge History of China, Vol. 7, Part 1: *The Ming Dynasty, 1368–1644* (1988), Frederick W. Mote and Denis Twitchett, eds., is a detailed narrative history of the dynasty. An excellent, succinct analysis of the Ming state is provided by Charles O. Hucker, *The Traditional Chinese State in Ming Times, 1364–1644* (1961).

A number of studies on social and economic history begin with the Ming but also include later history. A useful survey of major topics complete with excellent suggestions for further reading is Lloyd E. Eastman, *Family, Fields, and Ancestors* (1988). Hilary J. Beattie, *Land and Lineage in China: A Study of T'ung-ch'eng Country: An-hwei, in the Ming and Ch'ing Dynasties* (1979), is a major contribution to social history. For an introduction to the examination system as it operated in late traditional China, see Ichisada Miyazaki, *China's Examination Hell: The Civil Service Examinations of Imperial China* (1976), trans. Conrad Schirokauer. Specifically focused on the Ming is John Meskill, *Academies in Ming China: A Historical Essay* (1982). An authoritative study of an important subject is Ray Huang, *Taxation and Government Finance in 16th Century Ming China* (1974). A real treasure house of information is the monumental *Dictionary of Ming Biography 1368–1644*, 2 vols. (1976), edited by L. Carrington Goodrich and Chaoying Fang.

Wm. Theodore de Bary, *Neo-Confucian Orthodoxy and the Learning of the Mind-and-Heart* (1981), takes Neo-Confucianism from the Song to the Ming and beyond. A landmark in the study of Ming thought was the publication of Wm. Theodore de Bary, et al., *Self and Society in Ming Thought* (1970). On Wang Yangming there are two complementary studies: Julia Ching, *To Acquire Wisdom: The Way of Wang Yang-ming* (1976), and Tu Wei-ming, *Neo-Confucian Thought in Action: Wang Yang-ming's Youth (1472–1509)* (1976). Also see Wing-tsit Chan, trans., *Instructions for Practical Living and other Neo-Confucian Writings by Wang Yang-ming* (1963), and the same author's, "Wang Yang-ming: Western Studies and an Annotated Bibliography," *Philosophy East and West* 12 (January 1972) 75–92. Good books on late Ming thought include Wm. Theodore de Bary et al., *The Unfolding of Neo-Confucianism* (1975); Edward Ch'ien, *Chiao Hung and the Restructuring of Neo-Confucian Thought in the Late Ming* (1985), and Irene Bloom, ed. and trans., *Knowledge Painfully Ac-*

quired: *The K'un-chih chi by Lo Ch'in-shu* (1987). Judith A. Berling, *The Syncretic Religion of Lin Chao-en* (1980), is important for students of intellectual history as well as of religion.

Literature provides fascinating vignettes of Ming life as well as insights into Ming sensibilities. For translations see the *Indiana Companion to Chinese Literature* (under "General Works," in Section 4). Andrew H. Plaks, *The Four Masterworks of the Ming Novel* (1987), is superb. For painting see two books by James Cahill, *Parting at the Shore: Chinese Painting of the Early and Middle Ming Dynasty, 1368–1580* (1978) and *The Distant Mountains: Chinese Painting of the Late Ming Dynasty 1570–1644* (1982).

First Encounters

An excellent introduction to the initial contacts between modern Europe and East Asia is provided by George Sansom, *The Western World and Japan* (1950). A well-written, informative account is C. R. Boxer, *The Christian Century in Japan* (1951). Also see Michael Cooper, S. J., *They Came to Japan — An Anthology of European Reports on Japan, 1543–1640* (1965), and George Ellison, *Deus Destroyed: The Image of Christianity in Early Modern Japan* (1973). For China, Jacques Gernet, *China and the Christian Impact: A Conflict of Cultures* (1982), trans. Janet Lloyd, repays a close reading. Also see L. J. Gallagher, trans., *China in the Sixteenth Century: The Journals of Matteo Ricci* (1953). Jonathan D. Spence, *The Memory Palace of Matteo Ricci* (1984), is a fascinating exercise in comparative history. European knowledge of Asia in early modern times and European reactions to Asian cultures and peoples is the subject of an exhaustive multivolume work still in progress: Donald Lach, *Asia in the Making of Europe* (1965 –). For the influence on each other of European and East Asian art from the sixteenth to the twentieth century, see Michael Sullivan, *The Meeting of Eastern and Western Art* (1973, 1989).

Qing

On the establishment of China's last dynasty there is the scholarly and thoughtful account by Frederick Wakeman, Jr., *The Great Enterprise: The Manchu Reconstruction of Imperial Order in Seventeenth-Century China* 2 vols. (1985), a major work and itself a great enterprise. Also see Lawrence Kessler, *K'ang-hsi and the Consolidation of Ch'ing Rule, 1661–1684* (1976). For the dynasty's two greatest emperors see Jonathan Spence, *Emperor of China: Self-Portrait of K'ang-hsi* (1974), and Harold L. Kahn, *Monarchy in the Emperor's Eyes: Image and Reality in the Ch'ien-lung Reign* (1971). Arthur W. Hummel, ed., *Eminent Chinese of the Ch'ing Period*, 2 vols. (1943), remains a valuable resource.

As noted under "Part III," there are a number of fine studies that consider the Qing as well as the Ming. One not mentioned there is the collection of essays edited by G. William Skinner, *The City in Late Imperial China* (1977). To gain a sense of the texture of local government, see Huang Liu-hung, *A Complete Book Concerning Happiness and Benevolence: A Manual for Local Magistrates in Seventeenth Century China* (1984), trans. and ed. Djang Chu. For an excellent source for additional references on government as well as other topics, see the "selected readings" in Susan Naquin and

Evelyn S. Rawski, *Chinese Society in the Eighteenth Century* (1987). This ambitious synthesis by two leading scholars is a logical place to begin further reading on the social history of late imperial China.

As usual, much can be learned about a period from its art. James Cahill, *The Compelling Image: Nature and Style in Seventeenth Century Chinese Painting* (1982), is an admirable book, fully worthy of its subject. The texture of ordinary life is brilliantly conveyed by Jonathan Spence in *Death of Woman Wang* (1978). For a literary analysis of China's greatest novel, see Andrew H. Plaks, *Archetype and Allegory in the Dream of the Red Chamber* (1976). Arthur Waley, *Yuan Mei: Eighteenth Century Chinese Poet* (1970), is a sensitively drawn portrait. For translations of representative Qing verse, see Irving Y. Lo and William Schultz, eds., *Waiting for the Unicorn: Poems and Lyrics of China's Last Dynasty, 1644–1911* (1986). For further readings on literature consult the *Indiana Companion* and the book by Naquin and Rawski noted in the preceding paragraph.

R. Kent Guy, *The Emperor's Four Treasures: Scholars and the State in the Late Ch'ien-lung Era* (1987), is illuminating on both scholars and state. On intellectual history see Wm. Theodore de Bary, et al., *The Unfolding of Neo-Confucianism* (1975), Thomas A. Metzger, *Escape from Predicament: Neo-Confucianism and China's Evolving Political Culture* (1977), David S. Nivison, *The Life and Thought of Chang Hsüehch'eng* (1966), and the bibliography in Naquin and Rawski.

PART IV CHINA IN THE MODERN WORLD

Paul A. Cohen, *Discovering History in China: American Historical Writing on the Recent Chinese Part* (1984), is a thoughtful account of some of the constructs and concerns underlying American Chinese Studies. Volumes 10 through 13 of *The Cambridge History of China* (1976–1986), all edited or co-edited by John K. Fairbank, deal with this period and include bibliographic essays. Accordingly, the following will emphasize recent publication. One of these is Fairbank's own summation, *The Great Chinese Revolution, 1800–1985* (1986).

A book that offers a new perspective on early Sino-Western relations is Jane Kate Leonard, *Wei Yuan and China's Rediscovery of the Maritime World* (1984). Some of the denizens of the maritime world are studied in Dian H. Murray, *Pirates of the South China Coast, 1796–1889* (1984). For Chinese relations with two major foreign countries see Warren I. Cohen, ed., *New Frontiers in American East Asian Relations* (1983), and Akira Iriye, ed., *The Chinese and Japanese: Essays in Political and Cultural Interactions* (1980).

A fine book that summarizes much research even as it breaks new ground is William T. Rowe, *Hankow: Commerce and Society in a Chinese City, 1796–1889* (1984). Also highly recommended is the same author's "Approaches to Modern Chinese Social History," in Oliver Zunz, ed., *Reliving the Past: The World of Social History* (1985), pp. 236–96. Susan Mann, "Urbanization and Historical Change in China," *Modern China* 10 No. 1 (1984): 79–113, reviews American and Chinese approaches to the study of urbanization. Philip C. C. Huang, *The Peasant Economy and Social Change in North China* (1985), is a major work rich in stimulating interpretations. Yen-p'ing Hao, *The Commercial Revolution in Nineteenth Century China* (1986), is an authoritative account of the modern sector. An overview of recent scholarship in the thriving field of mission studies is provided by Murray A. Rubinstein, "Christianity in China: One Scholar's Perspective of the State of Research in China Mission and China Christian History, 1964–86," in *Newsletter for Modern Chinese History* (Academica Sinica, Taipei), No. 4 (Sept. 1987): 111–43. Historians have increasingly turned to local history in their search for answers to major questions of social and political history. A fine example of the genre is Mary B. Rankin, *Elite Activism and Political Transformation in China: Zhejiang Province, 1865–1911* (1986).

The study of modern Chinese intellectual history has been deeply influenced by the brilliant writings of Joseph Levenson, especially his *Confucian China and Its Modern-Fate*, 3 vols. (1958–65). An excellent example of what can be accomplished by a master in the field of intellectual biography is Benjamin Schwartz, *In Search of Wealth and Power: Yen Fu and the West* (1964). More recently, James R. Pusey, *China and Charles Darwin* (1983), is a major book on a major theme. Another important book by a scholar who has made notable contributions to our understanding of Chinese intellectual history is Chang Hao, *Chinese Intellectuals in Crisis: Search for Order and Meaning, 1890–1911* (1987).

Luke S. K. Kwong, *A Mosaic of the Hundred Days* (1984), lays some myths to rest while new light on the Boxers is shed by Joseph P. Esherick, *The Origins of the Boxer Uprising* (1987). Two of the leading figures during the last decade of the Qing are examined in Daniel H. Bays, *China Enters the Twentieth Century: Chang Chih-tung and the Issues of a New Age, 1895–1909* (1978), and Stephen R. MacKinnon, *Power and Politics in Late Imperial China, 1901–1908* (1980).

PART V POST-IMPERIAL CHINA

Republican China is the subject of Volumes 11 and 12 of *The Cambridge History*. Also see Lloyd E. Eastman, *Seeds of Destruction: Nationalist China in War and Revolution* (1984), and his *Family, Fields, and Ancestors*, already mentioned above. For additional readings on an important topic see "Warlord Studies," a review essay by Diana Lary in *Modern China* VI, No. 4 (1980): 439–70. A recent contribution to cultural history is Ralph Crozier, *Art and Revolution in Modern China: The Lingnan (Cantonese) School of Painting, 1906–1951* (1988).

An excellent account of the various approaches scholars have used in their attempts to analyze the Chinese revolution is provided by the introduction to Kathleen Hartford and Steven M. Goldstein, eds., *Single Sparks: China's Rural Revolutions* (1989). Volume 14 of *The Cambridge History* (1987), ed. Roderick MacFarquar and John K. Fairbank, deals with the People's Republic from 1949 to 1965 and contains discussions of bibliography.

A leading student of ideological developments in China is Maurice Meisner, whose most recent book is *Marxism, Maoism, and Utopianism: Eight Essays* (1982). A major topic is examined in James L. Watson, ed., *Class and Social Stratification in Post-Revolution China* (1984). *Popular Chinese Literature and Performing Arts in the People's Republic of China, 1949–79* (1984), ed. Bonnie S. McDougall, is another valuable collection of essays. To date, two volumes have appeared of Roderick MacFarquar, *The Origins of the Cultural Revolution* (1979–) but no definite study of these turbulent years themselves has yet appeared. A book that combines personal experience with analysis is David and Nancy D. Milton. *The Wind Will Not Subside: Years in Revolu-*

tionary China, 1964–1969 (1976). Tang Tsou, *The Cultural Revolution and Post-Mao Reforms: A Historical Perspective* (1986), is a valuable collection of articles by a leading political scientist interested in theory. The fallout of the Cultural Revolution years can be sampled in *Mao's Harvest: Voices from China's New Generation* (1983), ed. Helen F. Siu and Zelda Stern. Also see Yue Daiyun and Carolyn Wakeman, *To the Storm: The Odyssey of a Revolutionary Chinese Woman* (1985), a gripping personal account.

A book that belongs on everyone's list is Richard P. Madsen, *Morality and Power in a Chinese Village* (1984). The empirical basis is an outstanding village study by Anita Chan, Richard Madsen, and Jonathan Unger, *Chen Village: The Recent History of a Peasant Community* (1984). Zhang Xinxin and Sang Ye, *Chinese Lives: An Oral History of Contemporary China* (1987), ed. W. J. E. Jenner and Delia Davin, is a collection of personal vignettes, windows into life in China today.

Travel accounts generally reveal as much about the traveler as they do about China, and it would be interesting to compare systematically the reports of recent visitors with those of foreigners who visited China in earlier times. Among the most engaging of the contemporary books are those by professional writers (Simon de Beauvoir, Alberto Moravia, Colin Thubron), those by journalists with Chinese experience (Edgar Snow, Seymour Topping), and those by specialists in Chinese studies (Ross Terrill, Simon Leys, Orville Schell). Especially noteworthy are books by those who have resided in China for a time as university teachers (Tani E. Barlow and Donald M. Lowe), journalists (Fox Butterfield, David Bonavia) or embassy officials (Robert Garside).

A good way to keep up with current developments is in the pages of *The China Quarterly*. Economic development has first priority in Deng Xiaoping's China so *The Political Economy of Reform in Post-Mao China* (1985), ed. Elizabeth J. Perry and Christine Wong, is especially welcome. For the countryside, also see Ashwani Saith, *The Re-emergence of the Chinese Peasantry: Aspects of Rural Decollectivisation* (1987). John P. Burns and Stanley Rosen, eds., *Policy Conflicts in Post-Mao China: A Documentary Survey with Analysis* (1986), is very useful. An important and depeply troubling book is Vaclav Smil, *The Bad Earth: Environmental Degradation in China* (1984). Energy policy is the focus of a fine study of how Chinese politics operate: Kenneth Lieberthal and Michael Oksenberg, *Policy Making in China: Leaders, Structures, and Process* (1988).

Much can also be learned from literature and the arts. See Ellen J. Laing, *The Winking Owl: Art in the People's Republic of China* (1988), Joan L. Cohen, *The New Chinese Painting, 1949–1986* (1987), and Jeffrey C. Kinkley, ed., *After Mao: Chinese Literature and Society, 1978–1981* (1985).

The Cambridge History volume does not include Taiwan (which will be discussed in Volume 15). A good place to begin reading about contemporary developments is Thomas B. Gold, *State and Society in the Taiwan Miracle* (1986). For earlier social history see Johanna M. Meskill, *A Chinese Pioneer Family: The Lins of Wu-feng, Taiwan, 1729–1895* (1979).

Copyrights and Acknowledgments

GEORGE ALLEN & UNWIN LTD   For three lines of poetry from *The Book of Songs*, edited and translated by Arthur Waley. Reprinted by permission of George Allen & Unwin Ltd.

COLUMBIA UNIVERSITY PRESS   For a table of the Five Agents system from *Sources of Chinese Tradition*, vol. I, compiled by Wm. Theodore de Bary, Wing-tsit Chan, and Burton Watson; for a poem by Wang Wei from *Chinese Lyricism; Shih Poetry from the Second to the Twelfth Century*, translated by Burton Watson; for an excerpt from a rhapsody by Sima Xiangru from *Chinese Rhyme-Prose*, translated by Burton Watson; and for "Reading the Poetry of Meng Chiao — First of Two Poems" from *Su Tung-p'o*, translated by Burton Watson. All reprinted by permission of Columbia University Press.

DOUBLEDAY & COMPANY, INC.   For a poem by Li Bo and "An Old Charcoal Seller" by Bo Juyi, both from *Sunflower Splendor*, edited by Liu Wu-chi and Irving Yucheng Lo. Copyright © 1975 by Liu Wu-chi and Irving Yucheng Lo. All reprinted by permission of Doubleday & Company, Inc.

RICHARD EDWARDS   For five lines of poetry translated by Tseng Yu-Ho, from *The Art of Wen Cheng-ming* by Richard Edwards. Published by the University of Michigan Museum of Art, 1976. Reprinted by permission of Richard Edwards.

GROVE PRESS, INC.   For "In Reply to a Poem from Cishan, Thanking Me for the Gift of Song and Yuan Lyrics I Had Printed" by Wang Pengyun, from *Anthology of Chinese Literature*, vol. II, edited by Cyril Birch. Copyright © 1972 by Grove Press, Inc. Used by permission of Grove Weidenfeld. And for three lines of poetry from *The Book of Songs*, edited and translated by Arthur Waley (Grove Press, 1960).

HARVARD UNIVERSITY PRESS   For a poem by Ch'in Kuan from Kojiro Yoshikawa, *An Introduction to Sung Poetry*, translated by Burton Watson (Harvard-Yenching Institute Monograph Series 17). Copyright 1967 by the Harvard-Yenching Institute. Reprinted by permission of Harvard University Press.

INDIANA UNIVERSITY PRESS   For a poem by Tao Jian and two other poetry excerpts from *An Introduction to Chinese Literature* by Liu Wu-chi (Indiana University Press, 1966). Reprinted by permission of Indiana University Press.

OXFORD UNIVERSITY PRESS   For a poem by Mao Zedong translated from the Chinese by Michael Bullock and Jerome Ch'en, from *Mao and the Chinese Revolution* by Jerome Ch'en, © Oxford University Press 1965. Reprinted by permission of Oxford University Press.

PENGUIN BOOKS LTD   For "To My Younger Brother" by Du Fu, from *Poems of the Late T'ang*, translated by A. C. Graham (Penguin Classics, 1965). Copyright © A. C. Graham, 1965. Reprinted by permission of Penguin Books Ltd.

RANDOM HOUSE, INC.   For a poem by Yuan Kejia from *The Chinese Literary Scene*, edited by Kai-yu Hsu. Copyright © 1975 by Kai-yu Hsu. Reprinted by permission of Random House, Inc.

ERIC SACKHEIM   For two lines by Lu Ji from *The Silent Zero, in Search of Sound: An Anthology of Chinese Poems from the Beginning through the Sixth Century*, translated by Eric Sackheim (Grossman, 1968). Reprinted by permission of Eric Sackheim.

ROBERT M. SOMERS   For material from "The Collapse of the T'ang Order" by Robert M. Somers. Reprinted by permission of Robert M. Somers.

CHARLES E. TUTTLE CO., INC.   For two lines of poetry from *The Great Cultural Revolution in China*, compiled and edited by the Asia Research Center; and for a poem from *Poems by Wang Wei*, translated by Chang Yin-nan and Lewis C. Walmsley. All reprinted by permission of Charles E. Tuttle Co., Inc.

TWAYNE PUBLISHERS   For two lines of poetry by Du Fu from A. R. Davis, *Tu Fu*. Reprinted by permission of Twayne Publishers.

UNIVERSITY OF CALIFORNIA PRESS   For a poem from *Chinese Poetry: Major Modes and Genres* by Wai-lim Yip. Copyright © 1976 by The Regents of the University of California; reprinted by permission of the University of California Press.

Illustration Credits

Index

Page numbers in *italics* refer to illustrations.